EXTRATERRITORIAL

MATTHEW HART

EXTRATERRITORIAL

A Political Geography of Contemporary Fiction

Columbia University Press / *New York*

Columbia University Press
Publishers Since 1893
New York   Chichester, West Sussex
cup.columbia.edu

Library of Congress Cataloging-in-Publication Data

Names: Hart, Matthew, 1974– author.
Title: Extraterritorial : a political geography of contemporary fiction /
Matthew Hart.
Description: New York : Columbia University Press, 2020. |
Includes bibliographical references and index.
Identifiers: LCCN 2019053214 (print) | LCCN 2019053215 (ebook) |
ISBN 9780231188388 (hardback) | ISBN 9780231188395 (paperback) |
ISBN 9780231547802 (ebook)
Subjects: LCSH: Fiction—21st century—History and criticism—Theory, etc. |
Political geography.
Classification: LCC PN3331 .H356 2020 (print) | LCC PN3331 (ebook) |
DDC 809.3—dc23
LC record available at https://lccn.loc.gov/2019053214
LC ebook record available at https://lccn.loc.gov/2019053215

Columbia University Press books are printed on permanent and
durable acid-free paper.

Printed in the United States of America

Cover design: Chang Jae Lee

CONTENTS

ACKNOWLEDGMENTS

My first and greatest debt, now and for two decades, is to the artist and poet Summer Jellison Hart. Summer didn't type a word of this manuscript, I promise, but not one bit of my work would be possible without the sustaining force of her love and partnership.

To our son, Connery, the bravest of all souls, who has traversed universes while I've been writing this book: you're amazing. I love you. Thanks for teaching me every day the importance of changing and enduring.

I began thinking about extraterritoriality during my last year at the University of Illinois, Urbana-Champaign, when my former student, Dr. Tania Lown-Hecht, asked me to direct an independent study on the work of W. G. Sebald. That happy semester of reading and talking led, eventually, to our coauthored article, "The Extraterritorial Poetics of W. G. Sebald," which was later published in *Modern Fiction Studies*. I owe a debt to Tania for those early conversations, without which this book might not have taken shape. My thanks, also, to Tania for permission to reuse some parts I wrote for our article in the conclusion to this book.

Extraterritorial was written at Columbia University, with the assistance of generous fellowship support from the Faculty of Arts and Sciences,

Columbia College, and the Heyman Center for the Humanities. The costs of research trips to the United Kingdom were partially met by two Summer Research Grants from the Office of the Executive Vice President for Arts and Sciences, and by a Lenfest Junior Faculty Development Award. When, as I began writing this book, my wife and son were both struggling with health crises, Nicholas Dames secured me a compassionate course release that made it possible for me to care for my family, advise my grad students, and not give up research entirely.

My sincere appreciation to the many staff members of Columbia's Department of English and Comparative Literature for all their labors on my behalf, especially to Pamela Rodman, who stands behind everything we do as a department.

Here's a thing I love about Columbia: my colleagues are unabashedly committed to sustaining a creative and self-critical intellectual community, devoted to the highest standards of interdisciplinary humanistic research. Over the years, I have received invaluable feedback, some of it even requested, from Jenny Davidson, Brent Hayes Edwards, Marianne Hirsch, Bruce Robbins, Joey Slaughter, Gayatri Chakravorty Spivak, and Gauri Viswanathan. This book is much better, I think, for their interventions.

Early research for chapters 1, 4, and 5 was made much easier by auditing two doctoral classes offered in sister departments at Columbia: Professor Susan Pedersen's course The Modern State in Theory and Practice and Professor Eugenia Lean's Colloquium on Modern Chinese History. My sincere thanks to Susan and Eugenia for giving me the opportunity to learn from them and their students. All historical and theoretical errors and omissions are, naturally, my own.

Several parts of *Extraterritorial* debuted in Columbia University workshops and seminars. Thanks to Mark Mazower and Eileen Gillooly for inviting me to present an early draft of chapter 5 in the Heyman Center for the Humanities works-in-progress series. Adam Tooze offered a trenchant reading of chapter 1 when I presented it in the Columbia University Seminar on Literary Theory; later that night, Adam helped me reorder and revise crucial parts of that chapter and my introduction. Chapter 2's critique of Agamben's political theory debuted in the Columbia University Seminar in Cultural Memory. A later version of chapter 5 was improved by the attention of students and colleagues at the Department of English and Comparative Literature's works-in-progress series. And a late draft of chapter 3 was revised with the help of generous feedback from the 2017–18 Heyman Center Fellows.

In the end, it's impossible to enumerate all the ways Columbia's scholarly community shaped this book at every stage of its development. So let me just note that this list leaves out my two most sustaining Columbia relationships: the intelligence and comradeship of my students, especially in my graduate seminars on contemporary literature and literary theory; and, supreme among colleagues, Sarah Cole. I'm willing to bet that nobody reading this book has had a better mentor. Whatever hour I've written or texted, whatever problem I've asked her to help solve, whatever the argumentative cul-de-sac I've driven myself toward, Sarah has been there for me, my work, and my family. She rocks.

Outside Columbia, I've been fortunate to present parts of every chapter of this book in invited talks where my ideas have been tested and improved through conversations both pleasant and tough. For invitations, smart questions, and good company, my sincere thanks to Joseph Valente, University at Buffalo; Frances Ferguson, University of Chicago; Nico Israel, CUNY Graduate Center; Nancy Armstrong, Duke University; Douglas Mao, Johns Hopkins University; Benjamin Kohlmann, University of Hamburg; Miles Osgood, Harvard University; Jini Kim Watson and Peter Nicholls, New York University; Jonathan Eburne, Pennsylvania State University; Joseph Jeon, Pomona College; Sara Marcus, Princeton University; Rebecca L. Walkowitz, Rutgers University; Peter Simonsen, University of Southern Denmark; Mrinalini Chakravroty, University of Virginia; and Seo Hee Im, Yale University. My sincere thanks also to the many students whose questions and comments made those trips intellectually productive, as well as to the administrative staff members who booked tickets, cut checks, and tolerated my questions and procrastinations.

Finally, to my friends and colleagues distant and near, who together realize the truth that intellectual life happens in company. My endless gratitude to Jessica Hallock, a beloved friend with the sharpest editorial eye: nobody showed more appetite for actually *reading* drafts of this book and nobody's red pen was wielded to greater effect. My sincerest admiration to my *Literature Now* partners, David James and Rebecca L. Walkowitz, who embody all the best professional virtues. A huge toast to my collaborators on the ASAP Motherboard and MSA executive committee, who keep teaching me about leaving the world better than you found it. Likewise, to the junior faculty crew at Columbia, whose ranks I've finally left but whose company I adore, especially Austin Graham, Dustin Stewart, and Dennis Tenen. To Cristobal Silva and Anahid Nersessian, who headed west along the way. To the poet K. B. Thors, vulgar machinist extraordinaire and the best long-distance writing partner a boy ever had. To the New York crew—Gloria Fisk, Kristin Meyer, and Jason Watt—whose company sustained me as this manuscript was belatedly coming together. And to my dispersed academic family, all of them dearly missed, who will deservedly drag me for leaving them out of this overlong list of abiding friendships and unpayable debts. I love you all.

* * *

Some sections of *Extraterritorial* were previously published as articles in scholarly journals, to which I am grateful for permission to reprint. Parts of chapter 1 were published as "Threshold to the Kingdom: the Airport is a Border and the Border is a Volume," in *Criticism* 57, no. 2 (Spring 2015): 173–89. Parts of chapter 5 were published as "Something Extraordinary Keeps Happening: J. G. Ballard's Enclave World," *NOVEL: A Forum on Fiction* 51, no. 2 (2018): 272–91. This book's conclusion reproduces, in highly different form, some sections I wrote for Matthew Hart and Tania-Lown Hecht, "The Extraterritorial Poetics of W. G. Sebald," *Modern Fiction Studies* 58, no. 2 (Summer 2012): 214–38. For permission to reproduce images, my sincere thanks to Mayaan Amir and Ruti Sela, Katja Novitskova, Sean Snyder, and Mark Wallinger.

EXTRATERRITORIAL

INTRODUCTION

Four Types of Extraterritoriality

Let the cracks between things widen until they are no longer cracks but the new places for things. That was where they were now.

—COLSON WHITEHEAD, *ZONE ONE*

THE SOMEWHAT FREE SEAS

I'm watching a video of a single-masted sloop moving slowly across the Eastern Mediterranean. Its course is matched by another small vessel. The two boats are joined by more than their common speed and direction. They are tethered by a beam of light, with the sail of the first boat acting as the screen against which the second projects a video (fig. 0.1).

The video shows many things. A half-naked man wearing antlers; burning vehicles in a desert landscape; scenes of dancing; portraits of women wearing hijab. Later, I watch another video of a video being projected onto a sail. In this short sequence, a woman wearing black is framed against a blue background. She walks from left to right along what might be a wall, the edge of a stage, a balance beam, or a tightrope. It is hard to tell: the rectangular image of the video projection is imperfectly framed on the triangular mainsail and, in any case, the sloop on which that sail is rigged lies some distance away from our documenting videographer. I can't work out whether the creases in the video's blue background mean that the original footage was shot opposite a ruffled curtain or tent wall, or whether the

FIGURE 0.1 *Exterritory Project* screening on the boat sails, 2009.

Credit: Ruti Sela and Mayaan Amir.

mainsail that's acting as a screen has started to luff in the wind. The distinction between image and support is blurred. So are the borders between the work, its exhibition, and its documentation. I can't distinguish between the actions and intentions of artist and curator, curator and documentarian, curatorial team and sailor, sailor and marine environment. Finally, just before the woman reaches the right-hand edge of the sail, she falls or jumps down. We know she does not actually drop into the sea but, for a second, the thought is irresistible.

The videos I'm describing are part of Exterritory Project, a curatorial initiative begun in 2009 by Ruti Sela and Mayaan Amir, two Israeli artists who in 2011 were awarded a UNESCO prize for fostering cultural dialogue in the Middle East. Sela and Amir's immediate goal was to find a way to curate artistic events and seminars in the context of the ongoing Palestinian boycott of Israeli cultural institutions.[1] In particular, they were frustrated by the difficulty of finding a mutually accessible and agreeable space to show a compilation of video artworks, *Wild West*, by Arab and Jewish artists joined by a common interest in "questions of boundaries" and "hyper-national claims."[2] Not wanting to exhibit in Europe or the United States—beyond the boycott zone but distant from their home region—they struck upon the idea of showing *Wild West* on the free seas. "Exterritorial waters," they hoped, might serve "as an autonomic area that can bypass laws of territory and can allow at least temporarily the postponement of arbitrary stipulations." Describing a 2010 event, Sela and Amir suggest that the oceanic "exterritory" might be an appropriate space for "reconciliation meetings" between artists from conflict zones.

International waters have long symbolized the possibility of free space. In his famous early work of maritime law, *Mare Liberum* (1609), Hugo Grotius argues on behalf of the Dutch East India Company that the world's oceans ought to be open to navigation by all and subject to the jurisdiction of none.[3] From this distinction between geographies that are alienable and those that are not comes a fundamental opposition between closed (territorial) and open (extraterritorial) space. This legal distinction is central to a rich history of thinking, artistic and philosophical as well as jurisprudential, about global or transnational spaces that might exist beyond sovereignty or nationhood: geographies, to quote one recent humanistic critic, that give rise to an "extraterritorial imagination" in which the limits of the social and political world are put to the test.[4]

It's with such ideas in play that Sela and Amir invited artists, writers, and curators to join them for their 2009 event on the mare liberum of the Mediterranean. In June 2010, they organized a more ambitious miniarmada, exhibiting over fifty artworks in the international waters between Israel and Cyprus. In what has become a kind of signature image of *Exterritory Project,* both events featured the projection of video works upon the sails of small yachts.[5] This curatorial practice poses an aesthetic question: How might the seas operate as an exhibition space? In exhibiting at sea, the curators transfer artworks into new contexts, creating an event somewhere between traveling exhibition, site-specific happening, and institutional critique. But the curators' own comments about *Exterritory Project* also emphasize the continuity between the aesthetic qualities of maritime space and their own political commitments: "What kinds of images 'benefit' from being unstable?" they ask. "What types of images can survive a space in which borders are constantly changing?"[6]

This book is about artistic and literary works set in and about extraterritorial zones. It is about the condition that Gerhard Richter defines, in appropriately shifty terms, as "existing in a territory beyond territory, belonging to a territory while at the same time being 'extra' or superfluous to it."[7] The images projected in the first *Exterritory Project* events certainly demonstrate such instability. But this is not because international waters exist simply *beyond* the national state and its laws, which is another way of saying that extraterritoriality is not, in fact, the antithesis of territorial power. In reality, the complicated "international" status of the open oceans proves one of the central points of this book: that what we think of as "global" space is the product of agreements, conflicts, and compromises between national states. By studying the art and literature of the extraterritorial we can better understand how the putatively global culture of the twenty-first century occupies a political geography that is only located *outside* borders, states, and nations by being simultaneously *within* them.

This is pretty abstract stuff, so let's get back to the Mediterranean. Sela and Amir's homology between "autonomic" images and free ocean spaces requires that they simplify the real complexities of maritime law. As Amir put it in an interview with *Art Dubai*, *Exterritory Project* depends on an idea of the ocean as a heterotopic zone that "exists outside a place" and possesses "the power to delay and neutralise the whole power-relations present in a culture."[8] But the seas in which *Exterritory Project* sails are the same ones in which on 31 May 2010 the Israeli Defense Force (IDF) boarded and seized a Free Gaza Movement aid flotilla: a civilian convoy, at that point in international waters seventy-two nautical miles from land, that was attempting to break the Israeli blockade of Gaza.[9] In that incident, the freedoms of navigation enshrined in the Law of the Sea were trumped by the Israeli state's unilateral projection of power beyond its territorial waters. In this event, rather than witnessing the neutralization or suspension of political sovereignty within maritime space, what people observed was a state's unilateral decision to project its power beyond borders at the expense of a multilateral agreement among all states to rescind jurisdictional claims over areas of salt water a long way from land.

This problem is hardly specific to the Israeli-Palestinian struggle, or to violent conflict in general. This is because, even when navies aren't seizing civilian vessels in international waters, the oceans of the world are not divided nicely between unfree and free, national and international.[10] A recent European Parliament report comments that maritime law has historically embodied "a constant tension between tendencies in favour of freedom and those in favour of exclusivity"; it also worries that the politics of the present have been "dominated by positions that favour exclusive rights" and by the increasing geographical extension of state sovereignty.[11] The seas aren't so free—and perhaps they never were. Grotius's foundational legal account of the open seas in *Mare Liberum* was, after all, moderated by his later claim, in *On the Law of War and Peace* (1625), that territorial claims to oceanic space may be made through "the instrumentality of person if, for example, a fleet, which is an army afloat, is stationed at some point of the sea."[12] Maritime law represents an uneasy compromise between open and closed kinds of legal space: the territorial seas extend twelve miles from most coastlines, though plenty of exceptions hold for geographies in which maximal territorial claims would result in conflicting or overlapping borders.

And so, to repeat: exterritoriality and territoriality are not opposites—or, if they are, they're the kind of opposites that attract. If every state with a Mediterranean coastline were to make the maximum jurisdictional claims technically allowed under international law, that sea would contain no "free" space at all.[13] As it is, the friendly and rivalrous states around the Middle Sea have seen fit to negotiate with one another so as to keep open the Mediterranean's international waters. In this, they are no doubt encouraged by other states from other regions, some of them with powerful military forces and strong desires to navigate strategic corridors such as the Suez Canal and Black Sea; by nonstate actors such as fishing, energy, and logistics companies; and by their own strategic and ideological commitments to transnational institutions and international law. To exercise sovereignty within an international system means choosing when and how to *refrain* from claiming territorial jurisdiction as well as deciding to assert it. There is no zero-sum relation between political power and its territorial expression.

A primary motivation behind *Extraterritorial* is the conviction that artists, authors, and academics would benefit from a more complex historical and theoretical understanding of the political geography in which we live. Over the last few decades, it has become a kind of academic orthodoxy to say that studying contemporary culture means taking a global or transnational perspective, even to say that twenty-first-century artworks are "global" in some intrinsic sense.[14] It doesn't follow from this that academic critics have done with particular detail; few would deny the centrality of local, regional, and national expertise to any scholarly sort of cultural criticism.[15] Yet it's now hard to imagine a serious account of twenty-first-century art and literature that would not grapple with, even if it did not begin from, the question of the global. That might mean, as in book history or literary sociology, attending to the absorption of publishing and book retail within a small group of vertically integrated transnational media corporations—a development that has led not to the homogenization of cultural life, but to increased specialization and diversification.[16] Or, in art history, it might mean the way Miwon Kwon conceives of the contemporary arts as an affective and epistemological means through which we might grasp the "contemporaneity of histories from around the world" as a "disjunctive yet continuous intellectual horizon, integral to the understanding of the present (as a whole)."[17] Or it might mean, as scholars have been arguing about for years now, supplementing the study of national and regional literatures with global or world literatures.[18] In sum, the field is rife with planetary scales and ambitions.

And yet our globalizing critical tool kit remains inadequate for the interpretation of individual texts and the analysis of culture at scale. The concept and practice of extraterritoriality represent possible solutions to such inadequacy. In the pages to follow, I show how critics of contemporary art and literature have neglected the role played by the state in the production of international and transnational space. They have done so, in part, because of a "sovereignty-territory ideal" in which state and nation are identified with a fetishized form of territorial authority, both broadly cultural and more narrowly political. As a result, almost any crack or gradation in a state's political geography gets misrepresented as a crisis in its very being or purpose.[19] The truth, however, is that state sovereignty helps produce international and transnational relations—and it's this truth that the art and literature of the extraterritorial helps us to see.

AN ARGUMENT OF THREE PARTS

Extraterritorial makes three interlinked claims, the first literary-critical, the second broadly historical, and the third conceptual.

 1. *The contemporary novel mediates human geographic experience, with extraterritorial spaces giving rise to extraterritorial forms.*

 My first argument centers on the proposition that geography is not just a topic (topos) of the novel but an active force that shapes it from within. As Robert Tally has explored, there is a long tradition of thinking about writers—especially writers in narrative genres—as akin to cartographers. "Like the mapmaker," Tally explains, "the writer must survey territory, determining which features of a given landscape to include, to emphasize, or to diminish. . . . The writer must establish the scale and the shape, no less of the narrative than of the places in it . . . [and] must determine the degree to which a given representation of a place refers to any 'real' place in the geo- graphical world."[20] But texts are more than the sum of their makers' cartographic efforts. Because readers inhabit real and imagined geographies—cities of the mind, as well as places of everyday lives—they bring to the texts they read a wide array of spatial memories and experiences. The real spaces often represented in texts also possess histories that are irreducible to any one telling or evocation. Finally, the social, economic, and, as this book studies in particular, political dimensions of geographic experience exert pressures and set limits upon the forms and themes of artistic production in the present. For all these reasons, critical readers attuned to geography must, as Tally has it, develop "a form of reading that focuses attention on space and spatiality in the texts under consideration. . . . [but that also pays] attention to the changing spatial or geographical formations that affect literary and cultural productions."[21] There is no literary geography that is not also a materialist literary history.

Influenced by such literary-geographic criticism, *Extraterritorial* focuses on the aesthetic representation of spaces such as airports, consular zones, freeports, detention camps, gated communities, and the oceans. These spaces have one central thing in common: within them, the puncturing and graduation of territorial sovereignty doesn't erase state power but extends it throughout putatively "global" space. Through discussions of writing by contemporary novelists as different as China Miéville and Hilary Mantel, as well as selected developments within the contemporary arts more broadly, the following chapters explore how extraterritorial geographies shape cultural objects in large and small ways. In chapter 5, for instance, we ask why all of J. G. Ballard's late fictions are set in the same kind of urban enclave—and why he insists that every part of his large and diverse oeuvre ought to be understood as recreating the extraterritorial International Settlement of Shanghai.

But extraterritoriality also has crucial effects at the micro level of novelistic language, form, and genre. For that reason, chapter 3 analyzes the temporalizing diction of Emily St. John Mandel's postapocalyptic novel *Station Eleven* (2014), where events are repeatedly described in terms of distance in time from the collapse of our modern systems of international travel and telecommunications. And it links that linguistic pattern to a broader trend within the postapocalyptic genre, in which an increasing number of such novels are set in an archipelagic geography in which characters move uneasily between isolated settlements set in lawless and ungoverned space. Extraterritoriality is, in this way, sometimes the overt subject of the novels studied in this book. But extraterritoriality is also part of the deep symbolic architecture of novels that ostensibly have nothing to do with that topic. In such instances, it emerges as the subject not of the novel's story but of its forms. The future of contemporary fiction is neither "global" nor "national," my analyses suggest, but trending extraterritorial.

As this last claim suggests, however, this book's literary-critical argument is hollow without an underlying historical conjecture:

2. *The political geography of twenty-first-century life is increasingly extraterritorial.*

In arguing thus, *Extraterritorial* draws on much work in spatial theory and political geography. Felicity D. Scott, for instance, has recently argued that post-1960s architectural space might be described in terms of the proliferation of "outlaw territories," including "semi-utopian 'open ends' for social experimentation," as well as sites about which few people would have utopian aspirations, including "refugee, detention, and resettlement camps" as well as "company headquarters and social scientific laboratories."[22] More broadly, I draw on the work of architectural and spatial theorist Eyal Weizman, who defines any human-occupied or -influenced space as a "political plastic" (or "politics in matter") that can be considered "a map of the relation between all the forces that shaped it."[23] More than providing one useful way to think of rural, urban, and other spaces as intrinsically politicized, Weizman also provides evidence for the claim that the political plastic of contemporary life is taking extraterritorial shape. Writing with Ines Gleisman and Anselm Franke, he argues that extraterritoriality underlies and explains a pervasive condition in which we experience "contemporary political space" in general as having been "shattered."[24] Far from surfing in a borderless world of global flows, or sitting securely in a bounded and grounded sovereign territory, the twenty-first-century political subject is, they claim, forced to inhabit and traverse "discontinuous territorial fragments set-apart and fortified by makeshift barriers, temporary boundaries, or invisible security apparatuses. . . . a territorial patchwork of introvert enclaves located side by side, each within the other, simultaneously and in unprecedented proximities" (n.p.).

This book does not argue that extraterritoriality is *the* determinative framework for understanding the present; its chapters do, however, provide evidence for the sorts of empirical claims made by Scott and Weizman. An important supplementary part of that project, therefore, is the argument ventured in chapter 1 but implicit throughout this book: that the so-called Westphalian nation-state that developed in early modern Europe has been afforded a falsely normative character in much cultural and political theory about the state and globalization. By focusing on extraterritoriality, we can better understand globalization as the long historical project of national institutions and elites.

But what is extraterritoriality, anyway? This definitional question is the main subject of this introduction and is best explained by my third and final major claim:

3. *Extraterritoriality is constituted by the interrelation between two antithetical pairs:* open/closed *and* spatial/personal.

To some writers and artists, such as Sela and Amir, extraterritoriality can designate openness or freedom; to others, as we shall see, it signifies imprisonment or subjugation. Some of us carry extraterritoriality with us as an aspect of our persons; others travel into and out of extraterritorial geographies. It is this fundamental dynamism that makes an extraterritorial zone like an embassy such a useful kind of space: an open door to some and a walled fortress to others, a piece of foreign space, but one rooted in the personal inviolability of an ambassador. Extraterritoriality is not one thing. It is a set of practices through which states govern populations by punching holes in their own political plastic, by stretching out into spaces formally governed by others, or by pooling and sharing jurisdictions and competencies. It denotes how states facilitate the production of international spaces by relaxing their authority over territory, preferring instead to claim sovereignty over persons. And, for sure, "extraterritorial" sometimes describes situations in which formal or effective territorial control breaks down. For some scholars, extraterritoriality is a feature of ubiquitous contemporary phenomena such as the internet, dispersed across actual and virtual space, but still also subject to localized "structural forces."[25] For others, its meanings are embodied by exceptional locations such as the Central Intelligence Agency's post-9/11 "black sites" in Poland and Lithuania, in which terrorist suspects were tortured in extralegal hells.[26] Finally, for others still, "extraterritorial" evokes the possibility of wilderness or outer space geographies inhospitable to human settlement and yet vulnerable to our actions.[27]

By attending to the extraterritorial as a contradictory idea and complex historical practice, this book moves beyond zero-sum accounts of global culture, in which every growth or innovation of a transnational kind is seen as an inevitable net loss for state or nation—and every assertion of state power is seen as the victory of "real" citizens or "real" communities against the fever dreams of "globalists." Along the way, this book explains what the many different kinds of extraterritorial zone and experience have in common. Although previous writers on this subject have contributed much to the theory and history of extraterritoriality, they have largely done so from within aesthetic and disciplinary silos, with the result that they've been able to avoid having to reconcile the contradictory aspects of extraterritorial space and personhood.[28] This book will bring together, but not wholly synthesize, those disjunct parts. Ultimately, it is the antithetical character of the extraterritorial that explains why it has become such a powerful figure for contemporary writers and artists, who delight in the way it confounds the boundaries between foreign and familiar, fixed and free, person and place.

By testing these three theses, *Extraterritorial* develops a historical theory of extraterritorial space, elaborates the aesthetic forms that history takes, and argues that we can understand the national and global dimensions of contemporary culture more completely by studying its extraterritorial aspect. That process of understanding begins by more fully developing my last thesis, about the antithetical character of extraterritoriality.

FOUR TYPES OF EXTRATERRITORIALITY

As we've seen, the extraterritorial can be invested with the power to liberate. But what then of a place like the United States' military detention facility at

Guantánamo Bay, Cuba, which has been rightly described as an "extra-territorial space" that, because it is neither fully within nor without the United States, enables the "suspension of law" as "a permanent technique of rule"?[29] In *Exterritory Project*, artists carve out for themselves a space of temporary relief from occupation and armed struggle; in Guantánamo, men are tortured and detained without trial or hope of release. Should one resist the extraterritorial, or run into it?

The answer is *neither*. There is no question that we ought to resist what is happening in Guantánamo Bay. But that's not because it's an extraterritorial zone; it's because torture and indefinite detention are crimes against humanity.

But neither is extraterritoriality an actor's category, possessing no fundamental qualities. Rather, the tension between free and unfree values is basic to extraterritoriality. Extraterritoriality is neither free nor unfree, but defined by the opposition between the values *open* and *closed*.

Next, to *open/closed* we must add another such pairing, which this time identifies the relationship between two different sorts of extraterritorial object: *person* and *space*. Sometimes extraterritoriality is a property of individual people, in the sense that it inheres in someone's legal and political personhood.[30] Consider a member of a UN diplomatic mission in New York. Wherever that person travels or abides, she is, by virtue of the 1946 Convention on the Privileges and Immunities of the United Nations, immune from the domestic law of the United States. And this is the case even though neither her home country nor the United Nations make any legal or political claim to the ground beneath her feet.[31] Such a person can wander about New York while always being somehow "at home," displaced out of territorial space into an alternate jurisdictional and political universe, exactly the size of her body.

In what follows, we'll call this quality *extraterritoriality of person*. But, in other instances, extraterritoriality can be understood as a property of space itself, such that most everyone who enters an extraterritorial zone crosses into a new jurisdictional system or political regime. Imagine now that you're a tourist visiting UN headquarters. The headquarters district is an extraterritorial space with respect to the United States, legally "inviolable" and under the "control and authority" of the UN Secretary General and General Assembly.[32] Article 3, Section 8, of the 1947 Headquarters Agreement gives the United Nations the power to "make regulations . . . necessary for the full operations of its functions" and to refuse to apply any US law inconsistent with those regulations. The complication, however, is that, just as our foreign diplomat friend is, when walking home through Manhattan, say, at once immune from US law and still very much within US territory, so is the headquarters district's inviolability hardly absolute. For instance, the Headquarters Agreement's lines about setting aside US laws immediately follow two earlier clauses in which the headquarters district is described as otherwise subject to the full range of federal, New York State, and New York City laws, and in which people within the district (at least, those people not protected by personal diplomatic immunities) are placed under the jurisdiction of the relevant US courts.[33] The United Nations has the power to refuse persons entry to the headquarters district, and to expel them from its premises; but it has neither control over its own external security nor the ability to sell or otherwise dispose of the land on which its various buildings sit.[34] The district is thus outside the United States for certain legal and political purposes, but it is never wholly beyond the de jure and de facto power of municipal, state, and federal courts and government agencies. In extraterritorial zones, the geography of power is divisible, graduated, and disaggregated, but rarely is that power wholly canceled and rarely is it cleanly transferred, as if flipped completely from one nation to another.

Just as the alternate political valences of the extraterritorial often overlap, so is there often no wall between its personal and spatial aspects. Because it raises questions about who has authority over what people in which locations, the idea of an extraterritorial person makes sense only if the world is already a kind of political multiverse, made up of many territories, and not a universe in which a single source of authority prevails everywhere.[35] In a perpetual and universal empire, there are neither exiles nor ambassadors. But in a world of many states, in which the power of one country depends in part on its citizens' ability to move within another, extraterritoriality of person becomes inextricable from extraterritoriality of place.

In the same vein, though flowing in the other direction, extraterritoriality of place can be produced by the actions of extraterritorial persons. For example, in Renaissance Europe, the consular immunities initially restricted to diplomatic ambassadors gradually became a property held in common by the ambassador's household, beginning with his family and servants but eventually extending to the physical space of the consular dwelling.[36] More broadly, any time a person moves within political or jurisdictional space, she invites the possibility of a change in her relation to other people, to various collectives or institutions, or to her own past. In the wake of World War II, the experience of exile led the Jewish intellectual Siegfried Kracauer to adopt the language of extraterritoriality to evoke how, first, the stripping of his citizenship rights in Germany and, later, his forced migration to France and the United States left him feeling personally adrift in space and time.[37] Not all such experiences involve the formal ascription of extraterritorial personhood, or a physical movement across a space like a consular zone. But even when "extraterritorial" is more metaphor than literal fact—and this book is full of instances in which authors and artists transpose historical facts into metaphorical figures—we witness the same overlapping and overdetermination of qualities of place and person.

The word "extraterritorial" was imported to English almost unchanged from juridical Latin. The *OED* gives its etymology quite simply: "Modern Latin phrase *extrā territōrium* outside the territory." The dictionary's first quoted example comes from Grotius's *On the Law of War and Peace*, which refers to the legal fiction through which an ambassador might be present in one country but, in the eyes of the law, be presumed never to have left the state he represents.[38] Ambassadorial or consular inviolability is a primary example of an extraterritoriality of person—but one that is, from the start, inexplicable without the prior spatial division of the globe on political lines. Thus, although Barbara Woodward, the current British ambassador to China, might be attending a trade fair in Chengdu, hundreds of miles from her embassy in Beijing, for the purposes of law she remains forever as if outside Chinese territory, in a transparent and portable bubble of Englishness.[39]

An extraterritorial person is not simply located outside a territory: she is poised between places and potencies, between responsibilities to host and sovereign, at once in a free legal space and still subject to the border-hopping reach of her political masters. It will be important, in the next chapter, to ask what it means to belong to a territory, rather than to just be on some piece of land. For now, we should merely note that extraterritoriality is not limited to ambassadors. For instance, another way of defining that term is as the "operation of laws upon persons existing beyond the limits of the enacting state or nation but who are still amenable to its laws."[40] In this definition, states extend their jurisdiction spatially, across seas and over borders, but they do so only so as to claim authority over certain individual persons or groups of persons. This kind of extraterritoriality applies to relatively uncontroversial legal instruments, such as reciprocal extradition treaties that prevent defendants escaping from justice in one country by fleeing to another; but it also covers the novel ways in which national legislatures have increasingly extended their courts' jurisdictions overseas. Thus, since 2004 US government employees have come under federal or military law while serving abroad—and not only diplomats and soldiers, but also civilian contractors employed by private companies.[41] In response to criminal and strategic threats that exceed national boundaries, countries such as the United Kingdom have expanded the number and nature of the unilateral jurisdictional claims they make over their nationals abroad. The Terrorism Act 2000, for instance, makes it an offense for a British person to incite someone to commit a terrorist act overseas, even providing for the unusual circumstance in which that act would be illegal in the United Kingdom but lawful in the country in which it's actually performed.[42] Likewise the Foreign Corrupt Practices Act, which gives the United States the ability to prosecute even non-US persons or corporations for business practices that are illegal in the United States but might not be in the place they take place.[43] In such legislation, the spatial extension of state power rests upon the idea that political space is divisible not just by borders and buildings, but by making distinctions at the level of the person.

AN ORDINARY SORT OF EXCEPTION

Extraterritoriality is ordinary, yet always exceptional.

Grotius's use of *extrā territōrium* to describe the legal immunity of ambassadors was a useful bit of lexical kit for early modern jurists, its growing popularity partly due to its use in Georg Friedrich von Marten's influential 1788 treatise *The Law of Nations*.[44] By the nineteenth century, "extraterritorial" had become a standard legal term, albeit one authors tried regularly to improve.[45] But extraterritoriality isn't always rooted in something as august as ambassadorial inviolability. Consider the "capitulations" negotiated between Christian Europeans and the Ottoman Empire from the fourteenth century onward. In these agreements, which got their Latinate name from the chapters (*capitulum*) into which they were divided, economic and political dispensations were granted to non-Muslim foreigners residing and trading in Ottoman lands.[46] A merchant from Genoa might, for instance, enjoy preferential tax breaks, be allowed to practice Christianity, and even bring or defend legal actions under the law of his home city. Unlike ambassadorial extraterritoriality, however, the forms of legal personhood enshrined in the capitulations tended to apply generally to whole groups of foreigners, not just to a diplomatic elite. They also weren't necessarily matters of international relations, since nonstate leaders, such as the communal head of a foreign trading community, could negotiate them locally. Finally, the privileges capitulations allowed often weren't absolute: they might expire or be renegotiated, while extraterritorial status in regard to, say, import duties wouldn't usually be extended to a fundamental aspect of Ottoman political sovereignty such as paying tribute to the sultan.[47] Such examples show how extraterritorial concepts and practices can become an ordinary part of human life, shaping everyday matters such as where and in what manner one lives, does business, or prays.

We can now say two more things for certain: as a phenomenon in the law, extraterritoriality is historically and socially variable, and, given that variability, it's much more than a phenomenon in the law. The ordinariness of the extraterritorial lies, in part, in the ease with which it can be mobilized to describe everyday experiences of many kinds. But, more important, its everydayness stems from the proliferation, across past and present social space, of many sorts of "quasi-extraterritorial" zone in which national law may not be suspended but in which there occur other sorts of territorial disaggregation. These quasi-zones include areas such as international airports, in which sovereignty claims are not relaxed but exceptions are made within criminal, fiscal, and immigration law. They also include areas for which the language of political geography has mostly figurative significance—for instance, the business parks and retirement communities that litter Ballard's late novels. When extraterritoriality gets evoked in these contexts, it evokes both more and less than the question of one's formal relationship to the state or international law. By reactivating, whether consciously or not, the Latin root *terra* (land) in "territory," the metaphorical extension of "extraterritorial" depends on the way our everyday talk about territory is inevitably associated with other experiences of being in or out of place, feeling grounded or ungrounded, and dwelling at home or sojourning away.

This book is not, then, a parsimonious project, in which the goal is to decide which places and people are properly extraterritorial. And yet, even given this plural perspective, it's still never quite right to describe extraterritoriality as *merely* ordinary, as if it represents no kind of exception from anything like a rule. One reason is because, even today, territorial geographies and experiences are still exceedingly common. Although I write these words in the wake of the biggest refugee crisis since World War II, and at a time when US news channels are full of angry chatter about caravans of migrants, most people still live in one country most of the time. Indeed, this resistant (if not quite residual) historical reality partly explains why the Italian philosopher Giorgo Agamben identifies the refugee as "the sole category in which it is possible today to perceive the forms and limits" of an emergent form of political community in which states might become an "extraterritorial space," with all citizens and noncitizens in an equal "position of exodus or refuge."[48] Extraterritorial personhood depends, from the start, on the relationship between exception and the rule, with the extra territorial person being the outlier and the supposed expectation being that jurisdictions extend throughout a whole national territory and include all the people within that territory. "Although many forms of political order have existed in times past," reads an early sentence in a history of extraterritoriality in US law, "the dominant form today is the sovereign, territorial state."[49] There is a close historical connection, which I address in the next chapter, between the emergence of a modern European system of international relations, the supposedly normative status of territorial sovereignty in that system, and the formalization of historically diverse forms of legal personhood into modern extraterritorial practices. These three phenomena—international relations, the Westphalian state, and the extraterritorial exception—aren't triplets or necessary relations, but they do keep company.

Thus, although extraterritoriality is an increasingly important aspect of contemporary political geography, the paradox remains that, as a concept and practice, it depends upon the association between legitimate power and localizable space.[50] This is why in US law, for instance, extraterritoriality is often defined negatively. Supreme Court Justice Oliver Wendell Holmes opined in the amusingly named *American Banana* case of 1909 that "the general and almost universal rule is that the character of an act as lawful or unlawful must be determined wholly by the law of the country where the act is done" and that, "in case of doubt," it ought to be assumed that any statute is "confined in its operation and effect to the territorial limits over which the lawmaker has general and legitimate power."[51] This is what lawyers call the "presumption against extraterritoriality," and it draws on a notion of lawful political authority that assumes that to rule is to rule over a limited space and only within that space.

Justice Holmes's conception of territorial sovereignty is powerful, pervasive, and often honored in the breach.[52] His negative definition remains valuable, then, because it forces us to recognize how extraterritoriality is produced in and through an international system made up of many states, the sovereignties of which are defined, however imperfectly, by natural and artificial geographic borders.[53] When I say that extraterritoriality is both ordinary and extraordinary, I therefore mean that it expresses and manages the contradictions that result between the attempt to root lawful authority in an integrated territory and the knowledge that, if territorial integrity is to mean much within a system of many peoples and rivalrous powers, we must not only let strangers in: we must sometimes allow them to live in their own house, with their own companions, and according to their own rules.[54]

A LITTLE LIGHT HAUNTING

The word "extraterritorial" is a minor ghost in the lexicon of critical theory, lightly haunting the canons of speculative criticism, and generally employed as if it's synonymous with the *open* pole of the *open/closed* dyad. A stray use by Roland Barthes provides the characteristic note: "How can anyone believe that a given work is an object independent of the psyche and the personal history of the critic studying it, with regards to which he enjoys a sort of extraterritorial status [droit d'extéritorialité]?"[55]

As Barthes employs it, the word *extéritorialité* has leaped clear of its legalistic and political meanings, becoming instead a largely topological concept.[56] Barthes yokes *extéritorialité* to an argument about the impossibility of critical disinterestedness: we cannot exist wholly outside or apart from our critical objects, says Barthes, because they are too much part of our person. If it were possible to be extraterritorial, in Barthes's sense, then we would be able to stand outside or away from the gravity of our own psychology and history. In this section, I trace how, in the existing humanistic work about the extraterritorial, that term is regularly used by theorists and critics as a simplified figure for exceeding or evacuating experiences of locatedness, commitment, and determination.

Let's begin with a brief passage from Fredric Jameson's "Postmodernism, or, The Cultural Logic of Late Capitalism" (1984). On the way to demanding new cognitive maps of the postmodern world, Jameson pauses to consider how multinational capital has "penetrated and colonized . . . precapitalist enclaves" that once afforded "extraterritorial . . . footholds for critical effectivity."[57] In these phrases, "extraterritorial" designates lost islands of resistance. The examples Jameson gives of such footholds ("Nature and the Unconscious") are not in themselves geographic, but the type of problem with which he is concerned explains his use of insistently spatial rhetoric. That problem is spatial in two senses. First, Jameson addresses, like Barthes, the topological problem of critical distance—namely, how can we get outside a postmodern culture that is characterized by its capacity to absorb and appropriate contrary forms or ideas? Second, Jameson argues that multinational capitalism is engaged in a new two-part process of enclosure, spreading across new nations and extending more completely through the social fabric of the countries in which it has already taken root. He calls this "the third great original capitalist expansion around the globe." Thus, while Jameson may use "extraterritorial" figuratively, it's not a trivial spatial figure. For Jameson, "extraterritorial" connotes a lost utopian outside to capital. It's consistent with his long interest in thinking about utopia from the perspective of space, whether in his analysis of science fiction as a "spatial genre"[58] or in his distinction between the radically closed and systematized space of the "properly Utopian program" and the openness of a merely reform-minded "Utopian impulse."[59] For Jameson, the extraterritorial figures forth an "other space," outside the dominant politico-economic order.

Zygmunt Bauman's globalization theory offers another variation on this theme. Discussing twenty-first-century tourism, Bauman deploys "extraterritorial" as a moniker for what he calls "nowherevilles": consumer bubbles built for traveling foreign elites, luxury resort enclaves that are "impermeable and invulnerable, immune to . . . local idiosyncrasies."[60] We'll return to this kind of space later on, via J. G. Ballard novels such as *Cocaine Nights* (1996). For now, the bigger point is that Bauman also attaches "extraterritorial" not just to tourist enclaves but to another kind of spatial image or process altogether—that is, to the idea that globalization means the transcendence of territorial boundaries and the decline of an international state system in which territory was once "the most coveted of resources," but in which "strength and weakness, threat and security have become now, essentially, *extraterritorial issues that evade territorial solutions.*"[61] In a sentence curious for its implicit circularity, he later declares that the terrorists behind the attacks of 11 September 2001 epitomize this condition: "Being a phenomenon of the era of globalisation," these men are said to be "by definition extra-territorial."[62]

Barthes, Jameson, and Bauman hardly offer strong theories of the extra-territorial. But their uses of the term line up nicely with the major literary-critical precedent for this book, George Steiner's *Extraterritorial: Papers on the Literature and Language Revolution* (1974). In Steiner's book, the idea that "extraterritorial" names a cultural and geographic outside is combined with a vision of the writer's semisovereign dominion over that other space.[63] The extraterritorial is not just *open*; it is a field of open play made by and for the literary author.

Vladimir Nabokov is, for Steiner, exemplary of such extraterritorial panache: "A great writer driven from language to language by social upheaval and war is an apt symbol for the age of the refugee. No exile is more radical, no feat of adaptation and new life more demanding."[64] In tracing Nabokov's migrations from St Petersburg to New York, and from Russian to English, Steiner describes a poetics in which artistic form is activated and transformed by the movement across and within languages. Such a personally extraterritorial literature doesn't transcend place altogether: as with the bilingualism of Samuel Beckett, Nabokov's fiction rather expresses a rootlessness nourished by the capacity to feel at home in many places. But, while such artistic extraterritoriality takes shape within the biographical and historical horizon of "the age of the refugee," Steiner emphasizes the power of the creative act to transcend any determinate relation to place or grounded authority (11).[65]

It's not all sunlit uplands and émigré creativity. Steiner admits the "tireless, aggrieved insistence" with which Nabokov lamented how the "political barbarism of the century made him an exile" (7). But if history is the experience of necessity, then, for Steiner, art triumphantly shows that necessity is, in the end, not sufficient.[66] Against his reluctant admission of Nabokov's historical grievance, Steiner develops a critical idiom in which the great modern artist is anything but a powerless refugee: "Whereas so many other language exiles clung desperately to the artifice of their native tongue or fell silent, Nabokov moved into successive languages like a travelling potentate" (7). The image is of the artist as a nomadic sovereign, his power enlarged, not canceled, by the fact of making a home on the road. We can imagine this artist rolling up to some caravanserai of language, a retinue of memories and forms drawing out behind him. There, he drinks deep from the wells of a temporary home—just his latest linguistic shelter. After a spell, he moves on, having transformed the place by which he has also been changed.

Steiner's phrase "travelling potentate" is no accidental metaphor. It signals art's victory over the epoch of territorial power and national culture. Early in his book, Steiner suggests that writers such as Heinrich Heine and Oscar Wilde, at home as they are in more than one language, represent the true essence of the modern in literature. Before and alongside multilingual modernity, he positions the classical and medieval periods, in which literatures and literary sensibilities were shaped by the vigorous interaction of two, three, or more languages. The historical aberration within this pattern comes, he implies, in the eighteenth and nineteenth centuries, with the "nationalist mystique of the *writer enraciné*" (4). This localization of literary genius has innocent roots in the untranslatable vernacular energies of a William Shakespeare or Michel de Montaigne but Steiner regrets that it leads, ultimately, to a Romantic idealization of the writer as "at home in the language of his production, but displaced or hesitant at the frontier" (4). The extraterritorial writer therefore represents more than a passing alternative to the poet of national spirit; Nabokov and Beckett signal twentieth-century literature's liberation from the literary-historical cul-de-sac of Romantic nationalism. Such an aesthetic might be occasioned by the territorial struggles of the two world wars, but Steiner's writer unhoused by war is mostly liberated to wander across language, singing the untruth of identity. For Steiner, artistic extraterritoriality has only a negative relation to "the "political barbarism of the century."

But this salutary outlook is only possible when we forget that extraterritoriality is not only *open* but *closed*. Thus, while Steiner may be right about the poetics of exile as they have developed since Ovid and Dante, his argument is based on an historically thin understanding. Likewise, there are in fact two spatial movements or logics in Bauman's evocation of the extraterritorial: a hollowing out of national space into culture-less enclaves, and an epochal leap beyond the territorial state. Those movements are joined by the way they both degrade localized forms of authority or identity, working to similar ends by different means. Bauman does not to my knowledge comment on the alternate spatial logics implicit in his different uses of this one word, but perhaps that is because he is not actually describing two distinct movements. The creation of an enclave within national space requires an initial movement over, under, or through a preexisting boundary between the national and the foreign.[67] There is no making of an enclave without the prior traversal of a boundary—and yet (here is the key point) not all movements across boundaries are ethically or politically neutral.

Consider the period between June 2002 and January 2006, when José Padilla was declared an "enemy combatant" and held, without the right to a habeas corpus hearing, on the Naval Consolidated Brig in Charleston, South Carolina. Despite being a US citizen, imprisoned on a US military vessel in US territorial waters, Padilla was, as a matter of law, marooned within an extraterritorial zone in which, by virtue of his identification as an "enemy combatant," he lay beyond the jurisdiction of any US court.

The existence of extraterritorial people and places proves only that the geography of power is not formalistic and binary; it is not a matter of present or not, integral or not, inside or outside. Extraterritorial people and places are not harbingers of failed statehood, or of an incipiently borderless and cosmopolitan planetary culture, or of the state's relentless and uncheckable potency or reach. Extraterritorial figures and practices mediate pervasive and long-familiar tensions between territorial (*closed*) and nonterritorial (*open*) forces and interests. There is, thus, a profound difference between extraterritoriality and non- or aterritoriality. If artists and scholars were to remember this, the social and political claims they make for their work might be smaller and less optimistic, but they would be more persuasive.[68]

POLITICAL GEOGRAPHY AND LITERARY FORM

This book builds on recent work in critical literary geography, especially as that scholarly subfield attends, as Andrew Thacker has explained it, to the way "materiality, history, and power" inflect the production of social space and how space signifies in writing: "To think geographically about literary and cultural texts," writes Thacker, "means to understand them in material locations, locations that can and should be examined historically and with an awareness of how diverse spaces can reflect, produce or resist forms of power."[69]

More narrowly, by engaging the political geography of extraterritoriality, I hope to enlarge our critical knowledge of novelistic *setting*—a crucial but somewhat undertheorized aspect of prose fiction. In his classic theory of the chronotope, a narrative form in which "spatial and temporal indicators are fused into one carefully thought-out whole," Mikhail Bakhtin showed that the spatiotemporal dimensions of the novel can be especially visible to the critic of genre, who can chart the distribution of plots and settings, noting when and where they cluster in recognizable and, ultimately, institutionalized and self-authorizing patterns.[70] For this reason, several of the chapters that follow take up specific contemporary genres or subgenres: speculative fiction, for instance, as well postapocalyptic and historical novels. As I explain fully in chapters 2 and 3, my approach is to consider setting as more than the inert where and when of the text. Setting is an active formal principle in the novel: it both shapes and is shaped by other formal elements such as diction, narrative voice, point of view, character, plot, and authors' knowing deployment of generic tropes. Where texts are set in extraterritorial zones such as detention camps or international cities, those fictional locations directly evoke this book's central thematic and historical interests; together, such places comprise a partial inventory of the contemporary world's extraterritorial shape. But settings also have an allegorical or metaphorical function, in which they translate between disjunct places and times, many of which—a family home in Tudor London, for instance, or an administrative center of government—don't initially appear to float free of state or nation. Finally, because extraterritoriality is, as we've seen, a feature of persons as well as of spaces, the settings analyzed in this book are often interesting because of how they affect qualities of voice and character. In literary form, as well as law and politics, the boundary between places and persons proves highly permeable. My critical analyses of contemporary fiction respect the fundamental duality of extraterritoriality itself, which is never less than a property of individuals as well as geographies.

My interest in extraterritorial forms, as well as spaces and histories, determines the organization and orientation of this book. Chapter 1, "Zone," focuses on contemporary art and political history. Its job is twofold: to explain and illustrate the historical inextricability of territorial and extraterritorial forms of governance, and to give a first example of how extraterritorial spaces give rise to peculiar aesthetic effects.

The historical argument about territoriality dominates the middle sections of the chapter, which dispute the normative historical character of the Westphalian state. Idealized accounts of territorial statehood, I argue, lead us to mistake globalization as a crisis for the national state, when much of what passes for that "crisis" is in fact perfectly ordinary. As a result, cultural theorists and critics have tended to miss, or misrepresent, the extent to which the phenomena we group together under labels such as "globalization" are often the products or projects of sovereign states and national elites.

The aesthetic implications of this history are suggested through two examples from contemporary art. First, I tell a story about the Geneva Freeport: a tax-free warehouse and point of sale for an unfathomably large number of contemporary artworks, which has also been the basis for recent theories about the contemporaneity of twenty-first-century art, including a "Duty-Free" or "Freeportist" aesthetic attributed to so-called postinternet artworks that exist mostly in remediated form on the internet. Moving to more overtly political art, the chapter's closing section exemplifies my arguments about the historically ordinary status of extraterritorial geographies by analyzing three works by British artist Mark Wallinger. Each of those pieces engages a different kind of extraterritorial zone: an area of relaxed obligation within Jewish religious law; an "exclusion zone" through which the British state regulates constitutional and common law rights to free speech; and the three-dimensional border zone of the international airport, in which sovereignty is radically disaggregated so as to manage human migration and enforce state security policies. Wallinger's reimagination of each kind of zone enriches our historical understanding of how globalization develops through the planned subdivision of sovereign space; it also illustrates how different sort of extraterritorial space require developments in and across different media and materials, from sculpture through installation and video.

With chapter 2, "City-State," we move on to the terrain of contemporary fiction, asking why China Miéville's speculative fictions are so regularly set in internally fractured city-states. Formally, the chapter considers the relation between setting, strategies of novelistic world-creation, and Miéville's commitment to what he calls "the weird of genre." Theoretically, it engages the most influential current philosophical account of extraterritoriality: Giorgio Agamben's political theory, in which the extraterritorial logic of the "inclusive exclusion" is held to be decisive for sovereignty in general. The chapter is highly skeptical about this argument, only the medium for its critique is novelistic, centering as it does on the philosophical implications of the city-state setting of Miéville's *The City & the City* (2009), which I read as an allegorical polemic against theories, like Agamben's, that identify sovereignty as the power to give the law to others without their consent. In Miéville's extraterritorial fictions, political power is inherently decentralized and pluralistic, neither exceptional nor liberatory, and subject most of all to the winds of capital.

Chapter 3, "String Theory," poses a literary-historical question: Why are so many recent postapocalyptic novels set in archipelagic landscapes? To answer this question, the chapter considers more than ten English-language examples, showing how twenty-first-century innovators in the postapocalyptic novel subgenre accentuate and magnify a quality common to many forms of romance narrative: the division of the story-world into city and wilderness, with the plot being generated in and through the characters' journeys between one kind of redoubt and another. Building on this analytical survey, the chapter features extended close readings that draw out particular kinds of exterritorial formal effect. Analyzing the world-making and narrative voice in Chang-rae Lee's *On Such a Full Sea* (2014), I explain its strange combination of certainty and sketchiness as a function of its fractured political geography. Reading the temporalizing diction of

Mandel's *Station Eleven*, I link that novel's verbal tics and tropes to its simplified landscape: a fence, a fire, and *out there*. And considering Margaret Atwood's *MaddAddam* trilogy (2003–13), I explain how its proliferation of proper nouns adds color to an otherwise abstract global economy, one in which national states have disappeared but the compulsion to mark and protect territory is as prevalent as ever. Although any empirical claim about the postapocalyptic genre as such would require testing against even more titles, my medium-scale analysis buttresses this book's claim about the influence of extraterritorial political geographies on the development of contemporary novelistic form.

Following two chapters about speculative fictions, chapter 4, "The Border That Is Not a Border," considers the historical novel. Franco Moretti has argued that classic European historical novels of the nineteenth century are disproportionately set in proximity to borders—frontiers that are then abolished or affirmed in order to symbolize the integrity of the national state. In contemporary variants, by contrast, the privileged generic space is the unrecognized or indistinct frontier, which is diffused throughout the territory and, far from being abolished, remains essential to the working of contemporary political life. We begin with Hilary Mantel's *Wolf Hall* (2009), which locates international conflict not at the edges of the territory but throughout national space, and particularly in the personal space of the household of Thomas Cromwell, King Henry VIII's chief minister during a key decade of the English Reformation. It traces that dynamic as it works out in the novel's plot, and in Mantel's historiographical commitment to the idea that Cromwell initiated a revolution in English state-formation, but it also focuses on Mantel's unusual deployment of the epithet "person" and, especially, on her adoption of a close third-person narrative style in which Cromwell's identification by the pronoun "he" is curiously pronounced. When we attend to these formal traits, a novel that initially seems to be about territorial sovereignty turns out to be about Cromwell's extraordinary extraterritoriality of person.

Chapter 4's second part considers Amitav Ghosh's *Ibis* trilogy (2008–15), a self-consciously globalizing novel that draws together several stories from the years before and during the 1839–42 Opium War between Britain and

China. Ghosh's trilogy—and especially its middle part, *River of Smoke* (2011)—draws directly on nineteenth-century documents that depict the Opium War as a struggle between two sorts of empire: an antique Chinese system of universal sovereignty and a British-dominated system of nominally equal territorial states. Ghosh rejects the formal equality of the international system as the mask of Western privilege and imperialist impunity, positioning the Opium War as a key event in what historians such as Kenneth Pomeranz have called the "great divergence" between Europe and Asia. Against both sorts of empire, his historical fiction celebrates instead the obscure extraterritorial enclave of "Fanqui-town," Canton's foreign trading colony in the years before the war. Against the classic historical novel's nation-making verve, Ghosh gives us a version of the genre that is formally and ideological unassimilable to any one national, ethnic, or linguistic tradition.

Chapter 5, "Settlement," finally moves us from space to time. Developing the previous chapter's interest in novels set on the South China Sea coast, its particular setting is the Shanghai International Settlement between the world wars. And its peculiar concern is how, in Western accounts of that time and place, extraterritorial spaces give rise to *extratemporal* aesthetic effects. The chapter begins with a contemporary photo essay about Shanghai Links, a luxury development that consciously replicates the style and political economy of the International Settlement. It then moves, via interwar British and Chinese texts about extraterritoriality in interwar Shanghai, to Kazuo Ishiguro's *When We Were Orphans* (2000), which depicts interwar Shanghai through a poetics of simultaneity and anachronism that inheres at the level of genre as much as plot and character. The chapter's final section then focuses on the late work of J. G. Ballard, explaining how and why his last four novels are all fundamentally the same "extraordinary ordinary" story about extraterritorial spaces, in which the semicolonial city of Shanghai is programmatically recreated as the future past of a catastrophic present. That programmatic rewriting gives rise to a novelistic poetics in which the untimely effects of combined and uneven political and economic development are felt at every formal level, from image and prosody through setting, plot, and character. It also, and once again, testifies to the extraterritorial directions of some of the most radical and influential Anglophone fictions.

Finally, the conclusion, "The Extraterritorial Novel," speculates about the implications of this book's arguments for the study of the novel in general. The conclusion's main example comes from W. G. Sebald, for whom extraterritoriality functions as a richly overdetermined metaphor. Via Sebald, Siegfried Kracauer, and György Lukács's theory that the novel is the genre most associated with the "transcendental homelessness" of modern life, the epilogue considers the idea the contemporary novel is an inherently extraterritorial genre. In the end, I conclude, there's nothing essentially extraterritorial about contemporary fiction. As a student of the historical social sciences, I have learned to reject the reduction of extraterritoriality to any one particular political function or value; and, as a literary critic with a commitment to historical social analysis, I refuse to idealize novelistic form and genre, preferring instead to embrace its wonderful mutability and contingency.

Extraterritorial sketches an ad hoc cultural map of an increasingly archipelagic world. It adds to methodological debates by showing how a political geography of literature can and should remain attuned to the literariness of the novel form. Beyond its more narrowly academic ambitions, *Extraterritorial* asks how and why institutions and citizens share and subdivide real and imaginary spaces in the making of transnational culture. By examining extraterritorial space, we learn how supposedly global forces produce not frictionless flows but a fractured landscape of gated communities, mobile border regimes, and insular solidarities. We learn why such extraterritorial fracturing is one of globalization's conditions of possibility. And we gain an artistic vocabulary through which to envision this complex and changing present. Uniting political, geographical, and literary insights, *Extraterritorial* essays the shape of the twenty-first century. It is in that spirit that we must now move beyond introductory framing and definitions.

It is time to enter the freeport zone.

1

ZONE

It is as if the modern system of rule, having expanded spatially and functionally as far as it could, has nowhere to go but "forward" towards an entirely new system of rule or "backward" towards early modern or even pre-modern forms of war or state-making.

—GIOVANNI ARRIGHI, *THE LONG TWENTIETH CENTURY*

"They come for the security and stay for the tax treatment."[1] David Segal's quip about the superrich arrives a little way into his *New York Times* story about the strange institution known as the Geneva Freeport: a vast warehouse home to an unfathomably large collection of art objects, all sheltered from sales tax and customs duties. In this age of market volatility and low interest rates, the very wealthy have developed a habit of investing in collectible commodities rather than financial securities.[2] The valuable objects they purchase are then stored in armored and climate-controlled vaults, safe from thieves and the elements: unlooked-at, but appreciating in value. Segal's story begins with a tale about a room stacked high with Picassos; in the next vault, someone is counting gold bars.

According to one expert, the Geneva Freeport functions as a "clearing house" for the international art trade, with "more than half of art traded globally through auctions and direct sales" moving through its vaults.[3] But nobody really knows how many artworks are stored or sold there, and no one can guess at their value. This is because the Freeport's privacy policies, compounding lax Swiss regulations regarding the identification of objects and owners, mean that even insurance conglomerates cannot calculate the extent of their clients' holdings.[4] The Geneva Freeport's status as an onshore tax suspension zone relies on the legal fiction that items stored within it are still technically in transit, even if the owner bought them there and never intends to remove them from storage.[5] A painting or case of wine might be sold, stored, and then sold again without ever leaving the Freeport and without ever incurring local sales or importation taxes. The Freeport is a "fiscal no-man's land," a loophole within one area of the state's traditional sovereign competency.[6] There could hardly be a better example of how a putatively global cultural sphere is produced by the circulation of people and things within a disaggregated legal and political geography.

In this chapter, I substantiate this book's main empirical claims: that in countries such as the United Kingdom, people live within a disaggregated political geography; that this geography is crucial to the functioning of what we call "globalization"; and that the history and theory of extraterritoriality helps us better understand both those facts. The chapter contests the historically normative status of the Westphalian territorial state, with the uncanny result—as my epigraph from Giovanni Arrighi suggests—that our present age sometimes appears to us as qualitatively new, but at other times like the rebirth of feudal or early modern forms of parcelized sovereignty. Cultural theories of globalization often depend on a mistaken identification of the nation-state with an ideal-type conception of territorial sovereignty. As a result, historically ordinary practices of territorial pooling, merging, and self-dividing are misdescribed as symptoms of crisis or transformative change. Far from representing a utopian outside to the state, extraterritoriality is inseparable from the very notion of territorial order.

This isn't a merely social scientific argument. In order to properly account for phenomena such as the global art market, we need to grapple with aspects of our shared history that can appreciate the functional spatial interdependence of the territorial and extraterritorial—and this is especially important if we're to measure globalization's aesthetic effects. That functional spatial interdependence is memorably articulated in Keller Easterling's *Extrastatecraft* (2014), the title of which is a portmanteau word describing the actions of private and semiprivate agents that operate "outside of, in addition to, and sometimes in partnership with" states.[7] Easterling is interested in the kinds of architectures made possible by infrastructural systems such as telecommunications networks, export processing zones, and other sorts of freeports or free cities, the many varieties of which she gathers under the generalizing noun "zone." The zone, she writes, is the "dominant software for making urban space" today.[8] Its distinctness in the way it depends on "a cocktail of enticements and legal exemptions" that are given spatial form by the drawing of a boundary between the zone and the nation in which it located, whose territorial integrity it interrupts, but upon whose authority its survival depends.[9] Because of this extraterritorial doubleness, a place such as the Dubai International Finance Center (DIFC)—an independent "Financial Free Zone" within the United Arab Emirates, with distinct civil and commercial laws based on English jurisprudence—does in some senses lie "beyond the reach of the state." But the DIFC stands apart only to the extent that such separation allows it to function as an "essential partner. . . . that strengthens the state by serving as its proxy or camouflage."[10] The zone is a "site of multiple, overlapping, or nested forms of sovereignty, where domestic and transnational jurisdictions collide."[11] It is a paradigmatic example of an extraterritorial space that occupies a position *outside within* the juridico-political space of the territorial state. Such a zone is the infrastructural materialization of the principles of "graduated sovereignty" that Aihwa Ong describes as a contemporary alternative to Westphalian concepts of sovereign government that overemphasize the importance of juridico-political centralization and territorial integration.[12]

The pages to come develop these arguments in a several contexts, providing evidence in the form of a variety of actual and imagined extraterritorial sites, from international airports to the Jewish religious enclaves called *eruvim*. The second half of the chapter then features an extended analysis of three recent works by the British artist Mark Wallinger: the Turner Prize–winning gallery installation, *State Britain* (2007); an outdoor conceptual sculpture, *Zone* (2007); and a video work, *Threshold to the Kingdom* (2000). These different pieces in different media share Wallinger's pervasive wit and fascination with the multiplication and internalization of borders. Taken together, they dramatize how states such as the United Kingdom have developed novel ways to subdivide and graduate territorial sovereignty so as to manage phenomena as diverse as immigration, international security, and internal dissent. Wallinger's artwork doesn't just protest against contemporary bordering regimes. It tests the adequacy of different visual forms and media for embodying or representing the many different kinds of borders, which today exist not at the edges of national space but throughout the territory. For now, though, we begin not with contemporary art as such; we return, instead, to the Freeport and to the aesthetic implications of its role in the international art market.

THE FREEPORT IN THEORY AND PRACTICE

Over the last decades, the Geneva Freeport facility has been joined by similar operations in Luxembourg and Singapore, while a new "Freeport of Culture" has been advertised as opening soon in Beijing. The first three of these facilities are not really competitors, since they are all, to one degree or another, projects of Yves Bouvier: Swiss proprietor of the logistics company Natural Le Coultre and a central figure in the highly specialized industry that links art removals and storage to the networks of art dealers, middlemen, and buyers who together underwrite the multibillion dollar international art trade.[13]

The complexity and obscurity of the freeport system makes it an obvious target of interest for anyone studying the political economy of contemporary culture. Yet recent criticism about the freeport trend shows significant interest in the facilities' aesthetic implications, as well as their economic function. In his *New Yorker* essay, Sam Knight explains that freeports offer "few tax advantages and scarcely any security features that a standard bonded warehouse cannot provide."[14] The attraction of facilities like the one in Geneva lies, he says, in the way they combine fiscal benefits with other, more specialized, attributes—most obviously, their operators' expertise in moving and storing artworks, but also their ability to cultivate a manner and environment pleasing to collectors and dealers: "The ultra-rich don't want just another warehouse," Knight explains, before quoting Bouvier himself: 'If you buy a painting for a hundred million, what do you want? You want to feel well. . . . Why else do people travel in first class?'" The freeport has thus become its own species of cultural and "lifestyle" realm—a zone of consumption, leisure, and display that's neither the same as the white cubes of Chelsea or Cork Street, nor identical to the hyperarchitectural volumes of international art museums, but that partakes of both, as well as the concierge culture of luxury hotel travel. The Singapore Freeport features a generous tax regime, cutting-edge security, and high-tech fire control and environmental systems. But equal care has also been put into the design of its lighting, furnishings, and interiors, as well as in the selection of artworks for its lobby area.[15] The managing director of Le Freeport in Luxembourg describes his facility as "the best alternative to owning your own museum."[16] And he seems, at least, to be putting his mouth where his mouth is. The "Facilities" page at Le Freeport's website is designed so that one learns about its "stunning architectural and aesthetic features" before being informed about its "safe and secure storage for works of art."[17]

Two recent pieces in the art theory journal *E-Flux* also make the case for a fuller kind of "duty-free aesthetics," in which the freeport's functional and economic centrality to the twenty-first-century art market is linked to arguments about the contemporaneity of contemporary art. In the second of those articles, Stefan Heidenreich uses the label "freeportism" to describe the supposed phenomenon in which new artworks are placed into freeport storage as soon as they are sold, sometimes before they are even exhibited, so that the act of disappearing into a tax-free black box becomes a constitutive element of the work itself. This alleged formal feature is then linked to a broader "post-internet" style in which artistic practice shuttles back and forth between virtual and material realms, with the work as a whole only coming together through its secondary mediation on the internet.[18] Heidenreich gives the example of Katja Novitskova's sculptures, in which she lifts images from the Web, manipulates them onscreen, displays them in galleries and museums as digital prints on aluminum sculptural forms, and then restores them to online circulation by posting installation view photographs on Instagram (fig. 1.1). These are works about which Novitskova says "you take certain elements from pre-existing environments . . . and you

FIGURE 1.1 *Hydrothermal Potential* (Lost City), 2015. Digital print
on two layers of aluminum, cutout display, 219 x 50 x 35 cm |
86 1/4 x 19 2/3 x 13 3/4 in.

Photo by: Katja Novitskova. *Image courtesy*: the artist and Kraupa-Tuskany Zeidler.

combine them in a way that creates new entities, almost like new life forms."[19] At the same time, while her images, so Novitskova says, "need to be materialised,"[20] she remains an artist for whom preparing a gallery show means sketching "not just the ideas I have around the exhibition or single works, but the potential visual documentation of it."[21]

Heidenreich presents no evidence that Novitskova's sculptures peculiarly congregate in freeport vaults—and the same goes for "post-internet" art in general, which may or may not be piling up in Geneva, Luxembourg, or Singapore. (The truth is, no one can say.) Still, Heidenreich claims this lack of proof isn't important:

> What matters is the speculative approach that leads venture collectors to invest in these assets. In order to claim their future value, artworks have to fit the site of non-exhibition at a freeport. The better objects are optimized for [circulation] through social media images, the more they adapt to the requirements of freeportism. The secondary layer of online-existence allows the "real" object to be completely withdrawn, buried in a wooden coffin.[22]

In Heidenreich's account, the aesthetic signature of freeportism is that the born-digital artwork can take physical shape (and thus becomes available for purchase and storage as a collectible commodity) while still continuing to accrue value through an online second life, which persists independently of whether that object happens to be exhibited, or bought and sold in public view.[23] "Freeportism" is thus adapted to two different kinds of extraterritoriality: the realm of the internet—poised between a virtual nowhere and a physical telecommunications infrastructure of server farms, packet-switching stations, fiber-optic networks, and satellites—and the fiscal and specular black hole of the freeport, at once within a national community and outside its customs and excise zone.[24]

While Heidenreich's speculations are perhaps too clever by half, Hito Steyerl's meditation on "Duty-Free Art" (2015) rests on more solid ground. Originally commissioned as a lecture by Artists Space New York, then published in *E-Flux*, and now collected as the title essay of her book

Duty-Free Art: Art in the Age of Planetary Civil War (2017), Steyerl's argument proceeds by way of paratactic juxtaposition. She connects the Geneva Freeport directly or indirectly to an array of different places, objects, and texts, including a Turkish national art museum turned into a refugee camp and a painting by Muammar Gaddafi's son. The piece is full of startling connections. It closes with the intriguing proposition that the freeport be read as an allegory for the possibility of autonomous art in the present age: "Duty-free art ought to *have no duty*—no duty to perform, to represent, to teach, to embody value."[25] Even more, as with Sela and Amir's vision of a heterotopic oceanic zone in *Exterritory Project*, Steyerl wonders whether the freeport might model the possibility of *political* autonomy in a context in which countries such as Switzerland "proclaim national culture" while building "gated communities for high-net-worth individuals, much like microversions of failed states."[26] Once again, extraterritorial space stands in for the possibility that one might step outside the realm of existing obligations or commitments.

Most central to our purpose, however, is the passage in which Steyerl links the Geneva Freeport to one of the central premises of Peter Osborne's influential book, *Anywhere or Not at All: Philosophy of Contemporary Art* (2013). This is the proposition that the very idea of contemporaneity involves a spatialized "fiction" of temporal copresence—that is, the fiction of being together (*con*) in time (*tempus*). Osborne argues, moreover, that under conditions of economic globalization any story of temporal copresence must be geopolitical in nature, imagining not just how human social life shares a common *when* but also a communal *where*.[27] It's not just that telling the story of contemporary art requires telling a story about the global art trade; about the artist as world-traveling celebrity; about the global movement in art students, professors, curators, and other recipients of institutional patronage; or about a pervasive aesthetic of hybridization, in which the conjoining or blending of disparate cultural elements has become the official signature of the artist-as-migrant. Osborne admits the importance of all of these elements. But his argument is really predicated on an idea about the utopian dimension of art in the twenty-first century: the thesis that art can provide a conceptual model in which human beings share, in symbolic terms if not in actual fact, a coherent, if disjunctive, social world. Osborne therefore suggests that the lines of global social interconnectedness that characterize works such as the Atlas Group projects of Lebanese artist Walid Raad should be understood as "a stand-in for the missing political collectivity of the globally transnational."[28] The downside to this utopian "stand-in" is that we need it because the "globally transnational" has so far only been realized in the dystopian form of global capitalism. Outside the market, "there is no socially actual shared subject-position" from the standpoint of which the present can be lived completely.[29] Art allows us to imagine a global commons that does not exist in practice; that is the key to its contemporaneity in an unevenly globalized age.

Steyerl turns to Osborne's argument right before discussing the Geneva Freeport. "Contemporary art shows us the lack of a (global) time and space," she writes. "It projects a fictional unity onto a variety of different ideas of time and space, thus providing a common surface where there is none."[30] Both Steyerl and Osborne invoke contemporary art as a proxy for an otherwise absent global commons. But Steyerl goes one step further, connecting the fictional unity of art and social space to the way the global art market depends, at the infrastructural level, on the creation of zones such as the Geneva Freeport, which enable international commerce by puncturing and graduating territorial space.[31] This is also where her musings on the freeport zone as a utopian figure for political autonomy collide with her clear-eyed sense of who actually benefits from the freeport industry. Duty-free art is global, Steyerl says, because it combines "a proliferation of locations" with a legal regime that allows the very wealthy to escape "accountability" for their crimes and obligations.[32] Duty-free art therefore gives us a decidedly mixed perspective upon what Osborne calls the "single historical time of the present."[33] In its disjunctive totality, as in its extraterritorial mixing of liberatory openness and occulted secrecy, the freeport figures forth both the dystopia of market-driven inequality and the utopia of the globally expansive artistic imagination.

BEYOND THE TERRITORIAL GIVEN

The freeport tells us something that will prove central to all subsequent chapters of this book: extraterritorial spaces can possess their own aesthetic affects. They are not just allegorical or homological reference points for artistic works that are ostensibly about other things. The job of the next three short sections, however, will be to explain such spaces historically and theoretically. Such an explanation matters because ahistorical accounts of territorial statehood corrupt our understanding of the present. They blind us to aspects of our shared history that are incompatible with the "sovereignty-territory ideal," in which state power in general is mistakenly identified with having power over land.[34] As a result, such explanations mislead us into thinking of globalization as an absolute crisis for the state when, in reality, much of what passes for that "crisis" is historically ordinary.

To better understand extraterritorial space, it is useful to turn to a concept that the radical public law scholar John Griffiths dubs "legal pluralism." Griffiths argues that entities like the Geneva Freeport (or, rather, the legal principles that make it possible) are not the exception but the rule: "Legal pluralism is the fact. Legal centralism is a myth, an ideal, a claim, an illusion."[35] We don't sufficiently notice this practical reality, he claims, because it is obscured by an ideology of legal centralism according to which the law "is and should be the law of the state, uniform for all persons, exclusive of all other law, and administered by a single set of state institutions."[36] For Griffiths, the idea that the law is singular and identifiable with an equally singular state is a mere doxa that pales against "the omnipresent, normal situation," in which social life is structured by multiple legal codes and institutions—for instance, of religious groups, castes, clans, professions, trade unions, and political parties.[37] He admits that the law of the state might assume a coercive and dominating power within a society, but, he contends, that doesn't mean that state law is theoretically dispositive, the only fact worth describing, or singular in its operations or claims to authority. "Always the stern logic of theory seems to imply that the dominating institution is absolute," writes Harold Laski, Griffiths's predecessor at the London School of Economics.[38] For the legal pluralist, the devil lies in the difference between domination and absolute power. That's a distinction that seems relevant to a place such as the Geneva Freeport, in which the state creates a loophole within its fiscal and customs regime so as to liberate the speculative energies of art collectors, gallerists, and logistics companies.

The problem with theories of legal pluralism is that they beg questions of coherence and hierarchy: How do all these legal codes hang together? Can we really compare a voluntary code such as the bylaws of a union local to, say, federal labor law? If the union's bylaws clashed with federal law, wouldn't the state carry the day? Most important, if the Swiss or Genevan authorities wanted to close the loophole that underwrites the Freeport, couldn't they zip it tight?

I don't invoke Griffiths's strong theory of legal pluralism, then, so as to endorse it but to suggest how the problem of extraterritoriality is continuous with a broader stratum of scholarly debate about the singularity, or otherwise, of state power. In what follows, I am guided by Michael Mann's argument that the various competencies of the law and government are at once "entwined" and "nonsystemic."[39] In the second volume of *The Sources of Social Power*, Mann argues that, "far from being singular and centralized, modern states are polymorphous power networks" that include what he calls "diverse crystallizations" of power.[40] Most centrally, he argues that state power includes distinct military, political, ideological, and economic dimensions but that the state as such is irreducible to any one such source of authority or legitimacy. Mann uses the chemical metaphor of the "polymorph" to describe how forms of social and political power belong to different systems simultaneously: "States have multiple institutions, charged with multiple tasks, mobilizing constituencies both through their territories and geopolitically."[41] The modern state as it developed in Europe is generally territorial and, because it exists in a world of other states with which it has formally equal relations, it can typically be defined from the "outside in."[42] The state's territorial extension gives it a kind of semiautonomy as an "arena" or "place" in and through which power operates.[43] And yet even this political space lacks final unity: "Whatever centrality, whatever private rationality, the state possesses, it is also impure, different parts of its body politic open to penetration by diverse power networks."[44] In this way, my argument in what follows tips its hand toward the idea that state sovereignty is divisible. In so doing, however, I focus not on the hierarchical arrangement of political institutions or laws within a single state but, rather, on the way social and political space can tolerate multiple geographies of affiliation and authority, both as a result of the interactions between states and in terms of the disposition of authority within an individual community.

My argument therefore contravenes the jurisprudential presumption against extraterritoriality that we encountered in the last chapter, which asserts that a nation's laws apply only within its territory and are legitimate for that very reason. That sort of doctrine is associated with the so-called Westphalian state, which takes its name from the 1648 Peace of Westphalia: a pair of treaties, signed at Münster and Osnabrück in Germany, that ended the Thirty Years' War and became retrospectively the symbolic origin of the modern interstate system. The idea of a Westphalian state is now indelibly associated with the doctrine that political sovereignty involves the right to geographically exclude "external sources of authority both *de jure* and *de facto*," as well as the principle that at "the international level this implies that states follow the rule of non-intervention in the internal affairs of others."[45] As recent history in places such as Syria and Ukraine shows, these doctrines of territorial exclusivity and nonintervention tend to be honored in the breach as much as the observance. It's also been said with good reason that the peace treaties of 1648 represent less a sea change in international relations than a convenient reference point for a slow and uneven process of geopolitical development in which European monarchies gradually began to conceive of themselves as exercising sovereignty over territories, rather than over persons.[46] Nevertheless, despite being debunked or criticized many times before now, the term "Westphalia" still names an ideal-type version of an interstate system. And, in that system, legitimate political authority is defined in and through relations between exclusive and territorially inviolable sovereignties, rather than by deferring to a patchwork of local competencies or a grand suprastate authority, such as an emperor or pontiff, located above individual peoples or places.[47]

So, how did we get to Westphalia? It helps to begin with the concept of territoriality as such. Friedrich Kratochwil's much-cited article on territorial communities defines them as "built upon the recognition of mutual rights subject to a common law within a given territory."[48] That statement rather verges on circularity, so it's helpful that Kratochwil also contrasts territorial groups with nomadic societies organized according to kinship systems and principles of movement rather than the grouping of nations or peoples within demarcated areas.[49] Moreover, this antithesis between territorial and kinship-based forms of authority and organization has a long and influential history. Emile Durkheim, to give just one example, argues that human societies progressively advanced from internally undifferentiated hordes, to communities organized around the politico-familial unit of the clan, to those structured around the "occupational milieu" of the division of labor.[50] If, for Durkheim, modernity is characterized by such progressive sociological differentiation, then the route toward modernity goes through territorial organization and stratification. Durkheim contrasts polities organized according to tribal or familial consanguinity to the organizational logic that, in his system, succeeds them: the "artificial" arrangement of peoples by territorial separation.[51] These territorial divisions are at first local or regional in nature but, as local jargons and dialects give way to national languages, and as provincial governments agglomerate into the organs of the national state, they become both larger and less grounded in "the nature of things."[52] What matters for Durkheim is not the specific quality of one's social or political relation to a particular piece of land, but the simple fact that over time the logic of social and political differentiation becomes territorial rather than familial.[53]

Despite its teleological character, Durkheim's narrative indicates the pervasiveness of the association between community formation and territorial division. Stuart Elden likewise begins his genealogical study of the concept of territory with Jean-Jacques Rousseau's *Discourse on the Origin and Basis of Inequality Among Men* (1755) and its famous assertion: "The first man who fenced off a plot of land [enclose un terrain], thought of saying *this is mine*, and found people simple enough to believe him, was the real founder of civil society."[54] To exercise legitimate authority, such stories would have us believe, is to claim ownership over some particular plot of earth. Elden traces forms of territorial thought back to ancient Greek literature and Hebrew scripture. In the main, though, he emphasizes the relative newness of territorial sovereignty—a political technology that depends for its development on such diverse factors as Pope Boniface VIII's 1302 distinction between the "two swords" of temporal and spiritual government and the late medieval growth of bureaucratic administration and systems of taxation. Territoriality has a long history, Elden knows, but his story of its hot embrace with political sovereignty really picks up in the thirteenth and fourteenth centuries. Saskia Sassen likewise argues that modern forms of territorial government did not emerge *ab novo* out of the nonterritorial sovereignties (feudal, imperial, papal) of the European late Middle Ages. The territorial and national state developed, instead, from capabilities that were intrinsic to medieval politics and society, including the way that the new cities and towns of Europe, identifying with the nation and the monarchy more readily than the local manor house and landowners, emerged contemporaneously with monarchical claims to forms of divinely inspired sovereignty previously restricted to the Bishop of Rome.[55] Elden and Sassen pit their analyses against accounts of territoriality that would see the modern state as inherently distinct from the feudalist order that Perry Anderson described as possessing an "inextricably superimposed and tangled [political map], in which different juridical instances were geographically interwoven and stratified, and plural allegiances, asymmetrical suzerainties and anomalous enclaves abounded."[56] The point, however, is that, no matter how nuanced their analyses, these theorists all affirm the idea that European political modernity is defined, if only in part, by the association between legitimate political authority and its spatial extension.

It is this same association between sovereignty and territory that the adjective "Westphalian" most typically describes. There was, naturally, rather more and less than a theoretical question at stake in 1648. The negotiating parties at Münster and Osnabrück weren't concerned with refining the conceptual vocabulary of international relations theory but with ending a long and terrible war to their own advantage. Still, in academic and popular writing, the Westphalian settlement remains associated with a trinity of concepts that continue to shape scholarly assumptions about the political geography of the present. That trinity might be represented by the shorthand "state," "sovereignty," and "territoriality," with each term presumed to lead necessarily to the next, such that to be a state is to be sovereign and to be sovereign is to be territorially inviolate. This conceptual trinity therefore encourages us to see territoriality and extraterritoriality as simple antitheses, with the latter figuring as an exceptional outside to the territorial norm. But this position is both factually mistaken and theoretically obtuse. It cannot account for territorial states' historical willingness to use extraterritorial practices in pursuit of their strategic goals, whether by extending their power across international borders, negotiating to limit that extension in order to make free or international space, or creating jurisdictional lacunae within their own territory. It mistakes the "extra-" in "extraterritorial" as marking a pure outside, rather than a dialectical condition of being *outside within*.

For an example of the territorial trinity at work, we can turn to Leo Gross's influential 1948 article "The Peace of Westphalia, 1648–1948." As its title suggests, Gross's essay compares the Westphalian treaties of three centuries before with the UN Charter that was then three years old. For Gross, these foundational moments in international relations together define a just world system "based on *states*," which are characterized by "untrammelled *sovereignty*" enshrined in "certain *territories*."[57]

In one respect, Gross's trinity seems eminently appropriate to its times. The UN Charter was in part premised, as Article 2 of that document explains, on principles of sovereign equality that proscribed violations by threat or force against the territorial integrity of member states.[58] But Gross doesn't stop with the suggestion that the agreements of 1648 and 1945 share a common basis in principles of de jure political equality realized in the de facto observation of territorial borders. He further asserts that the treaties of 1648 provide the "ratio scripta" (written reason) that underlies the new post–World War II epoch. With the Allied victory and the founding of the United Nations, Gross declares that the Westphalian trinity of statehood, sovereignty, and territoriality has once again resumed its historic position as the "majestic portal which leads from the old world into the new."[59]

Such confidence came to seem misplaced almost as soon as the Cold War set in. Less than a decade after Gross wrote his encomium to Westphalia, John H. Herz would argue that the development of aerial nuclear weapons, with their power to "by-pass the shell protecting a two-dimensional territory," presaged the obliteration of "the very meaning of [the political] unit and [its putative] unity."[60] Looking back on the founding of the United Nations from the perspective of the 1990s, Giovanni Arrighi similarly argues that the post-1945 international institutions that Gross saw as the apotheosis of Westphalian principles were part of an ongoing dialectic of territorial expansion and supersession. For Arrighi, the restoration of territorial sovereignty following World War II's "unprecedented violation of the principles, norms, and rules of the Westphalia system" was followed by a cycle of US hegemony that established new institutions such as the International Monetary Fund (IMF), which themselves placed powerful practical limitations on the sovereignty rights that the UN Charter ostensibly affirms.[61] Rather than signaling the continuity between a Westphalian old order and the new, Arrighi sees 1945 as a moment of consolidation in a new hegemonic cycle within the world system:

> Once again, expansion had involved supersession. The supersession of the Westphalia system by [British] free-trade imperialism [of the nineteenth century] was real but partial. The principles, norms, and rules of behavior restored by the Congress of Vienna [1814–15] left considerable leeway to the members of the inter-state system on how to organize their domestic and international relations. Free trade impinged on the sovereignty of rulers, but the latter's ability to "delink" from the trade and power networks of the hegemonic state if they so chose remained considerable. . . . In comparison with free-trade imperialism, the institutions of US hegemony have considerably restricted the rights and powers of sovereign states to organize relations with other states and with their own subjects as they see fit.[62]

Similar judgments can be found everywhere in academic and popular literature about the prospects for the territorial state in an age of multinational capitalism, many of them portending that Westphalian norms no longer apply to a world in which terrestrial borders appear to matter less and less. This was especially the case during the heady days of 1990s globalization theory. Jean-Marie Guéhenno wrote then of the collapse of the "territorial given" in international relations: now that wealth is increasingly abstract and immaterial, he argued, power no longer depends on the relations of spatial proximity and integrity that structured the modern state.[63] In Arjun Appadurai's anthropology of the present, territorial sovereignty was said to persist as the mere "ideoscape" through which beleaguered national states seek to "repatriate," at the level of ideas and images, the dispersed facts of transnationally dispersed economic production.[64] Appadurai hypothesized that the 1990s inaugurated a new era of "sovereignty without territoriality" in which the attachment of political authority to land, once considered the fundamental source of power and legitimacy, was more than just in doubt. Far from possessing normative force, Appadurai declared, territoriality had become the "key site" of crisis in a nation-state system that was said to be on its "last legs."[65]

NEITHER WESTPHALIA NOR THE GLOBE

It is now two decades since the boosterish 1990s—and the territorial state isn't finished yet. Luckily, it's possible to set aside the hyperbolic aspects of globalization theory and still puncture the myth of Westphalia. The key, here as before, is not to reduce territorial statehood to a fetishistic illusion or hypostatize it as an irreducible norm of political modernity. As we have seen, phenomena such as the Geneva Freeport and Dubai International Finance Center illustrate the way states today will willingly puncture and subdivide their sovereign territory without giving up their claims to supremacy within such zones. And, historically, the balance between territorial and extraterritorial practices of rule has always been dynamic. In *The Long Twentieth Century*, Arrighi argues that the Westphalian system's hegemonic authority began to wane long ago, during the nineteenth-century era of

British-led free-trade imperialism.[66] Supposed Westphalian norms were briefly reasserted after 1918, in the Wilsonian and Leninist moment of national self-determination; but, as we have already seen, they were superseded again by the events of World War II and the postwar creation of transnational institutions that enabled and legitimized the globalized industrial and, especially, financial and banking system. Arrighi's argument does not, however, commit one to a non- or antiterritorial political geography. He describes world history since the seventeenth century as structured by a negotiation between the consolidation of political and economic power within territorial borders and a contrary process in which the state form is expanded, creating many more states or state-like bodies, and then, in a dialectical reversal, superseded by hegemonic systems of increasing comprehensiveness that mitigate against exclusive sovereignty rights.[67] The name of the animating force behind those new hegemonic formations is the market. The transnational capitalism of the period since the 1980s does not, Arrighi admits, prosper "by thrusting its roots more deeply into the lower layers of material life"; rather, it works "by pulling them out" (25). That system couldn't first flourish, however, without a creative synthesis between territoriality and the market. Even if they represent contrary modes of rule, from the perspective of the historical *longue durée*, world market and territorial state have never operated in isolation but only in and through their interrelation.[68]

Arrighi's world history connects both halves of extraterritoriality's double discourse. If the system of territorial states is actually defined by the dialectic between what John Gerard Ruggie calls "spaces-of-places" and "spaces-of-flows," then it soon becomes clear how extraterritorial spaces play an important part in mediating this self-divided geography of power.[69] In *Lineages of the Absolutist State*, Perry Anderson describes the uneven development of an interstate system in which feudalism's spatially disaggregated political economy slowly contracted into centralized monarchical states. This process, which he dates to the period between the late fifteenth and mid-seventeenth centuries, was therefore also the time in which governments experimented with "the establishment of the novel institutions of reciprocal fixed embassies abroad, permanent chancelleries for foreign relations, and secret diplomatic communications and reports, shielded by the new concept of extra-territoriality."[70] In this history, extraterritoriality cannot be described as either the evacuation of state power or its brute extension. Rather, a range of extraterritorial practices—not just embassies but many kinds of zone in which territorial sovereignty is suspended or subdivided—help manage the tension inherent within the fact that a state's ability to act in the world rests on the power and authority it gains through prior identification with a specific territory.

In a similar spirit, Ruggie describes the period of globalization as characterized not by the eclipse of territorial sovereignty but by its irregular "unbundling," by which he means the paradoxical fixing of political and economic power in "nonterritorial functional" spaces such as freeports and the headquarters of international institutions such as NATO and the United Nations. Such zones don't negate territorial authority but localize "dimensions of collective existence that territorial rulers recognize to be irreducibly transterritorial in character."[71] Ruggie identifies the extraterritorial space of the embassy as just the first and most durable instantiation of a type of political geography in which claims of territorial sovereignty are relaxed so that international relations can be managed or brought into being. He is, moreover, far from alone in his emphasis on economic globalization's unbundling of territorial space. Sassen, for instance, writes that the "master normativity" of the Westphalian state is over, if it ever existed, but she holds that global capitalism, far from being inherently toxic to territorial forms of governance or authority, in fact often depends upon them.[72] An economy dominated by transnational corporations could never have come about, she argues, without the use of typically state-based capabilities such as legal and regulatory systems, schools and universities, emergency services, and energy and transportation infrastructure.[73] Moreover, it is *within* the national and still significantly territorial state, Sassen claims, that "the most complex meanings" of the global are currently being produced and debated.[74] This doesn't mean that the national state has not been transformed over the last decades; it means that we ought to avoid lapsing into a naïve "global-national duality," where world and state are "conceived as a mutually exclusive set of terrains where the national economy or state loses what the global economy gains."[75] Sassen emphasizes that the geography of globalization is incomplete: neither "diffuse" nor "all-encompassing."[76] Likewise, national territorial space was never total or fully integral.[77] Extraterritoriality is premised on exactly this dialectic between interlocking systems that are often described as if they're absolute or complete, but that don't only depend on one another—they often occupy the same space.

A NOTE ON THE "POST"-WESTPHALIAN

Given all this, it's tempting to say that we live in a post-Westphalian world, in which territorial sovereignty is irrelevant, or becoming so. But, in a world of zones and freeports, that's not true.

In her study of the post-9/11 surge in building border fences, Wendy Brown insists that if we speak of a "post-Westphalian" moment, we must remember that "the prefix 'post' signifies a formation that is *temporally after but not over* that to which it is affixed."[78] This is an important qualification, consistent with the significant role that territorial forms of authority and affiliation play in all the novels and artworks discussed in this book. And yet we can't quite stop at "post-Westphalian," even in Brown's qualified sense of the meaning of the phrase, for that very term perpetuates the inflated status of 1648 and all that. If one objection to the Westphalian is that it is out of date, another is that it never amounted to much in the first place.

The idea of a Westphalian order is modernist, Eurocentric, and so struggles to explain juridico-political systems from other places and times. Although the subsequent chapters of this book center on novels written in or about Britain and North America since the 1980s, they are often set in the historical past or imagined futures and are therefore defined by speculative retrospection or retrospective speculation. One cannot write criticism about such literary objects by assuming that putative Western norms travel easily throughout time and space. James Scott, to give one example from recent scholarship, tells of Southeast Asian principles of warfare and governance more concerned with sovereignty over human labor power than with the politicization of social space. He then quotes the bafflement of British colonial administrators when confronted by juridical norms and governmental practices that didn't identify authority over people with authority over land.[79] The forms of extraterritoriality studied in this book clearly don't apply everywhere and at all times—for instance, during the nineteenth century's uneven transition from informal empire to formal colonialism in Africa, the kinds of legal immunity and political authority enjoyed by chartered commercial and trading companies were quite distinct from those that functioned in Shanghai.[80] The historical extraterritorial forms studied in this book are contingent and, while they illustrate and underwrite important contemporary developments, cannot tell the entire truth about any reality. The same goes for supposed Westphalian norms, which non-Eurocentric histories soon show to be provincial and contingent.

But the problem with the post-Westphalian isn't reducible to the fact that this supposed political norm didn't hold everywhere outside the West. Even in Europe, states and sovereigns continued to conceive of political power in nonterritorial ways. Extraterritorial forms of sovereignty may have puzzled the British colonial administrators cited by Scott, but their masters in Whitehall were quite open to the possibility. Consider the treaty port system, which prevailed in the major trading cities of the South China Sea coast in the century after 1842. As we will discuss in chapter 5, the treaty port system deployed a pre-Westphalian concept of legal personality (the idea that juridical space can be as small as a single person) as a technology of empire that granted legal impunity to foreign merchant-adventurers. Chinese nationalist writers of the early twentieth century saw this as a deliberate policy of underdevelopment: an anachronistic revival of antique political principles that betrayed the spirit of modernity and fostered the sense that Asia was a zone of semicivilized backwardness.[81] The treaty port system reveals that British legal space was not isomorphic with the national territory of the United Kingdom, a fact not only enshrined in international agreements such as the 1842 Treaty of Nanjing but in domestic legislation such as the Foreign Jurisdiction Act of 1843. Shanghai's International Settlement, as well as similar European concessions and factories elsewhere in Asia, were never formal colonies. The International Settlement was always

Chinese soil. And yet the central precincts of Shanghai still became an extraterritorial enclave in which British citizens enjoyed many of the legal protections and privileges granted their fellow citizens at home or in Crown Colonies such as Hong Kong and Singapore. The treaty port system was also consistent, at least initially, with patterns of Qing Empire legal thought and practice that were sympathetic to the divisibility of juridical space and to the proposition that different sovereignty regimes might apply to different social or ethnic groups.[82] A historical practice such as consular jurisdiction in China cannot therefore be reconciled with the presumption that the history of the United Kingdom's overseas empire, or the histories of the peoples and nations that empire benefited or exploited, are explicable in Westphalian terms.

And perhaps even the Peace of Westphalia was not properly Westphalian. Some international relations theorists have identified what they call a "Westphalian myth" in which the historical meanings of the 1648 treaties have been reduced to a set of ideological bromides about territorial integrity and nonintervention. Andreas Osiander attributes this simplification, in part, to the effect of nineteenth- and twentieth-century nationalisms that retrospectively described the Westphalian settlement as a triumph of state particularism over universal empire. The result, he claims, is a vision of European international relations misleadingly fixated on territorial sovereignty, as if it were the telos of political modernity.[83] Benno Teschke similarly objects that, rather than inaugurating a modern system of international relations, the Westphalian peace ought to be understood as the consolidation of longstanding patterns of interdynastic absolutist power, not as the emergence of some new political order.[84] This argument is consistent with Anderson's thesis that European absolutism of the seventeenth century was doubly determined by the copresence of a feudal political order and a commodity economy.[85] Absolutist regimes in Europe certainly launched programs of territorial integration and centralization that undercut feudalism's spatial "'detotalization' of sovereignty," but the new Westphalian order did not wholly break from an early modern political geography characterized by "a vertically articulated system of parcellized sovereignty and scalar property."[86] The ideal type of the territorial state fails the test of universality whether one looks to the present, the past, the east, or the west.

Again, why does this matter? Because the Westphalian myth idealizes territorial sovereignty in the past, it causes us to mistake present-day developments such as the Geneva Freeport, which continue a long history of extraterritorial governance, for the end of sovereignty, statehood, or border regimes in general. And if the Westphalian myth is real, extraterritoriality becomes no more than an anomaly or exception—nothing more or less than the state's aggressive extroversion or utopian antithesis. This is a version of what international relations theorists call the territorial trap: an epistemological double bind in which an idealization of territorial statehood—and especially a fixation on its presence or absence, rather than its actual complexities—causes us to mistake territoriality for the antithesis of the global. Following John Agnew, who first named the territorial trap, this book emphasizes the "the interaction between global and local (including state-territorial) processes of political-economic structuration."[87] Extraterritoriality is among the earliest, most significant, and still developing practices through which that local/global interaction has been institutionalized and mediated. It is for this reason that it is so valuable as a historical lens, theoretical concept, and symbolic figure for understanding the present. The final two sections of this chapter show how the artist Mark Wallinger gives critical form to the political geography that the noun "Westphalia" so badly misnames. In beginning to tell that story, we return to one of the cities in which the 1648 treaties were signed.

THE DIFFERENCE A LINE MAKES

Mark Wallinger created his vast and ephemeral public sculptural work, *Zone*, in 2007 for the Skulptur Projekte, a public art event held every ten years in Münster. The sculpture began when Wallinger took a map of the city, plonked a saucer upon it, and drew a circle roughly describing its center. Moving from the flat space of the map to the three dimensions of lived geography, he then took several miles of fishing line and, by attaching it to streetlamps, buildings, trees, and other elevated structures, created a barely visible frontier describing a new temporary enclave within the city.

Zone does not directly evoke state borders, or even municipal ones. Its inspiration is the Jewish religious boundaries called *eruvim*. An *eruv* is a physical boundary that encloses apparently public domain so as to make it private. Taking its name from the Hebrew for "mixing," an eruv moderates religious strictures governing what actions or tasks can be performed on the Jewish Sabbath—for instance, to allow the carrying of certain objects outside the home.

An eruv can be demarcated by the walls of existing structures; by features of the natural landscape such as rivers, hills, or the coastline of an island; or by something as insubstantial as a wire strung between utility poles—thus, Wallinger's fishing line constructions in *Zone*.[88] Eruvim are common to many parts of the world with significant populations of observant Jews and are often unnoticed by non-Jewish citizens, who may have no idea that they live within or near such an enclave. The Harvard University Pluralism Project counts four major eruvim in and around the cities of Boston and Cambridge.[89] The greater part of the island of Manhattan (the New York City borough in which I sit as I write these words) is contained within an eruv. The northwest London eruv likewise carves out a zone of religious exemption in several square miles between Hampstead, Finchley, Hendon, and Cricklewood.[90]

Wallinger's *Zone* isn't really an eruv. It has no status in Jewish law, and it doesn't observe the many strictures (some debated, some generally accepted) that determine whether such a structure is or isn't authoritative. Despite this, *Zone* possesses a memorial function as weighty as its parts are light. By constructing the ghost of a semi-invisible Jewish enclave within the city, *Zone* draws attention to the history of Jewish residence and anti-Semitic racism in Münster. In particular, it evokes the genocidal period between 1933 and 1945, during which a Jewish community of some 558 persons was reduced by murder, deportation, and exile to almost nothing. According to the historians of Yad Vashem, during the period of Nazi rule between 264 and 280 Jews emigrated from Münster and 247 to 288 were killed in the camps. Only 24 of those sent to places such as Theresienstadt and the Riga Ghetto are said to have survived.[91] *Zone* says nothing directly about this history; a simple strung line enclosing an arbitrarily chosen circle of municipal land, it possesses no obviously denotative historical content. It is impossible to miss, however, the way that its silent allusion to the boundary between public and private spheres evokes the exterminated Jewish households of Münster, the stripping away of Jews' public selves as German citizens during the Third Reich, and the violent invasion and expropriation of their private dreams and possessions. *Zone* encloses an extraterritorial space not in a narrowly political sense but so as to commemorate the nonidentity of even the most apparently unitary and self-identical human geographies. In this respect, it takes its place among the many countermonuments to the Nazi's genocidal victims, which seek to acknowledge the dead without naturalizing or idealizing their memories, and without assimilating them to ethnonational ideologies.[92]

But *Zone* is concerned with more than one kind of passing away. It's important, in this context, that Wallinger should have made *Zone* where he did. Münster's history of anti-Semitism is far from exceptional; many cities, in Germany and elsewhere, own a piece of that terrible experience. But, as we have seen, in 1648 Münster was, with Osnabrück, one of two cities in which representatives of Europe's belligerent powers sealed the Peace of Westphalia. By sketching a new religio-legal geography upon the city, Wallinger's *Zone* reminds us of the ways in which, centuries after the Westphalian treaties established the supposed norm of *cuius regio, eius religio* (whose realm, his religion), the social and legal space of the modern state remains criss-crossed by multiple geographies of affiliation and obligation.[93] *Zone* therefore recalls us to the fact that, even in a geopolitical order in which states generally recognize no law superior to their own, their territories have long been home to multiple forms of religious jurisprudence. In Europe, the canon law of the various Christian traditions provides the most central example, with Halakah, Dharmaśāstra, and Sharia law also playing their role.[94] In colonial states such as British India, forms of religious law and personhood were written into the official judicial system;

indeed, Griffiths traces the modern form of legal pluralism to 1772, when the East India Company legislated for parallel Hindu and Islamic systems of property and family law within the colonies governed by that company-state.[95]

The world depicted in Wallinger's artworks resembles neither a jigsaw of exclusive territories nor a borderless sphere.[96] In several of his signature works from the early years of this century, frontiers proliferate and are internalized, multiplying from the edges of the nation to its center. In these artworks, we have not moved emphatically beyond the territorial state; rather, new walls and enclaves stripe and puncture its geography. In Wallinger's artwork, borders between territories do not represent the edges of geopolitical planes but mutable three-dimensional volumes.[97] In the video installation *Threshold to the Kingdom* (2000), as we shall see, the space of the international airport emerges as an extraterritorial border within which people sojourn and even live. As such, the airport exemplifies an historical trend in which borders have proliferated and become distended, appearing not merely at the edges of territories but within and throughout. "No longer entirely situated at the outer limit of the territories," writes Étienne Balibar, these days borders "are dispersed a little everywhere, wherever the movement of information, people, and things is happening and is controlled."[98]

To say this is, on one level, just to define the border as such. As Balibar has written elsewhere, in a system of nation-states borders are inevitably "internalized by individuals," becoming "inner borders" that constitute the national subject but are, paradoxically, also "invisible borders, situated everywhere and nowhere."[99] It is nevertheless true that the present age is defined less by the disappearance of borders into the subjective realm, or by what Brown calls their theatricalized and compensatory fortification, than by the border's differentiation and multiplication.[100] Consider, in this vein, the fact that the United Kingdom now operates border controls in France and Belgium, and that many aspects of border and immigration control have been effectively privatized by being made the responsibility of airlines, hoteliers, proprietors of Internet cafés, and the like.[101] Consider that the US Border Patrol now routinely operates immigration and customs checkpoints, both permanent and "tactical," between twenty-five and one hundred miles north of the border with Mexico and as many as one hundred miles south of the border with Canada.[102] This is what Balibar has in mind when he writes, somewhat paradoxically, that borders "are no longer *at the border,* an institutional site that can be materialized on the ground and inscribed on a map, where one sovereignty *ends* and another begins."[103] Borders are now distributed throughout national territories because of, among other things, "a transformation of the means of international communication, which has relativized the functions of the *port of entry,* revalorized internal controls, creating within each territory *zones of transit* and transition."[104]

Airports such as the one represented in *Threshold to the Kingdom* are at the center of these changes. In the 1990s, to give a rather dramatic example, French immigration law specified that asylum seekers could be detained in the "international zone" of ports and airports while the merits of their claims were assessed. Such legislation created a vastly expanded transit area that, at Roissy-Charles de Gaulle airport, for instance, was extended (in law, if not in material fact) to a hotel clearly outside the airport's usual area of customs and border controls. This hotel was, from a strictly legal perspective, rendered outside of French sovereign territory while still remaining under the control of the French republic; indeed, the very existence of that juridically projected transit area depends on the divisibility of the legal notions of sovereignty, jurisdiction, and control—concepts that, from a normatively Westphalian perspective, are assumed to be inseparable. In this way, potential asylees were made subject to French immigration law and therefore able to be detained or deported, without ever having been considered emigrants to France. Asylum seekers were thus unable to avail themselves of French or EU constitutional protections.[105] Developments such as these epitomize the "differential operation" of the border in the present age—a political, legal, cultural, and experiential volume that, in a wonderfully pregnant phrase, Balibar describes as having become an "extraordinarily viscous spatio-temporal zone," at once ubiquitous and heterogeneous.[106]

Wallinger's persistent interest in the visual poetics of the border is suggested by the subtitle of his book *The Russian Linesman: Frontiers, Borders, and Thresholds*, a documentary supplement to his 2009 Hayward Gallery touring exhibition of the same name. The title refers to a football official, Tofik Bakhramov (actually an Azerbaijani), who on 30 July 1966 ruled that Geoff Hurst's extratime shot had crossed West Germany's goal line, thereby ensuring England's victory in the final of that year's World Cup. (What a difference a line makes!) *The Russian Linesman*'s interest in geopolitical borders is made explicit in those parts of the book depicting militarized frontiers such as the UN-designated "Green Line" between the Greek and Turkish halves of Cyprus. At other points, as with his reproduction of Joanna Kane's photographs of nineteenth-century life masks, Wallinger appears to be interested in metaphorical kinds of border: between photography and painting, for instance, or morbidity and vivacity. In some of the volume's most arresting moments, the literal and metaphorical join together. Thus, excerpts from the dramatic airport defection scene of Rudolf Nureyev's autobiography, in which he makes a balletic leap to freedom into the arms of some French policemen, are juxtaposed with a photograph of his tomb, "covered with the representation of a Kilim rug to signify this bisexual, exiled outsider as Tatar, Muslim, nomadic and stateless."[107]

Wallinger's catholic sense of what counts as a border or threshold extends to the form and structure of his book, which features a dazzling range of materials. Next to his own autobiographical and critical writings, Wallinger collects extracts from sources as diverse as newspaper stories, lyric poetry, and Richard Ellman's biography of James Joyce. Alongside documentation and reproductions of his own artworks, he gathers sundry images such as a high-resolution photograph of mountains on Mars, taken by a NASA robot in 1997; Caravaggio's *The Incredulity of Saint Thomas*, painted in oils circa 1601–2; and a 1956 stereoscopic photograph titled *The Queen Visits Her People in Nigeria II, Her Majesty at Itu Leper Colony*. This technique of multimedia anthologization—familiar from writers as different as John Berger, Teresa Hak Kyung Cha, and W. G. Sebald—involves something like a simultaneous dislocation and localization of materials and meanings. Anthologization localizes meaning because Wallinger's visual and textual miscellany is oriented around the common theme of the border or threshold, even if only by the fact of his own examples' ingathering between the cardboard frontiers of the book's covers. But anthologization also dislocates meaning because this centripetal interpretive act is one that the reader must perform herself, working against the sheer variety of *The Russian Linesman*'s inclusions and pushing back against Wallinger's apparent refusal to rule in or rule out.

The Russian Linesman thus invokes a poetics of interstitiality that is so persistent in contemporary artistic discourse as to have become almost banal. Borders here figure in two directions: they are barriers to movement and thought, evidence of injustice and blockage. We die and are stopped; we cannot always follow Nureyev in dancing to freedom. At the same time, borders are not only obstacles to be scaled; we don't only leap over or despite them. While they undoubtedly frustrate the carrying over of people and ideas, borders also and inevitably create new opportunities for transgression and transformation. The border, scholars have been telling us for years, is an impasse and an entryway, a contradictory zone of separation and mixing.[108]

And so, however interesting we might find its parts or sequences, there's something a bit too familiar about *The Russian Linesman*'s dallying in the interstices. The same can't be said about *State Britain* (2007), the monumental work for which Wallinger was awarded the Turner Prize, probably the most prestigious award available to younger British artists. Here, the poetics of liminality carries specific historical weight and articulates concrete political stakes. For almost eight months, the grand Duveen Galleries of London's Tate Britain art museum were home to what looked like a highly emotional protest against Britain's participation in the Iraq and Afghanistan wars (fig. 1.2). In actual fact, *State Britain* was political speech at one remove: a meticulous recreation of the late Brian Haw's famous peace vigil in Parliament Square, London.

Haw's protest began in June 2001. Initially targeted against the long-running UN sanctions regime against Iraq, it ended only in 2011, when Haw became too sick to continue living and sleeping outdoors. Within a few months of its beginning, the vigil grew to represent broad public disillusion with the United Kingdom's post-9/11 wars and, eventually, public anger about how new domestic security legislation was being used to silence

FIGURE 1.2 Mark Wallinger, State Britain, Duveen Galleries, 15 January–27 August, 2007, Mark Wallinger. Provenance.

Photo copyright © Tate.

antigovernment dissent.[109] Wallinger admired Haw for his dedication to all these causes. His recreation of Haw's many posters and banners, in all their weather-beaten particularity, commemorates the activist's legendary stamina and purity of principle.

But *State Britain* isn't merely commemorative; it also dramatizes the malleable relationship between political geography and criminal law. Although Haw's encampment was initially modest, it soon became notorious for its size and obtrusiveness. At its peak, the protest stretched across forty-four meters on a location directly across from the Palace of Westminster, from which vantage point Haw would harangue members of Parliament on a megaphone audible from within the Commons chamber. Westminster City Council failed in 2002 to remove the encampment on the grounds that it obstructed public rights of way; but, eventually, in May 2006, the Metropolitan Police dismantled all but a small remnant. Their legal pretext was the "exclusion zone" newly delimited in the 2005 Serious Organized Crime and Police Act (SOCPA). This controversial act contained a provision banning unauthorized political demonstrations within a kilometer of the Palace of Westminster.[110] As the home secretary admitted at the time, this was the proverbial "sledgehammer to break a nut"—a new piece of criminal law, aimed at one intransigent citizen, which in its attempt to remove that citizen from within sight and sound of Parliament, created a new lacuna within the juridical space of the capital.[111]

This is where we arrive at *State Britain*'s key formal element, which, through a formal gesture that resembles *Zone*'s bare strung line in space, likewise pushes the work beyond commemorative reconstruction. Alongside the remade encampment, Wallinger applied a line of black tape, running across the floor of the Duveen Galleries, that demarcated the actual geographic border of SOCPA's exclusion zone: the legal sledgehammer that the state used to break Haw's protest and so remove it from view. *State Britain* marks and depends upon the coincidence between Tate Britain's location almost exactly a kilometer south of Parliament and the new geography of the security state. The *State Britain* installation is positioned and oriented within the gallery so that it sits just inside—that is, on the unlawful side—of SOCPA's geographic distinction between free and regulated zones of speech and assembly. The black tape marks a kind of internal amity line between one zone of English legal space and another.[112] It describes a circle that has its origin at the Palace of Westminster and a circumference that bisects the Duveen Galleries.[113]

State Britain maps and trespasses against Parliament's power to create zones of legal exemption within national space. To be sure, SOCPA does not wholly suspend constitutional and common law rights of speech and assembly, but, like an inside-out version of the free speech zones that have become common at political conventions in the United States, it has rendered traditional English liberties geographically divisible.[114] This is a fact that *State Britain* doesn't simply utter or imitate; it's immanent within the work's most basic formal elements—the drawing of a line and the arrangement of objects in space. The very decision to recreate Haw's encampment at Tate Britain, and so to give the work its somewhat cornily punning title, would be incomprehensible without Wallinger's understanding that the rights of citizens are not only renegotiated at the border between one territory and another. The uneven spatial distribution of power makes citizenship rights negotiable even at the very center of the polis.

THRESHOLD TO THE KINGDOM

State Britain builds specific legal and political content into the generalized poetics of liminality articulated in *The Russian Linesman*. Beginning from the premise that we live within and between many sorts of frontiers, it dramatizes how states enlarge their authority by graduating and dividing their sovereign territory, creating multiple sorts of legal and political regime within national space. Considered in this way, it connects at a theoretical and topical level with the new sorts of legislative activity that enabled, to give one further example, the detention of the Brazilian citizen David Miranda at Heathrow Airport on 18 August 2013.

Miranda's detention was an aftereffect of the Edward Snowden diplomatic melodrama, in which, despite vociferous US complaints, the renegade intelligence analyst and whistleblower spent thirty-nine days in the legal limbo of the international arrivals hall of Sheremetyevo International Airport. Snowden was trapped in the airport because, having arrived in Moscow en route to Cuba from Hong Kong, he was informed that the US government had canceled his passport, which prevented him from boarding his next flight. He remained safe in the airport, however, because the Russian government was able to insist that, despite having disembarked from his plane, Snowden had not passed through immigration control and thus could not be deported or arrested by the Russian state, or molested by the agents of any foreign power.[115] Eventually, Snowden was granted political asylum in Russia and was admitted to the country on a foreign visa.

The Miranda case was, by comparison with Snowden's, a rather minor airport theatrical. It nevertheless demonstrates that the legal ambiguities intrinsic to port areas are as available to liberal democracies such as the United Kingdom as they are to authoritarian states such as Russia.

Miranda is the partner and colleague of the journalist and activist Glenn Greenwald, and he was held at Heathrow as he traveled home from a meeting in Berlin with Greenwald's collaborator, documentary filmmaker Laura Poitras. While in Berlin, Miranda received from Poitras thousands of classified computer files that Snowden had stolen from the US National Security Administration. It was to secure these files that the British Security Service (MI5) detained Miranda as he passed through Heathrow. His detention lasted only nine hours, but he was denied access to legal representation, and all his electronic equipment was confiscated. In any other part of Great Britain other than a port or border area, Miranda's detention would have been flagrantly illegal.

Miranda was held at Heathrow under Schedule 7 of the Terrorism Act 2000, which created a new police authority to question and detain people in a port or border area.[116] Much of the early reporting in the British press focused on the fact that Schedule 7 stops do not require judicial authorization or a standard of reasonable suspicion, as well as on the appropriateness of using antiterrorism legislation to detain a person engaged in a journalistic enterprise.[117] The key part of the puzzle for us, however, is the way Schedule 7 creates a jurisdictional space specific to ports and border areas. The legal distinction between ports and other areas of national territory is not new to the Terrorism Act 2000: the Immigration Act 1971, for instance, stipulates that: "A person arriving in the United Kingdom by ship or aircraft shall . . . be deemed not to enter the United Kingdom unless and until he disembarks, and on disembarkation at a port shall further be deemed not to enter the United Kingdom so long as he remains in such area at the port as may be approved for this purpose by an immigration officer."[118] What is new in the Terrorism Act 2000 is the way that the identification of the airport as an extraterritorial zone provides the basis for an extension of police powers that would breach police procedures and human rights law if they were extended to the nation as a whole. Indeed, the geographical specificity of the Schedule 7 powers underwrote Lord Justice Laws's 2014 rejection of Miranda's petition for judicial review of his detention: Schedule 7 did not contravene the European Convention of Human Rights, Laws argued, precisely because it was limited in scope, and it was limited in scope because it demarcated a legal-geographical line between the border area and public space in general.[119] The principle of territorial disaggregation through which the government circumscribes (and so justifies) extraordinary police powers is invoked by Lord Justice Laws as the reason why that power is proportional, and, therefore, legal.

The Miranda case clearly illustrates how the innovations in legal space dramatized by *State Britain* take particular shape in airports. Nor is this simply a matter of the exigencies of antiterrorist or counterespionage law. Justine Lloyd has written of the airport as a space in which the "border becomes uncanny," leading to "a moment of individuation that takes place not at the edge of national territory, but in the heart of the global city."[120] She roots this quality in the legal and administrative distinction within airports between "airside" and "landside" spaces, the former of which she describes as extraterritorial zones with respect to customs and immigration law. More than this, she explains how this basic distinction has been expanded and exacerbated by developments such as the UK government's deployment of immigration checks in Budapest airport and by the German government's designation of the Frankfurt-Main airport as a "legally declared detention zone" for asylum seekers.[121] In all these instances, the airport, far from marking a two-dimensional line between national and international space, becomes a disaggregated legal-political volume in which different regimes of rights and obligations apply to different kinds of persons and in which certain aspects of national law may or may not apply depending on where in the airport you happen to be.

These issues are given haunting and poetic shape in the final artwork I will consider in this chapter: Wallinger's *Threshold to the Kingdom*, which was filmed in 1998 and first exhibited in 2000. *Threshold* has two main elements. The first consists of slow-motion footage of international travelers arriving at London City Airport, each sequence fading out and in as a new group of arrivals clear customs and passport control. In exhibition format, the video is set to loop back after slightly more than eleven minutes, so that this sequence of arrivals and fade-outs is potentially endless. The second key element is a soundtrack consisting of a recording of Gregorio Allegri's *Miserere*, a seventeenth-century setting of Psalm 51, "Have Mercy on Me,

O God." This exquisite piece of choral polyphony was traditionally used in the Vatican's Tenebrae service during Easter Week and was for many years forbidden on pain of excommunication from being copied or sung outside the Sistine Chapel. Legend has it that the *Miserere* only became publicly available after Wolfgang Amadeus Mozart transcribed it from memory in April 1770. From the start, then, *Threshold* brings together several sorts of exceptional space, actual and metaphorical: the cloistered chapel within the Papal city-state; the transit zone between leaving an airplane and formally entering a country; and the difference between a mental space marked by musical genius and the mind that merely holds a tune.

For all the apparent simplicity of its construction, there's complex formal labor going on in *Threshold*. Wallinger says that his use of slow-motion footage involved an implied "rebuke to the presumed *gravitas* of Bill Viola's decelerated videos."[122] And so it is. Even mashed-up against its astonishingly lovely soundtrack, the visual track of *Threshold* remains studiedly dull, with Wallinger refusing to transmute monotony into sublimity. His camera stays fixed, never tracking to follow a traveler and inquire where she is going. His lighting is dimly institutional and his single shot is imperfectly framed, neither tight enough on the door to crowd out the visual noise of planters and pedestrian barriers nor wide enough to give a full sense of setting and context.

This antigravitational quality also affects *Threshold*'s engagement with its manifest religious content. What's impossible to miss about this work is that its structural overlay of music and video produces a Christian allegory in which the traveler's cross-border movement figures forth another form of transport: the soul's migration between this world and the next. For international arrivals, read the pearly gates. *Threshold* implies a Dantean odyssey between this mortal coil (signified by the unseen country of departure), purgatory (the implied interstitial zone of passport control and customs) and the heaven of the arrivals hall. This reading is, moreover, consistent with Wallinger's broader interest in the rhetoric of revelation and salvation—explored, for instance, in the two other video works, *Fly* (2000) and *On an Operating Table* (1998), the footage for which he shot on the same day as *Threshold*, as well as other pieces from the same period—for example, the statue *Ecce Homo* (1999) or *The Word in the Desert* photographic series (2000). And yet we can't stop with the Christian allegory. In the end, the antiaesthetic quality of the visual track undercuts, rather than folds into, the *Miserere*'s aspirations toward sublime comedy. The religious reading is irresistible but not sufficient.

Within and before Wallinger's sacralization of international travel lie more literal referents, which are never absorbed within its eschatological register: the banal, securitized architecture of the airport and the gloomy, self-absorbed faces of the travelers, who have completed the move from airside to landside. The photographic eye in *Threshold* resembles less the omniscient perspective of a divine judge than of a low-resolution surveillance camera. Wallinger explains to Mark Herbert that he once thought he was afraid of flying but then realized he was scared of the airport itself: "It was that incredible scrutiny, the state examining one, which you don't feel anywhere else. The powerful relief you feel when you finally reach home, or the state you're hoping to reach, seems rather like confession and absolution."[123] In the same way that not everybody gets into heaven, so is the threshold between the arrivals halls and the nation-state the province of properly documented sheep, not undocumented goats. *Threshold to the Kingdom* thus conjoins the test or judgment implied by political citizenship with the audiovisual rhetoric of Christian eschatology, but it does so in a way that disenchants and, so, ultimately redirects us to the secular world. The grainy quality of the footage and the unmoving eye of the camera drive home this sense of *Threshold* as documenting a scene of routine social and political election. It is this securitized everydayness that explains why Wallinger's travelers appear so boring and insubstantial. They are not ghosts; they are nothings. They are not paranoid; they are merely observed. They do not protest; they are barely even asked to acquiesce. They are lucky enough to carry their citizenship lightly.

Wallinger's travelers have been judged; their very arrival testifies to the fact that judgment is taking place. But, having been chosen, the travelers' job in *Threshold* is to depart the center of the action. *Threshold to the Kingdom* isn't ultimately about the travelers, or even the arrivals hall into which they emerge with every fade and cut. As its title suggests, *Threshold* focuses on the partially seen transit zone, the doors to which lie at the center of its unmoving vision. The purgatorial space of the threshold is the zone that Gaston Bachelard described as "painful on both sides" and that Jacques Derrida articulated as the point at which hospitality reveals its secret kinship with hostility, even as it expresses an ethical relation in which the host might open himself up to await his guest "as a liberator, his emancipator."[124] The threshold is the space of entrance that is also a space of election and judgment; it is the volume framed and exposed by the alternately yawning and grinding jaws of the security door. It is not a doorway, precisely, but a zone of indeterminate dimensions that we glimpse only briefly from our position within national space. This is why, once they become the elect, Wallinger's travelers no longer hold our gaze. By the time we see them they are already blessedly null. Our eyes are locked instead upon the operations of an extraterritorial zone that remains only partly visible, the power of which resides in its ability to be at once strange and familiar, at once within and outside the kingdom.

Where are we once we have left the plane but not yet passed passport control? Where are we in the freeport and the exclusion zone? What does "Westphalia" fail to name? There is a threshold to the kingdom: a zone of plural and disaggregated authority. It is more common than you think, and it reveals a geography of power that is all the more real for being anything but singular or exceptional.

2

CITY-STATE

By some chaos of democracy . . .

—CHINA MIÉVILLE, *IRON COUNCIL*

C hina Miéville (b. 1972) is arguably the foremost British exponent of the "new weird" tendency in the novel, a writer who makes no bones about his deep investment in science fiction (SF), fantasy, and other "paraliterary" genres.[1] He is also, this chapter argues, a crucial thinker about the political geography of the present. In particular, Miéville's writing weirdly addresses the most prominent current theory of extraterritoriality: Giorgio Agamben's deployment of the spatial logic of "inclusive exclusion," which forms an important part of his *Homo Sacer* series of books and has had wide influence among scholars of contemporary politics and culture. It's now time to face Agamben's work more fully, albeit through the medium of Miéville's fiction. For although this chapter is indeed an essay in political theory, it is also a study of how novels produce knowledge about themselves and the world.

For all the diversity of China Miéville's works, his fiction is immediately recognizable. Beyond signature elements such as his obsessions with rubbish, cephalopods, Victoriana, and the prefix "Ab-," Miéville is famous for his fabulously baroque sentences, love of obscure words, and neologistic ways: "turingware," "handlinger," "grindylow," "floak," "pavonine," and "moldywarpe," for example.[2] Nor is this a superficial kind of linguistic glamour. The Australian novelist Kirsten Tranter wisely describes how, in the way Miéville's "syntax and verb forms . . . push against the boundaries of convention and sense," his novels enact "on a formal level [their] thematic preoccupation" with radical social change.[3] There are few more linguistically inventive and politically committed writers at work today, and probably no British writer since the late Anthony Burgess and Doris Lessing who writes so widely across so many genres, or takes such consistent pleasure in creating alternate worlds by inventing lexical facts.

I'm interested, however, in a less remarked-upon feature of Miéville's fiction, which doesn't dwell at the level of the sentence or word. This chapter and those that follow focus on narrative setting—that is, on how the internal force of an imaginative geography shapes a novel's wider form and themes. Setting is more than a frame in which actions occur, more than the "ground" against which the "figure" of character is made visible, and more than a proxy for "atmosphere" or "tone."[4] In the novels discussed in this book, space is thematized and thereby evinces Mieke Bal's description of how narrative setting can become "an object of presentation itself, for its own sake. . . . an acting place rather than the place of action."[5] In particular, Miéville's settings epitomize this book's vision of a world the political plastic of which is at once torn and involuted. In a recent retrospective on weird fiction, Roger Luckhurst celebrates Miéville as the creator of secondary worlds in which borders "refuse to act like simple lines but become multiple and mobile."[6] Miéville isn't alone in this. When M. John Harrison initiated a discussion about the term "new weird" in 2003, he also helped bring into new perspective a comparatively "Old" strain of weird fiction, much of which—for instance, in the stories of Arthur Machen or William Hope Hodgson—evokes or takes place in the unstable border-zones between disjunct realms.[7] In this capacity, Luckhurst says, Miéville's settings are "typical of the weird, but also speak to a contemporary era of globalization" in which—and here he quotes Sandro Mezzadra and Brett Neilson—"borders 'are often subject to shifting and unpredictable patterns of mobility and overlapping, appearing and disappearing.'"[8] In another recent essay, Luckhurst draws a line between the characteristic settings of the "post-genre fantastic" ("strange spatial zones, weird topologies that produce anomalies, destroy category and dissolve or reconstitute identities") and the way novels set in such spaces continually stage "their own dissolution of the law of genre."[9]

In this same way, narrative settings in Miéville novels are never less than errant. His spaces are divided and permeable, on the move, and generally massive—massively strange, and also just tending to grossness and complexity.[10] In Miéville's fiction, as in the work of other new-weird writers like Jeff VanderMeer and Brian Catling, the mutuality between genre and setting becomes an occasion not for the reproduction of familiar sorts of narrative space, but for an occult riot that transforms both space and the narrative media through which settings are shaped and represented. This chapter begins with its central example, the 2009 hybrid noir novel *The City & the City*; it then considers the relationship between setting, secondary world creation, and genre across several key works from Miéville's oeuvre; and, finally, it returns to *The City & the City* by way of Agamben's political theory and Miéville's own academic work in international relations. At the literary-critical level, the chapter's main job is to show how Miéville's signature style is the perfect narrative medium for representing the weird that is the extraterritorial city-state.

THE WAIST OF AN HOURGLASS

The City & The City is, in one way, a familiar type of story. It's a first-person detective novel that follows Inspector Tyador Borlú through a murder case, beginning with the discovery of a woman's body and ending with his pursuit of those responsible for killing her. The primary complication for Borlú's investigation comes from a series of jurisdictional disputes, which cause him to get entangled in a messy turf war between rival political factions and police forces. Imagine any crime story in which a city cop gets in a turf war with the state police or the FBI, or in which a routine murder inquiry uncovers a rat's nest of municipal corruption. Imagine all this told by a middle-aged cop on the Extreme Crime Squad: a respected detective, maybe losing a step but still up to the job, perennially single or serially monogamous but a good boss to his beat cop female sidekick. That kind of story.

But this is more or less where familiar territory ends. At the end of the murder plot, for instance, Borlú recovers a valuable artifact (and murder weapon) that may be a magical object, may be some kind of unknown ancient technology, or may just be a MacGuffin, designed to create an occult reverberation but otherwise simply move the plot along. At the level of style, Miéville mixes genres and modes to strikingly original effect, drawing from police procedurals, Cold War noir, the paranoid SF thriller à la Philip K. Dick, and the gnomic absurdity of Franz Kafka's *The Castle*, among much else. But the novel's biggest deviation from the regular detective story has its roots in that jurisdictional dispute, which turns out decisively strange.

The City & the City is set in and between the fictional cities of Besźel and Ul Qoma, somewhere in post-1989 Central Europe. The relationship between the cities is distinctively weird, in both the literary and colloquial senses. Ul Qoman buildings sit on the same streets as Besź structures, separated by elements of culture—different patterns or wealth or poverty, of Slavic or Ottoman style—but by no visible political or municipal borders. Two groups of citizens share the same plazas and parks; two sets of cars drive the same streets, obeying two different traffic codes; men and women walk around rigorously "seeing" their own people and places and even more rigorously "unseeing" the foreign presence among which they live so intimately. "Grosstopically," as Borlú puts it in one of his creator's signature neologisms, the cities share the same physical geography, the same brute topology.[11] Juridically and existentially, however, they occupy different "realms" (*CC* 70). Besźel and Ul Qoma join at only two points. They share a common external border with the European state (or states, we don't know) in which they are landlocked like some freak-show Luxembourg: "A single line in existential legality as well as mere metal fact" (61). But, most of all, there's Copula Hall: the governmental seat of both city-states, at the heart of which lie rooms "that were in neither or both cities, that were in *Copula Hall only*" (131; emphasis in original). Here is a perfect image for the extraterritorial in its most mobile and general sense: spaces that are not inside or outside one territory or another but are in both by virtue of being in neither.

The image of these rooms in Copula Hall recalls a beautiful and disturbing moment in the novel *Austerlitz*, by the British-resident German author W. G. Sebald. That novel's title character is describing the gigantic stone Palace of Justice in Brussels. The grand city building is said to contain "corridors and stairways leading nowhere, and doorless rooms and halls where no one would ever set foot, empty spaces surrounded by walls and representing the innermost secret of all sanctioned authority."[12] It is a space at once vacant and impenetrable: an absurd but potent zone of law at the center of Europe's administrative heart. The authority of this space, as with those strange chambers in Copula Hall, doesn't stem from its visibility, or from its openness to the public in whose name it has been built. Its importance derives from its apparent impossibility.[13] Unlike the rooms in Copula Hall, the blind spaces in the Palace of Justice do not seem to be, in a legal or political sense, actually extraterritorial; nevertheless, their doorless vacancy speaks to the way that Sebald appears to locate the secret of sovereignty and the law in what Agamben calls "a zone of indifference, where inside and outside do not exclude each other but rather blur with each other."[14] In the Palace of Justice and Copula Hall, the putative unity of law, territory, and citizenry collapses into an extraterritorial topology in which sovereignty fills in "empty spaces surrounded by walls."

The City & the City imagines what would happen if that extraterritorial topology was to become a general property of urban space. One immediate effect of that change is that people would need to coin new words so as to describe their new world. Thus, in *The City & the City*, sovereignty can be "total" (completely local to whichever city one happens to be in), "alter" (totally other: acknowledged foreign land), "crosshatched" (variegated, such that the cities' territorial claims are shared, partial, or interrupted), or a sphere of "dissensus" (an area of contested sovereignty, about which the cities cannot agree). And even these new words won't suffice to describe the complexity of social and political life in *The City & the City*. Since one can "see" across the almost perpetually present border at millions of points, and since the proscription to "unsee" one's foreign neighbors has the force of law, both cities' citizens can cross from the total into the alter without moving—that is, they can trespass upon foreign juridical space through a simple sensory act. At one point, Borlú briefly notices a woman standing near the crime scene he is working. Then he corrects himself: "With a hard start, I realised that she was not on GunterStrász at all, and that I should not have seen her" (12). A single urban space can contain two—or three, maybe four, maybe more—jurisdictional regimes. In Besźel and Ul Qoma, there is no way of counting the number of borders and no way of definitively mapping their orientations, what they leave in and leave out. Even more than the airport zones discussed in the preceding chapter, these cities *are* borders; they are made of such lines and such volumes.

Such is the stage upon which *The City & the City*'s characters move. This is how Borlú describes the relation between the cities and Copula Hall, not to mention the strained relation between juridical space and lived experience in the two cities:

> If someone needed to go to a house physically next door to their own, but in a neighboring city, it was in a different road in an unfriendly power. That is what foreigners rarely understand. A Besź dweller cannot walk a few paces next door into an alter house without breach.
>
> But pass through Copula Hall and she or he might leave Besźel, and at the end of the hall come back to exactly (corporeally) where they had just been, but in another country, a tourist, a marvelling visitor, to a street that shared the latitude-longitude of their own address, a street they had never visited before, whose architecture they had always unseen, to the Ul Qoman house sitting next to and a whole city away from their own building, unvisible, there now they had come through, all the way across the Breach, back home.
>
> Copula Hall like the waist of an hourglass, the point of ingress and egress, the navel between the cities. (70)

"Copula" derives from the Latin "to fasten" or "fit," an etymology that survives in the way grammarians use "copula" to describe words such as "is," which join subject and predicate, noun and verb. But the "navel" that is Copula Hall is obviously a point of separation as well as a conjunction. It marks the cities like the belly button marks the humans in Aristophanes's story from Plato's *Symposium*—an origin myth for the existence of love, in which people used to be monstrous spherical beings before the gods cut them in half and they were doomed to spend their lives longing for the lost half of their "original nature."[15] The navel was formed, Aristophanes has it, when Apollo stretched and smoothed human skin to cover the wound left by Zeus's sword, leaving just a "few wrinkles around the stomach" to "be a reminder of what happened long ago." In this same way, Copula Hall is both suture and injury; the point through which transit between the two cities is possible, but also a further hole in their spatial fabric, and a reminder of what might once have been whole.

Still, however neat Miéville's allusion, the citizens of Besźel and Ul Qoma lack any such origin myth. Their historians don't know how or why the cities entered into their intimate nonembrace, and nobody really agrees whether unity, separation, or this ambivalent state in-between represents their fundamental nature. The people of both cities call their prehistory the time before "cleavage," which everyone in the cities also knows has a double meaning as "split or convergence" (87). Some in the cities—they call them "Unifs," for "unificationists"—want to join that which they believe to have been rent asunder. Others wave nationalist banners, trying to force the cities further apart, or conquer one in the name of the other. The plot of the novel is driven by the tensions that are intrinsic to a densely populated space that is at once one, two—and more than two.

Why more than two? As Borlú implies in his description of the cities' weird geography, between Besźel and Ul Qoma lies "Breach." And, in Borlu's world, the word "breach" does double work as uncapitalized verb and proper noun. The verb refers to unsanctioned movements between the cities' two realms: for instance, if a person in Ul Qoma were to walk into a shop in Besźel, she'd be very clearly guilty of breaching. But, equally, when Borlú fails to "unsee" the Ul Qoman woman who is "not on GunterStrász," he breaches in one of the petty ways that occur every day. Since city cops like Borlú or his Ul Qoman counterparts can't police transgressions across a border they're not even allowed to observe, that job must fall to a third power. The proper noun "Breach" (sometimes "the Breach") refers to that interstitial third authority—a kind of semioccult police force, somewhere between the Furies and the Feds, which regulates the boundary between Besźel and Ul Qoma.[16] In this way, Breach can clearly be seen as an allegorical figure for the "borderline" form of sovereignty theorized by Carl Schmitt after the example of Jean Bodin. Breach is a figure of awesome and arbitrary force, which polices the border between the cities from a position that is at once outside of them but in no other territory either. At a point early in the novel, Borlú recalls the moment from his childhood when he first saw Breach at work. An Ul Qoman motorist, navigating a cross-hatched stretch of road, loses control and crashes into a storefront in the other city, killing a Besź pedestrian. Then this happens:

> In seconds, the Breach came. Shapes, figures, some of whom perhaps had been there but who nonetheless seemed to coalesce from spaces between smoke from the accident, moving too fast it seemed to be clearly seen, moving with authority and power so absolute that within seconds they had controlled, contained, the area of the intrusion. Their powers were almost impossible. . . . closing out outsiders, sealing off a zone inside of which, their quick actions still visible though child-me so afraid to see them, Breach, organising, cauterising, restoring. (66)

There's something magical about Breach, the agents of which appear out of nowhere to seal off a kind of nowhere-space. Breach is the embodiment of what Schmitt writes about when he describes political theory as depending on "secularized theological concepts" and compares the idea of sovereign authority to the miracles of Christ.[17] Schmitt's analogy depends on the fact that miracles demonstrate the existence of the divine within nature by subverting natural laws—thus, Lazarus rises from the grave, the stink of four days' burial upon him, his body still bound and wrapped, so that the sensual weight and reality of death comes to attest to Christ's power over creation.[18] Likewise, for Schmitt, the sovereign's power doesn't derive from its identity with the law but from standing outside of it. Bodin described "the main point of sovereign majesty" as consisting in "giving the law to subjects in general without their consent."[19] Schmitt likewise calls the sovereign one who "stands outside the normally valid legal system [but] nevertheless belongs to it, for it is he who decides whether the constitution needs to be suspended."[20] This is a sentence that, because it identifies the sovereign with the one who *decides*, explains why Schmitt's theory is regularly called *decisionist*. And because Schmitt and Agamben both conceive of sovereignty as the exception that proves the rule, their kind of theory is also called *exceptionalist*. "Sovereign," says Schmitt, "is he who *decides* upon the *exception*."[21]

By analogy, then, Breach is miraculous and powerful because it exists outside of Beszel and Ul Qoma while still belonging to the cities. The most fundamental legal norm in Beszel and Ul Qoma is the prohibition against breaching. And yet Breach enforces that taboo by existing within what Borlú, who at the end of the novel becomes one of its officers, calls "the interstice" (312). Breach occupies the breach that it proscribes. To exist in Breach is to be, as one of its agents asserts, "beyond law . . . where *decision* lies" (246; italics added).

There's no coincidence here; the allegory between Breach and the power of sovereign decision is strong, if—as is always the case with allegories—hardly exact. After all, my analysis simply explains why Miéville himself called *The City & the City* an imaginative riposte to the "bullshit exceptionalism of Schmitt and Agamben."[22]

MIÉVILLE, METROPOLITAN

We return to bullshit exceptionalism later on. First, we should consider the political geography of Beszel/Ul Qoma as something more than a philosophical allegory.

Miéville is a profoundly political person who disapproves of critics turning his novels into political exempla. In an interview published in the paperback edition of *The City & The City*, he complains about "allegorical" interpretations that seek "a 'master code' to 'solve' the story, to work out what it's 'about' or, worse, what it's 'really about'" (320). Such analyses, which would compare the two cities to East and West Berlin, or to Sarajevo in the 1990s, read not "too much" into the story, he says, but "too little," refusing a rich account of the text as an aesthetic world in its own right (320–21).

How, then, to square that complaint with my thesis that *The City & the City*'s Breach allegorizes the supposed secular miracle of sovereign decision? For one thing, Miéville's not opposed to all kinds of figurative interpretation. He embraces metaphor as a "fractally fecund" figure for reading and writing, insisting only that his creations exceed any single interpretation (321). He writes of the fantasy monsters he sometimes creates that, while they surely "demand decoding," they'll only remain "worthy of their own monstrosity" by refusing to become fully legible.[23] What he objects to is readers who would substitute typological reason for the topographic richness of weird worlds. Speaking in an interview, he insists that the connections and connotations that inevitably develop in the mind of a reader should not "ride roughshod" over the "internal consistency" of the secondary world, reducing a live figure to an allegorical deathmask.[24] The analysis that follows tries to avoid that kind of reduction—unless by "reduction" one means not oversimplification but the way a cook intensifies the flavor of a sauce by bringing out that which is rightly peculiar to it.

One way to begin is to note that cleaved city-states are general across Miéville's fiction. Consider the relationship between London and its "Abcity," UnLondon, in the young adult novel, *Un Lun Dun* (2008): "Abcities have existed at least as long as the cities," explains a talking book to the novel's heroine and ab-heroine: "Each dreams the other."[25] The short story "Reports of Certain Events in London" likewise tells of an urban sect that tracks the appearance of "Viae Ferae" such as Varmin Way. These are feral alleys and pathways that suddenly appear within streetscapes that were once "total" (although the story doesn't use that word). More than just streets, the feral pathways are uncouth parts of a living geography: ripping their way into the streetscape of London, they demonstrate that its spatial fabric is far from seamless or inviolable.[26] This sense that space is vibrant and

multiple also characterizes the city-state of New Crobuzon, the central setting of Miéville's breakthrough novel, *Perdido Street Station* (2000), the
first part of his prize-winning Bas-Lag trilogy and credited as a signature
work of the "new weird."[27] New Crobuzon is a fantastic metropolis, full of
ghettos and suburbs and secret realms, some of them "beyond the reach"
of the government and dependent on a "self-appointed network of postal
workers, sanitary engineers, even a kind of law."[28] Even the railway termi-
nus after which *Perdido Street Station* is named is compared to a town unto
itself, a self-governing enclave that's home to New Crobuzon's embassy
quarter as well as its version of the Pentagon (*IC* 368–69). Meanwhile, New
Crobuzon sits within, even as it struggles to dominate, a vast fictional map
in which huge stretches of terrain are not just, in the words of *Perdido Street
Station*'s scientist hero, "*beyond our power*" but in the most basic sense
"*unknowable*" to the people of the city (*PSS* 231–32; italics in original). There
is no way to describe the imaginative geography of Bas-Lag as a mere container for the arrangement of peoples and plots. It is a geography in which
"the land, and the air, and time are sick" (*IC* 270); it is at once natural, "ab-
natural," and the product of social making and remaking (477). Bas-Lag is
a savage literary world, torqued and broken, which torques and breaks the
characters it holds in space. Its very dynamism compels us to reconsider the
difference between character and setting, person and place.

Above all, in Bas-Lag, there is Armada, the floating pirate cosmopolis
at the heart of *The Scar* (2002), the middle part of the trilogy. Armada is a
city made of ships, big and small, all lashed together and joined by bridges
and walkways. As it sails across the oceans of Bas-Lag, constrained by no
permanent place or border, we might at first mistake Armada for something
like *Exterritory Project*'s experiments on the free seas. Better yet, we might
connect it to the "pirate utopias" limned by the postanarchist writer Peter
Lamborn Wilson.[29] In fact, Miéville has strongly criticized the fantasy
that we might escape state power by taking to the sea, especially when
that dream is articulated in the mode of libertarian fantasy: "It is a lunatic
syllogism: 'I dislike the state: The state is made of land: Therefore I dislike
the land.' Water is a solvent, dissolving 'political' (state) power, leaving
only 'economics' behind."[30] And yet, for all his derision, Miéville clearly

understands how pirate and maroon communities once inspired those seeking to escape state despotisms—and, in *The Scar*, Armada embodies exactly
that freedom for plenty of its residents. It's not just that many Armadans
are on the run from New Crobuzon or other terrestrial powers; Armada
is, as Carl Freedman notes, also a place of comparative liberality and
equality, which by the end of the novel witnesses a successful popular
revolution against its leading faction.[31] In this, it represents a genuine point
of political difference from New Crobuzon, which in the final part of the
Bas-Lag trilogy, *Iron Council* (2004), is the site of a viciously repressed
uprising.

Moving free of terrestrial empires, the pirate city-state roams the seas.
Its geographic and political mobility has obvious cultural analogues and
consequences—for instance, its official librarians are charged with collecting books in all tongues, while its diverse peoples and species get by in the
placeless maritime pidgin called Salt. And yet there's nothing finally romantic about Armada's wanderings. From the perspective of New Crobuzon's
governing oligarchy, the whole place is a kind of great externality. It's not
just that Armada is a bizarre congeries of hulks and boats: an island of
human settlement, untidy and windswept in a far vaster ocean. The bigger
issue is that, as pirates, the Armadans are considered *hostes humani generis*—
the enemy of all humankind and so beyond the pale of the law.[32] Armada
isn't just outside, or opposed to, one or another territorial state; as an outlaw nation it represents the juridico-political other against which the community of laws in general defines itself.

But that's just Armada from the outside. By contrast, the view from
within is congruent with territorial political authority. Armada is subdivided into several "femto-states" called "ridings." The term "riding" evokes
the English county of Yorkshire's historic northern and southern parts,
while the prefix "femto" designates a factor of ten to the power of negative
fifteen—so, more simply, states that are *really, really small*.[33] What's more,
each of these miniature polities boasts its own leaders and characteristic
form of government: "Curhouse's democracy, Jhour's solar queendom, the
'absolutist benevolence' of Garwater, the Brucolac's protectorate" (*S* 223). If,

from the outside, Armada is a pirate utopia beyond the pale of the law as such, from the inside it looks like an exercise in territorially organized administrative pluralism, with each geographically delimited riding operating according to its own political and legal norms and interests. There's therefore a complicated dance going on in *The Scar*, with Armada at once embodying the possibility of life beyond territorial statehood and functioning as a miniature family of nations unto itself. At one point in that novel, the whole world of Bas-Lag is called a "Fractured Land" (393). It's a phrase that applies to Armada's internal political geography as much as to the possibility that, somewhere in Miéville's fantastic secondary world, there might exist a place beyond the state.

This habit of geopolitical splintering and resplintering pertains even to the final part of the Bas-Lag trilogy, *Iron Council*. I say "even" because large parts of that novel read like a western, structured around a series of epic quests into and out of badlands areas populated by renegade bandits, mysterious horsemen, restive natives, and rebellious sex workers.[34] *Iron Council* is named, moreover, after a perpetually moving train, the riders of which lay down tracks ahead of the engine, while other workers pull up the rails on which it has just moved. The train was once the project of the Transcontinental Railroad Trust (TRT), which dreamed of connecting New Crobuzon to the far reaches of its empire. While under construction, however, the TRT's workers downed their tools and went into full revolt, seizing the train as the symbol and home for a new political community. The perpetual train thus figures as a utopian figure for a city-state gone feral: an extraordinary model for a community improbably but irresistibly in process. "The train carries its track with it, picking it up and laying it down," intones Miéville's third-person narrator, as the Iron Council escapes into Bas-Lag's western wilderness: "A sliver, a moment of railroad. No longer a line split through time, but contingent and fleeting, recurring beneath the train, leaving only its footprint" (262). In its locomotion, as much as its radical democracy, the forever moving-and-making train is central to *Iron Council's* thematic opposition between the repressive oligarchy of New Crobuzon—"greatest city-state in the world" (332)—and the volatile puissance of a revolutionary community, symbolized here as a perpetual motion machine for the production of constituent power, never fully constituted into its other.[35]

As with Armada's status as a mobile outside to New Crobuzon's territorial order, there's a lot to say for this analysis—and yet, again, just as the inside and outside of Armada exist in tension with one another, so does *Iron Council*'s symbolic opposition between stasis and movement need adjusting. The Iron Council isn't just a principle of movement but "a town moving" (*IC* 261), or, in a winningly oxymoronic phrase, a "vagrant sanctuary"— which is to say, a sanctuary for vagrants that remains safe by being vagrant itself (272). In the terms outlined earlier in this book, that vagrant sanctuary brings together the two types of extraterritoriality of person and of place. For some years, free in the West, the train even comes close to settling down, repeatedly circling the same ellipse of track as it winds between friendly homesteads and fields, "neither sedentary nor nomadic, describing its home" (341). The Iron Council is not the negation of territorial governance but something else: an extraterritorial refusal to choose. The train runs over and remakes common sense ideas about what it means to rule over land, to rule over people, or to refuse to be ruled at all.

In the end, the Iron Council never stops being a species of city-state: a "renegopolis" and a "republic" (*IC* 348, 513). Its difference from New Crobuzon has something to do with its vehicular motion but, most crucially, inheres in the city-train's egalitarian potential, such as the way its founders try to eliminate the gap between sovereign and citizenry: "The town and its government were one" (348). It's not the Iron Council's extraterritoriality that marks the biggest difference between it and New Crobuzon: it is its socialism. The tale of the train's rebellion is told from the perspective of the golem-maker Judah Low, who first works for the TRT as something akin to an ethnographer-scout, quits in disgust at his complicity in the destruction of an aboriginal community, is drawn inexorably back to the railroad as a gambler and a laborer, and finally joins the uprising. Judah loves and fights for the Iron Council, with his magic proving vital to its survival, and yet Judah leaves the train almost as soon as it secures its freedom in the West, inevitably returning to New Crobuzon. He is a man who "carries

New Crobuzon within him," if only in the sense that it has taught him to
"[see] everything as a city" (271–72). And there's no reason, moreover, to
believe that Judah's perspective is wrong. Bas-Lag breeds cities and subci-
ties, throwing up contested urban zones of authority as quickly as the Iron
Council throws down and tears up its tracks.[36]

In the Bas-Lag books, settings that at first seem to escape territorial
determination eventually reach a complicated sort of accommodation with
it. What's more, this pattern doesn't only apply to the Bas-Lag books. In
his most clearly SF novel *Embassytown* (2011), Miéville flies us light years
across the weird geography of "immer space," a zone somewhere between
dimensions that allows humans and other species to travel vast distances
among the stars. Most of the story takes place, however, not in immer space
but in Embassytown, a small colonial enclave on an alien planet at the edge
of the map of known space.

Embassytown is an entrepôt colony governed by consular officials from
a humanoid empire called Bremen. It's the hometown of the protagonist,
Avice, who has returned after many years spent wandering in immer
space. Avice describes Embassytown as a "ghetto city" (*E* 82) marked by the
proliferation of "interzones" (13, 132). As its name suggests, it is an extraterritorial city-state in which a multinational and multispecies population
are considered "juridically Bremeni," even as they exist on a hostile alien
planet at the pleasure of their "Hosts," an insectoid race called the Arieki,
whose language is notorious for its complexity and who were initially wholly
nonplussed by the Bremenis' attempts at establishing diplomatic and trading relations. As the novel progresses, Embassytown also becomes an out-
right "narcocracy," with its colonists locked in a fatally parasitic supplier/
addict relationship with the Hosts (*E* 106). By playing with the Orientalist
discourse of racial and linguistic otherness, alluding to doctrines of consular jurisdiction and personal extraterritoriality and evoking the idea of
"narcocracy," Miéville invites his readers to think about Embassytown in
relation to the subject of chapters 4 and 5: the ports of the South China Sea
region during the heyday of the opium trade. At the same time, Bremen is
a rather fecklessly mercantile power that is named not after one of the great
European imperial powers but after the German Free Hanseatic City of

that name—which is to say, it evokes the parcelized political geography of the Holy Roman Empire rather than the Westphalian state system or the universal empire associated with the Church in Rome. *Embassytown*'s symbols of human empire thus point, in one direction, toward Euro-American semicolonialism in East Asia and, in the other, toward Europe's early modern history of city-states and subnational confederations. The two historical allusions both evoke the limit-condition of the extraterritorial, suggesting alternatives to the neatly antithetical dreams of the territorial state and the borderless universal empire of capital or God.

Miéville's oeuvre thus draws a map of imaginary Monacos, a star chart of Singapores. His settings reduce what Aristotle called political partnership to its Western ideal type: the city-state or urban polis.[37] His novels possess this restricted and formalized political geography not because he's a metropolitan chauvinist (though he is a Londoner through and through) but so as to model political struggle in its abstract complexity.[38] As such, his plots become intensely political, not just because by restricting political life to an urban center he's able to dramatically intensify factional and ideological strife, but because his stories are haunted by a literary-philosophical tradition of urban dreaming that would include Plato's *Republic*, Thomas More's *Utopia*, Tommaso Campanella's *The City of the Sun*, and Italo Calvino's *Invisible Cities*, among others.

Still, if Miéville reduces the territorial nation-state to a version of the classical polis, such reduction takes place within secondary worlds that are otherwise agonistic and internally subdivided. In *Iron Council*, New Crobuzon's governing oligarchy is challenged by the revolutionary Collective, whose partisans declare that there are "two powers in this city" and rename their working-class neighborhoods "the Free Territories" (402). Employing language that directly evokes Schmitt's decisionist theory of sovereignty (and that oddly predicts a famous George W. Bush remark from April 2006) the Collective's partisans declare: "Parliament ain't the only decider in New Crobuzon any more" (364).[39] While the Collective's life as "an alternative city-state" (463) is crushed by the oligarchy's military, Iron Council is far from the only alternative space in the Bas-Lag trilogy: at no point in the trilogy does New Crobuzon lack what *Iron Council*'s narrator calls "alternative structures" of social and political life (82). In this sense, Armada's convolutions in *The Scar* are even more fundamental to Bas-Lag's narrative world, since they depend, as we have seen, on a double dissection of political space. First, around the floating polis, a line is drawn in nature between the city-state and an extraterritorial maritime nowhere—a line that mirrors a further division between the community of laws and the enemies of all humankind. Next, a further series of lines are drawn throughout the city itself, dividing administrative regime from administrative regime. The simplification of political life to the urban polis really ought to clarify the distinction between external and internal borders. But, in Miéville's city-states, that is exactly the border that becomes hardest to judge. Do the edges of the city-state called Armada lie between its floating fabric and the water in which it moves, or between the different constituencies of its federated whole? Is Iron Council the negation of territorial power, or the sign of its persistence, or itself an internally fractured sort of territory, or all of the above? Is the power that decides in New Crobuzon identical with its government? If Miéville's initial reduction of political geography to a world of city-states can be described as a kind of imaginative localization, then the way he creates internal borders within and through those polities represents the dislocation of that prior localization.

DUNGEON MASTERS' DEVICES

Miéville's settings aren't abstract theoretical experiments; they are the products of novelistic craft. The work of secondary world creation is central to Miéville's compositional practice, as it is to many writers who work in speculative traditions. In interviews, he has spoken about how the idea for New Crobuzon emerged first from a sense of mood that was initially conceived as something like a mental tableau, not yet thrown into the time of narrative. From that psychogeographic mise-en-scène, Miéville began to create maps, actual and cognitive, as well as "histories, time lines, things like that. . . . stuff that may or may not actually find its way into the novel."[40]

85

An enthusiast of role-playing games (RPGs) as a boy, Miéville continues to practice the strategies of secondary world creation that link the game designer to the novelist. It's even possible that this compositional practice has aftereffects in the documentary record of his reception. For, while it may be true that only *Perdido Street Station* among his books comes with an authorized frontispiece map, the internet is rife with weird cartography of Bas-Lag and other worlds.[41] These are the product of reading communities that, long attuned to the production of extracanonical paratexts, together amount to the refracted mirror image of Miéville's own techniques of literary world-making.

Imaginative systematization is much more than the literary equivalent of avoiding continuity errors; it is key, Miéville contends, to the quiddity of speculative subgenres. Although my next chapter, partly about Chang-rae Lee's *On Such a Full Sea* (2014), provides reason to doubt the strict connection between systematicity and speculative world-making, Miéville himself is adamant that the reader's ability to surrender herself to "the impossible, the weird, that characterizes genre" depends upon the methodical construction of alternate literary worlds.[42] This doesn't mean, as theorists of SF have sometimes claimed, that the weird must be commensurate with the real—the idea that, even if intelligent giant squids don't *really* live in the British Museum (the premise of Miéville's *Kraken* [2010]), our imaginative versions of them must still not contradict fundamental laws of nature or reason. The systematic has no necessary relation to the real. Jules Verne famously complained about H. G. Wells: "He goes to Mars in an airship, which he constructs of a metal which does away with the law of gravitation. *Ça c'est très joli,* . . . but show me this metal. Let him produce it."[43] But Miéville has no truck with such reality checks; he revels in the unlikely, the incredible, and the sheer otherness of what he calls the "abcanny."[44] Like Wells, he thinks that Verne misses the point: the novelist has no obligation to truth or reason beyond that which is necessary to "domesticate the impossible hypothesis" and so lend any scenario the agreement of plausibility.[45] The novelist's brief is to speculative possibilities, not logical ones. Building on Wells's position, Miéville therefore insists that the "cognitive" aspect of SF lies not in its fidelity to scientific fact or method but, rather, in the social compact between readers and writers in which the *resemblance* of reason substitutes for the authority of science. What Wells talked about as the power to domesticate the unfamiliar, Miéville describes as "a function of (textual) charismatic authority" that allows one to surrender to the fantastic and weird "as-if cognitively."[46]

This isn't just a question of setting, as if the speculative text's charismatic authority depends simply on drawing maps properly. It's also a matter of style and theme. Consider, in this context, the obvious consonance between Miéville's depiction of a fractured world of city-states and his tendency towards generic mixing and confabulation. His complex political geography, with its mobile borders, its holes and defiles, takes an aesthetic form deserving similar description. More than this, his settings are, in an important sense, constructed out of genre elements—stock characters, tropes, and situations inherited, consciously and unconsciously, from a thousand forebears, including everything from pulp novelists, paracanonical representatives of the old weird such as H. P. Lovecraft, and literary giants like Herman Melville, whose *Moby-Dick* lies very close to the submarine surface of Miéville's *Railsea* (2012). For this reason, when Miéville talks about systematization, he's not just talking about maps, timelines, and other dungeon master's devices; he's thinking about the interaction between RPG-style systematization and what he describes as a kind of Surrealist literary image, "as unreal and affecting as possible," which stimulates systematization but ensures that the literary fact is never reducible to any one spot on a chart or map.[47] This is the difference between the creation of a literary world and the construction of lists and handbooks: it's the difference between actually playing an RPG and only reading the handbooks.

In one sense, this description applies to most novelistic settings, which involve far more than mere geography, natural or built—more even than elements such as weather, qualities of light and darkness, or the kinds of intangible properties critics attempt to capture when they talk about "atmosphere" or "mood." Into the category *setting*, Seymour Chatman rightly suggests, we must also put minor characters such as the masses of troops from different nations that, in Kurt Vonnegut's *Slaughterhouse-Five* (1969), Billy Pilgrim encounters in a beet field beside the Elbe.[48] Setting is, for these reasons, a strange sort of formal concept. It is both straightforwardly spatiotemporal (the when and the where of the *fabula*) and a capacious container for all those narrative existents that are not primary characters and that are not therefore elevated by interiority, or by any kind of narrative agency that transcends, however briefly or in part, determination by geography and history. Many of those elements will be "generic," in the sense that they're typical rather than derivative. This is the sense in which the rural manor in a Irish "big house" novel such as Elizabeth Bowen's *The Last September* (1929) is both a fully realized aesthetic location in its own right—an extraordinary creation, partly based on the author's own home, possessing unique historic and atmospheric qualities—and the equally artful synthesis of formal logics and tropes that go back as far as the gothic novels of Maria Edgeworth.[49]

Miéville's settings radicalize this common generic logic, a point we can best illustrate via the "steampunk" aesthetic with which he was associated in the early years of his reception. As is well known, steampunk mixes the technological marvels of SF with the camp strangeness of magical fantasy.[50] It breeds genres together, moreover, within fictional worlds that are more industrial and retrospective (steam engines, dirigibles, revolutionary shades of 1848) than digital and futuristic. It is in this sense that steampunk implies more than a surface aesthetic: corsets worn with welding goggles or laptops finished in walnut and brass. This hybrid style implies a story-world constructed out of the knowing collision of generic traits and chronotopes.

The signature qualities of Miéville's version of steampunk are best illustrated by the "Remade." Remades are monstrous humans who were once criminals or dissidents—or, really, anyone New Crobuzon's oligarchs consider dangerous or disposable. After being condemned by the state to "punishment factories," their bodies are rebuilt by sorcerer-scientists known as "bio-thaumaturges," who transform human anatomy using a mixture of magic, mechanics, and biomedicine. Some Remades are cruelly enhanced for hard labor: powered by steam engines, moving on wheels or tracks, wielding mechanical limbs that crush, lift, or grab. Other kinds of remaking are functionally useless, explicable only as savage somatic perversions after the pattern of Dante's *contrapasso*—thus, when an impoverished woman is convicted of infanticide, she is remade with her dead daughter's fat little arms grafted onto her temples. Mutilated and transformed, the Remade human is stripped of her political rights and dignity, then condemned to some combination of imprisonment, indentured servitude, or colonial exile. Some of the Remade rebel and escape and so become "fRreemades," living seminomadic lives of banditry or marronage.

Occasionally, as with *The Scar*'s Tanner Sack, a Remade character rises to the level of a main character. Sometimes, like the Iron Councillor Uzman, they occupy the kind of middle part that, in a cinematic remake, might be played by one of those character actors who are at once ubiquitous and barely famous. Most often, though, the Remades form a mute suffering mass. Outcasts from New Crobuzon society, they tend to be objects of description rather than the subject of narrative focalization. On just two pages of *Iron Council*, for instance, Miéville's narrator describes the following characters, all of them forced by indenture into building the railway and none of them to be encountered again: "A crawling man spiral-shelled in iron and venting smoke"; "bodies made of iron and rubber cables, and steam engine arms"; "a man whose front pullulates with scrawny arms, each from a corpse or amputation"; "a taller man, his face stoic, a fox stitched embedded in his chest from where it snarls and bites at him in permanent terror" (166–67). The fate of these men and women recalls the denial of citizenship embodied in outrages such as the Tuskegee syphilis studies and Josef Mengele's experiments at Auschwitz. More broadly, because their weird individuality is always cut across by their marked status as real abstractions— that is, as the representatives of a social class that is necessarily greater than the sum of its parts—the Remades also become a kind of species metaphor for the new proletarian bodies distended by the chymic forge of the real industrial revolution.

But Remaking isn't just, remember, a matter of industrial modernity gone wrong. Its marriage of meat and machinery is made possible by dark magic, as much as secular science. And while it's true that Remaking's cruelties signify social injustice, it also makes possible a liberating superhuman excess. Thus do we have not just the mutilated downtrodden, but also Jack Half-a-Prayer—a Robin Hood kind of fReemade, who terrorizes New

Crobuzon's elite using the power and charisma afforded him by his giant praying mantis limb.[51] With the Remade in mind, it's easy to see how the fictional world of New Crobuzon is created out of a similarly anarchic fusion of generic archetypes, drawn from the worlds of fantasy and SF: monster and robot, animal and machine. In its combination of magic and industry, Remaking complicates received wisdom about SF's forward-looking technologism and fantasy's evocation of a timeless prehistory. But because New Crobuzon is modeled on London during the industrial revolution, Miéville's chronotopical mash-up is in fact even more disordered than this description suggests. A hint lies in plain sight, in the name "steampunk," which grafts the 1980s genre term "cyberpunk," with all its high-tech associations, onto the rackety sensorium of coal-fired locomotion. The technologistic aspect of the Bas-Lag story-world is therefore just as available for nostalgic backward glances as are its knights and sorcerers. Likewise, thaumaturgy is as much an occult science as it is the harnessing of forces outside of nature and history, its practitioners studying at universities and conducting research and experiments alongside scientists and engineers. In steampunk, that is, SF gets linked to the past, but so is magical fantasy detached from its association with a consolatory historical conservatism.

Such mixing is at once temporal and generic. And it is crucial, finally, to Miéville's creation of a secondary world that is at once profoundly unequal and in a state of crisis and flux. The world of Bas-Lag is characterized by a kind of revolutionary stasis. In *The Scar*, for instance, a dour knight, Uther Doul, carries the "possible sword," a half-magical, half-technological marvel that adds the sum of all possible maneuvers to the single thrust or slash or parry the swordsman actually makes. Uther literally wields the sum of all possible acts. He is a walking metaphor for irresistible change or potential.

Uther harnesses such possibility, however, not to transform the world but to restore Armada to its historic function as a pirate city. Indeed, for all his commitment to social change, Miéville sometimes reads like one of the great contemporary novelists of the world-shattering *not yet*. This is a quality epitomized by the frustrated political revolution at the heart of *Iron Council*. At the end of that novel, the train arrives on the outskirts of New Crobuzon, rushing to support a revolution that was crushed while they were still on the way. Just before the train and its cadres are annihilated by the city-state's waiting armies, the train is stopped—literally frozen in time by powerful magic. Forever onrushing and yet permanently still, the *Iron Council* is left, in some of the novel's first and final words, in a state of *"always coming"* (1, 564; emphasis in original).

Miéville's generic fusions are aesthetic figures for the way New Crobuzon is poised, in thematic as well as literary-historical terms, between an occult past and a future we cannot fully imagine. Steampunk peoples and places are more than characters and settings; they're metafictional symbols for the contingency of genre, as well as building blocks for a story-world that embodies a similar weirdness and contingency. The sociology of Miéville's imagined locales combines with his generic promiscuity in a way that approaches identity more than homology. Bas-Lag *is* a revolution in stasis; it owns that identity by *being* the confabulation of contradictory generic chronotopes. In this, as in so much else, it doesn't so much exceed the simplifications of allegory, as it eats them.

AN EMPIRE OF SOVEREIGNTY

It's now time to ask whether some political position inheres in Miéville's weird city-states. That inquiry leads us back to Agamben and *The City & the City*.

Miéville's settings remind us of what the last chapter discussed at length: territorial sovereignty on national lines is a relative latecomer; "Westphalian" rule was only ever hegemonic, not absolute; and its waning does not predict the end of the nation-state. "The era of the crassest globaldegook is over," Miéville noted approvingly in 2007. "The supposed imminent demise of the state, the perforation, dissolution, and evaporation of its sovereignty and borders are asserted with considerably less vigor [now] than during the boosterish early 1990s."[52] But while the fantasy of a borderless and tension-less globalization has been exposed for the claptrap it was, that exposure does not mean a return to business as usual. Miéville might grow righteous against the globalist dreams of the antistatist right, but he knows that "the internationalization of capital" is real and that it manifests itself, in another echo of the previous chapter, not in the form of the border's overthrow but of its mobilization. The neoliberal dream is "not of open borders but mobile ones," he writes, "as ferociously exclusive as those of any other state, and more than most."[53]

The fact that Miéville so regularly builds his fictional worlds around the urban form of the classical polis encourages us to read them as thought experiments in the nature and operation of political power. And because these delimited sovereign realms are set within expansive narrative worlds, his novels also regularly evoke the very questions—about territoriality and its limits, and about the way we represent the geography of power—that concern me in this book. This novelistic tendency clearly connects to Miéville's identity as an erstwhile scholar of international relations, in which discipline he holds a doctorate from the London School of Economics.[54] His academic monograph, *Between Equal Rights* (2004), develops a commodity theory of international law first propounded by the Marxist intellectual Evgeny Pashukanis. Arguing that, under the conditions laid out in the modern system of international law, states "*interact as property owners—each state owns its own sovereign territory*," Miéville also analyzes "the role of state-sponsored international legislation in bleeding 'stateness' across national boundaries" and rejects the "simplistic assertion that globalisation is eroding the nation-state."[55]

Most interestingly for a reader of Miéville's fiction, his monograph also concludes that the concept of juridico-political authority must be historicized in terms of an "empire of sovereignty" that includes both the history of European imperialism and the era of anticolonial self-determination (*BER* 260–68). At this point building on the work of the "brilliant and sinister"[56] Carl Schmitt himself, Miéville understands the modern state system as the product of a legal nomos in which "the political and social order of a people becomes spatially visible" and in which "every new epoch in the coexistence of peoples, empires, and countries . . . is founded on new spatial divisions, new enclosures, and new spatial orders of the earth."[57] Although Miéville is careful to distinguish his position from what he calls

Schmitt's "austere idealist philosophy" (291), he derives from him an axiomatic connection between international relations, international law, and the divisibility of juridico-political space. Such a spatial division may be actual, as with the building of walls, but it may also be a line drawn on a map or in mental space. Schmitt's prime example of this is the creation of "amity lines" in the Americas, which separated a European sphere of supposed peace and law from a extraterritorial zone in which diplomatic and military norms no longer applied, and in which colonial rivals and colonized peoples could be attacked with impunity.[58] "No peace beyond the line," Francis Drake is supposed to have said (*BER* 180). While Miéville is cautious about whether lines of amity actually existed in the way Schmitt says they did, he takes from the German jurist a sense that the colonial construction of an "'agonal' zone beyond law was . . . invaluable and necessary" to the developing European system of territorial sovereignty (181).[59]

And so to Agamben, who also builds upon Schmitt's insight about the centrality of spatial division to the disposition of political sovereignty, and whose books and essays on this topic have become central to contemporary theories of extraterritoriality. It's curious, given that last fact, that Agamben has only rarely invoked the language of the extraterritorial directly—for instance, in his 1993 essay "Beyond Human Rights," and in a key passage of *Homo Sacer* (1995). In the latter text, he compares "the interval between death sentence and execution" in the Nazi camps to the fences that surrounded those zones. The comparison depends on the way both are said to delimit "an extratemporal and extraterritorial threshold in which the human body is separated from its normal political status and abandoned, in a state of exception, to the most extreme misfortunes."[60] The moment is brief, but its appearance in a sentence packed with core Agambenian keywords and topoi—the fenced-off camp, the ban or abandonment, the state of exception—suggests its importance to his political philosophy. We will explore the extratemporal in a later chapter that focuses on, among other topics, how the death of a parent might occur and yet be undone in Kazuo Ishiguro's *When We Were Orphans* (2000). For now, note how the figure of the extraterritorial gives topological form to the paradox which, for Agamben as for Schmitt, is central to sovereignty: that it "consists in the fact

[that] the sovereign is, at the same time, *outside* and *inside* the juridical order."[61] Agamben consistently explains the sovereign exception through spatial metaphors. Sovereignty is that which is *"taken outside (ex-capere),* and not simply excluded"; it is "an inclusive exclusion (which thus serves to include what is excluded)"; and it is the secret of a political system that "no longer orders forms of life and juridical rules in a determinate space" but is instead ordered around a *"dislocating localization."*[62] The extraterritorial space of the camp is the space of the *homo sacer*: the person reduced to biological existence, a species of outlaw who can be killed with impunity but who cannot, because he has no legal existence, be the victim of a murder or the object of a sacrifice.

The spatial form of the inclusive exclusion is suffused throughout the language and logic of *Homo Sacer* and *State of Exception*. That logic, which inverts the usual relation between exception and norm, has also proved extremely influential among contemporary theorists of extraterritoriality. Consider Keller Easterling's first book, *Enduring Innocence* (2005), the introductory paragraphs to which approvingly cite *Homo Sacer*'s "argument that the [concentration] camp is a place of legal exception or lawlessness," the form of which is traceable to other kinds of "legal lacuna or island entitled to special sovereignty or exemption from law."[63] At the very end of that chapter, Easterling quotes Agamben again, theorizing that the "structure of the camp" has now metamorphosed within "the *zone d'attentes* of our airports and certain outskirts of our cities."[64] Eyal Weizman's lecture "On Extraterritoriality" (2005) likewise dedicates an early paragraph to Agamben, who Weizman says is "well known for his writings on the state of exception, which goes hand in hand with extraterritoriality."[65] The Barcelona conference to which that lecture was delivered featured Agamben as a keynote speaker and led him to coedit a volume of essays, "Archipelago of Exceptions: Sovereignties of Extraterritoriality," many of which are deeply influenced by his work.[66] Likewise, a 2003 volume on extraterritoriality edited by Weizman and Anselm Franke contains an essay, "Extraterritorial Spaces and Camps," the first three citations of which all refer to Agamben's work.[67] It's easy to proliferate other instances in which Agamben's political philosophy has proved central to twenty-first-century theories of the extraterritorial—from studies of refugee camps in places as distinct as Palestine and Tanzania to the artist Trevor Paglen's investigation of military "black sites."[68] Although several of these authors criticize aspects of Agamben's thinking, they all understand extraterritoriality as a projection of sovereign power by means of the spatial logic of the "inclusive exclusion." Indeed, this proliferation of Agambenian examples in the secondary scholarship is only matched by the range of the philosopher's own figures for extraterritorial spatial relations: all those many zones of indistinction, thresholds of undecidability, localizations without order, and machines with empty centers, that litter the landscape of his prose.

When, as explained in the introduction, I use the language of the *outside within,* I share in this general indebtedness to Agamben. The difficulties with his theory emerge, however, when he tries to root his use of the extraterritorial in political history, rather than using it as a topological metaphor. Agamben argues that, far from being an aberration, or a betrayal of the norms we associate with liberal states, the Nazi *Laager* are key to the nature of political life since the middle of the nineteenth century. Schmitt argues that colonial amity lines define the modern political order; similarly, Agamben holds that the Nazi concentration camps epitomize the "hidden matrix or *nomos*" of Western political life since the liberal revolutions of the eighteenth and nineteenth centuries. The camp, he writes, is "the space that opens up when the state of exception starts to become the rule. In it, the state of exception, which was essentially a temporal suspension of the state of law, acquires a *permanent spatial arrangement.*"[69] To simplify a complicated argument greatly, the fenced-off camp embodies the way a supposedly temporary and abstract principle of emergency power has in fact become a fundamental aspect of political and juridical life. Created and governed by the state's most powerful and authoritative institutions, the camp becomes the exceptional zone in which liberal legal norms and practices are canceled and suspended. The camp's full historical emergence in the middle of the twentieth century signals the arrival, Agamben argues, of a permanent paradigm of government in which "law encompasses living being by means of its own suspension" and in which the moment of political action or decision shows itself to be autonomous of legal or moral norms.[70] Agamben's "extraterritorial" camp boundary is thus far more than a general spatial figure for a curious logical relation; the space of the camp is the historical and material shape taken by the sovereign exception when it (supposedly) becomes a paradigm for government. Against the liberal presumption that death camps and gulags represent the perversion of juridical norms, Agamben argues that such extraterritorial zones literalize the matrix of power that structures all forms of constituted power.

This proposition leads us to the most general, and the most curious, among Agamben's deployments of the extraterritorial—and one that hearkens back to the *open/closed* antithesis described in the introduction to this book. As we've seen, Agamben identifies the space of the camp with the coercive force of sovereignty itself. A fierce critic of the state and sovereign power in general, Agamben associates the camp most clearly with the figure of the police, whom he condemns as "not merely an administrative function of law enforcement" but, deploying yet another spatial metaphor, as "the place where the proximity and the almost constitutive exchange [quasi lo scambio costitutivo] between violence and right that characterizes the figure of the sovereign is shown."[71] Setting aside the oxymoronic "almost constitutive," it's clear that, if the extraterritorial is the zone defined by the police, in which violence and the law shake hands, then Agamben would be right to identify extraterritoriality with a coercive or "closed" political regime. But, in fact, Agamben's use of the extraterritorial points in two directions at once. In *Homo Sacer*, extraterritoriality is a kind of politico-geographical trap that any person would want to escape; but in the essay "Beyond Human Rights," it's also a kind of happy nonplace, beyond the reach of the state, to which political resistance might lead.

In "Beyond Human Rights," Agamben argues that, in an age of the refugee and mass migration, we should break with the idea that citizenship is, or ought to be, rooted in heredity and, thus, on "the trinity of state-nation-territory that is founded on that principle."[72] If, or when, that trinity were to break apart, the space of sovereignty would no longer be what Agamben calls "topographical"—which is to say, *territorial*, based on the idea that political authority is isomorphic with the demographic spread of a unitary population and with its uninterrupted extension in space. Instead, sovereignty would take *topological* form, as in the example of a Möbius strip, "where exterior and interior in-determine each other."[73] In such a context, an institution and an idea such as "Europe" might cease to be territorial and recompose itself as a chain of communities "that would articulate each other via a series of reciprocal extraterritorialities."[74] What this would mean in practice is hard to tell. We have only the suggestion that two different communities might, while "insisting on the same region," nevertheless remain "in a condition of exodus from each other."[75] Such communities wouldn't be organized around territorially limited citizenship rights but, rather, around what Agamben calls "the *refugium* (refuge) of the singular."[76] In this context, extraterritoriality is said to hold out the promise of a "model of new international relations" between polities that are not simply postnational, or post-Westphalian, but in which the putative connection between land, law, and violence has been severed in favor of some irreducible alterity.[77]

Here, then, are two types of extraterritoriality. In *Homo Sacer*, extraterritorial zones are lawless only in the sense that, within them, the law has no normative content and sovereign power exerts untrammeled power over life and death. In "Beyond Human Rights," by contrast, extraterritoriality has the power to puncture and "topologically [deform]" the whole idea of lawful sovereignty.[78] It's rare to see both of extraterritoriality's moral and ideological aspects in one philosopher's work, but that seems to be what we have on our hands.

Agamben's two-way extraterritoriality doesn't appear to stem from some infelicity of translation; nor is it just an error.[79] The darkly decisionist political philosophy of *Homo Sacer* is entirely congruent with the project of splintering the territorial state: the extraterritorial camp is the dystopian downside to the utopian upside of "Beyond Human Rights." If the state is reducible to the police, and if the police are identical with sovereign violence, then who wouldn't want to break all three with an extraterritorial hammer? Agamben's dual versions of the extraterritorial do not form either end of an antithesis. To adopt his own simile, they are the "in-determinate" sides of a Möbius strip. Together, they form an impossible singularity that holds together because it is defined through and against the same

Westphalian trinity we encountered in the last chapter: "State-nation-territory." Agamben believes that the extraterritorial camp always lies hidden inside the territorial state, no matter how liberal that state might otherwise appear. And, because he believes that the camp is always ready to emerge, as the inclusive exclusion of the state in general, he also believes that the formal and ideological trinity "state-nation-territory" is already exploded at heart. "Beyond Human Rights" seeks to harness that explosion's energy, liberating and revalorizing the occulted nomos of the political. In this context, the extraterritorial becomes a kind of topological *pharmakon*, at once the poison that is sovereignty and its cure.

BREACH AND THE BREACH IN BREACH

So what is "bullshit" about all of this? Miéville's impatience with decision-ist theories of sovereignty can be guessed at from *Between Equal Rights*. Early in that monograph, he attacks "command" theories of law in which the legal form is identified with the dictates of a monarch or other executive authority. Such a theory, he complains, "presumes an ideal-type definition of law—as the will of the sovereign—which is then used as a yardstick to examine reality. In other words [it does] not analyse reality, in all its complexity, but *judge* it" (18). In command theories, propositions are said to be lawful without reference to their substantive properties: the only thing that counts is whether the utterance in question can be identified, whether at the point of a gun or the end of a writ, as a sovereign command. From the perspective of command theories, the state itself is considered apart from its historical properties or development; it is merely the institutional space within which the sovereign happens to act (19).

Miéville doesn't have Agamben directly in mind when criticizing such ideas about the law.[80] Still, there remains a pronounced overlap between command theories and the strain of decisionist thought Agamben inherits from Schmitt—an overlap that Pavlos Eleftheriadis describes as inhering in the "implausible and unattractive" judgment that "law is a matter of violent imposition . . . [with] no legal limit. . . . No institution can prevail over the sovereign. In fact, law is not a matter of institutions at all."[81] If the sovereign can be, in the words of the agent of Breach, "beyond law, where decision lies," then identifying it as such tells us nothing else about the content or value of legal and political regimes or actions (*CC* 246). Agamben describes the extraterritorial space of the exception as "an empty space."[82] But, from Miéville's perspective, such emptiness is not in fact a property of politics or law—and it has nothing to do with the actual nature of sovereignty, its agents, or institutions. That empty zone is just all a philosopher can see when he sacrifices historical analysis for the formal description of abstract ideas. This is the lesson of *The City & the City*, as much as *Between Equal Rights*.

In Borlú's investigation into the death of Mahalia Geary, the key event is his decision to breach. Desperately chasing a suspect across the cities' cleaved jurisdictions, Borlú opts to break the law rather than let a murderer escape, and so he shoots his suspect across the invisible frontier between the cities. Almost as soon as the suspect's body has hit the ground, Borlú becomes the property of Breach:

> "*Breach.*" A grim-featured something gripped me so that there was no way I could break out, had I wanted to. I glimpsed dark shapes draped over the body of the killer I had killed. A voice close up to my ear. "*Breach.*" A force shoving me effortlessly out of my place, fast fast past candles of Besźel and the neon of Ul Qoma, in directions that made sense in neither city.
>
> "Breach," and then something touched me and I went under into black, out of waiting and all awareness, to the sound of that word. (*CC* 238; emphases in original)

From this point on, Borlú is no longer a citizen of Besźel. As the novel races toward its conclusion, he goes from being the prisoner of Breach to, eventually, its willing agent. In that guise, he uncovers the international conspiracy behind Mahalia's murder. He also preserves Breach's authority in the midst of a cities-wide challenge to its prerogatives, thereby maintaining the delicate jurisdictional balance between Besźel and Ul Qoma. Eventually, after the emergency dies down, Borlú is formally inducted into Breach, his diligent police work having affirmed Breach's status as a place "out of either town [but] into neither" (303).

In this sense, Borlú fulfills the detective's traditional functions as an agent of the prevailing moral and political order. But he doesn't become an angel of sovereignty, executing miracles from the zone between the cities' overlapping jurisdictions. Instead, his journey into Breach's breach demystifies that institution. As we read about Borlú's work in and for Breach, we see that it is ordinary, even vulnerable; it's not an ideal but an institution, inhabited by a bunch of civil servants who do their job with the same mix of habitual action and improvisatory panic as the rest of us. When Borlú first enters the precincts of Breach, recall, he saw it as a "void full of angry police" (*CC* 248). As the days go by, however, that void is populated and, soon, he stands amazed as he sees its agents argue, then vote, about how to conduct their investigations (259). Seen from within, Breach doesn't embody the singular and exceptional power of decision; its character and authority turn out to be the result of many decisions, made by many agents, some of them contradictory—just with all of them wrapped in the glamor of speed and cool gadgets. Borlú watches the agents of Breach "bickering and voting in their fast loose way" (265). From within, he can no longer unsee "the crude democracy of their methodology" and "their decentralised self-ordering" (280). Far from being a monarchical miracle, Breach turns out to be nothing more, nor less, than a disjoint and somewhat democratic bureaucracy. In the end, Breach is an institution among institutions, not the secret of power in general. And so it should be. For all its weirdness, *The City & the City* is a very good detective novel—and there are few good detective novels that do not, at some level, entertain the possibility that the police might do good.[83]

As it closes, *The City & the City* continues to thematize its political geography. Borlú is now an avatar of Breach, the citizen of an "community of bare, extra-city lives." He says he's not an upholder of "the law, or another law," but someone whose job is to "maintain the skin that holds the law in place." Breach is not, in fact, a void, nor does it live within a void. It is not what Agamben, thinking of the camp and of the state in general, calls a "kenomatic" space of nothing but lawless anomie.[84] Borlú tells us that the avatars of Breach are philosophical types and that they debate among themselves exactly "where it is that we live." The novel closes with Borlú's answer to that question, which he declares is the opinion of a liberal: "I live in the interstice, yes, but I live in both the city and the city" (312). Breach is a skin or membrane: it is thin, but like the organ that covers our bodies, it has volume and it is sensitive—a medium for feeling and touching, if not always for feeling the right thing in the right way.

Even more than this, Breach is not the only thing that might exist between the cities. In the previous two chapters, I aligned the argument of this book with theorists of the state, such as Michael Mann, who emphasize the plural and disaggregated nature of its power. *The City & the City* likewise raises the question of whether any political or legal authority could ever claim the singular and indivisible nature that Schmitt and Agamben afford to the sovereign decision. Mahalia's mistake, in *The City & the City*, is to become obsessed with the legend that a third city called Orcinny exists "between the other two," in the disputed zones: "When the old commune split," says Borlú as he explains this theory to his straight-talking sidekick, "it didn't split into two, it split into three. Orciny's the secret city. It runs things" (50). While Orciny turns out to be more of a real fraud than a true fiction, it bears noting that Breach's status as *the* exceptional power is put into question almost right from the start of the novel. If Orciny "runs things," then Breach is not a miracle but just one mystery among many, just one interstice in a possibly infinite series of interstitial powers. "If there's something else between Besźel and Ul Qoma," Borlú demands of a Breach agent late in the novel, "where does that leave you?" (246). The agent is silent and horrified. He recruits Borlú to Breach in part because, if Orciny were found to be real, it would devastate Breach's fragile authority as arbiter of the cities' rival jurisdictional claims. If Breach is like a god to the cities' ordinary citizens, then finding Orciny would be like discovering god's god.

For Miéville's readers, though, the truth of Orciny makes little difference to anyone except Mahalia, whose willingness to believe in the myth opens the way to her exploitation by her killers. In *The City & the City*, political gods don't exist and only bullshit philosophy believes in them. In Besźel and Ul Qoma, a city-state that seemed to be shaped like a miracle turns into something ordinary: a space defined by agonistic struggle and the lawful chaos of institutionalized democracy. Breach is still legible to us as a juridico-political allegory; it's just that, despite its initially Schmittian appearances, it turns out to be an allegory for sovereign power in all its non-magical activity. Once again, that passage from Sebald's *Austerlitz* comes to mind: the Palace of Justice in Brussels, with its hallways to nowhere and rooms with no doors. The palace's secret chambers are an excellent figure for the dark side of the legal order, but, in the end, Sebald characterizes the law as involving a compromise between an occulted power and the mix of good intentions and proud incompetence that is bourgeois civil society. In Sebald's Palace of Justice in *Austerlitz*, the dislocating localization of the law creates hidden alleys of human movement amid the dark cells of bare life. The palace is full of "creaking wooden stairs which gave the impression of being temporary structures," of obscure corners and empty rooms that the citizens of Brussels have converted from public halls into spaces of private enterprise: "tobacconists, a bookie's, a bar, and . . . a gentleman's lavatory."[85] Its jury-rigged and semiprivatized hallways are not just spaces of exceptional power but islands of tactical resistance to exactly that kind of claim to authority. These spaces are not empty zones in which sovereignty lurks, but places full of social life, however violent and unequal; the law is a human geography in which power is contested and negotiated.

The space of exception exists in the sphere of extraterritoriality. But so does the space of tactical maneuver. "A tactic is a calculated action," writes Michel de Certeau, "determined by the absence of a proper locus. . . . The space of a tactic is the space of the other. Thus it must play on and with a terrain imposed on it and organized by the law of a foreign power."[86] Subject to the law, yet never wholly determined by it, the extraterritorial geographies of Miéville's city-states are epitomized by these "dark cul-de-sacs," dead-end corridors piled with unwanted furniture, "as if someone had been obliged to hold out there in a state of siege."[87] What's more, as these examples show, even the law is far from singular. An understanding of juridico-political power as contingent and contested is at the center of Miéville's philosophical allegory. In *Between Equal Rights*, he argues that the lack of a single locus of sovereignty does not imply an absence of law. Coercive power is generally thought to be essential to the operations of the law, whether domestic or international, but a unitary or singularly overarching authority remains extrinsic to it (*BER* 129). Miéville holds that international law emerges not despite the absence of a single locus of sovereign authority but because of it: "The development of law as a system was evoked not by the requirements of the state, *but by the conditions for commercial relations between those tribes which were not under a single sphere of authority*."[88] He rejects the mordant clarity of the Agambenian position, which prefers the terrible singularity of the sovereign exception to the real complexities of social and political struggle. Agamben's spatial figure of the inclusive exclusion remains a powerful general frame for conceiving of the extraterritorial, especially as it helps undo the normative association between territoriality, citizenship, and nationality. But Agamben errs when he at once identifies the extraterritorial with the space of the camp and makes it the general historical nomos of sovereignty as such.

Good socialist that he is, Miéville will admit of only one power with the potential to synthesize the diverse strands and institutions of legal and political life—a power that applies to all his worlds, no matter how weird. When Borlú works out who is really responsible for Mahalia's murder, he discovers a transnational corporation seeking to accumulate wealth by exploiting the cities' quaint jurisdictional heritage and archeological riches. Instead of another wannabe sovereign actor, carving out a jurisdiction above and beyond the city and the city, we are left with an agent of capital, working toward ends that certainly have political effects but that possess no kind of Schmittian formal clarity. There are only two kinds of miracle in *The City & the City*: the magic of the commodity form and the ordinary wonder of human social and institutional commitment, bonds of friendship and duty that can't be reduced to the will to give the law to others without their consent, and that are weirder in practice than in theory.

3

STRING THEORY

That night, in the summer of Year Fifteen, Jeevan Chaudury was drink-ing wine by a river. The world was a string of settlements now and the settlements were all that mattered, the land itself no longer had a name

—EMILY ST. JOHN MANDEL, *STATION ELEVEN*

SETTING IS A KIND OF DESTINY

Is geography destiny? The Obama Administration worried that it was. The Department of Education's 2015 statement on "Equity of Opportunity" begins with some okay-then rhetoric from president Barack Obama's sec-ond inaugural address ("We are true to our creed when a little girl born into the bleakest poverty knows that she has the same chance to succeed as anybody else") and then lists the impediments to be overcome if that child is to "learn and achieve" in the same fullness as all Americans. After wealth and whether or not English is your first language, the third obstacle given is "zip code," the sequence of numbers by which the US Postal Service identifies a mailing address. The wrong address, the government clearly implies, makes it more likely that you will be poorly educated; it makes it more likely that your family and friends will be poorly educated; and it makes a poor education more difficult to escape or overcome.[1]

Though we might cavil at the way the Department of Education's state-ment implicitly conflates educational opportunity and social equality, there's little doubt that geography shapes positive inequalities of means as well as negative inequities of opportunity.[2] In a report on rural poverty, the US Department of Agriculture describes how "people living in poverty tend to be clustered in certain regions, counties, and neighborhoods rather than being spread evenly," with the effect that "economic conditions in very poor areas can create limited opportunities for poor residents that become self-perpetuating."[3] The US Census Bureau likewise uses statistical mapping to chart demographic fluctuations in the incidence of official poverty.[4]

The Census Bureau's maps show the uneven distribution of economic inequality across administrative space (the borders of state and county governments) as well as generational time (zero-to-seventeen-year-olds compared to those eighteen or over). These correlations once again suggest that poverty doesn't just happen to concentrate in certain areas of the country; the racially and socioeconomically segregated nature of US territory explains why poverty becomes persistent over time—why, that is, the spatial distribution of economic inequality is historically sticky, if not entirely static.[5]

None of this should be surprising. The United States has a widely acknowledged history of "redlining": a form of institutionalized prejudice in which government agencies, state-sponsored corporations, and private enterprises collude to distribute economic opportunities so as to systematically favor "new construction over existing dwellings, open land over developed areas, businessmen over blue-collar workers, whites over blacks, and native-born Americans over immigrants."[6] Public policy decisions have been made in such a way that the wrong kind of poor neighborhood tends to stay poor, often despite strenuous efforts to the contrary by local residents. The statistical maps produced by the Census Bureau are not, for this reason, simply two-dimensional charts. Read comparatively across time, they imply probable futures: stories about the fortunes of people in place, told in the terms suggested by their past. They're not novels, but they're not temporally flat, either, mere slices across socioeconomic space. If where you are in those maps doesn't absolutely predict where you'll go—well, your location definitely makes some destinations more likely than others.

This chapter extends the last one's concern with narrative setting in speculative fiction, its basic premise being that just as geography effects people's futures in the real world, so does a character's location have a determinative effect on where she goes and what she can see, say, or do along the way. The chapter's particular focus is the contemporary Anglophone postapocalyptic novel; and because I hope to say something general about that body of fiction, the chapter features discussions of more than ten examples and counterexamples—not distant reading, exactly, but an attempt at interpretation at medium scale.[7] But, because I also want to show how extraterritorial geographies can be the subject of a novel's style and form, not just its overt concern or theme, the chapter also features extended close readings of three recent texts: *On Such a Full Sea* (2014) by the Korean American author Chang-rae Lee, and two works by Canadian writers— the *MaddAddam* trilogy (1993–2013) by Margaret Atwood, one of the most prolific and critically celebrated novelists working today; and *Station Eleven* (2014) by Emily St. John Mandel, a younger author newly risen to prominence. These three examples are connected by their dates of publication and language of composition, by the fact of having been written by authors more often associated with "literary" forms of fiction rather than popular genres, and by being set on the North American continent in the near future.

My starting observation is that a significant number of such contemporary novels are set in political geographies that resemble island archipelagoes more than Westphalian territories. Such novels accentuate and magnify a quality inherent in many forms of romance genre: a tendency to divide the story-world into the city and the wilderness, with the revelation of character and theme strung out along the arduous journey from one kind of local settlement to another. Although this formal pattern didn't emerge in the twenty-first century, its present efflorescence represents a kind of collective aesthetic response—at once mimetic and self-consciously critical—to the changing nature of contemporary political space. Within books like the *MaddAddam* series, Westphalian territorial space is punctured and fragmented by powerful forces that operate on a planetary or even cosmic scale.

Such global causes, however, produce archipelagic effects: not planetary government but isolate settlements adrift in lawless space. This pattern is, of course, not wholly new: the idea that global catastrophes might produce parcelized political geographies can already be observed, for instance, in H. G. Wells's scientific romance *The War in the Air* (1908), in which the quadruple catastrophe of aerial warfare, economic crisis, famine, and pandemic disease leaves its protagonist living in a neofeudal England of little settlements and petty sovereignties. But there are two new aspects to the contemporary variant: first, a general emphasis on human-caused (anthropogenic) forms of social and, especially, ecological catastrophe; second, the way anthropogenic catastrophes tend to take place according to the timescale that Ernest Hemingway used to describe bankruptcy—gradually, and then suddenly—so that the time of disaster resembles the temporality of the very globalized political and economic order that is collapsing.[8]

For the writer of postapocalyptic fictions, moreover, extraterritorial spaces mediate more than the relationship between state and globalization (the argument of chapter 1), or the formal and conceptual parts of a political allegory about sovereignty in general (that of chapter 2). At a formal and thematic level, the internally contradictory nature of extraterritorial zones—at once spatial and personal, open and closed—enables the interrelation between everyday and fantastic kinds of character and experience. As types of narrative space, extraterritorial zones possess what Eric Hayot, in his theory of literary world-making, calls the "anthropological" quality common to literary genres that, at the level of setting, begin by positing a "double world."[9] First, there's the special geography of the world apart: the fortified encampments and company towns, for instance, that litter Octavia Butler's *Parable of the Sower* (1993); or, to cite Hayot's own example, the "Paradise Incorporated, and Highly Restricted" of Raymond Chandler's Idle Valley, the Los Angeles subdivision at the heart of *The Long Goodbye* (1953).[10] Notwithstanding the differences between post-apocalypse and the noir, or between 1950s suburbs and near-future wastelands, the same general spatial relation applies in all these examples. Against and around the exceptional zone, there exists a second world: the sociogeographic "whole" within which the extraordinary zone is at once contained and released.[11] In this same way, extraterritorial settlements are poised between being representative social microcosms and sites of spectacular difference, defined continually against what used to be or what lies beyond the walls. The line that describes the border around such a zone is the "aperture or bridge" that joins it, spatially and temporally, to the world outside, and it is also the wall or moat that allows us to see that world as distinct.[12] Herein lies the extra-territorial settlement's speculative formal promise: its capacity to at once define an extraordinary world and project it as ordinary. The *outside within* logic of the extraterritorial offers more than a way of negotiating different geographic scales, or of staging political conflict and decision-making. Extraterritorial settings are a literary technology for making the world differently while acting like that difference is ordinary—or, even, that it's a kind of destiny.

There's a long precedent for emphasizing the determining form of narrative setting, most powerfully apparent in the great realisms of the nineteenth century. Consider the theory of milieu that Erich Auerbach derives out of Honoré de Balzac's *La Père Goriot* (1834). Here, so Auerbach has it, Balzac presupposes an elementary harmony between setting and character. Such harmony produces a stylistic unity in which descriptions of person and place intermingle and implicate one another. And this intermingling of the human and the geographic becomes the narrative engine for powering a new kind of realism—an "atmospheric realism" in which setting becomes an "organic" and "demonic" entity, at once "total" and "necessary" to the novel's formal operations and affective qualities.[13] As with the generic ructions and constructions that make up Miéville's New Crobuzon, a milieu is far more than a geographic fact, and much more than a vessel for the containment of stories. A narrative effect itself, setting also produces and subtends other parts of the fiction not otherwise reducible to space and time. Auerbach inherits the language of milieu not just from Balzac, who uses the term in his preface to the *Comédie Humaine* (1842), but from the naturalistic philosophical framework of Hippolyte Taine's *Histoire de la littérature anglaise* (1863–64), with all that implies for how human personality might be shaped by the mutual constitution of space and society.[14] In the theory of milieu, in short, the gap between geography and destiny shrinks.

But the novel isn't synonymous with naturalism. What's more, we rightly celebrate great novelists for their capacity to conceive of the world differently, transforming their chosen medium as they do. This is especially true when it comes to the family of genres, including postapocalyptic fictions, that are commonly gathered together under the label "speculative." That term provokes a lot of critical disagreement, with Samuel R. Delany memorably describing it as "one of the numerous terms that numerous critics for numerous reasons have decided is inadequate for the numerous things that fall under it."[15] For some authors, such as Atwood, speculative fiction can be distinguished from science fiction (SF) or fantasy along an axis or realism or plausibility. Whereas she defines SF as denoting "books with things in them we can't yet do or begin to do," Atwood argues that novels such as her own *Oryx and Crake* (2003) create fictional worlds out of "means already more or less to hand."[16] They don't, therefore, ask us to believe in the unlikely or the impossible. By contrast, there are genre writers who suspect that, for Atwood and other late adopters, the "speculative" label is merely a gentrifying term, designed to launder the subcultural stink of the fantastic.[17] And, indeed, whatever associations individual writers or readers might have with that moniker, there are reasons to believe that its original adoption by editors and publishers in the 1960s was part of a marketing strategy designed to "separate certain fictional works and publishing efforts from the commercialism and the expectation of formulaic predictability that had accrued around the term science fiction."[18] From this perspective, the difference between speculative fiction and SF or fantasy proper is not rooted in objective formal or conceptual differences but in distinctions of taste, themselves based in a cultural economy of prestige. This view accords, moreover, with a more generally nominalist tendency in recent debates about literary genre, with SF in particular having been described not as a thing in itself but as the "discursive product of enrolment processes undertaken by numerous actants with different and at times conflicting agendas."[19] Genres, this argument holds, don't exist in an objective sense— just ways of talking genre and doing genre. There is "no such thing as science fiction," write Mark Bould and Sherryl Vint, not because authors and readers don't believe in its existence but because all the SF stories in the world, plus all the claims readers have made about them, don't add up to a single coherent discursive object to call by that name or any other.[20] And if SF doesn't exist, what price a baggy compromise object like speculative fiction?[21]

My taxonomical goals in this chapter are modest; I make no attempt to settle the question of whether abstract universals such as genres are objectively real, coherent discursive fabrications, or incoherent versions of the same. The literary-historical usefulness of the term "speculative" is connected to—not compromised by—its flexibility. "Speculative" describes, however incompletely, a congeries of genres and subgenres that, in addition to SF, also happens to include the particular concern of this chapter: postapocalyptic fiction.[22] It's the generic description that Atwood prefers for *MaddAddamm* and the only one that also comfortably includes *On Such a Full Sea*, *Station Eleven*, and the other examples in this chapter.

More broadly, I follow Theodore Martin in understanding genres as social and contingent—useful not just as ways of describing the enjoyably predictable features of a text but also of historicizing its relation to different moments of production and reception, as well as to literary history itself. Martin considers genre as having a mediating function that allows us to better understand the historicity, not just of one or two individual texts, but of the present itself: "Genre, he writes, "describes how aesthetic forms move cumulatively through history. The accretive history of a genre is a measure of both change and continuity, diachrony, and synchrony, pastness and presentness."[23] And, in this way, genre, by allowing us to observe the interplay of different historical moments, "offers a singular view of contemporary history not by highlighting what's new in it and not by exposing what's old-fashioned about it but by showing how the very idea of the contemporary emerges out of a constant negotiation between the two."[24] By tracking how writers of twenty-first-century postapocalyptic fictions have intensified a spatiotemporal feature long common within versions of romance genres, I hope to illustrate the extraterritorial dimensions of contemporary culture.

These two dimensions of genre—the historical and the speculative—come together in Octavia Butler's celebrated dystopian novel *The Parable of the Sower* (1993), the realistic tenor of which has seen it described as "Mundane SF."[25] *Parable* is surely based in clear-eyed observation of North American social facts; indeed, in its description of the United States' takeover by a right-wing neo-Christian populist, as well as in its evocation of the effects of anthropogenic climate change, it has been hailed as unusually perceptive about the direction of twenty-first-century US history.[26] And yet, for all its general plausibility, it reverberates in a register more prophetic than simply predictive. As a kind of odyssey about the extraterrestrial future of all humanity—a journey in which each step is taken on behalf of all people, not just its central group of California exiles—*Parable* has ancient precedents in epic and scripture. Its visionary quality is evidenced not just by its near-future setting but by the whole trilogy's (unfinished) orientation toward interstellar colonization. That cosmic ambition is further amplified by Butler's persistent recourse to the forms and language of prayer, hymn, and homily, with Lauren Olamina's story frequently interrupted by verses from the religious text she is writing, "Earthseed: The Books of the Living." The visionary aspect of Butler's late fiction finally inheres in its fundamental commitment to the idea that, in order to envision life differently, a person must first of all *move* in space, hopping from shelter to shelter, perhaps, but always out, into the open. Butler appears to suggest that, in order secure the future, one must, like Lauren Olamina and the generations of African American maroons, runaways, and migrants who preceded her, take a chance on the difference between here and there, the geographical past and the future uncertain. One must move north of a blasted gated community in Los Angeles, across the wilderness that is dystopian California, into the new community called Acorn, and, finally, out again—in the second part of the sequence, *Parable of the Talents* (1998), and the unfinished *Parable of the Trickster*—by way of peripatetic evangelizing into a new life in outer space.[27] When it comes to speculative fiction like Butler's, the extraterritorial space of the gated community or fortified camp isn't merely an abstract spatial figure or principle; the logic of the *outside within* gives shape to speculative fiction's constitutive back-and-forth movement between fantastic and everyday events, between visionary and quotidian perspectives, and between the stickiness that is *where you are* and the slipperiness that is *where you might be*.

WHERE YOU ARE

The gravitational force of being "where you are" is at the heart of Chang-rae Lee's speculative picaresque, *On Such a Full Sea* (2014).[28] Three chapters in, those words are spoken by Lee's heroine, a young woman called Fan, while she attends a wake. A popular boy from Fan's neighborhood has accidentally drowned. The boy was a friend of Reg, the father of Fan's unborn child, who has himself recently been kidnapped by the shadowy "director-ate" that runs things in the city of B-Mor—or, as we would call it today, Baltimore. The old city on the Patapsco River has been transformed by ecological disaster and the collapse of the United States as a going concern. No longer a shrinking municipality with a mixed economy, B-Mor has been retooled as a walled enclave with a singular purpose: the production and supply of clean foodstuffs to elite, and equally gated, "Charter" villages.[29] It is thus somewhere between a colony, one of Miéville's city-states, and the kind of production zone described by Easterling in her study of infra-structure space.[30] What's more, B-Mor hasn't just been walled off; it has been systematically repopulated. Today's African American majority has disappeared: B-Mor is now home to refugees from "New China" (*OFS* 13) who have settled in American cities that, having been already "abandoned" by their original residents, were saved from the general destruction through a social irony dubbed "preservation by absence" (18).

The story behind the New Chinese arrival in B-Mor is left obscure. *On Such a Full Sea* is narrated in the first-person plural, with events told from the perspective of all Fan's neighbors. But while this collective narrator is bound together by bonds of familiarity and ethnicity, such intimacy never adds up to much like historical memory. The B-Mors do not appear to possess much by way of administrative or ancestral records, nor do they have a tale of the tribe to fall back on. In fact, as I'll go on to show, the story we are reading is something like the B-Mor people's attempt to tell such a tale, or to imagine an alternative to it. In any case, the collective narrator does tell us that the enclave's residents were transported from China en masse almost a century before the undated present (14). We learn that the narrators' ancestors were "trucked out" of Xixu City, their original Chinese riverside home, just days before it was "razed" (1, 17). And we are given reason to think that the environmental apocalypse that has stripped B-Mor of its seasons (there are now only blistering summers and frigid winters, with the result that most people live underground) is part of the same worldwide disaster that poisoned Xixu City's water and turned its air into "a haze that you can almost smell" (1). This much seems clear.

Against such knowledge, we never find out whether the New Chinese "originals" were forced into migrating or whether they quit their polluted homeland voluntarily (15). The collective narrator never explains whether their arrival in "shiny silver company buses" means that their transportation across the globe was wholly the initiative of private actors or some kind of partnership between corporations and states. We don't even know whether their transfer to North America ought to be understood as a sign of Chinese global hegemony or of the collapse of all national governments. It's possible that Fan and her people are the human flotsam upon a new wave of Asian capital investment, as with the migrant workers who today populate Chinese-run businesses and development projects in states such as Uganda.[31] Then again, the mass transportation of Chinese people to North America—especially to a historically black city such as Baltimore, south of the Mason-Dixon Line—might also be read as an allegory of nineteenth-century coolie labor, in which Asian workers were shipped to the Western Hemisphere following the abolition of the Atlantic slave trade. All we know for sure is that here is an ethnic Chinese productive enclave, built on the ruins of a black-majority city, in a territory historically associated with slavery and racial segregation. In the opening pages of *On Such a Full Sea*, geography therefore emerges as a social and environmental fact that is at once determinative and obscure. People move, abruptly and a long way, for reasons we don't fully understand; but those same people move in groups, for reasons tied to the despoliation of the Earth, in the shadow of racial and colonial histories, to places they probably didn't choose—and in which they are now, anyway, stuck.

Fan is one of these obscurely emplaced immigrants. When she first says "where you are," she has been standing silently in shared grief with the dead boy's brother. Then this happens:

> At some point Fan left the boy's side and came down toward the buffet line. Most everyone noticed this and seemed to pause in what they were doing. And in a voice that surprised for its clarity and reach, she said quite oddly:
> Where you are.
> By now everybody had turned to her. Her hands were curled into loose fists and she said the words again, this time softer, as though she were speaking to herself rather than addressing any crowd. Again no one said a word. She then left via the back gate of the yard with those who had finished eating, leaving us to wonder what she was talking about. (30)

What Fan means by "where you are" quickly becomes the subject of debate. Some of her neighbors attribute to it wholly private meanings, unknown to the community at large; others dismiss it as "gibberish" or as "the beginning of a thought that Fan couldn't quite finish" (31). Most agree that it's the gnomic conclusion to some kind of sententia: "'Everything you desire can be found . . . ,'" or, "'Look not elsewhere but simply . . .'" (31; ellipses in original). Although none of these meanings stick, the narrator still identifies her utterance as the "point that the first signs of collective interest in Fan appeared" (31). Over the course of *On Such a Full Sea*, Fan will be transformed into an object of folk legend: a communally dreamed symbol for emergent feelings of social discontent and desire. It's typical of *On Such a Full Sea*'s narrative voice—typical, that is, of the way it speaks in an idiom at once diffuse and certain—that while no one ever decides what Fan means by "where you are," everyone attributes to it meanings consistent with "a feeling that she was, in fact, looking after us, perhaps even advising us about something crucial" (31).

"Where you are" is an unassimilated verbal artifact from a moment in which Fan has just begun her journey into legend. But while the phrase itself soon fades from the novel, reemerging only in the final pages, the language of location emphatically does not.[32] Already one of the B-Mors has suggested that "where you are" should be prefaced by, "'One's destiny lies not in the past nor the future but . . .'" (31). And, while the collective narrator quickly dismisses this strong association between geography and destiny, *On Such a Full Sea* remains sodden with deterministic spatial idioms and metaphors. For instance, in describing the futile ambitions of Harvey, a B-Mor resident who is struggling to pay for his wife's medical treatments, the narrator concludes: "There is no leaping of worlds in this world. Except for the rare case, the distance is too great" (51). Here, the rhetoric of distance provides a reliable metaphor for what might not be thought or attempted. Later still, Fan's exceptional qualities are again evoked through insistently spatial figures of grounding and freedom, limitation and extension:

> It's not that we're too fearful or comfortable, too cautious or reluctant, but that, as we have never experienced life *outside these bounds* . . . the *reach* of our thoughts has a *near ceiling*. Imagination might not be *limitless*. It's still *tethered to the universe of what we know*, and as wild as our dreams might be, we can't help but read them with the same *grounded* circumspection that *guided* our forebears when they *mapped out our walls*. Fan, though, made a *leap*, which was a startling thing in itself. (109; emphases added)

That "leap" is Fan's decision to leave B-Mor, stepping past the security gates and into the lawless ungoverned counties that lie between the city and the Charter villages. Fan's heroism lies in the way she is, by comparison with her neighbors and those she meets on her travels, neither "grounded" nor "bounded." Her mind is not restricted by the provincialism that defines the walled city of B-Mor, the insecure armed compounds she visits in the ungoverned counties, or the luxury gated communities of the Charters. Fan's vision is broader. Her actions exceed what the narrator celebrates as "the form of our excellent *contiguity*, a *rigorous closeness* that only rarely *oversteps* its bounds" (88; emphases added). At the beginning of the novel, the narrator describes Fan's peculiar skill as a diver in the tanks in which the B-Mor residents raise fish for export. She has the habit of staying underwater for ages, holding her breath for amazing lengths of time as if she were able to "transform not her but the composition of the realm, make it so the water could not harm her" (6). This skill is not the result of some superpower or evolutionary shift; it's just one more sign of what the narrator, in yet another spatial figure, calls Fan's "special conviction of the imagination," which allows her to "see how the world can sometimes split open, in just the way we hope" (6). Fan's visionary power lies in her ability to imagine her fractured and constrained world as "in fact, unbounded. Free" (6). She is this novel's heroine not because she transforms life in B-Mor or rescues her kidnapped lover or exposes the directorate's cruelties. (By the end of the novel she has accomplished none of these things.) Fan's heroism lies in her ability to see beyond her world's primary geographic division and act in accordance with that vision. She alone is able to see her world as one without losing her bearings or giving up her freedom.

THE WEIGHT OF REALITY

The systematic division of Fan's world into abandoned open counties, productive agroindustrial cities, and service-oriented Charter villages is established by page 2 of *On Such a Full Sea*. Yet, as with the facts behind the New Chinese migration, Lee's narrator doesn't tell us much about what caused the breakup of the erstwhile United States. We know that a private federated company established B-Mor, and not "the revolving cast of governmental bodies" that tried and failed to manage the country's collapse (19). We can also deduce that B-Mor isn't unique: other "abandoned cities" were settled around the same time by Chinese migrants, with one of them even identified as "D-Troy, the big midwestern facility" (42). The reader can also work out, if only by negative inference, that the archipelagic system in which B-Mor and D-Troy float as two large islands is not peculiarly American. That's why, at a point when Fan's central plotline is fairly well established, we learn that a group of B-Mors once traveled on their "once in a lifetime global" to Amsterdam, with the implication that it's one of the only cities in the world still "open to any who wish to visit" (98). The combination of parochial enclosures within ungoverned territories appears to be general across Lee's narrative geography. *On Such a Full Sea*'s spatial division of labor shapes a secondary world in which two sorts of enclave float in extraterritorial space.

Reviewing *On Such a Full Sea* in the British press, the great SF and fantasy author Ursula K. Le Guin complained about the sketchiness and inconsistency of that secondary world. Le Guin contrasts Lee's novel with works of "social science fiction" that strive hard, however allegorical their intentions and effects, to carry the "weight of reality."[33] And she is particularly annoyed by the way *On Such a Full Sea* depicts a world that is at once spatially broken and economically networked:

> A good many things in the novel were inexplicable to me, such as . . . how raw materials are produced and how, without trains or good highways, they manage to have coffee, petrol, electronic devices, food in plastic pouches, neoprene suits, plastic throwaway dishes and implements— unsustainably hi-tech luxuries that we in 2014 enjoy thanks to our immense global network of industrial production. In a broken, sporadic civilisation, where does all this stuff come from?[34]

Le Guin isn't the first critic to suggest that Lee's commitment to generic conventions is a bit half-hearted.[35] To the question "where does all this stuff come from?" let me therefore reply by quoting, from an early bit of exposition, a few of the narrator's words about how "truckers and Charters move about exclusively on . . . secured, fenced tollways that few counties drivers can afford, and are often banned from anyhow" (*OFS* 35).[36] One might still wonder how people manufacture or pay for packaged food, neoprene suits, and such like, but Lee has definitely thought about how those commodities might be delivered.

But, in the end, Le Guin's objection is, I think, misplaced. It's easy to imagine a version of *On Such a Full Sea* that spends more time worrying about, say, the infrastructure behind the aviation system Lee calls "globals." Lee's light hand with expository detail no doubt explains why some reviewers disagreed about fundamental aspects of his novel, such as whether it depicts the Chinese colonization of the United States or, rather, the American privatization of the American state.[37] And yet the expository sketchiness of *On Such a Full Sea* is not, in the end, a symptom of Lee's dallying in generic traditions he neither respects nor understands; it's an artful quality of his novel's collective narrative voice, the character of which is defined by where it cannot go, and what it must therefore imagine.[38] As that voice struggles to exceed its own parochial perspective, restricted in space and with limited knowledge of its past, it betrays how the story of Fan's journey outside B-Mor's walls is constructed out of gossip, guesswork, and the creative torque of oral tale telling. "We reshape the story even when we believe we are simply repeating it," the narrators opine in one of several meditations on how Fan becomes an object of myth for those left behind: "Our telling becomes an irrepressible vine whose hold becomes stronger than the originating stock and sometimes even topples it, replacing it altogether" (186). Because Fan never goes home and never finds Reg, her story is an odyssey without *nostos* and a quest without end.[39] In describing *On Such a Full Sea*'s expository gaps in this way, I'm not arbitrarily renaming a bug as a feature; this isn't a matter of perspective—or, at least, if it *is* a matter of perspective, it's only in the sense that the narrator's "irrepressible," but unresolvable, voice is the only perspective we get.

Le Guin is thus only narrowly correct to assert that *On Such a Full Sea* fails the test of social science fiction. It fails that test if we agree with her that a novel's capacity to "serve as warning or satire" depends on the systematic organization of its secondary world.[40] But, really, *On Such a Full Sea* is not an exercise in systematic world building. Yes, Lee's novel depicts a radically simplified political geography, but within that geography, feelings of certainty and ignorance, clarity and opacity, combine as an effect of point of view. Not systematic but partial knowledge rules the day: a view of, and from, distinct parts of an unseen whole, with those brief pools of experience and conjecture barely connected by a skein of gossip and projection. In *On Such a Full Sea*, there are only three types of space: City, County, and Charter. But the last two kinds of space are literally beyond the ken of the people that describe them to us—the Counties and the Charters lie on the other side of uncrossed borders that mark divisions in experience as well as mere spatial fact. For the narrator, there is B-Mor (known, grounded, consanguine) and then there is everywhere else. Lee's setting thereby structures and thematizes the dilemma faced by his collective narrator, as well as by the speculative novelist in general: How can we spin a tale that weaves together regions of likeness and unlikeness, knowing and unknowing, everyday experience and impossible incident? The novel's setting is not the sign of its failure to be a social allegory of the kind preferred by Le Guin. *On Such a Full Sea* is a social allegory shaped differently, structured by the mobile boundary between the speculative and the known, the open and the grounded, the wilderness and the city. Its social critique is directed less at the material conditions that broke and polluted Fan's world, than on the way the destiny that is geography produces, at the level of the narrator's collective consciousness, not certainty about one's place in the world but wistful anomie.

Because of the B-Mors' seclusion in their gated city, the story of Fan's odyssey without *nostos* represents a kind of speculative gamble on behalf of the narrator and their tribe—a shared imaginative wager that they, too, might escape the destiny that is geography. The sketchiness of *On Such a Full Sea*'s processes of secondary world-creation can't be considered apart from its narrators' attempts to escape what Le Guin calls the "weight of reality," thereby repeating—in the imagination, if not in actual fact—Fan's leap beyond the city's walls. In this novel, there is no contradiction between the narrative work of speculation and the possibility of geographic determination. Lee's narrators *must* speculate and mythologize, guess and aver, precisely because they are constrained by their "rigorous closeness" within the walls of B-Mor. We know a little about where Fan has come from. We are told one story about where she is. We can even make guesses as to where she goes at the novel's end. But, despite the simplified and determinative nature of Lee's extraterritorial world, we can only speculate as to the ultimate meanings of "where you are."

SIX CHARACTERISTICS OF WHERE WE ARE

I have described *On Such a Full Sea*'s archipelagic narrative geography in detail because, while its formal implications are unusual, its general spatial morphology is not. Consider, in this light, English author Sarah Hall's feminist novel *The Carhullan Army* (2007), published in the United States as *The Daughters of the North* and winner of the 2007 John Llewellyn Rhys Prize for fiction in the United Kingdom.

Hall's narrator-protagonist is known only as Sister, and, like Fan, her story begins when she escapes from the fenced-in "official zones" (here governed by a despotic "English Authority") and lights out for open lands.[41] Her goal in crossing the empty and untilled countryside is to reach another sort of enclosed settlement: not comfortable Charter villages but Carhullan, an isolated mountain farmhouse that is home to an Amazonian-style community of armed female revolutionaries. Because the Carhullan women live outside of the approved "designated sectors," they are judged to be "Unofficial" and "autonomous" (*DN* 15). They're not free citizens, however, but outlaws or *inimica*: exiled beyond the pale and protection of the law, they are not considered part of the commonwealth and can therefore be killed with impunity.[42] In Sister's near-future England, anthropogenic climate change has caused agricultural failure, epidemic disease, and global resource wars. To control the population and conserve resources, the English Authority has depopulated the countryside and confined its citizenry to fenced-in industrial zones within large ungoverned areas (7). "For years I had not been out of Rith," Sister muses on her way out her hometown: "The zones did not allow for transference" (9). The country governed by the English Authority has been reduced to what Carhullan's charismatic leader, Jackie, calls "a country of local regimes" (104). Small details differ, but this is the same basic political geography that we encountered in *On Such a Full Sea*: walled settlements surrounded by extraterritorial space.

Consider, in addition to Rith and Carhullan, the gated self-sufficient luxury towers and drought-stricken refugee camps that dot the desert landscapes of Paolo Bacigalupi's *The Water Knife* (2015), set in the US Southwest after the abolition of the right to interstate travel.[43] Or the "Alternative Zones" of Tech City/Wreck City in Jeanette Winterson's *The Stone Gods* (2007); the aforementioned camps and gated communities of Butler's *Parable* series; the internally segregated buried silos in Hugh Howey's *Wool* (2012), each utterly separated from the next, such that the inhabitants of every silo believe that they are the only survivors left on a scorched and uninhabited Earth. Then add to these settings the progressively shrinking geographic scale of each part of David Mitchell's *Cloud Atlas* (2004), which begins with an intercontinental maritime romance and ends with a postapocalyptic yarn set on Hawai'i, in an age in which only a dying elite have the technology to travel long distances.[44] The past two decades have witnessed a marked proliferation of such novels, in which systemic planetary events produce fractured and archipelagic novelistic maps, and in which characters' movements through narrative space are gradually reduced to the arduous transit between scattered redoubts.

By reading such novels together, six spatial characteristics emerge that collectively outline the extraterritorial narrative poetics explored in the rest of this chapter:

1. Recognizable territorial states are fractured and rendered noncontiguous.
2. Such fracturing is caused by large scale, always extranational and usually planetary, events or combinations of event—for example, global environmental catastrophe, pandemic disease, world war (often nuclear), systemic economic collapse. These events are usually human-caused, though occasionally they result from astronomical events such as asteroid strikes.
3. In this fracturing, human political space, rather than opening up, distills down to insular settlements: smaller than a country but bigger than a household, and not generally organized along kinship lines.

4. These insular settlements are situated within anarchic or lawless open spaces that are extraterritorial in the same way as the oceans: not beyond political power but subject to no single authority.

5. There is always more than one kind of insular settlement. The world is a political pluriverse, not a universe.

6. Insular settlements themselves turn out to be internally subdivided: punctured by rival sovereignty claims or crisscrossed by forms of life or authority that are not rooted in power over land. Even internally, the pluriverse rules.

Presented abstractly like this, you might think these criteria describe a noisy and crowded kind of narrative space. Yet they actually outline a creative logic through which novelistic setting becomes simpler and more clearly formalized, with relatively few sorts of location, sparse and clear relations among them, and plenty of open areas in which, most of the time, not much happens. Such geographical simplification is, of course, intrinsic to the novel, in which choosing and delineating a setting always involves distilling and selecting between a limited range of geographical possibilities. ("Really, universally," wrote Henry James, "relations stop nowhere, and the exquisite problem of the artist is eternally but to draw, by a geometry of his own, the circle within which they shall happily appear to do so.")[45] By drawing lines in space, limiting some movements and enabling others, writers are better able to elaborate relations between characters and plotlines, producing clear opportunities for symbolization and thematization: an eligible bachelor comes to town; Grandma moves in; a young woman strikes out upon her own. In the contemporary postapocalyptic novel, such spatial simplification also serves a larger purpose of allegorization, with the reduction of narrative space to isolated settlements enabling geography to stand out as the social abstraction of a general ill—neither symptom nor cause, exclusively, but a kind of materialized idea. The critic, meanwhile, benefits from the way that simplified and formally abstract narrative spaces enable comparison across and within generic groupings. And so, to return to this chapter's epigraph and title phrase, it's now time to test these six propositions by traveling along a string of settlements in open space, spread out like beads upon a fragile cord that threatens to break and scatter.

AN ARCHIPELAGO OF SMALL TOWNS

That epigraph about a string of settlements comes from Emily St. John Mandel's *Station Eleven*, a debut postapocalyptic novel by an author already acclaimed for work in other genres: "The world was a string of settlements now and the settlements were all that mattered, the land itself no longer had a name."[46] The cause of such destruction is the Georgia Flu, a deadly viral pandemic that, spreading along international air corridors, quickly kills billions and brings about what the surviving characters repeatedly call the total global "collapse" of civilization.[47] Such a collapse means living without a lot of things: "No more cities. . . . No more flights. . . . No more countries, all borders unmanned. . . . No more Internet" (31–32). The Georgia Flu doesn't quite bring the world to an end, but it kills off a hyperconnected and peripatetic way of twenty-first-century living.

Beyond mass death, the primary symptom of civilizational collapse in *Station Eleven* is the radical disaggregation of social and political space. In this novel's postapocalyptic world, the territorial state is done for, as are most of the means humans have developed for overcoming geographic distance: reliable roads, mechanized travel, the postal service, telecommunications. "Civilization in Year Twenty," the narrator explains, "was an archipelago of small towns," bound together by mutual sacrifice and hostility to outsiders (48). In this world, there are the barely populated settlements, the weed-choked and bandit-filled roads that hardly connect them, and the open space of the "interior" (56). Human life has reverted to some kind of primordial form: a fellowship, a fire, a fence, and *out there*.

Such an arrangement of narrative space is, again, not unprecedented. Still, *Station Eleven* is unusually serious about the way it characterizes the precollapse world through tropes of international flight and global telecommunication. Airplanes may connect the Georgia Flu's disease vectors, but that just clinches their fundamental importance to St. John Mandel's view of the precollapse present, which is positively defined by the global exchange of people, things, and signs. Among the novel's central characters are two Hollywood actors, famous throughout the world; a much-traveled English management consultant, educated in Canada and now resident in the United States; and an executive in the global shipping and logistics industry who "travels almost constantly between a dozen countries" (107). If anything, St. John Mandel pursues this theme almost too deliberately. Thus, the very first chapter set in the fallen world begins, "Twenty years after the end of air travel" (35). Later, an elderly survivor of the collapse silently remembers life two decades ago: "Incredible in retrospect, all of it, but especially the parts having to do with travel and communication. . . . These taken-for-granted miracles that had persisted all around them" (232–33).

If the world before the Flu is defined by the miracle of human communication, the world afterward is shaped by how hard it now is to traverse even short distances. *Station Eleven* features two main postapocalyptic plot-lines, both of them set in the upper Midwest of the former United States. The first centers on the Traveling Symphony, an itinerant band of actors and musicians who spend most of the novel picking their way across the dangerous area between two settlements, one hostile and the other unfamiliar. The second plotline narrates the founding and growth of a new community at Severn City Airport—the same settlement toward which the Symphony ends up traveling as it searches for two missing members. Once defined by transience and devoted to flight, the airport has now become a graveyard for grounded planes and a permanent home to several hundred people. One of the planes is even a kind of winged mausoleum, full of the bodies of flu victims who were quarantined onboard. So, while the airport city represents stalled mobility, the Symphony is a slowly trundling metaphor for the residual possibility of communication across space and time. The Symphony obviously evokes the minstrels and traveling shows of an earlier era, its performances demonstrating the players' commitment to the idea that "survival is insufficient" by performing the plays of Shakespeare and works from the European classical repertoire (58). In this way, the Symphony embodies more than the simple fact of communication across space:

it carries us across the absolute geographical space of the area in and around its own "territory" (36), and it transports us back in time and space to a moment when people were able to believe that culture represented more than the obvious flipside to barbarism. Through both movements, one spatial, the other temporal, it translates the aesthetic language and values of a world that's gone—traveling shows, European high culture, repertory companies—into the rag-tag practices of a new human era.

With few exceptions, the chronologically later parts of *Station Eleven*'s episodic narrative are characterized by the same simplified, fractured, and deterministic spatial imaginary that we saw in *On Such a Full Sea*.[48] Thus, in the fifteenth year after the collapse, a Frenchman long stranded in Western Michigan says to a Symphony member: "If you were to talk about the other towns you've passed through, that would count as news to us. The world's become so local, hasn't it?" (*SE* 108). (The Frenchman runs a circulating library and is trying to start a newspaper.) In Year Twenty, the children born after the Flu are shown "maps and globes, the lines of borders that the Internet had transcended" (262). They can understand "dots on maps—*here*—but even the teenagers were confused by the lines" (262; emphasis in original). Neither the virtual transcendence of space nor the neat arrangement of political geography into territorial blocs makes any sense to children born without the internet, nation-states, or international relations. In *Station Eleven*, a planet-wide epidemic event has erased geopolitical distinctions, and the result isn't free movement but its opposite: the production of a few fixed points strung out in space, the obstacles between them harsher and more numerous than ever.

Station Eleven hardly neglects other parts of the postapocalyptic taken-for-granted: the deaths that a few pills would prevent, the revival of handicrafts and hand-to-hand combat, the bad teeth, the endless venison for dinner. Still, no other civilizational change resonates as much in *Station Eleven* as the fall from global movement into local insularity. St. John Mandel even takes special care to include the classic postapocalyptic trope, repeated at least five times in case we miss it, of a multilane highway clogged with abandoned cars.[49]

Perhaps most interestingly, St. John Mandel carefully maps her novel's spatial division between globe and archipelago onto the equally fundamental temporal breach between pre- and postapocalyptic times. *Station Eleven* begins on Day Zero, a winter evening on some unspecified date in the present. That date, on which the pandemic flu goes global, becomes the temporal hinge point between our world and what comes after. It even marks the start of a new calendar: "Day One, Day Two, Day Forty-eight, Day Ninety, any expectation of a return to normalcy long gone by now, then Year One, Year Two, Year Three. Time had been reset by catastrophe" (231). The trope of time reset by catastrophe is common to postapocalyptic fiction. Neal Stephenson's *Seveneves* (2015), for instance, creates an entirely new dating system out of its inaugural, world-destroying event, while Jeff Long's technobiblical plague thriller *Year Zero* (2003) draws both its title and its fervid millennial sensibility from that same calendrical conceit. And why not? If French revolutionaries and Italian fascists can enshrine a new era, why not the survivors of civilizational collapse?

Ubiquitous feature or not, *Station Eleven* has a remarkably developed manner of temporal marking and sorting. The characters themselves understand things in terms of narrative beginnings and endings: "Jeevan was crushed by a sudden certainty that this was it, that this illness . . . was going to be the divide between a *before* and *after*, a line drawn through his life" (20; italics in original). And not only characters use the language of "Day One" and "Year Two." The third-person narrator possesses that idiomatic tic long before it becomes a general habit of characters' speech. "This is well before the Georgia Flu," the narrator explains as she describes a meeting between two lovers. "Civilization won't collapse for another fourteen years" (71). The opening of chapter 16 states that its events took place "twenty six years after" the events of the previous chapter, "and fifteen years after the Georgia Flu" (108). "A year before the Georgia Flu," we read in the first sentence of chapter 17, "Arthur and Clark met for dinner in London" (110).

A closer look at the distribution of temporal language in *Station Eleven* suggests how obsessed it is with marking time. All told, thirty-one of *Station Eleven*'s fifty-five short chapters (56.4 percent) begin with a strong temporal referent—by which I mean that, in each case, one of the chapter's first three sentences establishes how much time has passed, or is yet to come, between the events being narrated and an incident we've either read about or have been told to expect.[50] Some of these temporalizing phrases do perfectly ordinary narrative business, as with the opening of chapter 48: "Three days after Kirsten and August had become separated from the Symphony . . . Kirsten woke up abruptly with tears in her eyes" (283). But that's only sometimes true. Of the thirty-one chapter openings that establish this kind of temporal relation, fully twenty-one of them (67.7 percent of the subset, or 38.2 percent of all chapter openings in the novel) refer to the collapse, either by invoking the new calendar directly or by similarly explicit means: "'Read me something,' Jeevan said, on the fifty-eighth day" (186).

The temporalizing quality of the narrator's diction is heightened by the way such phrases cluster in the opening sentences of chapters. Looked at quickly, *Station Eleven* resembles the kind of contemporary narrative that fashions a "global" whole out of the networked interlacing of otherwise disjunct characters, settings, and plots.[51] Alexander Beecroft explains how, in multiplot movies like Alejandro González Iñárritu's *Babel* (2006), as well as in novels like *Cloud Atlas*, lines of coincidence and association—created by the transfer of objects, by physical proximity or similarity, or by other relationships that extend across time and space—connect the novel's discrete plotlines and protagonists. These coincidences and connections amount, Beecroft says, to globalizing strategies of "narrative entrelacement."[52] Such entrelacement exists in *Station Eleven*, too—most especially in the hand-drawn comic book that passes from character to character, linking strangers together across the proliferating boundaries that exist between eras and settlements. More often than not, though, *Station Eleven*'s lines of connection are interrupted by the narrator's repeated lexical reassertion of the temporal breach between before and after, such that the work of globalizing entrelacement is abruptly broken by the way the worldwide pandemic produces extraterritorial space. The historically earlier chapters of *Station Eleven* describe a recognizable society, at once systemically "global" and socially provincial—which is to say, white, middle-class, Anglophone, and North American. But then, interrupting this uneven social whole, there is the "changed world" (37), the "altered world" (57). The post-collapse chapters of *Station Eleven* take place in an "orangeless world" of small towns in what used to be Michigan: isolate communities that lack the means to ship tropical fruit from what once was Florida (243). *Station Eleven*'s split temporal axis is given meaning and substance by its geographical elaboration. Before, the possibility of the globe; after, the difficult journey home. Before, mobility; after, string and locality.

DYSTOPIAN FICTION AND TOTAL SPACE

On Such a Full Sea and *Station Eleven* epitomize the archipelagic narrative space-time that I'm concerned with in this chapter. Still, these narrative features would tell us nothing if they were simply a general feature of speculative fiction. But a brief consideration of other kinds of literary geography shows that's not the case

In George Orwell's *Nineteen Eighty-Four* (1949), to take a very famous example, the allegorical simplification of political space tends toward totalization, not fragmentation. In Orwell's dystopia, the armored jigsaw of the Westphalian interstate system has morphed into the three massive territorial blocs of Oceania, Eurasia, and Eastasia. According to the forbidden tract that Winston Smith reads at one point in the novel, only the "disputed areas" at the poles and equator are left open: imperial free-fire zones for waging permanent limited war, they are the ungoverned exception to the Earth's division into massive territorial blocs.[53] The central zones of Oceania and the other superstates are, by comparison with the disputed areas, practically "inviolate" from enemy threats because, as machines for the production and consumption of goods, they are all so big as to be effectively "self-contained."[54] Such territorial massification is the geopolitical counterpart to Orwell's bleak vision of systematized totalitarian power. In *Nineteen Eighty-Four*, the (vertical) concentration of power within the institutions of the party-state takes (horizontal) expression in the form of the Earth's division into self-sufficient territorial blocs. The geopolitical space of *Nineteen Eighty-Four* is just as simplified as that of *On Such a Full Sea*, but it takes a different shape and obeys a different scalar logic.

Some narratives offer yet more radical versions of total space. Consider J. G. Ballard's "The Concentration City" (1957). In this paranoiac short story, densely populated urban structures cover the entirety of a planet, which is now wholly wrapped around in the ribboned gray honeycomb of human construction: "Noon talk on Millionth Street," read the opening lines: "Sorry, these are the West Millions. You want West 9775335th Street East."[55] In Concentration City, the idea of "free space" is "a contradiction in terms," while the notion that humans might fly free through the air in machines is taken as evidence of psychosis (*CSB* 25). The City's authorities assume that their municipality is isomorphic with space and time itself; there is no space that is not City territory and no time when the City wasn't everything that is the case. As the City expands its terrain through history and geography, human memory and reason contract in turn.

Of course, no system is perfect and even dystopian narratives marked by the trope of territorial massification leave room for envelopes of human movement—moments of freedom without which, after all, the business of plot development would become quite hard. In *Nineteen Eighty-Four*, Winston's apartment contains a sliver of space outside the range of the telescreen's watching eye. The protagonist of Concentration City can't convince anyone to believe they'll ever see "free space," but his therapist does eventually admit that it's a theoretical possibility. However, these exceptions only further confirm the rule: in these speculative fictions, setting tends toward the construction of new geopolitical totalities, not dispersed insularities. If the contemporary postapocalyptic novel takes extraterritorial form, that either has something to do with that specialized genre itself, or with the world that we live in at present. While my six spatial principles show up in many examples of postapocalyptic fiction, they aren't innate to speculative fiction.

THE EXTRATERRITORIAL BY
JOHN MORRESSY

And so, to fully account for those six principles, we must combine generic analysis with historical reasoning. A first step in that process is to acknowledge that archipelagic settings show up in other speculative genres. The perfect example here is John Morressy's *The Extraterritorial* (1977), a popular SF novel written as part of the *Laser Books* series, a short-lived subscription initiative of the romance publisher Harlequin. No surprise given its title, *The Extraterritorial* evokes many of the spatial and political phenomena so far analyzed in this book. The title refers to the protagonist, Martin Selkirk, a soldier who fights the United States' dirty wars overseas. It therefore evokes both the idea of a place beyond US territory and those forms of legal personality discussed in the introduction—for instance, in the Military Extraterritorial Jurisdiction Act (2000), which puts US service personnel and civilian contractors under US jurisdiction, no matter where in the world they might be.[56] More generally, *The Extraterritorial* is set in the wake of what its prologue dubs "the chaos and fear that marked the closing years of the late twentieth century."[57] In its twenty-first-century world, the United States has been "literally" (which is to say, "politically") torn apart (*E* 7). At the novel's opening, the East Coast is run by a despotic technocratic "Association" that has supplanted State and Federal governments, with "the rest of the country . . . abandoned to the Outlanders who prowled the ravaged midlands" behind a militarized "Barrier" stretching from the Great Lakes to the Gulf of Mexico (7). Travel beyond the Barrier, or overseas, is strictly forbidden, while even the cities of the east are riddled with internal borders and no-go areas: under "Operation Beltline," the Association has divided all urban areas into three sectors comprising elite institutions and personnel, industrial facilities, and non-Association workers and the unemployed (26). In this secondary world, "the very concept of a single, unified nation" has disintegrated (134).

This hardly exhausts the extraterritorial resonances of *The Extraterritorial*. As Morressy's gimcrack plot gathers steam, Selkirk joins a rebel cadre, the Counterforce, that is opposed to Association rule; later, he breaks with the rebels and travels beyond the Barrier in attempt to ally with the Outlanders, who don't so much oppose the Association as, like the Carhullan women, live beyond any jurisdiction whatsoever: "First the Association, then the Counterforce, now the Outies," Selkirk remarks in one of the novel's final lines; "I guess there's always work in this world for an extraterritorial" (190). This last quip doesn't only mean that Selkirk has once again adopted his characteristic position of internal exile and geographical estrangement, like an armed version of one of Nabokov's *hotelmenschen*. Selkirk's personal extraterritoriality is more general, its characteristic quality being his refusal of any and all attempts to consolidate power and personhood in space. He thinks of himself as an extraterritorial because he used to travel abroad in a capsule of portable legal impunity, and he still thinks of himself that way because he now lives in a world in which territorial states have collapsed. But Selkirk is also extraterritorial in a more complete sense. He resists any and all authoritative stabilizations of political power, whether in the personal language of citizenship or the collective idioms of class identity or national belonging. "Suddenly, for just an instance," Selkirk feels as he takes his first steps of rebellion, "he was two men at once, living two simultaneous scenes, each as real as the other" (68). Like all good Cold War heroes, Selkirk is most authentic when he chooses individual self-exile over group belonging.

The novel's settings allegorize this ideological fantasy in unmistakably spatial ways, with every act of rebellion propelling Selkirk into a new alliance in a correspondingly new geography: from the luxurious Association zones into the poor parts of the city, from the urban slums into the depopulated areas and secret facilities in which the Association does its nefarious business, and, finally, out beyond the Barrier. In this sense, *The Extraterritorial* is not so much a dystopian novel in a simple sense as what Margaret Atwood calls "ustopian," a word she coins so as to capture the way that, in her reading and writing experience, "the imagined perfect society and its opposite" inevitably contain "a latent version of the other."[58] This ustopian generic irony takes acute form in Morressy's *The Extraterritorial*, being epitomized in the way Selkirk loathes the Association's divide-and-rule tactics but still repeatedly revolts from any identification of power over people with power over territories. He hates the new world because it's fallen apart at the seams but, like Fan in *On Such a Full Sea*, he can't conceive of a good and free life defined by any ethos of citizenship, consanguinity, or closeness.

THE WATERLESS FLOOD

The Extraterritorial is, thus, rather too perfectly extraterritorial for a forty-year-old novel. And, for that reason, it poses a problem for my argument: extraterritorial geographies may not be intrinsic to speculative genres, but neither are they exclusive to postapocalyptic fiction, or to novels and stories written in the last decade or two. So what marks the difference between *The Extraterritorial* and a contemporary postapocalyptic novel such as *Station Eleven*?

We've already discussed, in the introduction and chapter 1, the long history of extraterritoriality, its inseparability from doctrines and practices of territorial rule, and the way it shifts between being a property of places and of persons. There should be no surprise, then, at Morressy's willingness or ability to play with the history of extraterritorial personhood, or at his sense that extraterritoriality works well as a metaphor for conditions of exile, both geographic and existential. Morressy's book came out only a year after George Steiner's *Extraterritorial: Papers on the Language Revolution* (1976), which, as we have seen, likewise develops the idea of the extraterritorial person, able to endure a "civilization of semi-barbarism" by remaining "eccentric" and "aloof."[59]

In a similar vein, Atwood contends that there's a long connection between ustopian fictions and divided and isolate spaces: "Like Plato's seminal Atlantis and the Avalon of Arthurian romances," she argues, such novelistic regions are "typically located on islands to be found just out of reach of the real maps, like the utopia in the book of that name by Thomas More."[60] For Atwood, speculative fiction responds to the historical development of secular rationality, which undermined faith in religious alternative geographies (the *Paradiso* and *Inferno*, Eden and Abbadon) and underwrote the scientific mapping of the New World and the oceanic vastness. Hounded by reason, ustopia migrated in space and time: "First it went underground, to the traditional location of under-the-hill fairylands."[61] Next, "once the Earth's structure had been more fully described by geologists," it shifted to the kinds of peripheral space epitomized by the racially exoticized African settings of H. Rider Haggard's bestselling imperial romances.[62] But once even those irrational extraterritories had become "too thoroughly mapped," the space of ustopia had to shift again: to "an outer space far beyond our system, or to a parallel universe, or to a past so long ago that all traces of it have been obliterated; or to the future, also an unknown."[63] At each moment in Atwood's historical story, ustopian fictions migrate to the edges of known history and space, into zones rife with arbitrary boundaries and islands of difference, in which speculative narratives fill in the gaps between what could and what might be said.

It's important not to apply Atwood's developmental chronology too literally. (What price, for instance, Wells's *The Island of Dr. Moreau* [1896], which combines the two sorts of narrative space Atwood associates with Thomas More and Rider Haggard? Or the same author's *The Time Machine* [1895], in which the traveler's leap into the future is followed soon after by his descent into the Morlocks' troglodytic realm?) And yet, for all that it might simplify the literary-historical intertwining of genres, topoi, and tropes, Atwood's ustopian proposition remains useful. Her proposition that "dire cartographies" are common to speculative fictions allows us to venture, once again, this chapter's central hypothesis: that contemporary writers, rather than inventing the postapocalyptic novel's archipelagic dynamics, have intensified and formalized a tendency toward spatial thematization and disaggregation common to the genre but not definitive of it.[64]

The most important "contemporary" feature of novels like *Station Eleven* lies in the way they emphasize the global production of archipelagic insularity. The fact that people live in petty towns like Severn City Airport is hardly unprecedented; neither is the fact that areas between domestic or urban centers tend to be lightly regulated areas of narrative possibility. (The plots of *Oedipus Rex* and *Don Quixote* both depend, for all their differences, on this basic opposition between home and away.) The peculiar thing about *Station Eleven* is the self-conscious manner in which it *does* tend to insist upon the unparalleled nature of the events it narrates. One popular way of accomplishing this topical effect is to make the apocalypse the result of anthropogenic climate change—as with "cli-fi" or "climate fiction" stories such as Bacigalupi's *The Water Knife*. Another approach, epitomized by *Station Eleven*, is to emphasize how natural disasters are facilitated and exacerbated by signature aspects of twenty-first-century political economy— and not just air travel but by population mobility, increased cross-border trade, urbanization, the spread of information technologies, climate change, deforestation, and water shortages.[65] Above all, novels such as *Station Eleven* combine the topos of anthropogenic catastrophe with the kinds of space-time compression ("the annihilation of space through time") that David Harvey considers characteristic of globalization in its neoliberal phase.[66] In this global chronotope, events in one part of narrative space don't just reverberate throughout the planetary network but take effect *everywhere* and *all at once*. The thing that occurs in an instant is the end of everywhere and all that we know.

In *Station Eleven* the Georgia Flu moves quickly, but only as fast as its human hosts can get on planes and fly. Not so the pandemic event in Atwood's *MaddAddam* trilogy, in which a plague deliberately unleashed by a human scientist called Crake breaks out across every major population center at once, spread through the medium of a globally marketed luxury consumer object: a sex pill called BlyssPluss that is the purported commercial spin-off of scientific investigations into extending human life. Combining temporal instantaneity with geographic simultaneity, *MaddAddam*'s "waterless flood" is a nihilist parody of globalist "just-in-time" manufacturing and commodity-delivery systems, as well as a nightmare version of an ecologist's vision of planetary connectedness.[67] In the waterless flood, a scientific attempt to escape time through human immortality leads to something close to the extinction of time itself. Time doesn't come close to dying because humans are made extinct—after all, someone has to survive to tell the tale, or have the tale told about them. But humanity is, through the planetary reach of the waterless flood, finally subjected, for the first time since Noah, to the judgment of a singular event. Here is death everywhere, for everyone, all at once—one world, united by disaster. Again, there are natural, as well as narratological limits to such instantaneity: just as some characters have to subsist, even a fast-acting disease needs time to incubate and spread. But the core temporal effect of the BlyssPluss plague lies in the way Atwood combines elements of plot, setting, and secondary-world creation so as to radically shorten the spatiotemporal distance between epidemiological cause and apocalyptic effect.[68] And she does this, in *Oryx and Crake*, by rooting the erstwhile natural event of pandemic disease in plausible aspects of contemporary political economy: a massively consolidated pharmaceutical industry, insufficiently regulated by national or transnational agencies, with operations all over the world; a sales and marketing sector capable of launching and promoting new products in every country on the same day; and a global logistics industry capable of delivering commodities at sufficient distance and scale to realize the marketers' dreams.

The geographic imaginary of the *MaddAddam* trilogy has every one of our six formal and narrative characteristics. Atwood's secondary world is, as Le Guin notes in her review of its second part, *The Year of the Flood* (2009), strangely unmarked in time and place: "The setting may be the upper Midwest of the US or Canada, but there is no geography, no history."[69] But in other ways the trilogy's general setting is well developed. Atwood's characters don't go to Starbucks, for example, but they don't frequent independent coffeehouses or some improbably anonymous chain, either. Instead, Atwood invents her own alternate brand reality, the Happicuppa franchise, complete with its own corporate lexicon and place in the novel's rich history of corporate malfeasance. This isn't the only example of Atwood's worldmaking labor. NooSkins, HelthWyzer, the Watson-Crick Institute, Secret Burgers, Slink, Rarity, Tails, Martha Graham Academy, ChickieNobs, EXTINCTATHON, RejoovenEsense, AnooYoo, Painball, the CorpsSeCorps: the *MaddAddam* trilogy is so rich in neologistic proper nouns that it reads, at times, like a narrative machine for the production of cutely named corporations, commodities, and communities. In this way, the trilogy's background lack of geopolitical reference combines with tremendous specificity and ingenuity at the level of its imagined social and economic world. While *On Such a Full Sea* remains enigmatic, poised halfway between simplification and fabulation, the *MaddAddam* books provide a richly detailed novelistic geography—just one in which branding identities matter more than geopolitical relations. Le Guin puts her finger on this difference when she attributes *The Year of the Flood*'s disinterest in certain kinds of detail to the fact that, in that novel, "no national governments appear to be functioning. . . . The Corporations, and particularly their security arm CorpSeCorps, are in total control."[70] The disappearance of the national state, which in Atwood's trilogy has become fully absorbed within a variant of neoliberal technocapitalism, takes away the novelist's need to embed her setting in any kind of recognizable Westphalian political space.

In the *MaddAddam* trilogy, political geography has been privatized along with the police but, consistent with her arguments about the spatial implications of ustopian fictions, territorial division and subdivision remain central to life under the waves of the waterless flood. In a paratextual preface to the trilogy's last volume, *MaddAddam* (2013), Atwood reintroduces us to Jimmy, protagonist of *Oryx and Crake*, and a major secondary character in the other two books: "In his pre-plague life, Snowman was Jimmy. His world was divided into the Compounds—fortified Corporations containing the technocrat elite that controlled society through their collective security arm, the CorpSeCorps—and the pleeblands outside Compound walls, where the rest of society lived, shopped, and scammed, in their slums, their suburbs, and their malls" (*MA* xiii–xiv). Atwood consistently links her vision of privatized insularity to the deep narrative roots of the romance. A long time before he became Snowman, living up a tree in a depopulated Earth, Jimmy listened to his father compare life in their walled compound to "days of knights and dragons . . . castles, with high walls and drawbridges and slots on the ramparts" (*OC* 28). And by the end of *Oryx and Crake*, Jimmy has indeed become a star player in a bloody kind of romantic melodrama, trying and failing to reset the apocalypse from within the castle keep of

Crake's laboratory compound. In any case, Atwood is happy to let us know that she knows that her near-future setting evokes ancient, even mythic, forms of parcelized sovereign space. And, of course, she also shows us the other side of her enclosed slums and high-tech bubbles: the "no-man's-lands" that lie between Compounds and "pleeblands," as well as the interstitial areas that proliferate between the Compounds' onionskin layers of security. In *The Year of the Flood* we even learn that the wall that once separated the United States from Mexico has now moved north, so as to shut out the new internal refugees—in an unfunny joke, they are called the "Tex Mex"— who are fleeing north from drought and desertification. A vast expanse of erstwhile sovereign territory is stranded outside the parts of Atwood's urban archipelago of Compounds and pleeblands, in a massively expanded border area that is at once American territory and not.

Further details would be superfluous. Like *Station Eleven*, the *MaddAddam* trilogy is shaped—plot and character, as much as theme—by the back and forth between insular settlement and lawless open territory. But, unlike in *Station Eleven*, Atwood's trilogy doesn't tell a story about the supersession of global space by insular settlements, with the two sorts of geography following in sequence: first open, then closed. In the *MaddAddam* books, the temporal and geographic antitheses that structure *Station Eleven* overlap and interpenetrate. The waterless flood's destruction of territorial statehood was already implicit within the privatized and parcelized political geography that exists from the start of the trilogy, before the plague hits and even before the series' narrative action begins. Likewise, after the death of billions, the insular spatial dynamic of Compounds and pleeblands continues in new ways. Although the death of billions of humans erases prior legal distinctions between public and private space, as well as between one nation-state and another, Atwood's characters still cluster together, mark their turf, and learn that good fences make good neighbors. Toby and Ren, the central characters in *The Year of the Flood*, survive the plague because when the virus hits they're isolated in enclosed and privately secured buildings. And when, later in the novel, they join a group of human survivors, those people have already fenced off a piece of land for farming, which they

then spend much time and effort defending against incursions by geneti-
cally modified feral hogs. It's a point reinforced by fact that this land used
to be part of a public park, and therefore one of the few parts of the trilogy's preapocalyptic landscape still held in common. On the other side of
the flood, land remains alienable, subject to territorial enclosure and claim.

International relations also survive the plague—or, rather, a territorial-
ized form of interspecies relations takes their place. In *MaddAddam*, the
new human tribe who have enclosed that patch of parkland agree to an
informal treaty with those gene-modified hogs, who turn out to be formi-
dably intelligent. Having arranged a fragile détente, the novel's human
and animal characters then cooperate in order to track down and kill their
common enemy: a pair of murderous human ex-convicts, who have slaughtered hogs for food and taken one of the surviving humans hostage. This
newfound human/hog alliance is cemented, moreover, by the diplomatic
agency of a new species called "Crakers"—blue humanoid beings whom
Crake bioengineered in his laboratory compound and who alone can communicate with both people and hogs. And even though the Crakers live a
pacific communal existence in something approaching a state of nature,
they also participate in the novel's overall geographic-political regime by
marking their territory with urine.

As a result of their alliance, the humans stop hunting the hogs and
the hogs stop raiding the humans' garden. Faced with a shared external
threat, two social groups form an alliance that has the effect not just of
safeguarding one little garden, or one group of hogs, but of legitimating
territorial claims in general. Of course, it's not like nothing changes the
other side of the waterless flood; the usual survivalist strictures apply.
But, in the end, there's no parallel in the *MaddAddam* trilogy for *Station
Eleven*'s programmatic opposition between preapocalyptic movement and
postapocalyptic insularity, or for *On Such a Full Sea*'s strange narrative
geography, at once simplified and defined by the places its narrator can't
go. Whatever world comes after Atwood's end of the world, it remains
familiar in many respects. Before, a privatized realm of parcelized sovereignty in which internally divided walled settlements are separated by

no-man's-lands; after, fewer people, new creatures, and a privatized realm of parcelized sovereignty in which internally divided walled settlements are separated by no-man's-lands.

In this way, Atwood's trilogy offers an original solution to a basic tension within the end-of-the-world story. Stories about the apocalypse are concerned, at some basic level, with the possibility of transforming human existence, but they must also be able to explain why so much that is familiar about our world survives its dissolution. Why, when Atwood remakes the world after the death of most of humanity, does she not overwrite the social or biological impulse to mark and fight over territory? A different novelist might appeal to some basic animal nature, such that the persistence of territorial space either side of the waterless flood reminds us that we are, after all, nesting creatures. Or she might compose a political allegory about humanity's original crime against the commons. The ghosts of these plotlines survive in the *MaddAddam* trilogy, and it's true that all the sentient beings that survive the end of the world aspire to more communal, and less ecologically destructive, ways of living. Nevertheless, Atwood's main answer to this generic and geographical theodicy is to negate it, showing that the world's political geography either side of the waterless flood simply remains much as it was.[71] Once again, the capacity of extraterritorial narrative setting to contain and structure contrary elements—territorial zones and open space; a global event that produces islands adrift—also mediates the relationship between the old and the new, familiar and unfamiliar, where we are and where we might go.

It's in the nature of extraterritorial cartographies to be double-sided, at once familiar and unfamiliar, open and closed, simultaneously terrible and full of awesome possibility. In *On Such a Full Sea*, Fan's heroism lies in her ability to imagine a fractured world as whole, even as her "leap" beyond geography leaves the folk who tell and retell her story grasping for a certainty they can never attain. In *Station Eleven*, the apocalypse is, more than anything, a problem of and in communication across space—a thematization of narrative geography that shows up in a profound temporal opposition, infecting even the most ordinary sort of diegetic business, between the world either side of the "collapse." And, by the end of the *MaddAddam* trilogy, the abstracted and insular geography of twenty-first-century geopolitics has not disappeared but has distilled into its basic parts: one human tribe behind a fence, a new species pissing onto the earth. In all the books central to this chapter, geography may not be destiny, but it's trending extraterritorial.

4

A BORDER THAT IS NOT A BORDER

I n what country is *Wolf Hall* set?

In England, obviously. A hugely popular prize-winning novel about the "rise and rise" of Henry VIII's courtier Thomas Cromwell, Hilary Mantel's *Wolf Hall* (2009) takes place mostly in London and thereabouts: Westminster, Hampton Court, Whitehall—the kinds of places where royal marriages and religious reformations get made and unmade.[1]

But, seen another way, from the standpoint of its central historical crux, *Wolf Hall*'s location is harder to pin down. In this chapter, I engage Franco Moretti's geographical hypothesis about historical novels: that they tend to cluster *"away from the center"* and *"in the proximity of borders."*[2] In so doing, Moretti claims, the historical novel represents the disorderly spatial and temporal character of eighteenth- and early nineteenth-century states, which are not singular sorts of polity at all. By staging tales of treachery and adventure close to various internal and external borders, classic historical novels reveal the real developmental and territorial heterogeneity of the newly dominant nation-states of Europe. Thus, to cite the most classic example, the story of the Jacobite rising of 1745, as depicted in Walter Scott's *Waverley; or, 'Tis Sixty Years Since* (1814), doesn't just dramatize the disunited political character of Great Britain; it depicts the Scottish Highlands as a developmentally distinct historical zone, where antemodern (and antimodern) traditions and loyalties prevail.

The key quality of the classic historical novel, however, is that it depicts such social and political unevenness only then to abolish it at the levels of plot, character, and rhetoric.[3] It's in this way, by dramatizing the gradual overcoming of territorial and developmental borders, that the classic historical novel emerges as something like the symbolic narrative form of the national state.

But *Wolf Hall* does not unify the space-time of the English nation. It requires that we ask instead whether words such as "England" signify as territorial terms at all. To say that Mantel's novel mostly takes place in England is, thus, both perfectly true and a way of begging the question. In *Wolf Hall*, England is represented as the kind of space we saw in Mark Wallinger's *Threshold to the Kingdom* and in China Miéville's *The City & the City*: one in which international borders, far from existing at the edges of the country, have become distributed throughout public and private space. *Wolf Hall* is, formally and thematically, deeply interested in the history of English state formation. What's more, it's a novel in which the assertion of English political autonomy is predicated upon the country's openness to the European continent. It is, in this sense, a perfect consolatory fantasy for the age of Brexit, in which there exists no contradiction between European cosmopolitanism and English independence.

The first half of this chapter considers the political geography of the twenty-first-century historical novel via Mantel's *Wolf Hall*. The second half focuses on Amitav Ghosh's *Ibis* trilogy (2008–15), and especially that trilogy's middle part, *River of Smoke* (2011). Where *Wolf Hall* is deceptively insular, the *Ibis* novels, which are set in and around the first Anglo-Chinese Opium War of 1839–42, are programmatically transnational, featuring a multiethnic cast of characters who move between the Atlantic Ocean, Indian Ocean, and South China Sea, collecting languages, lovers, and cuisines as they sojourn and sail. The *Ibis* trilogy has been described by academic critics, inter alia, as an example of "world-forming literature"; as typical of the kind of multiplot narrative form through which the "plot of globalization" unspools; and even as that oxymoronic thing, "American World Literature."[4]

But the *Ibis* trilogy is not naïvely devoted to transnational connection. Ghosh draws directly on Victorian sources that depict the Opium War as a struggle between two politico-geographic ideal types: a Chinese Empire that assumes a kind of universal sovereignty, and an international state system made up of formally equal territorial blocs but within which Great Britain is hegemonic. And while Ghosh surely does not subscribe to any clean dichotomy between territorial sovereignty and extraterritorial empire, the *Ibis* trilogy certainly ends with the defeat of the Chinese—and so with the forced entrance of the Qing empire to an international state system based upon the presumption of formal equality between territorially limited states. By the end of *Flood of Fire* (2015), China is emphatically one state among many.

Still, the *Ibis* trilogy is much more and less than a story about the eclipse of one kind of imperialism by another. By the end of its almost 1,700 pages, the reader is left in no doubt that the formal equality offered to China by Britain masks a future of real inequality, with the defeated Qing empire now subject to exploitation by Western states and the smugglers and traders who attend them. In this vein, *River of Smoke*, in particular, poses itself against both sorts of empire, Asian and European, the one predicated on shaky notions of universal sovereignty and the other on a rigged competition for hegemony within an interstate system. Against those differently undesirable kinds of empire, *River of Smoke* affirms an extraterritorial exception: the foreign mercantile enclave at Canton that goes by the name "Fanqui-town," where people come together from all over the world to do cultural, economic, social, and sexual business. Among Fanqui-town's famous thirteen factories—warehouses and office spaces that, before the 1840s, were the only places in China that white foreigners could officially do business— Ghosh imagines a version of globality that can reconcile the reality of vernacular difference with the colonial subject's struggle for political freedom and equality.

Here we have two historical novels, then, in which the history of state formation and international relations is rewritten—and rewritten such that extraterritoriality functions not as the exception to the Westphalian norm than as a rule of political life in general. György Lukács famously argues that historical novels escape being mere romantic entertainments by bringing

"the past to life as the prehistory of the present."[5] These contemporary historical novels are just as attracted to border zones as were their Victorian
predecessors, but their works' salient formal and topical quality lies in the
way those borders are no longer found, as Moretti had it, *"away from the
center,"* but have become general throughout the territory. Mantel and
Ghosh keep faith with Lukács's claim that the literary depiction of the historical past depends on "a felt relationship to the present."[6] They do so,
though, not by reconciling bourgeois notions of progress with the reality
of a history forged in crisis (Lukács's thesis), or by traveling to frontier settings that affirm the integrity of the national home (Moretti's conjecture).
Wolf Hall and *River of Smoke* instead form part of the loose literary-historical
category that Caren Irr calls the "contemporary geopolitical novel"—a
diverse group of fictions in which "twenty-first-century authors have
returned to received genres and begun to overhaul them."[7] In so doing, Irr
argues, those authors "have paid special attention to those elements of the
political novel that were grounded in the increasingly dated ideal of the territorially defined sovereign nation."[8] The contemporaneousness of *Wolf
Hall* and *River of Smoke* is still immanent within what Moretti would call
their common "genre space." But that space has become an involute zone
in which distinctions between inside and outside, native and foreigner,
ancient and modern, are at once mobile and determinate, and in which, as
we previously saw with Chang-rae Lee's *On Such a Full Sea*, personal qualities of character, voice, and diction become inextricable from those of collective political space. Where are *Wolf Hall* and *River of Smoke* set? In the
world—which is to say, in a somewhere that is a somewhere because it faces
two directions.

WHAT ENGLAND IS

Wolf Hall mostly takes place between 1529 and 1535. During its first sections, Cromwell is a lawyer in service to Cardinal Thomas Wolsey, lord
chancellor of England and papal legate—the most powerful minister and

cleric in the land. Wolsey's great cause is to secure a papal annulment of Henry VIII's marriage to Katherine of Aragon, so that the king may marry Anne Boleyn. Wolsey fails, is humiliated and banished from court, and dies in ignominy. Cromwell, amazingly, not only survives his master's fall but goes on to accomplish what the cardinal could not. With Wolsey gone, he becomes the king's man. Proving himself as adept at court intrigue as he is at framing a law or raising a loan, he prospers mightily. By the end of *Wolf Hall*, Cromwell has ensured Anne's coronation as queen, secured the king's supremacy over the church, and, as a result, kick-started the legislative and economic engine of England's magisterial reformation. Not coincidentally, the novel ends with Cromwell's morally ambivalent but politically definitive victory over Sir Thomas More, who martyrs himself rather than swear an oath to Henry's supremacy.

This all sounds like high drama—and it is. Still, it is impossible to read *Wolf Hall* and not sense England's occult insularity in the early sixteenth century: a small country, full of ghosts, traumatized by decades of civil war, its statesmen forever playing off the powerful French against the even more powerful Holy Roman Emperor. When Cromwell's first master dies in disgrace, the narrator asks, "What was England before Wolsey? A little offshore island, poor and cold" (*WH* 260).[9] A few years later, when Cromwell is established at court, the narrator describes his importance to English government: "The courtiers see that he can shape events, mold them. He can contain the fears of other men, and give them a sense of solidity in a quaking world: this people, this dynasty, this miserable rainy island at the edge of the world" (522). The passage is written in the remarkable close third-person perspective that Mantel adopts throughout *Wolf Hall*, such that Cromwell is never more than a narrative object but never only that. The second sentence's progression—from Cromwell's pronominal person, outward to the "fears of other men," out again to the English people, the Anglo-Welsh Tudor dynasty, and, finally, the whole island of Britain—embodies the expansive scalar drama that epitomizes *Wolf Hall* in general. Cromwell, it turns out, is the ideal container within which personhood and stateness can interpenetrate and so become meaningful to one another. To return to the terms laid out in this book's introduction, a novel that seems, at first, to be about territorial sovereignty turns out to be about extraterritoriality of person.

Let's first explore why *Wolf Hall* initially seems to be about territorial sovereignty. For Cromwell, Henry's marriage crisis is an opportunity to make England into more than "a little offshore island" while preventing its absorption into some larger empire, whether secular or spiritual. Just a few pages before those lines describing the island at the edge of the world, Cromwell opines to Archbishop Thomas Cranmer that, rather than obeying the pope, the English people will "find it more natural to obey an English king, who will exercise his powers under Parliament and under God" (516–17). And, just a few paragraphs before that, in a passage of reported speech, Cromwell has been trying vainly to persuade More to recognize "the king's natural jurisdiction over the church" (515). The question of royal sovereignty lies at the heart of *Wolf Hall's* dynastic drama. While, for More, temporal rulers ought to tremble in the sight of Rome's universal jurisdiction over spiritual matters, for Cromwell, Henry's desire to marry Anne must be seized upon so as to install him as "sole and supreme head of [his] kingdom" (277).

While the question of royal supremacy is symbolically resolved by More's execution, it is initially introduced via the legal question of praemunire. The problem of praemunire was first codified during the reign of Richard II and concerns whether a kingdom can tolerate multiple sovereignty claims and, thus, whether there's a contradiction in English law between papal claims to universal spiritual jurisdiction and the monarch's claim to supremacy.[10] In the first third of *Wolf Hall*, this question applies most directly to the king's case against Cardinal Wolsey, whose dual allegiances to England and Rome embody the tension between territorial (English, temporal) and extraterritorial (Roman, spiritual) jurisdictions.[11] When Wolsey falls from grace, he is indicted under the statutes of praemunire for "asserting a foreign jurisdiction in the king's realm" and thereby assuming a position as *"alter rex"* (*WH* 153). (About this charge, the narrator notes wryly: "He is, he has always been, more imperious than the king. For that, if it is a crime, he is guilty" [153].) Still, even before writs are moved against Wolsey, we have already heard him described as "the man who ruled England" (50) and as having assumed the idiom of authority that ought to be peculiar to the king: "He used to say, 'The king will do such-and-such.' Then he began to say, 'We will do such-and-such.' Now he says, 'This is what I will do'" (28). Even when he is exiled into the north, the cardinal is accused of administering "a country within the country" (195). In the figure of Wolsey—butcher's son and aspirant pope, faithful servant and *alter rex*—we find embodied the period's constitutive tensions between distinct but overlapping power centers and sovereignty regimes. And in the legal question of praemunire we see one obvious way in which England in the 1520s was crisscrossed by different juridical zones: one territorial, its edges conterminous with the coastline and Scottish border, and the other extraterritorial, applying wherever the church asserts its rights and immunities.

One way of describing *Wolf Hall*, then, is as a lightly skeptical episode from English Whig history, in which a proto-Westphalian form of sovereignty emerges from the providential accidents of Henry's marriage bed. But, in fact, *Wolf Hall*'s historical argument is more complete than that. Mantel dedicates her novel to the historian Mary Robertson, until recently the curator of medieval and British historical manuscripts at the Huntington Library, where Mantel's own papers are collected. Robertson's doctoral thesis in history describes Cromwell's "Ministerial Household" as "an institution informally bridging the gap between a medieval civil service based ultimately on the king's own household and a modern bureaucratic civil service centered on the departments of state."[12] Robertson's scholarship is, moreover, avowedly influenced by G. R. Elton's political history, and especially by his book *The Tudor Revolution in Government* (1953), which she lauds as "magisterial" in the way it argues that there occurred a profound transformation in the nature of the state during Henry's reign.[13] "The plain fact," Elton thunders in the first pages of that book, "is that Henry VII ascended the throne of a medievally governed kingdom, while [Queen] Elizabeth [I] handed to her successor a country administered on modern lines."[14] And so he continues:

In the course of this transformation there was created a revised machinery of government whose principle was bureaucratic organization in the place of the personal control of the king, and national management rather than management of the king's estate. The reformed state was based on the rejection of the medieval conception of the kingdom as the king's estate, his private concern, properly administered by his private organization; it conceived its task to be national, its support and scope to be nation-wide, and its administrative needs, therefore, divorced from the king's household.[15]

Or, as Elton put it in *England Under the Tudors* (1955), "the essential ingredient of the Tudor revolution was the concept of national sovereignty."[16] For Elton, as for the historian dedicatee of *Wolf Hall*, the story of Cromwell's career is a story about the transformation of England into a unitary "Empire" defined in and through its autonomy from "the authority of any foreign potentates."[17]

Elton's revolutionary thesis is now more than sixty years old and has come in for sustained criticism.[18] Many subsequent historians see greater continuity between late medieval and Tudor government than does Elton, as well as less continuity between the dynastic state in which Cromwell worked and the fiscal-military states of the seventeenth and eighteenth centuries.[19] But, for our purposes, as readers intent on understanding *Wolf Hall* rather than political historians interested in the Tudor state, there are three elements worth noting in the arguments ventured by Elton and Robertson: first, they do see Henry VIII's reign as a period of real transformation in the English state, marked by a new conception of sovereign nationhood; second, they date the key moment of bureaucratic revolution to the period in which *Wolf Hall* is set; and, third, they argue that Cromwell's centrality to that process, as both an individual and as the head of a new sort of "ministerial household," has been neglected or caricatured.

Whether they're true or not, these conjectures shape *Wolf Hall*'s engagement with Tudor history. Mantel's Cromwell is not just set on resisting Rome for doctrinal reasons, or as a way of simply satisfying his king's sexual and dynastic desires—though neither of these are trivial concerns. When, in the spring of 1532, the Reformation Parliament begins to enact anticlerical legislation, a passage of exposition about Cromwell's plans to "[break] the resistance of the bishops" is prefaced by a paragraph ventriloquizing the deeper ambitions of our protagonist, about it being "time to say what England is, her scope and boundaries . . . her capacity for self-rule . . . what a king is, and what trust and guardianship he owes his people" (*WH* 338–39). This emphasis on righteous government as national government continues when, once again debating the differences between clerics and commoners, Cromwell insists to his rival Stephen Gardiner that, if he were to "look at any part of this kingdom," he would "find dereliction, destitution. There are men and women on the roads. . . . Believe me, Gardiner," Cromwell concludes in unusually passionate tones, "England can be otherwise" (539). The oaths that Cromwell designed to accompany the 1534 Act of Supremacy are presented as more than a "test of loyalty" to Henry; they are described as a means of joining together "the men of every burgh and village, and all women of any consequence" (574). The novel's diction, as it moves toward its end, becomes increasingly national and spatial, its figures reaching out to include "the people on the Scottish borders and the Welsh marches, the men of Cornwall as well as the men of Sussex and Kent" (574). Finally, in *Wolf Hall*'s very last scene, this process of territorial consolidation is thematized explicitly, at the level of governmental power-knowledge. As Cromwell plans the king's summer progress for 1535, he meditates on the need for "better maps" that will let him know "where the bridges are," "the distance between them," and "how far you are from the sea" (648–49). The magisterial religious reformation here becomes inseparable from the political project of making the nation, whether we conceive it as an object of popular identification, a commonwealth of subjects, or a knowable administrative entity.

And how is this new national state to be built? At Cromwell's hand. Robertson's influence on Mantel shows when we read in *Wolf Hall* that the gentry now send their sons to Cromwell in order "to learn statecraft" (*WH* 534). Likewise, our hero strives to transform his king from a "lord of generalities" to a ruler willing to "labour over detail," absorbing the information now streaming to him from new and reformed courts and councils: "All the families in England and what they have . . . down to the last watercourse and copse" (610). Those bureaucratic instruments themselves are now capable of "smooth and civil handover," their activities able to "roll on, whoever the personnel" (482). Moretti argues that one way the historical novel helps construct the imagined community of the nation is by symbolically resolving the social and developmental differences marked out by internal borders. In *Wolf Hall*, those borders begin to be managed out of existence by Cromwell's depersonalizing administrative genius. If this is the case, then there's no doubting where *Wolf Hall* is set: in an England that's becoming ever more itself.

SUCH A PERSON

But *Wolf Hall* would be boring if there were no limits to Cromwell's genius: no shades of light and dark to his character, no contradictions in his world. And my opening question about setting would also be *unusually* and not (as I hope) *usefully* dumb.

Whatever her historical commitments, Mantel understands that the administrative changes of the 1530s left untouched many aspects of late medieval government. This reality is best embodied in *Wolf Hall* by the glowering presence at court of Thomas Howard, Duke of Norfolk: a feudal prince in his own country, politically powerful, his speech lousy with Catholic oaths and his body rattling with holy relics.[20] More than that, power in *Wolf Hall* is, no matter what Elton says about its growing abstraction from the king's "personal control," still deeply bound up with Henry's individual charisma and authority. Whatever his accomplishments, Cromwell must continually trim his policy to predict the interests of the king.[21] And much of Henry's power remains rooted in his claim of right by way of heredity and (his father's) conquest, rather than through power invested in institutions such as Parliament or as an expression of popular will. As a result, *Wolf Hall* is full of worries about the king's two bodies, both of them—the corporeal and the political.[22] The novel's court intrigues are saturated with anxiety about Henry's reproductive capacity; with his own worries about getting old, injured, and fat; with the courtiers' clamoring to be physically close to the king's bulk, bedchamber, and chamber pot; and with their terror at the idea that he will expire while hunting or jousting: "'Suppose he dies?' Norfolk demands. . . . Then what?" (255). Above all, the king's person looms in our consciousness by dint of Cromwell's fearful knowledge that, as a lowborn man with no natural support among the aristocracy, his position will always be dicey. "What you are," Henry says to Cromwell on promoting him, "I make you. I alone" (360). And what the king's bodies make, they will inevitably mar. Such will be the story of *The Mirror and the Light*, the long-delayed final book in the trilogy, in which Cromwell falls from grace almost as quickly as he rose.

In fact, *Wolf Hall* is lousy with the language of personhood—so lousy, in fact, that the word "person" comes to rival "England" as its defining lexical totem. The Duke of Norfolk, who knows something about personal power, first introduces the language of personhood to the novel. Expecting deference from Cromwell but meeting only polite self-composure, he "bursts out, 'Damn it all, Cromwell, why are you such a . . . *person?*'" (163; ellipsis and emphasis in original). Later in the same chapter, when Cromwell presumes to correct one of Norfolk's commands, the Duke erupts: "You . . . person . . . you nobody from Hell, you whore-spawn, you cluster of evil, you lawyer" (187). It's a nicely weighted epithet, "person." It allows Norfolk to acknowledge Cromwell's unusual charisma and presence ("Thomas," says the king to his councilor, "it is like hugging a sea wall. What are you made of?" [513]). At the same time, "person" lets the noble Norfolk put a commoner in his place.

But although Norfolk introduces this lexical note, he doesn't control it. The epithet "person" expands and, in expanding, comes to affirm Cromwell's unflappable flexibility. As we should expect, Cromwell is the first to get in on the personhood act. When Bishop Gardiner spitefully asks what title he goes by, he replies "placidly": "A person. . . . The Duke of Norfolk says I'm a person" (232). Next, the narrator joins in, notarizing Cromwell's alliance with Cranmer in the sentence, "They embrace cautiously: Cambridge scholar, person from Putney" (241). Cranmer himself later complements Cromwell as "a person of great force of will" (278). Best of all, there's Cromwell's own meditation on personhood: "There are some people in this world," he thinks, "who like everything squared up and precise, and there are those who will allow some drift at the margins. He is both these kinds of person" (228). It's fitting that this thought occurs to Cromwell during a visit to Thomas More's house—fitting because, for Mantel, the sainted More is doomed by his terrifying certainty, while the equally ruthless Cromwell is redeemed by his ability, to borrow a phrase from Ali Smith, to "be both."[23]

As well as being produced by the novel's diction, Cromwell's labile personhood is also a function of *Wolf Hall*'s narrative voice. The narrator's close third-person perspective is, in itself, hardly unusual. Less common is Mantel's persistent use of the present tense, which performs the trick of making well-known historical events seem still in development, generating narrative tension where it might otherwise easily dissipate. (This is a perennial problem in historical novels about well-known events.) More unusually still, the narrator reinforces Cromwell's intense but flexible personhood by doubling and tripling down on the repetitive use of the pronominal "he." This is a lexical feature that's hard to demonstrate without reading the whole novel out loud—or, even better, without comparing *Wolf Hall* to the rest of Mantel's oeuvre.

But we can try. On one page of the long fourth chapter, the reader encounters three paragraphs describing Cromwell at work: "He sits at his desk, piled high with drawings," begins the first; "He opens a letter," begins the second; "He reads," begins the third (133). While we might feel that this narrator is unusually focused on everyday deskwork, the threefold pronominal pattern doesn't seem, by itself, unusual. The kicker is that, within these three short paragraphs, "he" is used to refer to Cromwell an additional twelve times. "He" always comes at the start of a sentence and is always followed by an action verb. There's a lot of "he" and "he" does a lot of stuff. Proper nouns are sometimes employed, but only to name other people or places: Cromwell's own name is never used. In all, Mantel's reiterative pronominal style produces a sense of omnipresent omnicompetence. After all that "he," Cromwell comes to seem less like any man, or everyman, and more like the only man we need.

Wolf Hall therefore contains two, apparently contrary, kinds of politico-geographic logic. The first, manifest at the level of its largely insular and metropolitan setting and reinforced by its implicit historical argument, is impersonal, predicated on the abstraction and extension of political authority across national space; the second, which inheres most fully in *Wolf Hall*'s diction and narrative voice, is individuated and individuating. The first works away at the kinds of internal border epitomized by the problem of praemunire; the second mitigates the novel's impression that political power will be invested in and across land, rather than in and over people. Territorial sovereignty, meet extraterritorial personhood.

But, of course, these logics are not really contrary, any more than modern conceptions of individual rights are antithetical to forms of territorial jurisdiction. In fact, the spatial and the personal come together in a passage I have already quoted: the narrator's assertion that Cromwell "can contain the fears of other men, and give them a sense of solidity in a quaking world: this people, this dynasty, this miserable rainy island at the edge of the world" (522). In this sentence, Cromwell's singular personal qualities allow people to feel rooted and, by feeling rooted, to locate themselves within a series of progressively expanding frames that end in geographic expressions: island, edge, world. The individuating power of extraterritorial personhood is, in *Wolf Hall*, the means through which territorial nationhood is symbolically produced.

FRANCE IS WHERE THEY HAVE WARS

Hilary Mantel's Thomas Cromwell traverses the edge of the world as a teenager, when he quits England for Europe after receiving such a beating from his father that he fears one or other of them will soon end up dead.[24] That passage in Cromwell's life is crucial to explaining how he becomes the kind of person he is—and, what's more, how the person he is formally unifies *Wolf Hall*'s different logics of power.

Cromwell departs England for France, "where they have wars," and eventually signs up as a mercenary soldier in Louis XII's army (13). This adventure ends in 1503 at the Battle of Garigliano, just north of Naples, when the French are soundly defeated by the Spanish. From there, he sojourns in Italy, eventually entering into service with the Florentine banking family of Francesco Frescobaldi, where he climbs from the kitchens to the countinghouse and beyond. At some point, he's engaged in English embassies to the Vatican, as well as in the Eastern Mediterranean trade. He spends time in Antwerp, earning a place in the networks of commercial and cultural exchange centered in that port city. Though much of Cromwell's life in Europe remains obscure, we know that he comes back to England, sometime in the 1510s, with knowledge of banking, trade, law, and Lutheranism. And we know that, added to his native English, the Welsh he's conned from his brother-in-law, and a youthful facility in Putney boatman's argot, he's now learned French, Italian, Latin, Spanish, and Flemish, and that he can "insult people in Castilian" (22) and add "Venetian endearments" to a letter "in the local dialect" (270). Newly repatriated, he finds he's "prone to start a sentence in one language and finish it in another" (41).

Cromwell the English state-maker is, also, Cromwell the multilingual agent of international finance, trade, and empire. He arranges loans on "the international market" and his judgment is trusted "here, in Calais, and in Antwerp" (90–91). Unlike the Earl of Northumberland, whom he outfoxes in a memorable scene, Cromwell knows that the world is no longer defined by feudal relations between lord and tenant, but that it is "run from Antwerp, from Florence," and "from Lisbon, where the ships with sails of silk drift west and are burned up in the sun" (378). This Cromwell gets homesick for Italy (109) and, when his fellow Londoners riot against foreigners, remembers that "he himself had not long been home" (174). Thomas More calls him "an Italian through and through"—he means, a Machiavel (567). But while More is wrong about Cromwell's character, as he is about most things in *Wolf Hall*, we know that our hero is not just "Thomas" but also "Tomos," "Tommaso," and "Thomaes" (71). He is a man who, when an Italian friend remarks that the English are odd, replies, "Christ, *aren't they*" (195; italics mine). On the day that his wife, Elizabeth, dies from the plague, Cromwell is away in the city, adding Polish to his gallimaufry of tongues (101).

Cromwell's identification with other peoples and cultures is crucial to Mantel's depiction of him as the omnicompetent shaper of a "remodeled society."[25] "I am always translating," he thinks to himself one day, "if not language to language, then person to person" (421). Thomas More may mistake the way that Cromwell is "Italian," but the reader knows that his nation-building enterprise is not built on doctrines of insular autarky. Thus, while Cromwell helps sever the spiritual links between England and Rome, he deepens the traffic between London and Florence, England and the Low Countries. As I argued in chapter 1, territorial sovereignty depends on relations of interdependence with foreign states; practically and theoretically, it means nothing without a conception of an interstate system, underwritten by legal notions of formal equality epitomized in the contractual exchange of commodities, as much as in emergent international diplomatic norms.

In saying this, I'm reiterating one of this book's central theoretical claims about the interdependence of extraterritorial forms of authority— even those professed with suicidal simplicity by Thomas More—and the notions of territorial sovereignty that emerged, in part, from the magisterial reformation's realignment of spiritual and temporal power. The myth of the Westphalian state has always been just that: a way of obscuring, to the detriment of ordinary people as well as academic accounts of global culture, how state sovereignty helps produce international and transnational relations. But I'm also trying to get at *Wolf Hall*'s formal geographical disposition, in which the unquestionable Englishness of that novel's plot, protagonist, and milieu is enabled by its openness to the world. For proof of that last proposition, let us turn back once last time to setting—to Cromwell's house at Austin Friars, where a motley crew of French servants, Flemish traders, and Italian bankers joins with a retinue of cosmopolitan English men and women to engender the economic and political policies that, in Elton's terms, created a new administration on national lines.

Austin Friars is a former monastic property turned into a city mansion. Economically and symbolically, it is aligned with London's incipiently bourgeois class of bankers, lawyers, and merchants, not with the grand country estates of Norfolk or Northumberland. In her notes to the Royal Shakespeare Company's stage adaptation of *Wolf Hall*, Mantel describes Austin Friars, possibly drawing on Robertson's doctoral thesis, as "a great ministerial household, a power centre, cosmopolitan and full of young men who were there to gain promotion."[26] At one point, midway in the story, Cromwell's chef complains to him: "I have Frenchmen, Germans, I have Florentiners, they all claim to know you and they all want their dinner to their own liking" (446). Earlier, faced with an argument among Austin Friars' women about religious reform, the narrator describes the household as "like the world in little," and then ventriloquizes Cromwell's thoughts about how he must teach his kinfolk and servants "the defensive art of facing both ways" (259). Austin Friars is the spatial embodiment of Cromwell's individual ability to be at once flexible and such a "person." It is the point at which the "he," "he," "he" of *Wolf Hall*'s narrative voice fully transmutes into a quality of setting.

So, where, in the end, is *Wolf Hall* set? In an England that is becoming more than ever itself, but through the actions of a person who is significantly Italian. Where is *Wolf Hall* set? In English courts and castles, and in a city household full of foreign languages and foods. Where is *Wolf Hall* set? Not at the edges of the territory but in a center that is its own kind of edge.

HISTORY IN THE PRESENT

Mantel denies that her goal in writing *Wolf Hall* was to rehabilitate Thomas Cromwell. "I do not run a Priory clinic for the dead," she jokes, alluding to the luxury drying-out clinic famous for rehabilitating the health and reputations of scandal-struck British celebrities.[27] Still, it's clear from her many

public comments about *Wolf Hall* and *Bring Up the Bodies* that she is motivated as much by "powerful curiosity" about Cromwell's life and character—
even from a "relish for his company"—as from the desire to engage twenty-
first-century realities directly, whether by developing an allegorical link
between Henry VIII's break with the Bishop of Rome and the United
Kingdom's recently completed project of withdrawing from the 1957 Treaty
of Rome, or, as I have tried to show here, through the more indirect means
of her novel's extraterritorial formal disposition.

That's not to say, however, that compelling parallels don't exist between
Mantel's sixteenth-century dynastic drama and the political geography of
the present. Perhaps the most important chapter in *Wolf Hall*'s marital plot
takes place in Calais, the "debatable land" that is Henry's only continental
possession and, thus, the last territorial evidence for his claim to be king
of France (402). In Mantel's telling, it is in Calais that Anne Boleyn finally
submits to Henry's caresses, committing him to marriage, bringing to a head
the break between England and Rome, and setting in play the politico-
erotic intrigue that will dominate the second half of *Wolf Hall* and the
entirety of *Bring Up the Bodies*. By setting that narrative breakthrough in
England's French enclave, Mantel once again foregrounds questions of political geography, including the way in which Henry's kingdom cannot be
reduced to a neatly Westphalian state, its jurisdictional borders nicely
aligned with the English mainland.

But setting this crucial chapter in Calais might also evoke, in the mind
of the twenty-first-century reader, a more contemporary space: the network
of refugee camps outside the Calais ports, which were until recently inhabited by migrants and asylees seeking access to Britain. These camps, the
most infamous of which was nicknamed "the Jungle," were on French soil
but, in an echo of the old walled enclave, were also patrolled by British
police officers. After migrants repeatedly managed to smuggle themselves
across to England on trains and boats, the camps were eventually separated
from the large international port complex by fences built by British contractors and paid for with UK government money. Twenty-first-century
Calais is no formal English enclave and after Brexit may well become

completely French from the standpoint of policing and security; for now, though, it's yet another space in which two states have opted to pool and merge powers and responsibilities so as to manage and blockade the human traffic produced by transnational economic and political conflict and insecurity. By comparison with this contemporary reality, the royal drama of *Wolf Hall* is a romantic memory: a turbulent episode in the uneven historical transition from one obsolete form of statehood to another. But *Wolf Hall*'s complex spatial dynamics don't just remind us of the constitutive tension between monarchical and papal authority, nor of extraterritoriality's spatial and personal aspects; it also evokes, however obliquely, our own period's ongoing disaggregation of politico-jurisdictional space—a process that, as we have seen throughout this book, is especially keenly felt in ports and border areas such as Calais, where people and objects pass from one territory to another.

Amitav Ghosh's *Ibis* trilogy is even more fully about ports and borderlands than *Wolf Hall*—and, perhaps as a result, has a more direct relationship to the present. Ghosh is on record about the "many curious parallels between the situation [depicted in the *Ibis* trilogy] and now."[28] These include the way that the United Kingdom, the dominant naval and economic power in the mid-nineteenth century, had a huge balance of payments deficit with the Chinese Empire under the Manchu Qing dynasty; likewise, the United States, today's Western superpower, is similarly in hock to the People's Republic of China.[29] Ghosh sees strong resonances between the hegemonic neoliberal capitalism of the early 2000s and nineteenth-century doctrines of Free Trade, which in the 1830s and 1840s became an ideological bludgeon to open Chinese markets to Western interests.[30] He has remarked that there exist "startlingly similar" qualities between the Opium War of 1839–42 and the Iraq war that begin in 2003,[31] not least because both sets of invaders share a proclivity for "mad evangelical" rhetoric in which promises of liberation mask "the most horrific violence."[32]

Finally, in *The Great Derangement*, Ghosh's nonfiction book about the imaginative challenges posed by anthropogenic climate change, he positions the First Opium War as a key event in Britain's imperialist policy of underdevelopment in India and China.[33] In this way, the *Ibis* novels' imaginative reconstruction of the Opium War's real history continues *The Great Derangement*'s argument that "the poor nations of the world are not poor because they were indolent or unwilling" but because "systems that were set up by brute force to ensure that poor nations remain always at a disadvantage in terms of wealth and power" (*GD* 110). The *Ibis* novels are not unidirectional allegories about the present. They are, however, part of a decolonizing intellectual project that seeks to reshape how nineteenth-century history has ethical and political meaning in the present. In the rest of this chapter, I explain how that work of reshaping is attempted—and how, as with the historical argument of *Wolf Hall*, it depends on the fictional representation of extraterritorial persons and places.

SINOLOGY, SETTING, SCALE

In *The Great Derangement*, Ghosh argues that the catastrophic effects of anthropogenic climate change feel to us like the fantastic acts of vengeful gods, unassimilable to the novel of everyday life. Climate change causes problems for the contemporary novelist, he says, because the modern novel depends on probabilistic rationality. Whereas earlier kinds of narrative fiction, "like those of *The Arabian Nights*, *The Journey to the West*, and *The Decameron*," were ready and willing to leap "blithely from one exceptional event to another," the modern novel, Ghosh says, depends upon "the concealment of those exceptional moments that serve as the motor of narrative" (*GD* 16–17). In making this argument Ghosh also draws on Moretti: not his argument about the political geography of the historical novel but his ideas about novelistic "fillers." These are everyday details, mostly appreciable at the level of description, that help conjure a fictional world but don't, in themselves, contribute towards the plot. In this way, Ghosh says, fillers midwife the novel into being "through the banishing of the improbable and the insertion of the everyday" (17).[34] As a result, the novel is said to resist the inclusion of extraordinary events such as those that presage the advent of the Anthropocene, when human beings attain the heretofore improbable power to effect the development of the Earth at a geological level.

Ghosh's argument about "fillers" and the novel is tendentious: if true, it applies not to the novel per se but to a restricted range of literary realisms such as emerged within the bourgeois literary cultures of nineteenth-century Britain and France.[35] I introduce it, like G. R. Elton's hypotheses about the Tudor state, not in order to endorse it but because, whether or not the novel is inherently probabilistic, Ghosh's venture into literary theory helps us better understand the formal and ideological project within which his own historical fiction takes shape. For the *Ibis* trilogy undoubtedly stretches the boundaries of representation; in *Sea of Poppies*, *River of Smoke*, and *Flood of Fire*, Ghosh attempts to transform the received aesthetic conventions of the historical novel into a vehicle capable of dealing with an expanded range of narrative events.

None of this means that the *Ibis* trilogy includes impossible or wholly unlikely phenomena, or that it's more than implicitly about anthropogenic climate change. While Ghosh has previously composed in speculative genres (see his 1995 SF novel, *The Calcutta Chromosome*), his historical fiction isn't mixed with magical fantasy or futurist yearnings.[36] The Opium War is extraordinary, in Ghosh's sense of that term, because his contention that the modern novel is defined by a bias toward the everyday involves a corollary move, which expands the grounds of his argument from probability to spatiotemporal scale. In short, Ghosh complains that the realist novel banishes the improbable in part because it favors novelistic settings that are generally defined by values of continuity and completeness: "Novels . . . conjure up worlds that become real precisely because of their finitude and distinctiveness. Within the mansion of serious fiction, no one will speak of how the continents were created; nor will they refer to the passage of thousands of years: connections and events on this scale appear not just unlikely but also absurd within the delimited horizon of a novel."[37] In this account, stories that take place on an expanded spatiotemporal scale are considered extraordinary not because they are unlikely or absurd; they just seem so when measured by formal and generic norms that accommodate settings of only a certain size, proportion, and complexity. Just as the realist novel supposedly cannot contemplate the fantastic or inexplicable, so, he says, does it struggle to contain stories told across continents and centuries.

For Ghosh, the novel is a representational technology that finds it difficult to represent phenomena that "mock the discontinuities and boundaries of the nation-state" (*GD* 62). He sees the novel as defined by the "boundedness of 'place,'" and, therefore, as incapable of "creating continuities of experience between Bengal and Louisiana, New York and Mumbai, Tibet and Alaska" (*GD* 62). It's not wholly clear why Ghosh thinks that "the mansion of serious fiction" doesn't include shelves full of novels in which connections are made across vast reaches of space and time.[38] (Nor is it obvious why he associates "place" only with a kind of absolute boundedness, rather than with forms of spatial relation that link one location to another.)[39] Yet, again, my purpose here isn't to quibble with this account of novelistic setting but to point out how the *Ibis* trilogy corresponds to Ghosh's description of what climate change demands of us imaginatively. Though the *Ibis* novels, of course, have their limits, they are not characterized by a primary commitment to spatiotemporal locality or boundedness.[40] Individually, and as a sequence, they create networks of narrative interconnection between continents, ecologies, and peoples. And they do that most clearly by projecting the Indian Ocean, in Isabel Hofmeyer's words, as a region defined by "layered and contradictory forms of sovereignty and belonging" that are "drawn outward by older networks of transnational trade and inward by the demands of the postcolonial nation-state."[41] The *Ibis* novels' historical reach isn't geological in nature, reaching back from the industrial revolution to the carboniferous period, more than three hundred million years ago. But they do depict the 1830s and 1840s as a historical hinge point in relations between the Global South and North: a moment in which the story of modernity, including the stories we have told ourselves about what it means to be modern, changed irrevocably, and that therefore continue to redound into the present. The Anthropocene poses, Ghosh says, a scalar kind of resistance to narration because "its essence consists of phenomenon that were long ago expelled from the territory of the novel—forces of unthinkable magnitude that create unbearably intimate connections over vast gaps in time and space" (*GD* 62). But, while the spatiotemporal scale of the *Ibis* trilogy's novelistic (extra)territory is measured in mere centuries of years and tens of thousands of miles, it is nevertheless constructed out of "intimate connections" forged across distances of time and space that no one person could cross by themselves.

Several critics have already described the *Ibis* trilogy as giving shape to events and experiences dispersed across great distances. In my last chapter, I drew on Alexander Beecroft's account of how techniques of "'multi-strand narration' [can be understood] as a means of representing the intricate and problematic ties that bind us together in the age of globalized capitalism."[42] And Beecroft's main example of globalizing entrelacement in fact comes from Ghosh's historical fiction. With their several plotlines spanning the Americas, Europe, and Asia, Beecroft describes the *Ibis* novels as offering "a networked model of social and economic interaction . . . where the links between former peripheries are as significant, and potentially as disruptive, as more familiar patterns of North-South relations."[43] Similarly, Paul Stasi has described *Sea of Poppies* as depicting "multiple subjective experiences in order to construct the larger truth of a global modernity that is one but uneven."[44] Discussing the same novel, Rudrani Gangopadhyay explains how its concluding maritime scenes, in which characters of different social and ethnonational backgrounds finally come together on the schooner *Ibis*, imagines a new kind of diaspora, "forged by the experience of crossing turbulent seas together."[45] There is no shortage of ways to describe the *Ibis* novels' form in terms of how they create tight intimacies out of vast distances.

The same applies to the trilogy's major characters and plotlines. The *Ibis* novels concern the three-way trade between Bengal, Mauritius, and Canton. Their interconnecting story arcs are shaped by the colonial traffic in people, commodities, and people as commodities—most especially the way that, during the 1830s, the British exchanged opium grown in Indian poppy fields for Chinese silver and tea. The third side of this triangle concerns the destructive effects of opium cash-crop farming on peasant agriculture in Bengal, which pushed peasant farmers off their traditional lands and led many of them to lives of indentured servitude in colonies that, until recently, had long exploited a workforce of African slaves. The various strands of this global economic system are then drawn together by the eponymous ship, *Ibis*, a former "black-birder," or slave-trading schooner, which at the beginning of *Sea of Poppies* is en route from the United States to Calcutta (Kolkata).[46] At the end of that novel, the *Ibis* carries a rebellious crew of prisoners and indentured laborers to Mauritius, where they will be expected to work in French-owned sugar plantations. In *Flood of Fire*, the Atlantic and Indian Ocean worlds of enforced labor are finally connected to the China trade when the *Ibis*, now retrofitted from slaver to cargo ship to opium smuggler, is sailed by Zachary Reid, a descendent of African slaves passing as white, on a mission to exploit the newly reopened opium trade in the Pearl River delta.

Ghosh bases his historical fiction in prodigious research, detailed in extensive bibliographic notes, as well as in the partial reconstruction of "The *Ibis* Chrestomathy," a dictionary of Indian vernacular idioms, Canton pidgin, and Laskari sailors' tongue that was first published as a paratextual supplement to *Sea of Poppies* and later included on the author's personal website.[47] Ghosh's research in primary documents, academic history, and nineteenth-century lexicons doesn't just enable his brand of didactic historical realism; it facilitates metafictional connections between the nineteenth-century setting of his novels and the twenty-first-century moment of their composition and reading. In the concluding paratextual materials to *Sea of Poppies*, the *Chrestomathy* is depicted as the work of the character Neel Rattan Hyder, a disgraced Indian zamindar said to be the great-great grandfather "of the present writer" (*SP* 502). Somewhat anachronistically, however, we see Neel begin work on the *Chrestomathy* not in *Sea of Poppies*—the volume to which that lexicon it is appended—but in the next book in the series, *River of Smoke*, where it is initially conceived as "*The Celestial Chrestomathy, Comprising a Complete Guide to and Glossary of the Language of Commerce in Southern China*" (*RS* 254). Later, however, we are told that Neel subsequently "gave up all hope of publishing his own *Celestial Chrestomathy* and took the work in a different direction"—but this is an event we learn about not in *River of Smoke* proper but in Ghosh's authorial acknowledgements to that book, which direct us towards "certain websites, including www.amitavghosh.com" (*RS* 520). And by the time we get to the final paratextual sections of *Flood of Fire*, Neel's archive of things written and collected has developed from a lexicographic project that initially formed a minor subplot of one novel into the archival basis upon which the trilogy's whole "history of the *Ibis* community" has supposedly been written.[48]

Through the progressive expansion of this metafictional reference work, Ghosh creates a textual and genealogical web that troubles distinctions between character and author, author and narrator, text and paratext, print culture and digital culture. Moreover, Ghosh's fictionalization of his own research labors blurs the line between the kinds of historical knowledge available to his nineteenth-century characters and those accessed by the author himself—a quality best evinced by the way the bibliographic notes to *Flood of Fire* are placed not under the subtitle "Acknowledgments," as in *River of Smoke*, but in an "Epilogue" that moves quickly from a list of historical sources that might have been available to a nineteenth-century researcher such as Neel and a compendium of twentieth- and twenty-first-century titles that Ghosh consulted but that his characters never could. In this way, Ghosh's paratexts do more than confuse the subjects of fiction and the objects of historical knowledge; they connect previously distinct historical periods and points of view, interrupting the temporal distinction between *then* and *now*, as well as the scalar distinction between *far* and *near*. Ghosh's research does more than help him generate characters, settings, and plots; it expands the referential horizon of novels that initially appear to belong securely in a particular period of the past.

But Ghosh's interest in historical knowledge extends beyond such period-busting play with sources and methods. Just as *Wolf Hall* is motivated by an historical conjecture about the long-term significance of Henrician state-making, so is the *Ibis* trilogy invested in the historiographical discourse that Sanjay Krishnan names "global anti-Eurocentrism," which contests the West's traditional sense of its own pre-eminence in narratives about how we became "global."[49] In *The Great Derangement*, Ghosh cites several times the work of Kenneth Pomeranz, one of the historians most associated with the project of critically reevaluating Eurocentric world histories. He places particular emphasis on Pomeranz's argument that the "great divergence" between the economies of Asia and Europe lies in the "purely contingent factor . . . that China's coal reserves, unlike Britain's, were not in easily accessible locations" (GD 96).[50] Against Eurocentric history, Ghosh argues that "modernity was not a 'virus' that spread from the West to the rest of the world. It was rather a 'global and conjunctural phenomenon,' with many iterations arising almost simultaneously in different parts of the world" (95).[51] As Beecroft argues, in being set at "a pivotal era in the history of European intervention in Asia, at the cusp of the Opium Wars and immediately before the Indian Rebellion of 1857, which will of course have the consequence of placing most of India under British rule," the Ibis trilogy "represents something like a narrativized version of [Pomeranz's] revisionist economic history."[52]

But, because the Ibis novels are written and published during a moment of Asian economic and geopolitical revival—the period that Giovanni Arrighi and others have called the first decades of a new "Asian century"—the historical narrative that Ghosh creates in fact has a double temporality. On the one hand, it is a story of historical foreclosure, defined by the failure of the Qing empire to assert its independence against British imperial violence: a story about the moment at which the West diverged from the East, and in which that "great divergence" was misdescribed as the difference between modernity and something ante-, non-, or antimodern. Yet, from the perspective of Pomeranz's global anti-Eurocentrism, the Ibis trilogy is only superficially tragic. It tells a tale of Chinese downfall that, far from being inexorable, is qualified by our knowledge of China's (and India's) twenty-first-century success. Lukács says that, in Scott, "historical necessity is always a resultant, never a presupposition; it is the tragic atmosphere of a period and not the object of the writer's reflections."[53] In the Ibis trilogy, Asian economic success in the present complicates the novel sequence's period specificity and sense of historical necessity.

And yet the Ibis trilogy also refuses historical Pollyannaism. Although Ghosh is deeply engaged with the world-making effects of the Indian

Ocean trade, his stories teach us that even oceanic histories are shaped by local forms of economic expediency and social exigency. The *Ibis* novels thereby imagine a version of a "global" economy that is not predicated on the planetary preponderance of a unilinear system of value. To borrow from Ritu Birla's study of vernacular capitalism in India, the *Ibis* novels "historicize the disembedding of the market from the social geographies of trade and credit, as well as . . . demonstrate the impossibility of such disembedding."[54] Through stories such as that of the rise and fall of the Parsi entrepreneur Seth Bahram Modi—a central figure in *River of Smoke*, who speculates on the opium market just as it is shut down by the Qing empire—the *Ibis* trilogy imagines how colonial law and economic practice give the lie to the supposedly "universal value system" of free trade.[55]

The participation of Indian merchants like Bahram in the imperial economy does not simply knit worlds together, as if the Canton trade erased distinctions of race or rank. In *River of Smoke*, the presence of South Asian merchants in the foreign enclave at Canton at once makes Indian subjects part of the same world as British, American, and Chinese persons *and* makes them newly aware of themselves as a national group: "Had they not left the subcontinent, their paths would not have crossed. . . . here, whether they liked it or not, there was no escaping [their] commonalities" (181). Meanwhile, as they grow in wealth and power, men like Bahram become newly aware of the limitations placed upon them by colonialism: "It is [Bahram's] misfortune," says Neel, "that he comes from a land where it is impossible even for the very best men to be true to themselves" (454). Even Bahram himself, despite being a generally accommodating fellow, argues that Indian merchants "have to move our businesses to places where the laws can't be changed to shut us out"—a proposition that means doing business outside of India, or outside of an India under British rule (423). Far from producing a unidimensional empire of the same, Ghosh's historical fiction positions the past, and the Asian century it prophesies, as one in which the regime of universal value depends on the production of difference in the form of inequality.

THE OPIUM WAR AND FORMAL INEQUALITY

That inequality is not, however, only a function of the structural imbalances that shape social relations *within* the British Empire; the narrative energy behind *River of Smoke* derives also from the conflict between what James Hevia calls "two imperial formations," one British and one Chinese, "each with universalistic pretensions."[56] It is here, notwithstanding the *Ibis* trilogy's more overtly transnational and didactic character, that Ghosh's historical fiction takes on politico-geographic implications similar to Mantel's. In Ghosh's literary reworking of the Opium War, Canton's Fanqui-town emerges as the alternative to two forms of imperial sovereignty, neither of them able to sustain human life in its diversity and fullness, and each violently opposed to the other. A little history should explain what I mean.

In January 1834, the British foreign secretary, Viscount Charles Palmerston, wrote to William, Lord Napier, the first chief superintendent of British trade in China. Napier's new position was necessitated by the 1833 abolition of the East India Company's trade monopoly in China, following which the regulation of British commercial activities in Asia came under direct control of the government in London. Among Napier's instructions was the injunction that, "in addition to the duty of protecting and fostering the trade of His Majesty's subjects with the port of Canton," he determine "whether it may not be practicable to extend that trade to other parts of the Chinese dominions."[57] In order to find this out, Napier was enjoined to establish "direct communications with the Imperial Court at Pekin [*sic*] . . . bearing constantly in mind, however, that particular caution and circumspection will be indispensable on this point, lest you should awaken the fears, or offend the prejudices, of the Chinese Government; and thus put to hazard even the existing opportunities of intercourse, by a precipitate attempt to extend them."[58]

As this last long qualification suggests, Napier's orders were roundly hedged. He was to try to extend the China trade beyond the Pearl River, but not to "leave Canton to visit Pekin, or any other parts of China."[59] He was to establish direct communications with the capital, but also to "abstain from entering into any new relations or negotiations with the Chinese authorities."[60] And so, shortly after arriving at Canton, Napier began to protest that Palmerston's January letter "instructs [him] to do one thing, a very material thing, and then deprives [him] of the means to do it."[61] He advocated instead an aggressive policy in which British naval power be used to "extort a Treaty which shall secure mutual advantage to China and to Europe"[62] by securing "the just rights, and [embracing] the interests, public and private, of all Europeans—not of [the] British alone but of all civilized people coming to trade according to principles of international law."[63] While Palmerston sought to extend the China trade through the gradual extension of communications, Napier wanted a grand diplomatic treaty, based in the reciprocal obligations of international law but accomplished through military force, and he wanted this not just because he believed it would place British trading relations on a surer economic footing but because it would modernize the basic ideological assumptions of Chinese political elites, whom he judged to be degraded and imbecilic, "dreaming themselves to be the only people on the earth, being entirely ignorant of the theory and practice of international law."[64] In short, he wanted to bomb the Chinese Empire into joining a geopolitical system in which political sovereignty is reciprocal and territorially limited.

In arguing thus, Napier drew on a long tradition of political thought about China during the late Qing empire—a discourse in which the struggle between China and its foreign antagonists gets figured as one between a static and traditional model of universal authority and a modern and dynamic interstate system. In this imaginary, the Chinese emperor is thought to conceive of himself as the sole sovereign, sitting at the center of a multinational tributary system and dominating a "China-centered sphere of Chinese cultural influence" in which no other state or civilization can claim parity.[65] As the Chinese historian Mao Haijian explains it, in this "'Heavenly Dynasty' (*tianchao*) conception of foreign relations," the world tended to be divided into three kinds of political geography. These were, first, China itself, or "'Heavenly Dynasty's primary realm' (*tianchao shang-guo*)"; second, the surrounding East Asian vassal states (*fan shu guo*) whose leaders "pledged allegiance to the Qing, sent tribute to the court, and accepted titles in return"; and, third, those "'regimes beyond civilization' (*hua wai ge bang*)," who were only permitted to trade with China through heavily regulated systems like the one at Canton and who, because they were not part of a tributary system defined by the superiority of the Qing emperor, were denied any right to establish "formal official relations."[66]

Napier's argument with the Foreign Office in London was as much shaped by his practical difficulties after arriving in Canton as by any philosophical disagreement about the nature of Qing sovereignty. Still, his early dispatches home demonstrate a political worldview steeped in a rhetoric of antediluvian Chinese otherness. In a letter of 26 July 1834, he writes of his arrival at Macao and subsequent journey upriver to Canton. Upon arriving in Fanqui-town, Napier's first official act was to attempt direct communication with Lu Kun, governor-general of Guangdong and Guanxi, via the delivery of a letter, translated into Chinese, confirming his royal commission from King William IV and announcing his orders to "protect and promote the British trade, which from the boundless extent of his Majesty's dominions, will bear the traffic of the world to the shores of the Emperor of China."[67] Lu Kun, however, refused to receive this letter; indeed, none of his subordinates would so much as touch it. Lu's objections, according to Napier, were threefold. First, the chief superintendent had arrived in Canton without securing prior permission. Before 1833, East India Company supercargoes were required to receive authorization before traveling from Macao to Canton and so, disturbed by the unannounced arrival of a new kind of British official, Lu insisted that he be given time to consult "imperial will" before acceding to any changes in the protocols regarding Sino-British relationships.[68] Second, since Napier's appointment concerned trading relations between China and Britain, Lu insisted that he ought not to address the governor but the Hong merchants, the guild of Chinese businessmen who were the designated channel for international trade and communication: "The great ministers of the Celestial Empire," reads the British translation of an edict sent by Lu to those same Hong merchants, "are not permitted to have intercourse with outside barbarians," especially not those whose business is the "petty affairs of commerce."[69] Finally, in a manner that Napier presumes to find grossly insulting, even the Hong merchants would not accept any communication addressed as a "letter," rather than a "petition."[70] The clear implication is that the formula "petition" properly identifies a communication from an inferior to a superior person, as from an official of Great Britain, a "regime beyond civilization," to a representative of the Chinese "Heavenly Dynasty."[71]

A stalemate ensued. Napier would not give up residence at Canton, which he believed gave him a strategic advantage he would not enjoy at Macao; he would not correspond via the Hong merchants, which he complained degraded the dignity of Britain in the eyes of the Chinese; and he would not stoop to *petition* anyone, since that would require him to admit that there was not a relation of diplomatic equality between himself and Lu Kun, between King William IV and the Daoguang emperor, and between the British and Chinese empires.[72] As Lydia H. Liu shows in her brilliant analysis of the language politics surrounding the Opium War, the other alleged insult that upset Napier was his supposed characterization as a "barbarian *eye*," with the Chinese character *yimu* (headman) being translated by the British in this pejorative manner, despite less offensive translations being available at the time. Liu describes how the character *yi* gets transformed, during the time of the Opium Wars, into what she calls "the super-sign *yi*/barbarian," which then comes to figure as a symbolic "threat to law and to the emergent order of international relations."[73] The British insistence that the Qing empire existed beyond the pale of international relations, and therefore needed to be forcibly brought within the orbit of the hegemonic world system, was greatly aided by complaints, such as those Napier repeatedly made in his dispatches home, that Qing officials had insulted his dignity as a representative of the Crown.

There are, however, good reasons to doubt whether Napier's difficulties really resulted from a basic contradiction between universal sovereignty and the interstate system. Recent scholarship argues that Qing conceptions of universal sovereignty were more "rhetorical" than actual and mostly aimed at consolidating domestic support for the regime as it encountered new foreign threats during a period of great internal stress.[74] For historians such as Joanna Waley-Cohen, Chinese emperors from the eighteenth century onwards were not committed to "isolationism. . . . hostility to innovation,. . . and [an] immutable sense of superiority" but, rather, to a flexible strategy of power unified by a "powerful reluctance to surrender authority or autonomy to any outsider or even to take a chance of doing so."[75] To refuse formal diplomatic relations, in this context, was not to remain insensible to the idea that political sovereignty might be understood differently in other countries; rather, it was to conduct diplomatic warfare by other means. James Hevia, similarly, argues against the assumption that "within the terms of Chinese culture there could be no true diplomacy (based as it must be on natural equality between sovereign states)."[76] He suggests, instead, that we ought to denaturalize the hegemonic status of international law as European diplomats such as Napier sought to affirm it in the run-up to the Opium War. What was at stake in Sino-British relations in the 1830s was not a conflict between tradition and modernity but, instead, a clash between coeval, if "mutually incompatible," understandings of "the meaning of sovereignty and the ways in which relations of power were constructed."[77]

Napier's struggles fall just outside the timeline of *River of Smoke*: he died of typhus only a few months after arriving in China, though not before ordering the bombardment of the Chinese forts at Whampoa, an act that demonstrated the murderous effectiveness of British artillery but failed to break Lu Kun's resolve. Napier's brief sojourn in Canton therefore figures only obliquely in Ghosh's story, when a group of foreign traders in Fanqui-town bet on the precise wording of his derogatory opinions about the Chinese (*RS* 392). And yet the idea that the conflict between China, Britain, and its allies can be described as a struggle over the terms of formal legal equality between states still plays a significant role in the *Ibis* trilogy, especially during *River of Smoke*'s denouement.

We see this most forcefully in the difficulties faced by Napier's successor, Captain Charles Elliot, plenipotentiary and chief superintendent of British trade from 1836 to 1841—a real historical figure and also a significant minor character in both *River of Smoke* and *Flood of Fire*. Midway through the former, Bahram converses with his Armenian friend Zadig Bey about the political situation in Canton. Zadig's status as a well-informed businessman, belonging to neither belligerent camp, affords Ghosh the opportunity for some historical exposition. He tells Bahram that, while the Chinese have historically "avoided violence and confrontation to a degree that is hard to imagine in any other country," they have recently taken a harder line with opium smugglers (*RS* 189). Zadig then narrates a story about an English smuggler who was expelled from China after his boat was stopped and his cargo confiscated. In response to the trader's deportation, the British sent warships up the Pearl River, threatening Chinese ships and fortifications. But then, Zadig continues, "you know what happened when Admiral Maitland came here with his fleet? The Chinese would meet neither the Admiral nor Captain Elliott [*sic*], the British Representative. It was the usual business about protocol and kotowing and all the rest" (189). Much later, when Commissioner Lin holds firm to his demand that the foreign traders in Fanqui-town surrender their stores of opium, Elliot addresses a meeting of besieged foreign smugglers. "Holding himself stiffly erect," he begins to address the gathered crowd (477). He tells of his "attempts to negotiate with Commissioner Lin," including "a letter addressed to the provincial authorities" that "was duly transmitted to the High Commissioner" (477–78). At first, this declaration elicits surprise, "for all present were aware that the provincial authorities had long refused to communicate directly with the British Representative" (478). But, of course, Elliot is eventually forced to admit that, no, he's not heard from the High Commissioner himself: Lin's reply has been sent "indirectly, by [way of] lesser officials, in a letter that quoted the Commissioner at great length" (478). When Elliot's official translator reads Lin's message out loud, Bahram begins to feel "the odd impression that he was listening not to the translator, but to some other voice that had taken command of the young man's mouth and lips, a voice that was at once completely reasonable and utterly implacable" (479). This is the voice of Lin Zexu—the only state official in the *Ibis* trilogy to earn anything like a sympathetic depiction. But Lin's implacable, reasonable voice does not come to Bahram directly but arrives through a chain of ventriloquism, translation, and quotation that is a perfect allegory for the game of telephone that is Sino-British diplomacy in prewar Canton. In *Rivers of Smoke*, international relations are only ever conducted in a manner at once oblique and ritualized—and that's because the meaning of terms like "international relations" is as much at stake in the struggle between Lin and Elliot as is the trade in opium itself.

EXTRATERRITORIAL CANTON

Elliot's difficulties in the realm of international relations are matched by his troubles within the anomalous legal-political zone that is Fanqui-town, where he can exert neither equality with the Chinese nor jurisdiction over his fellow Britons. As the political situation in Canton sours, Elliot tries to take control over the opium trade. As Ghosh tells the story, his actions meet with fierce resistance among British disciples of free trade, who argue that "there has never been any express diplomatic convention between England and China. *Ergo* [Elliot] is not invested with any consular powers" (*RS* 338). As a result, many of the foreign traders assume an even more radical kind of legal impunity than they will later be afforded in the postwar Treaties of Nanjing (1842) and Wanghia (1844). For while those treaties made Britons and Americans subject to the jurisdiction of their own diplomatic consuls, the Canton traders argue that they come under neither Chinese nor British legal authority.[78] When James Innes, a particularly determined opium runner, is asked to quit Canton by the Fanqui-town chamber of commerce, he therefore bellows in reply: "No, sir, I will not leave Canton and you cannot make me do it! Let me remind you that I am not a member of this Chamber. I am a free man, sir, and I obey no mortal voice" (319). This line of reasoning leads Elliot, in turn, to castigate the whole crew of opium traders as "outlaws" who believe that they "are exempt from the operation of all law, British and Chinese" (376).[79] And, indeed, when the opium traders are later challenged by the Weiyuen, the head of the Canton constabulary, about why they continue to flout Chinese imperial edicts, they appeal to the "custom for the foreign community in Canton to regulate itself" (460). Then, when the Weiyuen objects that "this custom holds only so long as you do not flout the laws of the land," the merchants reply that, "as

Englishmen and Americans, we enjoy certain freedoms under the laws of our own countries. These require us to be subject, in the first instance, to our own laws" (460). In Fanqui-town, hypocrisy abounds. Even though the Chinese state never officially relaxes its territorial claim to the ground on which Fanqui-town stands, foreigners like Innes are able, by making a series of irreconcilable claims to different kinds of extraterritorial person-hood, to align themselves with English law, Chinese law, or no law at all, whatever the search for profit appears to demand.

And yet Ghosh's Canton is never a formally extraterritorial place. By contrast with post-1842 enclaves such as the Shanghai International Set-tlement, the behavior of foreign residents in Canton in the 1830s was strictly controlled. In *River of Smoke*, one of our first accounts of life in the city comes from Fitcher Penrose, an English collector of Chinese plants, as he converses with a budding naturalist called Paulette Lambert. Penrose describes Can-ton as "the busiest, most crowded city I ever saw. The biggest too, bigger even than London. . . . a sea of houses and boats" (97). But while these sen-tences make Canton seem like an urban ocean of possibility, Fitcher's next remarks inform Paulette that she will never get to see it, because Chinese law forbids European women from going there (98). Paulette's disappoint-ment is real, and she has to be content with exploring the island of Hong Kong—at that point an obscure watering station some years from becoming Britain's major Chinese colony. The restrictions Fitcher describes were, likewise, real. Immanuel C. Y. Hsu reports that, in 1836, the foreign com-munity in Canton measured only 307 people, all of them men. (By contrast, the Portuguese-run settlement at Macao, just down the Pearl River delta from Canton, was home to 4,480 foreigners, of whom some 2,149 were women.)[80] Alongside the restrictions against female settlement, the foreign traders at Canton had to follow a list of twelve rules of behavior, many of them strictly enforced, which ran from a ban on foreign warships north of the Humen Straits; a prohibition on firearms; restrictions against move-ment beyond the neighborhood around the thirteen factories; and—most important—the limitation of all economic activity to a defined summer trading season during which buying and selling could only be conducted via the Hong monopoly.[81] And, of course, economic activity was constrained by the fact that, from 1757 to 1842, Canton was the only port through which European and American merchants could gain any legitimate access to China's vast internal markets.

Life in the Canton factories is thus marked, in the *Ibis* trilogy, by a peculiar mixture of license and constraint, freedom and limitation. In *Sea of Poppies*, Fanqui-town is first described in unpropitious terms: a "spit of land, just beyond the south western gates of the walled city," on which "the Aliens had been permitted to build a row of . . . narrow red-tiled buildings" (367). In this "one narrow enclave" were confined "extra-Celestial" beings such as the "'Red-faced' Aliens from England, 'Flowery-flag' Aliens from America"; sundry Dutch, French, Danes, and other Europeans; and also the "White-hatted Aliens—Parsis from Bombay" (367–78). Their alien status confirmed by their physical and legal isolation, the foreign inhabitants of Fanqui-town endure conditions of cultural, social, and economic privation quite different from the freedoms enjoyed by the many other kinds of foreign subject—including Buddhists from the subcontinent, as well as Muslims from Java, Malaysia, and Arabia—who have liberty to live within the great and diverse city of Canton proper.

Yet while these "extra-Celestial" foreigners' lives were undoubtedly restricted by Chinese state edicts, those restrictions weren't absolute, or always unwelcome. A queer character like Robin Chinnery, the fictional Anglo-Indian son of the real English painter George Chinnery, and the narrator of *River of Smoke*'s epistolary chapters, loves Fanqui-town in part because "nowhere else is there such a number of incorrigible bachelors" (159). Even for a heterosexual like Bahram, it takes only a short while to learn that the official proscription against women does not apply to the Dan boatpeople, whose sampans and lanteas lined the riverbanks alongside the factory settlement. (Over his many years in Fanqui-town, Bahram enjoys a love affair with a Dan woman, Chi-mei, with whom he fathers a child, Ah Fatt, who becomes a recurring character in all three parts of the trilogy.) More formally, neither Robin, Bahram, or future taipans such as William Jardine were considered to be under Chinese legal jurisdiction. As Pär Kristoffer Cassel explains, while the system of personal extraterritoriality that emerged after 1842 dramatically increased the sovereign immunity of European colonists, that power was built upon existing Chinese technologies of legal pluralism, in which different juridical regimes regularly applied to different social or ethnic groups. In the Canton factories, Qing law was applied only selectively to foreigners, and usually only in response to the most heinous sorts of criminal act, like murder. "From a Qing point of view," Cassel writes, "it was a privilege to submit to Chinese civilization and the Qing Code"; among foreign commentators, it was argued that the Qing Code "only applied to foreigners who voluntarily submitted to the imperial government and not to temporary sojourners" such as the Canton merchants.[82]

Certainly, in *River of Smoke*, the foreign merchants feel at once licensed and restricted by their position half inside and half outside the Chinese state. Because they are not given entry to the geographic sphere of Chinese law, enjoying the liberties as well as the responsibilities of an imperial subject, the Western merchants' physical and economic agency is constricted. But because the Chinese mostly avoid claiming jurisdiction over them, the thirteen factories of Fanqui-town also come to seem like a place beyond authority. This state of affairs doesn't mean that foreign states did not sometimes attempt to exert themselves in Fanqui-town. In *River of Smoke*, the various factories are described as being adorned with national flags that "look like gigantic lances, plunged into the soil of China" in such a way as to unambiguously connect private enterprise to the project of foreign imperialism (172).[83] And, at times, or so one free trader complains, the Canton chamber of commerce tries to act like a "shadow government," not just facilitating the commercial activities of its private members but seeming to assert "jurisdiction" over them (321). "House No. 1" in the British factory is even nicknamed "the Consulate" by the enclave's foreign residents (373).

Like so many of the zones, camps, and city-states discussed in this book, Ghosh's version of the Canton factory enclave is, thus, neither beyond sovereignty nor wholly subject to it. Culturally and socially, too, it is an interstitial place. In *Sea of Poppies*, the neighborhood in which Fanqui-town sits is described as at once aqueous and grounded: "So thickly settled that nobody could tell where the land stopped and the water began" (367). *River of Smoke* sounds the same notes. At one point, Robin goes to visit the studio of a Chinese painter who was once the student, or maybe a colleague or rival, of his famous English father. In the eyes of the elder Chinnery, Canton painters are guilty of producing "a *bastard* art"—a commercial aesthetic that obeys neither Chinese nor European techniques or tastes (*RS* 231). But to his illegitimate son, that bastard art is marvelous because it is "utterly *novel*"—and that novelty lies in the way that, "just as foreigners want pictures of Fanqui-town because it looks to them so indescribably Celestial, so too do the Chinese covet them because the same sight is in their eyes utterly Alien" (234; emphasis in original). Alien to all, Robin describes Fanqui-town, using extraterritorial similes familiar to us from the first chapters of this book, as "like a ship at sea" and "the last and greatest of all the world's caravanserais" (174). Cromwell's personhood is defined in part by his mastery of the art of facing both ways; Ghosh's Fanqui-town is itself because it belongs to nobody while being contested by all.

Such doubleness! But a doubleness that comes at a cost, and that remains contradictory. The central moral irony of the *Ibis* trilogy is, thus, that, while it is scathing about the economic and political practices that created Fanqui-town, it celebrates the cultural fact of this cosmopolitan caravanserai. We can tell this, above all, by the way *River of Smoke* mourns its loss.

The central Canton story of *River of Smoke* is embedded within a frame narrative that tells the story of how Deeti, the Indian peasant woman who is among the central characters in *Sea of Poppies*, finds and founds her family shrine on the island of Mauritius. The shrine, which Deeti and her family call a "Memory-Temple," is located in an old shelter for escaped slaves ("or marrons, as they were known in Kreol" [10]) and is adorned with paintings of the schooner *Ibis*, its multiethnic passengers and crew, and the key events in the ship's journey from India to Mauritius. In this way, the Memory-Temple symbolically embraces both the desire to collect ancestral memories around a common locale and the recognition that Deeti's family, like many others in the Indian Ocean basin, is defined and shaped by the fact of voluntary and involuntary diasporic movement. Toward the end of the opening frame, Neel comes to visit, kick-starting the novel's main action by telling the tale of how he and Ah Fatt escaped their imprisonment in the *Ibis* and made their way to Canton. At the end of the novel, we return to Neel and Deeti in Mauritius. Neel has spent the night reading a packet of Robin Chinnery's letters from Canton, which include a painting of Fanqui-town in flames.[84] This leads Deeti to ask whether he ever went back to Canton after the outbreak of the Opium War. Neel then tells of his return in 1868:

> The place was changed beyond recognition. The site of the Maidan was a scene of utter desolation: the factories were gone—hardly a brick was left standing upon another. A new foreign enclave had been constructed nearby, on a mudbank that had been reclaimed and filled in. It was called Shamian Island and the houses the Europeans had built there were nothing like the Thirteen Hongs. Nor was the atmosphere of the new enclave anything like that of the Fanqui-town of old. It was a typical "White Town" of the kind the British made everywhere they went—it was cut off from the city, and very few Chinese were allowed inside, only servants. The streets were clean and leafy, and the buildings were as staid and dull as the people inside them. But behind that façade of bland respectability the foreigners were importing more opium than ever from India. (*RS* 516)

The voice is Neel's but the perspective is at one with the author himself, who in an interview describes Fanqui-town in the 1830s as a "lost world" and contrasts it with its later replacement, which was "built under completely different circumstances, after European domination had been clearly established."[85] The conflict between England and China is now seen by historians such as Hevia as a struggle over the fundamental terms upon which international relations would take place; in a similar way, the very look and layout of the original Fanqui-town is shaped by a dynamic—and, in the 1830s, still unfinished—struggle between foreign and Chinese vernacular elements. Fanqui-town is the product of the West's unjust colonial exploitation of South and East Asia. Yet, in its legal and political ambivalences, as well as its multiethnic and multilingual mash-up, it embodies a kind of "global" experience that, by troubling the imperial logic of formal political equality between sovereign territorial actors, can acknowledge the facts of vernacular difference and the struggle to achieve social and political inequality.

BORDERS AND BORDERS THAT ARE NOT BORDERS

In these contemporary historical novels, the location and nature of political borders comes into question. In *Wolf Hall*, borders proliferate. As the English state struggles to define itself through and against the universal jurisdiction of the Roman Catholic church and its agents, Mantel's narrator develops an idiom and set of topoi that extend monarchical authority through national space. But, against its own territorializing logic, *Wolf Hall* also develops a powerfully individuating language, centering on the expression "person" and the ubiquitous pronominal "he." Cromwell's cosmopolitan personhood thus becomes, formally as much as narratively, the means through which the English state is reformed and the portal through which it opens onto the world. He can be the agent of territorial sovereignty because he is an extraterritorial person.

Amitav Ghosh has spoken before about the way borders move, imaginatively if not in actual fact. In an interview with the BBC World Service, he talks about his youthful desire to travel outside India and then explains that, although he once thought the border might be finally crossed and left behind, it simply reappears where you are, within the city or nation to which you've come.[86] In *River of Smoke*, though, Fanqui-town is more than a place to which people bring their own sense of belonging. It is an ambivalent zone on the verge of becoming a border. Captain Elliot's attempt to make Fanqui-town an area of real consular power and jurisdiction would transform it into a new threshold and limit between China and everywhere else—but this is exactly what Lin Zexu and the other Qing officials will not allow. Refusing to conduct diplomacy according to Westphalian norms, Lin and company refuse—for a while, at least—to allow Fanqui-town to become a place of formal diplomatic exchange. Fanqui-town remains within and apart, neither free from sovereign jurisdiction nor consistently governed by one set of laws. The *Ibis* trilogy is never only about the proliferation of borders within extraterritorial enclaves. It is also about the ways people and states fight over borders; it is about a space that one party desires to transform into a border between nations, but that another does not.

This chapter has discussed too few historical novels to venture an argument about them at the level of genre. We cannot say, with certainty, that the contemporary historical novel now generally gathers in the space of the extraterritory, not the proximity of the border. The generic implications of this chapter's argument are suggestive, and, for now, we will have to be content with that. Still, in moving us toward China and extraterritorial law in the context of Western imperialism, Ghosh's historical fiction introduces the crucial story that underpins this book's next and final chapter: the story of a political geography that was not produced by the willing suspension of sovereignty claims but by colonial policies in which foreign privilege was expressed in the form of extraterritorial personhood. That story now takes us to Shanghai, to its International Settlement, and to the genre-bending fictions of Kazuo Ishiguro and J. G. Ballard.

5

SETTLEMENT

Royal strolled around the shrouded furniture. He raised his stick and slashed at the stale air with the same stroke he had used against Ryder. At any moment a battalion of police would arrive and cart them all off to the nearest jail. Or would they? What played straight into the residents' hands was the remarkably self-contained nature of the high-rise, a self-administered enclave within the larger private domain of the development project.

—J. G. BALLARD, *HIGH-RISE*

SHANGHAI LINKS

Shanghai Links is a luxury expatriate community in the Pudong New Area of Shanghai, China's liveliest commercial metropolis and the setting for the novels discussed in this chapter. When it was planned in the early 1990s, Shanghai Links was the first Chinese real estate development to attract investment from Bankers Trust, a major US investment bank, as well as large US pension funds such as New York Life.[1] When it opened in 1998, Shanghai Links was supposed to feature a golf course designed by Jack Nicklaus; a first tract of 30 luxury homes, the materials for which had been imported from North America; roads and infrastructure for a further 470 such residences; and the second campus of the Shanghai American School, in which children receive English-language instruction following a Western-style curriculum.[2]

Shanghai Links was celebrated in the financial press as presaging a new era of capital investment in China—a sign that the expat community in Shanghai was growing and that the regulatory structures of the People's

Republic were now sufficiently robust to attract traditionally risk-averse US pension funds.[3] As it happened, though, Shanghai Links turned out to be a bad bet. Barry and Stuart Hansen, the Canadian businessmen behind the project, intended to fund the development by securitizing future leases on unbuilt houses and apartments.[4] But they were soon accused by their partners of having misrepresented the capital available to them—allegations that were later affirmed by the High Court in London.[5] The Hansens counterclaimed, alleging misbehavior by the local government and other state agencies, as well as by the multinational construction firms Bouygues SA and Pomerleau International, who had been awarded contracts to develop the site.[6] The work of construction went slowly, then stopped. Legal challenges also stalled, with the Hansens refusing to obey judgments in courts from as far apart as London and the Cayman Islands.[7] News reports suggest that the Shanghai city government was also dragging its feet, perhaps as a result of its own factional struggles.[8] When Sean Snyder, a Berlin-based American artist, photographed the site in 2002, Shanghai Links looked forlorn. Surrounded by chain-link fences dotted with half-built security towers, it looked less like a luxury community than a disused military base, or a prison camp after liberation by an invading army (fig. 5.1).

Snyder's photo-essay about Shanghai Links begins, in fact, not in his own millennial moment but in the nineteenth century—and, specifically, by referring to the Nanjing Treaty of 1842, which ended the First Opium War and established the initial legal basis for British extraterritorial jurisdiction in China. That treaty, in Snyder's account, began the process through which Shanghai was "divided into foreign districts" that, likewise, "divided the Chinese sections of the city with gates and walls."[9] He describes how these foreign enclaves, which eventually became known as the International Settlement and French Concession, were built "in accordance with Western standards, including paved Western-style streets, gas lighting, electricity, telephones, running water, automobiles, and streetcars."[10] Then, following this potted history of old Shanghai, he switches back to the present, interspersing his own descriptions with slogans drawn from a Shanghai Links advertising brochure, set off from the main text by the use of a bold and italic font:

When this development is finished, you'll never know
you are in China

Locals call the compound "the American Concession". . . . Shanghai Links is a guarded reconstruction of an upper-middle class North American community transposed onto Chinese soil overlooking the Yangtze River[11]

In Snyder's view, there's an unambiguous connection between Shanghai Links and the extraterritorial enclaves that dominated Shanghai between 1842 and the Japanese invasion of December 1941.[12] He thereby adds an artistic supplement to the work of scholars such as Pál Nyíri, who argues that the influence of the foreign concessions continues long after their formal abolition. For Nyíri, the economic reforms that have transformed China under Deng Xiaoping and his successors have revived a version of the

FIGURE 5.1 *Shanghai Links, Hua Xia Trip, 2002.*

Credit: Sean Snyder.

extraterritorial concessions; in particular, the political geography of the concession is replicated in the twenty-first-century infrastructural or special economic development zone, which operates as "a form of 'internal concession' within which foreign investors as well as their Chinese employees, in exchange for helping to develop the nation, [are] given greater economic and social freedom than elsewhere."[13] For Snyder, meanwhile, the afterlife of the erstwhile foreign concessions also links expatriate gated communities like Shanghai Links to the even larger archipelago of US military bases. This is not because Shanghai Links has, appearances aside, any kind of military function. Rather, as Snyder explains in another photoessay, "Temporary Occupation," Shanghai Links and US military bases are both transported oases of Western social and economic life. They exemplify a form of architectural development in which modular architectural commodities, from suburban housing stock to retail frontages, are shipped like the parts of a stage set for reassembly abroad, creating enclaves within which—as this chapter's epigraph from J. G. Ballard suggests— demographically discrete populations live in self-contained and self-administered enclaves, cut off from surrounding communities.[14] Like the historical extraterritorial enclave it so readily evokes, Shanghai Links thereby represents the broader neocolonial phenomenon that Mark Prince calls "the art of displacement": "Like international viruses," such strategies of development and design traverse the economic and infrastructural processes of transnational capitalism so as to "briefly inhabit any place regardless of its local make-up."[15]

Shanghai Links epitomizes the contemporary delinking of customary relationships between natural and built environments, population and territory, place and nation, production and consumption, that we have observed throughout this book, in both fictional and real geographies. It also evokes problems of historical anachrony and uneven development that are specific to the history of extraterritoriality in China. Shanghai Links is a new kind of speculative real estate development in a hypermodern city newly open to global capital; it is also the return of the semicolonial repressed. It embodies a future political geography in which the construction of global flows and networks is facilitated by the privatization of public space; it also shows how even hypercapitalist developments stall, stutter, and decay. In this way, Shanghai Links exemplifies the major theme of this chapter: the way that extraterritorial spaces give rise to extratemporal experiences. The interruption of the state's supposedly unitary political geography by the "anomalous zone" of the extraterritorial concession creates similar interruptions at the level of people's experiences of historical time.[16]

For writers like J. G. Ballard (1930–2009) and Kazuo Ishiguro (b. 1954), the persistence of the extraterritorial zone is a core fact of contemporary metropolitan life. Ballard, in particular, identifies the privatization and segregation of public space with developments in North America and Western Europe since the 1970s, but he says it was also evident in the International Settlement in which he grew up from 1930 to 1945. In a 2005 interview, Ballard spoke of how, "for reasons of security" and economic advantage, over the last few decades "middle-class professionals. . . . [have been] subtracting themselves from the whole [arena of] civic interactions that depend on them, virtually conducting an internal immigration."[17] In his 2008 autobiography, *Miracles of Life: Shanghai to Shepperton*, Ballard describes, in imagery highly reminiscent of Snyder's work, how "each foreign nationality in Shanghai built its houses in its own idiom—the French built Provençal villas and art deco mansions, the Germans Bauhaus white boxes, the English their half-timbered fantasies."[18] These are the kinds of details that Ballard will rely on as he situates his life in extraterritorial Shanghai as the alpha and omega of his imagination, with the power to connect the disparate parts of his oeuvre and unlock the dark heart of cultural life after World War II.

In what follows, I attend to the differences and continuities between the International Settlement and twenty-first-century enclosures like Shanghai Links. Following the last chapter's dive into British imperial history, this chapter analyzes contemporary artistic representations of Shanghai in the period between the world wars, when British power in China reached its peak and then rapidly collapsed. As Ballard and Ishiguro represent it, and as many others agree, the interwar period was one in which the paradoxes of imperialist extraterritoriality were palpably dynamic, both at the level of urban geography and in their effect on peoples' apprehension of historical time.[19] Yet this chapter is neither a study of Republican China nor of colonial politics and law. It rather asks why—and to what formal and thematic effect—two major contemporary novelists employ interwar Shanghai as the setting for their novels, short stories, memoirs, and screenplays. As in the last two chapters, my focus is on the way that political and personal histories of extraterritoriality manifest in narrative form.

So why are Ballard and Ishiguro interested in extraterritorial Shanghai? The obvious answer is biographical. Ishiguro's Japanese father was born in Shanghai between the wars. In interviews about *When We Were Orphans* (2000), a novel set in Shanghai between the turn of the century and the 1937 Japanese invasion of the Chinese-run precincts of the city, Ishiguro speaks of his fascination at learning that his apparently "sedentary" relatives "lived in this wild and exotic place."[20] As for Ballard, his celebrated autobiographical novel *Empire of the Sun* (1984)—adapted for the screen by Steven Spielberg in 1987—taught the world about his childhood in the International Settlement and adolescence in a Japanese detention center for Allied civilians. Although different novelists in many respects, Ballard and Ishiguro both transform extraterritorial Shanghai city into a novelistic space-time in which, to quote M. M. Bakhtin on the idea of the chronotope, "spatial and temporal indicators are fused. . . . Time, as it were, thickens, takes on flesh, becomes artistically visible; likewise, space becomes charged and responsive to the movements of time, plot and history."[21] In Shanghai narratives such as *Orphans* and *Empire*, the fractured and involuted qualities of the city's semicolonial geography give rise to complex heterochronic experiences. In this way, extraterritoriality emerges as a fictional space-time through which problems of combined and uneven development become newly visible. But to understand why that is so we must first, like Sean Snyder, take a step back in time—not to the nineteenth century in this case, but to the 1920s, when the Western rights of extraterritorial jurisdiction secured after the First Opium War were under attack from citizens of the new Republic of China.

POINTS OF DISTURBANCE

Writing in his Columbia University doctoral dissertation of 1925, the Chinese literary scholar and political scientist Shih Shun Liu dismissed the practice of extraterritorial jurisdiction as "incompatible with the modern conceptions of territorial sovereignty, on which the science of international law is founded."[22] Shih argued that extraterritoriality, which in China granted privileged foreign nationals personal immunity from national laws, had been born at a time "when the principle of sovereignty was unknown."[23] But Shih was writing in an age when—despite the Wilson administration's refusal to support Chinese demands at the 1919 Paris Peace Conference— the right to national self-determination had become the watchword of liberals and Leninists alike. In 1921, as a consequence of their defeat in World War I, Germany and the former Austria-Hungary were forced to renounce their claims to extraterritorial jurisdiction in China, and, in 1922, the Nine-Power Treaty included a solemn promise to "respect the sovereignty, the independence, and the territorial and administrative integrity of China."[24] In this historical context, Shih felt able to dismiss extraterritoriality as little more than the "yoke" of imperialism in China: with anticolonial nationalism unleashed upon the world, extraterritorial law had become a "decadent institution" that was "doomed to decay."[25]

We shouldn't be surprised at such severity. Shih's studies in the United States had been sponsored by the Chinese government at a time when that country's division between rival power centers at Beijing and Guangzhou was exacerbated by the domination of its trade, foreign relations, and urban geography by islands of extraterritorial jurisdiction governed by (and for) imperial powers such as Britain, France, Japan, and the United States.[26] These were the "treaty ports" that, from the middle of the nineteenth century, were China's main points of connection with Europe and the Americas. Foremost among the treaty ports was Shanghai, in which a few thousand foreign capitalists had created "a zone of European law and social practice" on the south China coast, within a city of two million Chinese.[27] This is the metropolis that, in a 1926 travel diary, Aldous Huxley described as "Bergson's *élan vital* in the raw. . . . Nothing more intensely living can be imagined."[28] In this kind of apostrophe, Shanghai figures as the kind of highly developed society that the British colonial jurist Francis Taylor Piggott had in mind when, in his 1892 treatise on *The Law Relating to Consular Jurisdiction and to Residence in Oriental Countries*, he warned of the many "points of disturbance" that would erupt when two complex systems of law, government, and trade come into contact within a putatively single political geography.[29] And so Shanghai is also the place that Huxley, drawing on a long and undistinguished tradition of Western Orientalism, could simultaneously describe as an ultracosmopolitan modern city and the fount of Asiatic timelessness: "A thousand years from now the seal cutters will still be engraving their seals, the ivory workers still sawing and polishing; the tailors still singing the merits of their cit and cloth, even as they do today."[30]

Shih Shun Liu didn't share Huxley's delight in China's supposed mix of antiquity and modernity. Any backwardness he would admit to was the result of deliberate structural underdevelopment, created by foreign states for the purposes of maintaining their political and commercial advantage. As Shih understands it, extraterritorial jurisdiction was founded in, and meant to extend, the unequal spatial distribution of power within a worldwide system of imperial capitalism. It represented the anachronistic survival, within the modern interstate system, of an ancient theory of legal personality, in which "racial consanguinity was treated as the sole basis of amenability to law. Thus, in the same country—and even in the same city at times—the Lombards lived under Lombard law, and the Romans under Roman law."[31] The West's resistance to full Chinese territorial sovereignty, he argues, produces the alleged civilizational backwardness that is then used to justify the system of extraterritorial jurisdiction in the first place. Extraterritoriality has so far been mostly visible in this book as a quality of legal and political space, but Shih Shun Liu apprehends it as simultaneously a crisis of heterochrony or untimeliness. In interwar China, the past is too much alive.

Extraterritoriality in China eventually ended in 1943; still, far from being fated to decay, enclaves such as the International Settlement persist across social and political space, as well as in the form of a literary chronotope that draws upon the past but is not defined by it. The chronotope of the extraterritorial enclave is, to return to Bakhtin, best understood not as a novelistic tool through which writers imagine the historical past, but as a critical "optic for reading texts as x-rays of the forces at work in the culture system from which they spring."[32] To read *Orphans* or *Empire* historically, as with the *Ibis* trilogy, is to understand them as histories of and for the present. Ishiguro and Ballard invest the chronotope of the Shanghai International Settlement with a contradictory range of narrative space-times. For Ishiguro, Shanghai is a place from which his orphans are exiled, but it is also the zone his protagonists carry around inside themselves. Because of this, characters such as Christopher Banks, the first-person narrator of *Orphans*, are defined by a double temporality in which they have been abandoned by the very people and places from which they still struggle to break free. In Ballard's *Empire*, meanwhile, the International Settlement embodies a kind of doomed futurity. Reflecting on the city's position close to the international dateline, the narrator declares Shanghai to be "a day ahead in time as in everything else."[33] Ballard has repeatedly described his childhood home as the epitome of today's globalized and hyperstratified megalopolises: his father, he says, called it "the most advanced city in the world."[34] *Empire*'s first sentence, likewise, is built around a long compound simile that suggests that Shanghai is uniquely the agent and victim of violent historical change: "Wars came early to Shanghai, overtaking each other like the tides that raced up the Yangtze and returned to this gaudy city all the coffins set adrift from the funeral piers of the Chinese Bund" (3). But while wars "come to" Shanghai without invitation, they not only come early, knowing they will be welcome; they bring back the death that already belongs to the "gaudy city." Within the tribute to the metropolitan future lies an essential morbidity.

Ishiguro's and Ballard's Shanghai fictions are defined by the violent copresence of temporal differences. They evoke what Ernst Bloch called the synchronism of the nonsynchronous—in German, *die Ungleichzeitigkeit des Gleichzeitigen*.[35] For Bloch, such temporal paradox was a central aspect of historical experience in general and of capitalist modernity in particular.[36]

But the temporal problem of *Ungleichzeitigkeit des Gleichzeitigen* is one that registers with peculiar intensity in the enclave city that Ballard described as having been "purpose-built by the West as a test-metropolis of the future" (*K* 233). In fact, Bloch well understood the relation between extraterritorial spaces and the simultaneously nonsynchronous. Writing about the way Germans in the 1930s seemed so vulnerable to the search for symbols of "transcendence in the past," he describes how fascist ideology carves out an "alogical space" within the state's social fabric—the kind of space in which, for instance, the "wishes and mythicisms" of "central Africa" might "[rise] up." This is a kind of nonsynchronism, Bloch decides, "that verges on extraterritoriality."[37]

SEMICOLONIAL SPACE-TIME

The treaty port system was created in 1842 by the Treaty of Nanjing, which ended the First Opium War and "opened" five cities—Canton (Guangzhou), Amoy (Xiamen), Fuzhou, Ningbo, and Shanghai—to British merchants, who were now free to reside within their precincts and trade with whomever they chose. The treaty is short and never uses "extraterritorial" or its synonyms. Instead, Article 2 grants the British Crown power to "appoint Superintendents or Consular Officers . . . to be the medium of communication between the Chinese Authorities and the said Merchants, and to see that the just Duties and other Dues of the Chinese Government as hereafter provided for, are duly discharged."[38] By mandating that official communication be mediated by British diplomatic officers, the treaty placed British merchants beyond the reach of Chinese law, enveloping them within the arms of domestic law even as they lived overseas. This position was clarified in the supplementary Treaty of the Bogue (1843), which explained: "Regarding the punishment of English criminals, the English Government will enact the laws necessary to attain that end, and the Consul will be empowered to put them in force; and regarding the punishment of Chinese criminals, these will be tried and punished by their own laws."[39] In the opinion of Shih Shun Liu's contemporary, Ching-Chun Wang, the 1843 treaty thus established a new "principle of 'unilateral' extraterritoriality" in China's relations with foreign powers.[40] This principle is "unilateral" because the syntactic and legal parallelism of the supplementary treaty's language obscures a greater inequality: "British subjects in China should be subject to British law and Chinese subjects in Great Britain also should be subject to British law . . . 'heads the foreigners win, tails the Chinese lose.'"[41]

The everyday effects of this system of extraterritorial legal personhood can be glimpsed in W. Somerset Maugham's "The Vice-Consul," one of fifty-eight prose sketches drawn from the English novelist's travels in China and collected in the volume *On a Chinese Screen* (1922). Because they established parallel and unequal systems of law within China, the unequal treaties caused jurisdictional complications when plaintiff and defendant were of different nationalities. Following the Second Opium War (1856–60), the general rule in China was to follow the maxim of *actor sequitur forum rei*, in which the plaintiff follows the defendant into her own court. Thus, if a Briton assaulted a Chinese, the case was heard by the British consul; if a Chinese was so accused, the case went before Chinese magistrates. This was the basis behind the so-called Mixed Court system, which prevailed in Shanghai from 1864 until 1927.[42] But just as the Treaty of Nanjing afforded Chinese citizens in Britain none of the extraterritorial rights enjoyed by Britons in China, so was this jurisdictional principle applied unequally. In Maugham's story, a young English vice-consul, recently promoted from "student-interpreter," visits a Chinese judge.[43] Maugham's portrait of the judge verges on stereotype. Portly and smiling, when he walks the short distance to his seat of justice, the judge "[assumes] instinctively the gravity proper to his office" (*OCS* 226). The unnamed criminal before the court has already been convicted and he, too, is drawn with an odd mixture of primitivism and punctiliousness. To the vice-consul, he appears as "a lissome creature that suggested the wild animal. . . . [with] eyes that did not slant as the Chinese eye is wrongly supposed to do, but were straight . . . unnaturally large and bright, fixed on those of the judge, [with] a terror that was horrible to see" (227). We do not learn what the criminal has done: he is merely asked to identify himself and suffer execution. But what is the

Englishman doing here? The only explanation can be that a capital crime has been committed against a Briton. For, although foreign consuls could try their fellow nationals in kingly solitude, when a Chinese defendant was accused of injuring a foreign plaintiff, "an 'assessor' (usually a junior consul official) of the plaintiff's nationality was allowed to sit alongside the Chinese magistrate during the proceedings."[44]

Maugham resists direct comment on this inequality. We learn instead about the vice-consul's shame at coming to identify with the fear of a condemned man who "could be no older than himself" (*OCS* 226–27). And we see the judge try to smile at the vice-consul after the execution, but all he can manage is "a grimace rather than a smile; it distorted painfully that fat good-humoured face" (229). Above all, we encounter the brittleness of a British imperial class that cannot admit to even the most complacently liberal hesitations. Thus does the vice-consul's bland meditation upon judicial killing—"how terrible it was to make an end of life deliberately" (229)—later give way before the forced bonhomie of the barroom banter in his whites-only colonial club:

> "Well," they said, "did you see the blighter shot?"
> "You bet I did," he said, in a loud and casual voice. (230)

In the way it exposes British condescension while hinting at a deeper crisis within the codes of imperial masculinity, "The Vice-Consul" explores a colonial ambivalence familiar to us from writers such as E. M. Forster. Its interest to us here, therefore, lies mostly in the way it illustrates the everyday effects of the structural inequalities that made the Treaty of Nanjing and the Treaty of the Bogue exemplary among the so-called unequal treaties, which together "encroached upon China's sovereign rights [and] reduced her to semi-colonial status" over the course of the century between the Opium War and World War II.[45]

But what does that term mean—"semicolonial"?[46] In Anglophone literary studies, this coinage is perhaps most familiar from Derek Attridge and Marjorie Howes's volume *Semicolonial Joyce* (2000), which considers, among other things, how James Joyce's oeuvre responds to the ambiguous political status of his Irish birthplace, which is simultaneously an "underdeveloped and deindustrialized" object of British power and somewhere that "helped build and maintain the British imperial system."[47] But in the Chinese context, "semicolonial" names a more complicated condition. Unlike Ireland, which was absorbed within a constitutional union with Great Britain between 1800 and 1922, the foreign settlements in China always coexisted with local sovereignty, no matter how much they offended or complicated it. "Semi-colonial" was used by Vladimir Lenin, in *Imperialism: the Highest Stage of Capitalism* (1916), to describe a "transitional form" of political economy, in which "finance capital is such a great . . . force in all economic and in all international relations, that it is capable of subjecting, and actually does subject, to itself even states enjoying the fullest political independence."[48] "Semicolonial" therefore describes a situation whereby foreign capital becomes hegemonic within a country that it does not dominate in political or military terms.[49] In the broadly Marxist anticolonial theory that developed in Asia and Eurasia between the world wars, semicolonialism also had at least three other major features. First, semicolonial China combined a predominantly agrarian peasant economy with pockets of industrial, commercial, and financial enterprise, especially in the treaty ports.[50] It was not merely "transitional," then, in the sense of being a way station between feudalism and capitalism; rather, it was constituted by the copresence of what might otherwise have been seen as historically antithetical modes of production. Second, as Mao Zedong pointed out in 1928, to this developmental asynchrony one should add the spatial interruptions forged by extraterritorial law:

It is a feature of semicolonial China that, since [1912] the various cliques of old and new warlords have waged incessant wars against one another, supported by imperialism from abroad and by the comprador and landlord classes at home. Such a phenomenon is to be found in none of the imperialist countries nor for that matter in any colony under direct imperialist rule, but only in a country like China which is under indirect imperialist rule. Two things account for its occurrence, namely, a localized agricultural economy (not a unified capitalist economy) and the imperialist policy of marking off spheres of influence in order to divide and exploit.[51]

Finally, semicolonialism in China involved multiple foreign powers (up to eighteen) that sometimes cooperated and sometimes competed. This in itself had unpredictable effects. In their cooperative mode, the foreign powers could establish what Shu-mei Shih calls "multiple layers of domination" over the Chinese; meanwhile, rivalries between these same countries "had the effect of exempting them of any responsibility or pretense to colonial benevolence."[52] Overall, the "sheer number of colonial powers in China prevented the constitution of a unified colonial state" and enabled a range of liberties—cultural, political, and economic—that were not always present in formal colonies such as Hong Kong or Singapore.[53]

At the level of Shanghai's urban geography, semicolonialism's most immediate effect was the creation of two foreign enclaves within the Chinese city: the nominally cosmopolitan (but actually British-dominated) International Settlement and the French Concession—unlike the International Settlement a colonial territory, over which France claimed sovereignty. British hegemony over the International Settlement, as we have seen, was not based on any territorial claim and, in this respect, was settled on a different legal basis than Crown Colonies such as Hong Kong or Singapore. For this reason, it's worth taking some time to explain how and why the International Settlement developed the way it did.

There is nothing in the idea of extraterritorial personhood that necessitates the creation of separate physical spaces—and certainly not on the scale of the International Settlement and French Concession, which by 1914 took up thirty-three square kilometers of the city center, including the major anchorages, diplomatic and commercial sectors, and richest residential neighborhoods.[54] Although the city's Chinese elite later came to regret it, the idea to house foreigners in their own enclaves was originally theirs. Marie-Claire Bergère explains that the unequal treaties of the 1840s "granted the right of residence to foreigners but did not make it clear where they should establish themselves."[55] Chinese officials therefore improvised a way of implementing the treaty rights that would respect Qing sovereignty, accommodate foreign demands for private property, and prevent conflict between ethnic groups. The result was the Land Regulations of 1845, which granted the British a segregated zone bordered by the Huangpu River to the west, the Chinese walled city to the south, and the Suzhou River to the north. The Land Regulations forbade Chinese nationals from owning property in the concessions; so long as they paid compensation to the original Chinese owners, foreigners were thereby able to gain perpetual leases to real estate.[56] The only other condition was that foreign residents paid an annual "rent" tax—a revenue that, beyond its fiscal significance, symbolized residual Chinese sovereignty. Herein we see the double nature of the International Settlement: a bordered zone of foreign impunity that simultaneously carves up and sits on top of Chinese territory, and a playground for legally untouchable imperialists that requires them to compensate the nation they exploit. As the Land Regulations were revised and expanded over the course of the century, the foreigners established their own systems of tax collection, founded a police force, and established public services and utilities. After 1854, the International Settlement boasted its own Shanghai Municipal Council, "a foreign political authority on Chinese soil" that was, bizarrely, not even directly answerable to the British Consul.[57] What began as a ghetto for foreign individuals therefore gradually became that oxymoronic thing: an extraterritorial statelet, a polis with no common citizenship, and a semisovereign semicolony that made no claim to the land beyond that represented by thousands of private real estate contracts.

In this way, Shanghai was divided into multiple jurisdictions, including the demimonde of the "External Roads Area" (or "badlands"), a Chinese neighborhood in which the Shanghai Municipal Council built streets, extended utility services and thus claimed the right to raise taxes and dispatch its police force.[58] To the International Settlement and French Concession, then, we can add the ambiguous phenomenon of this "extraconcessional" neighborhood: the edgeland's very own edgeland. In this ambiguously subdivided city, fugitives from Chinese justice thrived in plain sight, safe from molestation by local police who could not cross (often notional) borders staffed by French gendarmes or Sikh constables. One had to possess three different driving licenses to navigate the multiple jurisdictions of the city.[59] In André Malraux's *La Condition Humaine* (1933), a philosophical thriller about the 1927 communist uprising in Shanghai, the novel's polyglot crew of revolutionaries cross and recross "l'avenue des Deux Républiques" between the Chinese city they wish to enflame and the French Concession they despise but that provides them sanctuary from the forces of the Kuomintang.[60] And if the political geography of Shanghai was complicated in 1927, it became even more so after 1937, when the Chinese-governed sections of the city were occupied by the Japanese. From that point, the International Settlement and French Concession survived as a *gudao*, or "lone islet," within occupied China—a coinage that draws on the Mandarin words *"gu'er* (orphan) and *gujun* (lone army [of resisters])" and "can also mean a haven, an oasis that afforded protection in a realm of violence."[61] Although they remained areas of extraterritorial privilege, the foreign enclaves now offered refuge to Chinese citizens, businesses, and political interests (both nationalist and communist) seeking to escape the Japanese.[62] As Frederic Wakeman puts it, after 1937 Shanghai "became a contested battleground in and of itself, if only because Japan could not take the international sections over forcibly without risking war with England and the United States."[63] Such was the city that the narrator of *Empire of the Sun* describes as a landscape of "real war," a world away from the heraldry and heroics of the Battle of Britain. This is the world in which the distinction between political friend and enemy has been effectively dissolved: "In a real war no one knew which side he was on, and there were no flags or commentators or winners. In a real war, there were no enemies" (6).

Extraterritorial Shanghai is a good example of what Aihwa Ong, writing about a later stage in Asian political and economic development, calls "graduated sovereignty," in which the differential management of peoples— here, defined by the way Chinese and foreign residents of the same city were subject to different legal regimes—"variously regulate the forms of belonging (citizenship) and produce the condition of order and stability (sovereignty)."[64] For Ong, the ability to graduate sovereign claims, or render flexible the category of the citizen, represent fundamental aspects of the modern state system. These are practices that may be particularly valuable to governments today, given the new powers of global markets and transnational regulatory agencies, but, as we saw in chapter 1, the idea that sovereign territoriality can be subdivided is far from new—in fact, it is not the historical exception, but the rule.

For an interwar nationalist such as Shih Shun Liu, however, such a perspective was intolerable: for Shih, modernity means territoriality means indivisible sovereignty. And because of this, his invective against what he saw as the anachonristic and decadent institution of extraterritoriality comes to embody the very spatiotemporal contradictions it protests. Shu-mei Shih explains that the writings of interwar nationalists tend to be characterized by a distinction between the "metropolitan" and "colonial" aspects of Western modernity, a dichotomy in which metropolitan modernity was "prioritized as an object of emulation" while the actual colonial policies of metropolitan states remained objects of critique.[65] Thus, while demanding an end to foreign colonial privilege, nationalists such as Shih Shun Liu nevertheless position the Westphalian nation-state as the telos of political development. Moreover, by implicitly separating the metropolitan and colonial aspects of Western modernity, Shih Shun Liu subdivides the temporal structure of modernity itself. He argues that China is politically underdeveloped because extraterritoriality has been kept alive by the imperial powers in the pursuit of their own interests. In an ideal sense, then, extraterritoriality represents the Western betrayal of its own deep nature—for when a modern nation-state insists on extraterritorial privilege, it is no longer behaving authentically, no longer being essentially modern. At the same time, however, Shih knows very well that the Western powers defended extraterritoriality in China by insisting that Chinese norms and institutions were not fit to regulate modern commercial practices.[66] Therefore, from this perspective, it is only by preserving a premodern legal institution that Western powers can pursue the economic life of the modern nation-state. To be practically modern they must be inauthentically modern; to build their futures, they must exhume their past.[67]

This contradiction explains why, as interwar visitors from British observed, life among the British colonial classes in the extraterritorial concessions combined the trappings of modern cities with a parochial culture that seemed "backward" by their own metropolitan standards. Five years after Maugham wrote his sketches, Arthur Ransome described the British in Shanghai as having constructed "the Ulster of the East."[68] The phrase implies that the British settlers are, like the unionist protestants of Northern Ireland, as blind to the long-term interests of the British state as they are contemptuous of the rights of the Chinese. More than this, in their very provincialism, they have cut themselves off from the current of modernity:

> Whereas both England and China have been profoundly affected by the [First World War], the Shanghailanders behave and talk as if the events that have followed 1914 had passed, so far as they are concerned, in a different planet. For them the last important political event was the suppression of the Boxers. Europe is far away from them and China, at their very doors, seems almost as far. They seem to have lived in a comfortable but hermetically sealed and isolated glass case since 1901.[69]

The meanings of extraterritoriality are not unidirectional. In tearing the fabric of Chinese national space, extraterritorial law creates uncanny temporal lags and disturbances, even within the foreign concessions themselves. This is the condition that W. H. Auden and Christopher Isherwood observed when, visiting Hankow in 1938, they described the White Russians who sought refuge in the foreign concession there after the October Revolution: "They have all drifted here somehow . . . and here they must stop; nobody else will receive them. They have established an insecure right to exist—on Nansen passports, Chinese nationality-papers of doubtful validity, obsolete Tsarist identity-certificates as big as table-cloths, or simply their mere impoverished presence. . . . 'Their clocks, says Auden, 'stopped in 1917. It has been tea-time ever since.'"[70] Here, the refugees' "right to exist" is guaranteed by the Chinese Republic's division into a crazy quilt of sovereignties. And yet the sanctuary afforded by extraterritoriality condemns the White Russian to an existence out of time, as the citizen of an "obsolete" empire that died two decades ago. Auden's witticism exposes how, in semicolonial China, what Benedict Anderson famously dubbed the "homogeneous, empty time" of the nation actually includes all sorts of temporal pockets or loopholes.[71] Anderson describes how nationalism conceives of the nation-state as "a solid community moving steadily down (or up) history."[72] That imagined community moves up toward the future, and down into the ancestral past, although it is supposed to do so as a unity. But, viewed from the standpoint of the extraterritorial, this community appears far from "solid." Its spatial perforation also implies the interruption of its steady movement toward the future, just as a hole below the water line will compromise the navigation of even the stateliest ocean liner. To adapt Jacques Derrida's remark about Hamlet's father: extraterritoriality desynchronizes, it recalls us to anachrony.[73]

This is the paradox that Shih Shun Liu's nationalism aims to address. His goal is to reset the clock of history, liberating and modernizing the state by unifying the space-time of the Chinese Republic. And yet the problem for such a nationalist project, as we have seen throughout this book, is that far from territorial sovereignty being "distinctly fatal" to extraterritoriality, the two are in practice far from inimical.

ORPHAN CITY

How do the extratemporal effects of extraterritoriality in China show up in Ishiguro's *When We Were Orphans*, a novel written several decades after the treaty port system was ended by Japanese invasion and Chinese revolution?

Orphans is narrated by Christopher Banks, an Englishman who grows up in the International Settlement. After the disappearance of his father, an employee of a British firm involved in the illegal opium trade, and his mother, a campaigner against that same business, Banks is exiled to an unfamiliar England whose customs he learns by reproducing the "gestures, turns of phrase and exclamations" of his peers.[74] Banks is at once an alien in England and a creature of foreign privilege in Shanghai: the sense of extraterritorial impunity he enjoys in China follows him home in the form of cultural and psychic loneliness.

Banks is obsessed by the mystery of his parents' disappearances, which he begins to associate with the fate of global peace. Compelled by his traumatic childhood to solve riddles and uncover evil, Banks grows up to become a detective after the fashion of Albert Campion or Peter Wimsey. After becoming famous for solving several notorious society crimes, he returns to the International Settlement in 1937, its extraterritorial privilege now cruelly accentuated by the fighting between China and Japan, which rages throughout the city without yet touching this orphaned island (*gudao*) of relative peace and security. Banks's mission is to find his parents, whom he rather absurdly believes to be preserved in a semipermanent state of captivity, an extratemporal and extraterritorial bubble, untouched by the violence of war. After a nightmarish sojourn in the blasted slums of Chapei (*Zhabei*), he is forced to realize that his mission is doomed to fail, finally understanding that, for all its privilege, the International Settlement is, in the words of his Japanese friend Akira, a ridiculously "fragile" zone that he cannot save from a world at war (274).

The illusion that 1930s Shanghai might contain islands of détente or suspended animation reappears in Ishiguro's screenplay for *The White Countess*, a 2005 movie directed by James Ivory and the last film Ivory produced in his famous partnership with Ismail Merchant. This rather turgid period romance centers on a blind and world-weary American ex-diplomat, Todd Jackson (played by Ralph Fiennes), who installs a White Russian aristocrat, Sofia Belinskya (Natasha Richardson, in her final role), as the hostess of his new Shanghai nightclub. Jackson's ambition for his club, which he renames after his sad and lovely hostess, is for it to be a sanctuary from his old public life—not so much a place of "permanent tea-time" as a version of the decadent "floating world" that so seduced the artist Masuji Ono in Ishiguro's second novel.[75] But Jackson's club is much more than a space of idle play. Although he initially tells Belinskya that the heavy doors of the White Countess are intended to "keep out the world," he also schemes with a Japanese government agent, Mr. Matsuda (Hiroyuki Sanada), to invite that very same world inside. When Matsuda first visits the White Countess, Jackson complains "there's no political tension in here" and declares that, without this element, his club will remain a mere "confection."[76] Matsuda therefore agrees to populate the White Countess with representatives of Shanghai's warring factions, from Western business types to communist intellectuals, Kuomintang soldiers to Japanese sailors. The club comes alive, animated by the dangerous balance between these groups. Indeed, the White Countess succeeds as a nightclub by becoming an International Settlement in miniature: a cosmopolitan space, secured for a while by Jackson's semicolonial entrepreneurialism, but marked by what M. A. Abbas calls the "cosmopolitanism of extraterritoriality," in which "colonial experience [has] shattered the innocence of difference."[77] As an allegorical stand-in for semicolonial enclaves in general, the White Countess is a zone of contact and exchange that threatens always to fall back into the chaos of war. And, as a "floating world" that sleeps during the day, the nightclub exists at a half-remove from the daylight time of politics and commerce while always maintaining its connection to that world of stratagems and clock-watching. Until its always doubtful potential is swallowed up by the Japanese invasion, the White Countess thrives for a time as a demi-monde in the most literal sense of that term: neither unified with the space-time of the city nor fully separate from it.

The White Countess tends toward the fantastic in the bad sense, being compromised throughout by what one reviewer called "a saucer-eyed belief in the intrinsic interest-value of aristocrats and people wearing dinner jackets."[78] But, in a broader sense—and especially in *When We Were Orphans*—Ishiguro's Shanghai is the product of what he calls "sufficient and hard research" in postcolonial historiography, period guidebooks, and local histories.[79] He understands the peculiarities of semicolonialism in China, which he contrasts with South Asia, "where the British [were] officially in power and India [was] a colony."[80] In Shanghai: "We're talking about unofficial imperialism . . . where the foreigners had won this thing called 'extraterritoriality' which meant that they were not subject to Chinese law. . . .

You have rival powers—British, Japanese, American, all trying to dominate economically, industrially, to exploit China—but with none of that sense of responsibility that came with colonizing countries."[81]

Ishiguro also insists, however, that historical verisimilitude is not his primary artistic goal: "[Shanghai] is a landscape," he says in a 2001 interview, "that I am using for my imaginative purposes."[82] As he said about the mid-century English settings of *The Remains of the Day* (1989), Ishiguro recreates historical spaces and periods not for their own qualities but as a way of writing "about my generation and the world around me."[83] As with Ghosh's *Ibis* trilogy, the extraterritorial dimensions of *Orphans* escape any single historical determination. Indeed, *Orphans* is far from the first Ishiguro novel to invoke feelings of extraterritorial displacement. In *The Unconsoled* (1995), for instance, Charles Ryder checks into a hotel in an unnamed central European town, where he has the following experience:

> I was just starting to doze off when something suddenly made me open my eyes again and stare at the ceiling. I went on scrutinizing the ceiling for some time, then sat up on the bed and looked around, the sense of recognition growing stronger by the second. The room I was in, I realized, was the very room that had serves as my bedroom during the two years my parents and I had lived at my aunt's house on the borders of England and Wales. I looked again around the room, then, lowering myself back down, stared once more at the ceiling. It had been recently re-plastered and re-painted, its dimensions had been enlarged, the cornices had been removed, the decorations around the light fitting had been entirely altered. But it was unmistakably the same ceiling I had so often stared up at from my narrow creaking bed of those days.[84]

Here, Ishiguro's narrator spins an ever-more-unreliable tale in which the architecture of a foreign hotel, despite being "entirely altered" from the supposed memory of the original, is "the same" as a bedroom in a British private home. In Shao-Pin Luo's analysis, this scene represents the way Ryder clings to objects and places that, because he invests them with phantasmal memories of family and home, provide a form of psychic compensation for the interrelated conditions of exile and orphanhood: "Exiles are always eccentrics who feel their difference," writes Edward Said in a passage Luo quotes, "as a kind of orphanhood."[85] In this context, though, we would be wise to substitute "extraterritorial" for "exile"—a better name for this uncanny dream of home, which focuses on a borrowed room, in an aunt's house, on the mobile border between nations.

Similar symbols and stories predominate in *Orphans*. After his desertion, Banks finds no solace in England, a place of "lanes and meadows [he knows] only from *The Wind in the Willows*, or else the foggy streets of the Conan Doyle mysteries" (54). When, on the first day of his voyage to London, the young Banks is consoled by the kindly Colonel Chamberlain—"Cheer up. After all, you're going to England. You're going home"—he feels only resentment: "As I saw it, I was bound for a strange land where I did not know a soul, while the city steadily receding before me contained all I knew" (29–30). Like Ryder, the only English "home" that Banks enjoys is in the household of an aunt. Although Banks describes how he came to master the behavioral codes of the English public schoolboy, his schoolmates recall him differently. In the novel's opening scene, Banks meets James Osbourne, whom he remembers from school as an unusually "well-connected" boy who might have taught him "something of the way things worked" (7). Osbourne, however, dismisses such "well-connectedness" as the desperate idée fixe of a lonely child: "My goodness, you were such an odd bird" (5). This judgment puzzles Banks, "since [his] own memory is that [he] blended perfectly into school life" (7). Later, after returning to Shanghai, Banks arranges to meet Morgan, another old schoolmate, for dinner. Once again, while Banks remembers him as an outcast, Morgan offers a rather different account: "You know, we should have teamed up. The two miserable loners. . . . We wouldn't have felt so left out of things if we'd done that" (196, 195). Says Banks: "I turned to him in astonishment" (195). Ryder's nostalgia is undercut by the matter-of-factness with which he insists on the impossible; similarly, Banks's supposedly ordinary Englishness is rendered foreign and extraordinary by these rival memories of his childhood.

The dinner in the French Concession introduces the scene that most clearly mirrors Ryder's dream of extraterritorial orphanhood. Without saying anything about where they are going, Morgan takes Banks into the International Settlement.[86] Their destination, it turns out, is the house in which Banks once lived with his parents. Although Banks does not at first know where he is, he finds the smell of the house "oddly comforting" and is eventually able to conclude that, despite "vast restructuring" and his inability to conjure more than the "haziest picture" of how things used to be, he is standing in "what used to be the entrance hall of our old Shanghai house" (197–99). As in the passage from *The Unconsoled*, Banks's certainty is undermined by his diction, the tentative and haunted nature of which suspends the illusion of realism without ever quite overturning the conventions of verisimilitude. This Kafkaesque stylistic affect is further enhanced when the present owner of the house, a wealthy Chinese man called Mr. Lin, not only confirms Banks's impression that he has come "home" but immediately refers to an "agreement," the result of which is that Lin now has to uproot his own family and return the house to Banks (201). Banks ends up accepting this extraordinarily generous offer, despite the fact that his family never actually owned Lin's house (it was the property of his father's employer) and despite possessing only a "vague recollection concerning some such arrangement" (201). In the context of semicolonial Shanghai, the "agreement" between Banks and Mr. Lin reads as a miniature parable of the unequal treaties and the way they legalized, by imbuing foreign persons with extraordinary authority, the expropriation of Chinese land.

Banks's return trip to Shanghai is an attempt to redeem his parenthood and, as the novel's title suggests, to place his orphanhood back in the past. But orphanhood and political identity are linked at root in this novel, and, as a result, the orphan's loss is not so easy to recover. Brian Finney explains how, in Ishiguro's fiction, "to be orphaned . . . becomes a trope for transnational identity, for being exiled from one's fatherland and motherland."[87] And orphanhood, as Alexander M. Bain first explained in this context, has an even more specific political meaning in Japanese-occupied Shanghai, when the International Settlement was referred to by the Chinese as *gudao*.[88] These connotations are all present in *Orphans*, from Banks's fear of deracination, to the scene in which the international elite watch the fighting in Chapei from the temporarily secure island of their high-rise hotel, to the way in which Banks's sojourn in no-man's-land culminates in his hapless invasion of a ruined Chinese home, inhabited by an orphaned girl who has been abandoned amid the corpses of her family.

Orphans is a novel about being orphaned in—and by—an orphan city. It is also about the irresistible urge to restart the clock of childhood and return to the fairyland of home. In her study of the orphan figure in the English novel, Nina Auerbach writes of the orphan's fundamental knowledge that "you can't go home again."[89] But, in Ishiguro's novel, orphanhood signifies both the premature termination of childhood and its perpetuation into the time of adulthood. Ishiguro's orphans grow up too soon because they experience the loss of their parents as a loss of innocence; this is why Jennifer, the orphan Banks adopts in the British-set middle section of the novel, senses that he will abandon her before he himself knows. Yet, despite their losses, Ishiguro's orphans remain childish because they still somehow remain within fantasy worlds of privacy and naïveté. In one incident, Banks goes to visit Jennifer at her boarding school before leaving for Shanghai. She suddenly stops and says: "When you're at school, you forget. Just sometimes. You count the days until the holidays like the other girls do, and then you think you'll see Mother and Papa again" (*O* 158). And, in an interview, Ishiguro describes Banks as possessed by a "kind of Eden-like memory of a time when you were in that childhood 'bubble,' when adults and parents led you to believe that the world was a better, a nicer place."[90] We have seen already how interwar texts depict Shanghai as at once hypermodern and stalled in a permanent teatime. We have also seen how contemporaneous theories of semicolonialism described it as constituted by putatively antithetical developmental regimes. In Ishiguro's use of the orphan trope, age and youth, experience and innocence, cynicism and optimism, likewise become not so much opposites as the nonorientable surfaces of a Möbius strip.

That's what happens at the level of character and story, but what about the broader aesthetic dimensions of Ishiguro's orphan story? Finney links the childishness of Banks's mission—the idea that he can not only rescue his parents and restore his lost home but, in doing so, put right a great evil—to *Orphans*'s status as a parody of golden age detective fiction: an

interwar genre, associated with writers such as Agatha Christie and Doro-
thy L. Sayers, that is often characterized as assuming that one can expiate
collective guilt by assigning individual blame and so "represents a primitive
desire for a prelapsarian world of innocence."[91] This critical take accords with
accounts of the detective genre as one in which narrative closure is closely
tied to a logic of moral or ideological restoration. For one distinguished contemporary practitioner, P. D. James, the English detective novel concerns
"a problem . . . which is solved, not by luck or divine intervention, but by
human ingenuity, human intelligence, and human courage" and therefore
"confirms our hope that, despite some evidence to the contrary, we live in
a beneficent and moral universe."[92] Ishiguro has confirmed this sense that
the golden age detective novel represented "a very poignant escapism on the
part of a generation that knew full well that evil and suffering in the modern world wasn't about a master criminal or a clever vicar who was poison-
ing people."[93] In these accounts, the generic qualities of *Orphans* that draw
on the golden age detective novel line up with the image of the orphan as
that oxymoronic thing: a disillusioned naïf.

The association of the golden age detective novel with moral benefi-
cence or restored innocence conflate ethical and formalist kinds of critical
discourse—a comingling that can be explained with the help of Tzvetan
Todorov's account of the detective novel as containing two distinct sorts of
story. The first kind of story, Todorov says, is "that of the crime," and the
peculiar thing is that it's "in fact the story of an absence: its most accu-
rate characteristic is that it cannot be immediately present in the book."[94]
The second story, which is present in the book, is that of the investigation
itself. But that story is also weird, since it "has no importance in itself"; it
functions only to mediate between the reader and the untold "story of the
crime."[95] The detective novel comes to a close when these stories meet—
that is, when the absence of the first story and the nullity of the second are
catalyzed into the plenitude of a solution that offers aesthetic, cognitive,
and moral satisfaction. Most important for us, these twin stories are marked
by disjunct sorts of narrative time, which must also be made to coincide.
The story of the crime is located in the past, but the story of the investigation occupies the present and points toward a future solution. The first story

occupies what Todorov calls the time of "the fable (*story*)" rather than "the subject (*plot*)." In the time of the fable, "there is no inversion in time, actions follow their natural order; in the plot, the author can present results before their causes, the end before the beginning."[96] Of course, few detective stories fully adhere to this structuralist paradigm. Still, as long as we're content to examine the genre from a certain distance, the detective novel not only appears to be predicated on the idea that the crimes of the past can be redeemed through the detective's moral labor; it projects the fantasy that the postlapsarian time of literary modernity might be brought into harmonious alignment with the folk temporality of the fable.

Ishiguro has described his novel's plot and tone as balanced on the question of how long Banks "can hang on to his little vision of how to deal with the problems of life."[97] *Orphans* thus contains two competing modes of narrative time, embodied within Banks himself, with the orphan story's axiom that childhood is a foreign country undercut by (and in turn undercutting) the detective genre's implication that one can indeed go home again. As these metaphors suggest, the novel's narrative temporalities correspond to its political geography, such that space and time are fused within the chronotope of the orphan city. For Banks, China is the space of disenchantment: it is there that he is deserted, left to the care of false uncles and faraway aunts. It is in England that he finds success as a detective and is encouraged in his fantasy of redeeming the past. Just as Ishiguro forces these narrative temporalities to combine and conflict within the generic and psychic identity of his protagonist, so, in terms of plot and setting, does the extraterritorial space of Shanghai crash China into England and traduce any simple division between zones of domestic innocence and foreign disillusionment. For this reason, though we can honestly say that Banks's time in England confirms his belief in the supernaturally restorative powers of the detective, it remains true that this faith was first born in the International Settlement, when "day after day [Banks and Akira] invented and played out endless variations on the theme of [his] father's rescue" (*O* 113). And, in one final paradox, if the generic division between orphan narrative and detective story implies that England is potentially a paradise regained—a small green world in which the guilty can be punished—then this ignores the fact that Banks is utterly lonely in England and never stops thinking of Shanghai as his "home village" (274). In its strange blend of narrative times and places, *Orphans* develops a generic and characterological allegory for extraterritorial personhood. As a disillusioned naïf, Banks personifies the untimely extraterritorial space-time of interwar Shanghai, which becomes more than a geography, or a way of governing—it becomes something approaching a way of life. In Ishiguro's story of innocence lost and regained and lost again, extraterritorial space makes for no kind of home, but it is the only home you get.

THE ORDINARY EXTRAORDINARY
J. G. BALLARD

In J. G. Ballard's Shanghai narratives, this same sense of spatiotemporal disjuncture is complicated and exceeded—and, with Ballard, it's usually best to begin with excess. The strange thing about his Shanghai narratives, then, is that they occasion an encounter not with excess in the form of variety but as repetition.

For all Ballard's often-noted iconoclasm, there is arguably no contemporary novelist with a more recognizable sensibility and style. Reviews of his work have long emphasized, whether in approbation or condemnation, the way it reiterates a signature iconography: "Birds, low-flying aircraft, pool after empty swimming pool"; "low-flying aircraft, wrecked automobiles, drained swimming pools, abandoned hotels"; "empty swimming pools, abandoned hotels, deserted runways."[98] But Ballard's novels don't only feature a repetitive sequence of symbols and images; they're also built around an unusually restricted range of plots, characters, and settings. It's this combination of recursive qualities that explains why the lexicographers of the *Collins English Dictionary* thought to add "Ballardian" to their stock of adjectives.[99] Ballardian fiction transgresses but doesn't transcend; it resists definition but ends up in the dictionary.

Consider, for instance, his 1988 novella, *Running Wild*. In this strange innovation on the police procedural genre, the adult residents of a luxurious gated community have been messily slaughtered. Their children have all disappeared. Scotland Yard sends a forensic psychologist, Dr. Richard Greville, to investigate. A white Englishman of middling age, he's more Lestrade than Holmes, but he eventually deduces what the reader has sensed for a while: terrorized by their perfect lives, the children have murdered their parents and run off to an existence of feral militancy. "By a grim paradox," Greville writes in his final report, "the instrument of the parents' deaths was the devoted and caring regime which they had instituted."[100]

Now compare this to *Cocaine Nights*, a 1996 novel set in a British retirement community in Spain. Frank Prentice is a popular bar owner in that community, Estrella de Mar. But as the novel opens we learn that he's confessed to murder and looks set for a long stay in prison. His brother, Charles Prentice, a white Englishman of middling age, arrives in Spain to seek out the truth. More Hastings than Poirot, Charles slowly discovers that Frank has become embroiled in a bizarre psychosocial experiment in which Estrella de Mar—one link in a chain of expatriate enclaves so sleepy that, within them, time is said to have died—is being shocked back into life by the programmatic commission of criminal acts.[101] Such licensed psychopathy is, Frank's coconspirators say, the only defense against a civilizational descent into dementia.

The list could go on. The same basic plot, character types, and setting also characterize *Super Cannes* (2000; voluntary psychopathy in a corporate campus), *Millennium People* (2003; academics and media types rebel in a condo development); and Ballard's final novel, *Kingdom Come* (2006; petty-bourgeois rioting in a megamall). This is a programmatic novelistic project, the reiterative nature of which Ballard explained as the effect of his youth in extraterritorial Shanghai: "A large part of my fiction," Ballard wrote in his posthumously published memoir, "has been an attempt to evoke [Shanghai] by means other than memory."[102] Talking to Hans Ulrich Obrist in 2003, he described his memories of Shanghai as having developed into "a set of images and rhythms, dreams and expectations that are probably the basic operating formulas that govern my life to this day."[103] In particular, the enclave settings of much of his work evoke nothing so much as the extraterritorial precincts of his youth, and, as we saw in brief at the start of this chapter, the space-time of his fictionalized Shanghai is defined by a fossilized futurity redolent of the untimely semicolonial city.

The intriguing thing, however, is that Ballard's account of life in Shanghai—and particularly the account of Lunghua given in *Empire of the Sun* and elsewhere—contrasts greatly with that provided by his fellow internees. And so how, in the light of these discrepancies, can we better understand Ballard's claim, as Martin Amis explained it in a sympathetic newspaper interview and profile, that in writing the story of his youth in Shanghai he finally "[gave] shape to what shaped him?"[104] What does this claim really owe to the history of the orphan city?

Answering this last question requires exploring the terrain of the "ordinary extraordinary." By this I mean to evoke and rename a problem we encountered earlier in this book: the way speculative fiction confronts the problem of making bizarre events believable. This is certainly how Miéville, remember, describes weird and speculative genres, which he says begin by positing "something impossible" and then grant that impossibility "its own terms and systematicity."[105] This duality makes novels like *Cocaine Nights* at once "carnivalesque" and "rationalist," for they limn social upheaval even as they ascribe predictable causes to disorderly effects.[106]

The Ballardian version of this problem is that, while his novels depict worlds blown apart by violent criminality, they also render such violence ordinary. In his novel set in the French corporate campus, *Super-Cannes*, the libidinal frisson of mugging a stranger answers the dilemma of how one sustains life within "an Eden without a snake," a world denuded of temptation and, thus, of transgression and guilt.[107] "People are like children, they need constant stimulation," claims the Dionysian tennis pro, Bobby Crawford, in *Cocaine Nights*: "Name me a time when civic pride and the arts both flourished and there wasn't extensive crime."[108] In this way, the criminal acts that take place so often in Ballard's late fiction represent versions of therapeutic antigenic assault, as in a vaccine, on the overly regulated and somnolent social body of his Spanish expat community. Crime may be extraordinary, but, in Ballard's novels, it's not only performed against a backdrop of deadly ordinariness; crime only becomes meaningful when set within this problem of social blandness.

But when crime becomes programmatic, it risks losing its exceptional and antigenic status. Because criminal acts are therapeutic responses to a supposedly basic psychosocial problem, each unlawful act tends toward predictability and abstraction. There's obviously a difference of kind and degree between a petty cocaine deal and a murder. Still, taken as a whole—which is, after all, how we are encouraged to take them—the social and affective qualities that make any particular outrage outrageous here disappear before the generalizable fact of a generic transgress. At a certain point, it no longer really matters much what anybody actually *does*, only that they *ought not to be doing it*.

And things get more ordinary, still. For instance, because the late novel cycle reiterates the same few basic elements, predictability gets baked into its very aesthetic. I've described Ballard's fiction as often becoming programmatic in nature—and it's true, his double commitment to genre fiction and the post-Surrealist avant-garde clearly lends his work a recursive quality, the novels methodically working through a deliberately restricted range of formal and social types. But one could also say that the late novels are not just programmatic: they can be boring. It isn't just that their protagonists tend to blur together; the same is true of their antagonists. Wilder Penrose from *Super-Cannes* is a psychologist, while Bobby Crawford is a tennis pro, but they possess the same saturnine physicality, habit of speech-making, and gift for divining people's needs. Likewise, Dr. Tony Maxted, the psychiatrist figure in *Kingdom Come*, shares a muscular body with Penrose and a surname and profession with Dr. Harold Maxted, one of the adult victims in *Running Wild*, notwithstanding the fact that "Maxted" is a name familiar to Ballard readers from one of the surrogate father figures in *Empire of the Sun*. The qualities that make Ballard's late fictions unusual are the same ones that, over the course of a sequence like the one that stretches from *Cocaine Nights* to *Kingdom Come*, produce an aesthetic affect similar to that which Sianne Ngai calls "stuplimity," in which "astonishment is paradoxically mixed with boredom."[109]

The problem of extraordinary ordinariness is, at root, a variation on that of the exception and the rule. In *Cocaine Nights*, Bobby Crawford's criminal spree shakes up Estrella de Mar and is thus a kind of diversion from the norm. And yet Bobby isn't a revolutionary; he just believes criminality creates a better sort of retirement community. Ballard's antagonists don't advocate for revolutionary alternatives, unimaginable from within the penumbra of the present. They are more like Bodin's sovereign prince, who embodies the law by standing beyond it. We are back, here, with the kind of decisionist political thought that underlies the extraterritorial spatial relation that, as we saw in chapter 2, Giorgio Agamben calls "the exceptio," in which the thing excluded proves to be constitutive of that which it stands outside.[110]

An extraterritorial spatial logic therefore underlies Ballard's late settings, which, like the International Settlement in which he grew up, function as outsides within the inside of a territory. In *Millennium People*, the Chelsea Marina housing development is described as a "re-education" and "labour camp"; it is dubbed an "anomalous enclave" and, eventually, compared to a "republic."[111] In *Kingdom Come*, the Metro-Centre mall complex is described as a "Republic" as well as "a self-contained universe."[112] Yet as much as these places stand apart, like so many Liechtensteins piercing the British body politic, they also typify, as we have seen, what Ballard thought of as a wider process of social and economic enclosure, in which the professional and middle classes have emigrated from social and civic life by enclosing themselves in gated communities and campuses.

But Ballard's enclave settings have a more particular historical source and referent—in fact, Ballard himself repeatedly told us how to fix his enclave settings in space and time. The earliest version of this answer comes in a 1963 essay-manifesto, "Time, Memory, and Inner Space," in which the question "How far do the landscapes of one's childhood . . . provide an inescapable background to all one's imaginative writing?" prompts the answer that the future setting of his novel *The Drowned World* (1962) represents the "fusion of my childhood memories of Shanghai and those of my last ten years in London."[113] He writes of Shanghai that his earliest memories of the city all take place "during the annual long summer of floods, when the streets of the city were two or three feet deep in a brown silt-laden water, and where the surrounding countryside, in the center of the flood-table of the Yangtze, was an almost continuous mirror of drowned paddy fields and irrigation canals stirring sluggishly in the hot sunlight."[114] And, no doubt, his novels and stories make a great deal out of the symbolism of water out of place: not just drained swimming pools, but flooded fields, brackish drinking water, culverts and streams and great rivers clogged with the bodies of men and machines.

Following the critical and commercial success of *Empire of the Sun*, Ballard began to go further, arguing that his childhood memories supplied him with a kind of authorial firmware. This thesis is epitomized by his repeated use of the phrase "from Shanghai to Shepperton," which from the 1980s onward provided the title or subtitle to two memoirs and a collection of autobiographical journalism and was appropriated in 2006 for an academic conference on his work.[115] In that sibilant phrase, the city of Ballard's youth and the London suburb in which he lived for fifty years figure as original cause and sustaining effect of his personal and literary life. As Roger Luckhurst puts it in his crucial early book on Ballard, in the autobiographical narratives Shanghai becomes "a disjunct temporal zone" that projects the "future dissolution" of both Britain's colonial past and its "neo-colonial" present. In this untimely chronotope, the borders around the International Settlement describe "a strange loop of time [in which] memories of the past, as already future, maroon the present."[116] Ballard's settings all look the same, their creator says, because they are all allegories of Shanghai, reborn to us as the future past of a catastrophic present.

There's no gainsaying the literary effects of this autocritical gambit. The enclave zones of the late novels, circumscribed by boundaries and punctuated by gatehouses, very obviously evoke the borders of the International Settlement and Lunghua camp as they are depicted in *Empire*. Beyond even this, there's the way *The Kindness of Women*, the 1991 sequel and supplement to *Empire*, takes this spatial resemblance and makes it the basis for a grand autocritical myth in which every landscape in Ballard's fiction—European or Asian, earthly or extraterrestrial—is reworked into a transmuted memory of Lunghua. Thus, when that novel's first-person narrator, "Jim Ballard," is accused of mooning about the airfields and wetlands of East Anglia and West Canada wearing a "Lunghua look," he insists that what one person experiences as traumatic memory, another reinvents as a kind of poetry: "People create their own mythologies," he says, having just described a dead Turkish aviator, his plane suspended in the waters of a Canadian lake, as having flown "home" (*K* 106). Ballard has described *Kindness* as narrating "my life seen through the mirror of the fiction prompted by that life."[117] It is a metafictional novel, beginning in and often educing Shanghai, about a writer's impossible struggle to be "wholly done with the past" (311). That struggle is "impossible" because it involves trying to move beyond, through artistic means, the original violence that stimulates the protagonist's aesthetic imagination. This is an unlikely prospect for a Ballardian hero. After all, this is the author who insisted "psychopathology should be kept alive as a repository, probably the last repository, of the imagination."[118]

Being done with the past is also impossible in another sense. If *Kindness* narrates Jim's struggle to stop turning his trauma into art, then this plot-line collides directly with the novel's second metafictional aspect: the way it's constructed out of systematic allusions to the real Jim Ballard's body of fiction. Each chapter of *Kindness* evokes one of its author's best-known works. Thus, most obviously, the opening chapters conjure, rewrite, and supplement *Empire*. The chapter titled "The Exhibition" doesn't mention *Crash*, but that novel has been rightly described as its "invisible, radiating centre."[119] Most typically, *Kindness* will evoke a previous work without much distorting the weave of its own narrative. In the chapter titled "Magic World," for instance, Jim watches his children play in their new suburban home: "Water surrounded Shepperton—the river, the gravel lakes, and the reservoirs of the metropolitan water board whose high embankments formed the horizon of our lives. Once I told Miriam that we were living on the floor of a marine world that had invaded our minds, and that the people of Shepperton were a new form of aquatic mammal, creatures of a new *Water Babies*" (117).

There's nothing here too disruptively metadiegetic. Alert readers would soon notice, however, that Jim's *Water Babies* story recalls *The Drowned World*, the surreal postapocalyptic novel he would have been writing at this point in his life: a tale, set in 2145, in which human survivors of planetary flooding uncover the floor (it happens to be London) beneath the tropical lagoon in which they've gathered. At the end, *The Drowned World*'s protagonist, haunted by an "ancient organic memory," flees south into the sea, betting on the unfinished business of evolution and seeking rebirth as a "second Adam."[120]

All of this points back to Ballard's description of *Kindness* as "not just an autobiographical novel" but one "written with the full awareness of the fiction that that adult life generated."[121] What Jim experiences as a personal dilemma, *Kindness* restages at the level of an oeuvre. Ballard positions what happened in Shanghai as the tropological and topological key to a compulsively iterative literary world, including the one conjured by *Kindness* itself. That novel ends with a series of scenes that initially promise release from this cycle of repetition. Jim is in Los Angeles to attend the premiere of Stephen Spielberg's film adaptation of *Empire*. He imagines that seeing his childhood projected onscreen has freed him "in a profound catharsis": "All the powers of modern film had come together for this therapeutic exercise. The puzzle had solved itself; the mirror, as I had promised, had been broken from within" (*K* 341). Shortly before, he has finally consummated his passion for the White Russian nanny of his early adolescence: "We had both been wounded and corrupted by Shanghai . . . and by making love in this California hotel we would prove to each other that the wounds had healed" (339). And yet, as this unlikely fantasy suggests, the story doesn't end there. Jim and his partner, Cleo, take one last trip to the Pacific coast. They witness the launching of a papyrus boat modeled on Thor Heyerdahl's *Ra*, a "replica of a replica" that can't help but remind us of Spielberg's cinematic remaking of Ballard's own fictionalization of his childhood—especially since it, too, is being filmed by an onboard cameraman. Jim again muses that he's recovered the happiness lost to him as a child: "All the murdered dead of a world war had made their peace" (342). But this happy possibility is undercut by his description of the boat, which, beset by lively winds and waves, soon escapes its handlers and is last seen "setting a course across the Pacific, with only its shanghaied cameraman as a crew" (343). At the very same moment that *Kindness* imagines an end to Jim's "Lunghua look," it restores that compulsion to us in its invocation of a "shanghaied" imagination. Even as Jim claims that his Chinese puzzle has solved itself, he is unable to conceive of any other course than that which leads "towards the China shore" (343).

UNRELIABLE ORPHAN

The problem, though, is that Ballard is an unreliable witness to his past. His novels contain acknowledged instances of fictionalization, notably in the way *Empire of the Sun* writes Ballard's parents and sister out of his war story, formalizing and simplifying a complicated story of traumatic privation into another kind of orphan story. That novel is also clearly marred by stereotypical depictions of the Shanghainese as passive victims of a geopolitical struggle that they don't even try to direct or control. The British Library papers relating to Ballard's 1941–43 internment in the Japanese-run Lunghua Civilian Assembly Center also contain correspondence dismissive of basic elements of *Empire*. A letter from former internee F. T. Ranson criticizes core elements of that novel's narrative geography ("the Whangpoo [River] was not visible from the camp and anyway you say it was to the west when in fact it was to the east") and accuse Ballard of making up some events ("I never heard of any collaboration") and ignoring others: "There were escapes—Roy Scott and Louis (forget his name) made it to West China."[122] Above all, these correspondents dislike *Empire*'s "lurid" depiction of camp culture, in which British can-do spirit devolves into late imperial lassitude, and in which the protagonist identifies strongly with the Japanese who defeated the British: "I can't help being surprised that you should express admiration for the Japanese and at the same time report that they beat a coolie to death," writes G. S. Dunkley of Henley-on-Thames. "Morale in the camps was uniformly good and British internees were far from being remiss in carrying out the many menial jobs which had to be done."[123]

One can imagine Ballard disdaining these letters as the work of men inert to distinctions between fiction and history. I mention them not because they have surpassing evidentiary value but because they suggest how we might historicize Ballard's persistent recourse to the space of the exceptio in terms that aren't reducible to autocritical mythmaking.[124] By granting us a historical point of contrast outside the circle of Ballard's own life and oeuvre, the Lunghua folders provide grounds for speculation about what his enclave settings mean for the historicity of his fiction in general. And when we step outside the loop of Ballard's autointerpretation, we don't only learn more about his novels; those texts also tell us more about the worlds they represent, and in which they were made.

Ballard's representation of Lunghua agrees with the one provided by his fellow internees in one crucial way: that the camp was an enclave unto itself. The Ballard Papers include the files of William Braidwood, president of the British Residents' Association of Shanghai (BRA) during the Lunghua internment and Ballard's father's closest friend. Among Braidwood's files is a narrative history of Lunghua that refers to a Japanese mandate that the camp be self-governing and self-sufficient, even requiring that the internees must themselves punish any civilian who dares to escape from Japanese detention.[125] The Braidwood files also include much evidence of internee initiative and organizational capacity. Soon after internment began, the BRA instituted itself as a complex organism of camp government similar to the Shanghai Municipal Council in which Braidwood and many of his fellow inmates had served before the war. Before long, the BRA organized its myriad activities under departments of "Billeting, Kitchen, Public Works, Public Health, Hospital and Clinic, Stores and Canteen, Bank, Gardening and Camp Service."[126] The ambitious nature of camp governance can perhaps be measured by the narrative history's account of how its school, "Lunghwa Academy," provided "instruction in all general subjects up to Cambridge school leaving certificates and London Matriculation standards."[127]

Margaret Braidwood did not send her husband's files to Ballard until 1996, years after the publication of *Empire* and *Kindness*—though they were in his keep during the writing of *Miracles of Life*. Their value for us lies in the way they show how the space of the enclave can, without disturbing our sense of its exceptionality, be identified with very different kinds of social practice and ideological value than the extraordinary ordinariness of the disjunct zones we find in Ballard's novels. The BRA papers evidence Mark Mazower's complaint—aimed at Agamben's *Homo Sacer*—that exceptional zones, even in extrajudicial detention camps such as Lunghua, aren't only characterized by the reduction of *homo politicus* to a state of bare life.[128] Such zones can also be more ordinarily ordinary, in the limited sense that, even in straitened circumstances, people find ways to realize their social solidarities in a manner consistent with life beyond or before that zone. Mazower's point is that these gradations apply even to the system of Nazi Laager—and it isn't hard to extend that analysis to the less deadly and restrictive world of Lunghua.

The Braidwood files thus repeatedly affirm continuities across time, between Lunghua now and the Shanghai International Settlement as it was; as such, they minimize the present spatial and temporal break between life in Lunghua and lives lived in prewar Shanghai. Braidwood's Lunghua is still the exception that proves the rule, but not in the sense that the camp represents, as it would for Agamben, the localization of a state of affairs that is at once peculiar to the camp and general throughout society. No, for Braidwood, the camp is, like Ishiguro's White Countess, the present materialization of a *past* state of affairs: a historical bubble, filled with habits of thought and action that did not die with the International Settlement's fall, and that might continue after life in Lunghua also comes to an end.

Braidwood's reports are bureaucratic in nature, not introspective. His memos and histories nevertheless give the sense that, for this volunteer servant of the British Empire, principles of self-governance and mutual aid were more crucial facts of war than the internees' physical or mental suffering. There's obviously some measure of positive thinking going on; it helps, psychologically and politically, to act as though things can and will continue to be what they were, and mean what they did, before the collapse of semicolonial rule in Shanghai. But the Braidwood papers also contain something worth holding on to. That something is consistent with

Mazower's remarks about the way some camps are more exceptional than others, but it's even more in tune with Elaine Scarry's ethical contention that the "acts of thinking" that persist even within states of exception tend not to be recognized as such.[129] For Scarry, emergency zones need not be, as Agamben describes them, "kenomatic"—empty of law or reason.[130] As with the kinds of routinized thought that characterize the actions of paramedics, or that are enshrined in mutual aid contracts between towns vulnerable to natural disasters, the times and places of an emergency can be thick with moral and social consequence. "In an emergency," Scarry writes, "the habits of ordinary life may fall away, but other habits come into play, and determine whether the action performed is fatal or benign."[131] Against extraordinary ordinariness, where the exception becomes the rule, Scarry attends to the resilience and diversity of the ordinary itself. The habits of life that persist within an emergency are still, in a sense, exterior to it. But that constitutive exteriority is temporal, rather than strictly spatial, since emergency actions represent ways of acting and thinking decided upon in the part of the past that's ahead of events, before ordinary life became extraordinary.

Braidwood didn't always find it easy to be sanguine. Lunghua camp was, however we conceive of it, a terrible and unpredictable place. This difficulty is epitomized in a note from his narrative history, which now exists as a scrap of paper floating in a Mylar sleeve: "Barbed-wire surrounded the camp. On the whole the camp was a pleasant one with plenty of space and a number of trees."[132] It's a strangely affecting fragment, with its paratactic swing from barbed wire to open space and the bathos of its meager "number of trees," a quality enhanced by Braidwood's uncharacteristic lapse into semiredundancy, his repetition of the noun "camp" drawing attention to the disjuncture between the fragment's apostrophes. The fragment suggests something of the strain Braidwood must have experienced in pitting his indefatigable industry against the guards' violence, his compatriots' pain and restlessness, and Britain's retreat from empire. Something of the same tone creeps into his November 1945 address to the BRA, which leavens an admission of Britain's diminished global power with the promise that "Chinese leaders have frequently stated that foreign capital will be welcome and . . .

that foreign technicians [are] both necessary and welcome."[133] But it wasn't to be thus. After the 1949 revolution, both Braidwood and Ballard's father, James, were imprisoned by the Chinese and deported from the country. The chain of spatial and temporal continuities that Braidwood attempts to write and administer into being—colonial, wartime, postcolonial—could not be sustained in the context of world war, Chinese revolution, and British imperial retreat. Braidwood longs for continuity but what we get, again, is the synchonicity of the nonsynchronous: the extratemporal experience at the heart of the extraterritorial enclave.

The art of self-government didn't die in Lunghua, even if the end of the war did effectively conclude the semicolonial careers of men like William Braidwood and Ballard's father. The younger Ballard, however, will have none of their claims to continuity. It's no surprise that the political geography of Lunghua depicted in *Empire of the Sun* is determined by a violent power (Japanese and, later, American) that remains—spatially, synchronically—*outside within* the camp's precincts. Likewise, that novel associates Japanese captivity not with municipal solidarities but with situations in which "anyone who sacrificed himself for the others soon died too" (90). Rather than yearning for temporal continuity between prewar enclave and wartime camp, Ballard doubles down on the extratemporal. His Lunghua is a decidedly heterochronic zone, at once the continuation and demise of the prewar extraterritorial city. Lunghua is "my new Shanghai," Jim says in *Empire* (69). But the space-time of the war is also described by Jim as a "peculiar space"—and, here, the shift to past tense is important—that separates him from "the fifty year-long cocktail party that had been Shanghai" (55, 59).

Ballard's Lunghua is also anything but British, unless that noun names not a nationality but a condition of unacknowledged loss. Like Estrella de Mar, Lunghua may be full of British people, but its very existence signals a loss of national integrity: the "Dream of Empire" died, Ballard insists, with Japan's victories in Singapore, Hong Kong, and Shanghai.[134] The kinds of enclave space that persist in the late sequence are still scattered about the map, but they are increasingly privatized and they have come home, colonizing European space itself. More than that, Britain's defeat by the Japanese confirmed a reality that, for Ballard, the International Settlement had itself long symbolized. As he depicts it, that enclave was always a zone apart within the British Empire as much as the Chinese Republic. "With its newspapers in every language and scores of radio stations, Shanghai was a media city before its time," he writes: "90% Chinese" and "100% American-ised."[135] In *Miracles of Life*, Ballard says that at Lunghua he became an American patriot.[136] In *Empire*, the protagonist looks at his countrymen and realizes that "he was closer to the Japanese" (104). In his 1993 essay "First Impressions of London," Ballard wrote of how foreign the English capital appeared to him when he first saw it in 1946: "Like Bucharest with a hangover—heaps of rubble, an exhausted ferret-like people defeated by war and still deluded by Churchillian rhetoric."[137] Even in the 1990s, he insisted that such fantastic delusion was still going strong: "To understand London now one has to grasp the fact that in this city, as nowhere else in the world, World War II is still going on."[138] To insist on the spatial logic of the exceptio is, in this context, to insist—against Braidwood and his institutional-ized optimism—that the British myth of imperial wholeness, of historical continuity and integrity, was fractured at the root in Shanghai. When Bal-lard's Shanghai fictions insist on the geography of the outside within, they protest against a symbolic national geography and national history in which everything always "holds . . . together," no matter how drearily and no mat-ter what the cost.[139] The International Settlement and Lunghua are spatial figures for a Britain that is no longer identical with itself, and in extrater-ritorial Shanghai never was.

Lunghua is only ordinary—not the end of the world but just an episode to be endured—if one can first of all push back through time: back to a world more pleasant, with a number of trees, but a world that is false to Ballard. His enclave world subjects social space to an authority that stands outside: an authority that is alien, even extraordinary, and is therefore the very thing his protagonists desire or seek to be. Ballard's alert readers knew that already. But the Braidwood papers let us know it differently, as part of an historical argument about the fate of British imperial spaces and values, and not just as a claim about an author's psychopathology.

By examining Braidwood's alternate version of Lunghua, we can better understand how and why Ballard's settings so relentlessly extraterritorial-ize social and political space. The historical thrust of Ballard's oeuvre shouldn't be reduced to its topical subjects: war in the East, drugs on the Costa, malls in the Shires. His extraterritorial fiction is not only about the twenty-first-century world of condo developments and research campuses. In its narrative geography, as well as in its self-conscious puncturing of bourgeois values, it is directed against the extraordinary fact that, for the people among whom Ballard lived in Lunghua and after, a lost national past still seemed to be the ordinary business of life. Ballard's late sequence is a machine for the production of settings that dislocate social space and time, settings that open out onto his version of Lunghua but close the book on another. Within and behind the production of sameness in the form of a sequence lies the rupture that was Shanghai and Lunghua. The journey "from Shanghai to Shepperton" doesn't just establish a repetitive relation between juvenile social cause and adult literary effect. The preposition "from" also, and more simply, describes a movement between two very different places and states. For all the contemporary glamour of millennial fictions such as *Cocaine Nights*, they're not only compelled to repeat but, in repeating, to repeatedly disavow a colonial version of the historical past.

CONCLUSION

The Extraterritorial Novel

This book has studied spatial and personal aspects of extraterritorial experiences and artworks, and it has analyzed their liberatory and coercive features: their tendency to puncture as well as enclose. In the prose works of the late German writer W. G. Sebald, all four types of extraterritoriality are mobilized to strangely compelling effect, such that this book's central concept and keyword sometimes seems to float free of any singular historical determination.[1] It's thus with Sebald that I consider whether the novel itself can be called "extraterritorial."

Sebald's oeuvre affords us a powerful last example of the mutuality between extraterritoriality of place and person, as well as the way stories about extraterritorial place and personhood produce extratemporal artistic effects. In an early moment of a late essay on Vladimir Nabokov, Sebald describes the "young emigrants" who populate the Russian writer's early novels: "Unversehens auf die falsche Seite geraten, fristen sie in Mietszimmern und Pensionen als Luftsmenschen ein quasi extraterritoriales, irgendwie illegitimes Nachleben" (Unexpectedly finding themselves on the wrong side of the frontier, they are airy beings living a quasi-extraterritorial, somehow unlawful afterlife in rented rooms and boardinghouses).[2] To be extraterritorial in this way is not to be immune to politics or the law; it is to become an accidental outlaw occupying a suspended state between nations, between idea ("airy") and thing, and between staying ("afterlife") and going ("rented rooms"). Even though, in this passage, "extraterritoriales" hardly stands in for unalloyed freedom, everything about the sentence, including Sebald's qualifying phrases ("quasi-"; "irgendwie"), make its meanings broadly figurative. As a quality of "life" or "afterlife," extraterritoriality appears to express not a problem of jurisdiction but an affect of bereft cosmopolitanism. It's because of this kind of sentence that one critic implies that "extraterritorial" provides the keyword for the ethical dilemma at the heart of all Sebald's writing, asking: "How does one signal solidarity with the victims of Nazi genocide without denying one's own German origins?" The answer: "To live for thirty years in extraterritorial limbo."[3]

It's not a gratuitous connection. Sebald reaches for the word "extraterritorial" when describing sites that are emblematic of some of his most characteristic themes: war, immigration and exile, the destruction of natural and built environments, the relationship between personal and institutional memory, genocide, and more. The adjectival form of the word occurs, for example, in *The Emigrants* (1992), when Max Ferber, a Jewish refugee from the Nazis, calls his German homeland "a curiously extraterritorial place, inhabited by people whose faces are both lovely and dreadful."[4] It returns in *Austerlitz* (2001) in a description of the concentration camp at Theresienstadt as an "extra-territorial place" beyond law and mercy.[5] And, in *The Rings of Saturn*, the abandoned atomic testing site at Orford Ness in the English coastal county of Suffolk is introduced as having "an extraterritorial quality about it."[6] It's a suitable phrase for a place that locals call "the Island" but that is actually a shingle peninsula, only a short boat ride across the River Alde from Orford village and linked to the mainland a few miles to the north.

The extraterritorial seems, then, like a signature aspect of Sebald's oeuvre. And, if we turn for a minute to the work of his compatriot and fellow exile, Siegfried Kracauer (1889–1966), who also featured very briefly in this book's introduction, we can begin to see how this highly figurative and overdetermined kind of extraterritoriality might be connected to the novel as such.

In his biographical essay "The Extraterritorial Life of Siegfried Kracauer," Martin Jay quotes the address Kracauer appended to a letter he wrote to T. W. Adorno and Leo Lowenthal in the 1920s: "The headquarters of the transcendental homeless."[7] Following this clue, Jay associates Kracauer's interest in extraterritoriality with the "transcendental homelessness" that György Lukács says is characteristic of the modern novel in general.[8] In his *Theory of the Novel* (1916), Lukács argues that modernity is split between self and world, thought and action, social totality and representational forms.[9] In this context, the individual human subject is alienated and adrift at root—homeless in spirit, if not in actual fact. The novel registers this homelessness so exquisitely because, Lukács says, within it, aesthetic forms are split from the "transcendental structure of the form-giving subject."[10] In the novel, aesthetic form has become autonomous, a created totality in its own right, independent of a lost "totality of being" in which everything was once "already homogeneous" prior to being "contained by forms."[11] The novel's homelessness is the sign of a fracture within this "rounded" and integrated civilization, even the borders of which are "not different in essence from the contours of things" but marked "only relatively" and to preserve "a homogeneous system of adequate balances."[12]

Jay gathers several distinct aspects of Kracauer's life and thought under this figure of transcendental homelessness—the figure of an individual separated at root from a rounded and homogeneous world. There is Adorno's description of his friend's apparently Asiatic facial features as "extraterritorial," to which we can add Asja Lacis's description of him as "African" and Hans Mayer's suggestion that Kracauer looked like "a Japanese painted by an expressionist."[13] Most important, there is Kracauer's own sense of social exclusion, especially his victimization as a Jew after Hitler's rise to power, when he was systematically denied his profession as a journalist, stripped of his civil and political rights, and exiled from his home—first to France and then, making the journey through Spain that his friend Walter Benjamin couldn't complete, to the United States. The word "extraterritorial" is Kracauer's name for a general condition of marginality that realizes itself in an intellectual struggle to redeem "contingency from oblivion."[14] "Extraterritorial" denotes the breaking and decentering of the totality of being; it describes a quality of experience and thought in which the divisions between social categories have been made harder, more brittle, and therefore susceptible to fracture and rearrangement.

Most important in the context of our last chapter, such breakage and reordering applies to temporal as well as spatial experience. In his book *History: Last Things Before the Last* (1969), Kracauer inveighs against the idea that a great historian is a "son of his time."[15] Arguing that "the historian's 'historical and social environment' is not a fairly self-contained whole but a fragile compound of frequently inconsistent endeavors in flux," he contests what he calls "the whole assumption . . . that people actually 'belong' to their period."[16] Kracauer advocates instead for a "chronological extraterritoriality" that undoes historical present-mindedness by destroying the axiomatic link between historical periods and the characteristics of individuals and events.[17] As these passages imply, Kracauer doesn't seek to escape chronological extraterritoriality but, rather, to harness it for a revolutionary historiography that could resist becoming an instrument of capital, empire, or fascism. Indeed, Kracauer even tried to foster such extratemporality in his own person, notoriously refusing to admit his own true age.[18] His examples of chronological extraterritoriality come, above all, from the modern novel—for instance, from Marcel Proust's representation of reality as a palimpsest of memory and experience. Proust's narrative poetics, Kracauer writes, create a "near-vacuum of extraterritoriality," a "no-man's land" of style and sensibility in which a person is simultaneously present in historical time and withdrawn from it.[19] In Marcel's movements through and against history, Kracauer found the ideal model for extraterritorial personhood.

Had Kracauer lived to read Sebald, he would have had more grist to his mill. Sebald's observation about Nabokov's *Hotelmensch* is characteristic of his own narratives, which are persistently set on the road, on trains, in waiting rooms, or in temporary accommodations. This motif reaches its apogee in "Il ritorno in patria," the semiautobiographical conclusion to *Vertigo*. In this stilted but oddly moving narrative, the narrator returns to his child-hood village of "W." in southern Germany. Because this is a tale of home-coming, the reader stays alert for the pathos of return; in such a story, every place might reveal itself as a *lieu de mémoire*, rich in remembrance and association.[20] Instead, in a moment redolent of the bedroom scene in Ishiguro's *The Unconsoled*, Sebald's narrator tells us in his deadpan tone that the inn he's about to check into is one in which his family "had lived in rented accommodation . . . for several years."[21] It's a truly odd moment, in which the Odyssean voyager reaches his Ithaca only to note in passing that his home is a hotel and that, anyway, he can barely recognize the building, so changed is it now from the place he remembered.

Just as Sebald's narrators tend to be adrift in cultural and biographical space, so do they fail or refuse to "belong" to one temporal periods. In *Rings of Saturn*, the narrator journeys to the extraterritorial peninsula of Orford Ness by boat, the captain of which he mythologizes into a mute avatar of Charon, who rowed the dead across the rivers to Hades. Having crossed the River Alde, Sebald's narrator traverses an embankment and arrives on the Ness: "It was as if I were passing through an undiscovered country," he writes, "and I still remember that I felt, at the same time, both liberated and deeply despondent" (234/291). Not for the first time in his oeuvre, Sebald has recourse to Hamlet's famous metaphor for death as a kind of terra nullius, or outlaw territory.[22] The Ness's weird mix of desolations—natural and man-made, material and symbolic—finds a parallel in the narrator's feelings of being adrift in time as well as space: "Where and in what time I was that day at Orfordness I cannot say, even now as I write these words" (237/295).

In the end, however, Sebaldian extraterritoriality can't be equated with homelessness, transcendental or actual. With the exception of *Austerlitz*, Sebald's novels are peculiar novels—often more easily classifiable as trav-elogues, memoirs, or autofictions—but they don't finally fit the model of homelessness described by Lukács and translated into the language of extra-territoriality by Kracauer. Rather than suggesting the extraterritorial dimensions of the novel as such, Sebald returns us to where we began: with a vision of the extraterritorial as antithetical, contingent, and fully meaningful only in the light of some specific history. The first step in that journey back begins when we realize that Sebald is never entirely homeless.

Although home, for the narrator of *Vertigo* (1990), is a strange and unwelcoming hotel, it remains somewhere to which Sebald's narrators endlessly return. The extraterritorial feelings of the *Hotelmensch* signify an incomplete rupture: the double impossibility of ever going home or ever becoming completely homeless. John Zilcosky points out that "instead of providing accounts of nomadism, Sebald's stories [present] subjects who could *never become sufficiently uprooted.*"[23] As a metaphor for problems of cultural belonging, the legal and political language of extraterritoriality therefore stands in for Sebald's uncanny knowledge that homes—whether familial or political—are at once inescapable and intolerable. Here is an analogous dialectic, domesticated but structurally similar, to that which characterizes a subject of consular jurisdiction like the young Ballard—a figure who is both beyond the territory and a portable piece of sovereignty all to himself. Sebald's "extraterritorial" is more than literal, to be sure, but it still carries the weight of its material determinations. In invoking the extraterritorial as a figure for feelings of cultural estrangement, Sebald transforms the space of the transient home into a literary topos for his own ambivalent political relationship to postwar Germany: loyal in his disloyalty, maintaining his citizenship so as to mark the depth of his voluntary exile in Britain.

The Rings of Saturn's journey to Orford Ness illustrates well how Sebald expands and displaces the material histories of extraterritoriality while always keeping that history activated—if not at the forefront of our attention, then still lurking visible. His phrase "extra-territorial quality" doesn't just describe Orford Ness's natural and geological strangeness: remote but near, looking like the island it is not. The narrator says that, when he first visited in 1972, he thought the Ness "resembled a penal colony in the Far East" (*ROS* 233/290). The remark gets at the alien qualities of this windswept peninsula, the stony hump of which shelters the village of Orford from the frigid winds and tides of the North Sea. From the village, the view of the Ness itself is interrupted by low pasture, seemingly sunk below the level of the river and the beach; these verdant meadows were once part of

FIGURE 6.1 Atomic Weapons Research Establishment Laboratory 4, Orford Ness National Nature Reserve.

Credit: Matthew Hart.

an airfield, but squint and you might convince yourself that they're rice paddies. More than anything, the comparison to an Asian penal colony evokes the architectural vision of the two large concrete structures—Atomic Weapons Research Establishment (AWRE) Labs 4 and 5 (fig. 6.1)—that locals call "the pagodas" and that rise up, like ruined temples to some unknown god, from the stones. It takes little effort to imagine the Ness as a chunk of alien territory that has drifted down the Suffolk coast—and, actually, from a geological perspective that is exactly right. Sebald writes of the Ness that, "stone by stone, over a period of millennia, it had shifted down from the north across the mouth of the river Alde" (*ROS* 233/290).

Between World War I and the end of the Cold War, Orford Ness was a major weapons-testing site for the military and the AWRE. The Ness hosted the British Army's Experimental Flying Section during World War I and was the site of early developments in aerial bombing and gunnery, parachutes, aerial photography, and camouflage. In the 1930s and 1940s, the Ness was home to landmark Royal Air Force experiments with radar, rocketry, and bomb ballistics, including the testing of a 22,000-pound "earthquake bomb." In 1953, Orford Ness was selected as a major site for ballistics and environmental testing of Britain's independent nuclear bomb program.[24] During this period, the people of Orford were not only separated from "the Island" by the natural barrier of the Alde; they were kept out by fences and armed guards, by violent explosions and unaccountable noises, and by laws against the revelation of official secrets.

None of this makes Orford Ness a formally extraterritorial space: there's no doubt about the United Kingdom's jurisdiction, then or now, over the village and peninsula. But if we relax our definitional strictures for a bit, remembering that even supposedly inviolate zones like the UN headquarters don't embody an absolute outside to the territories from which they're carved, then the Ness's geographic and jurisdictional connection to Britain becomes exactly the point. Sebald's extraterritorial feelings about Orford Ness are not produced by separation alone but by the Ness's weird combination of integrity and isolation. Like many restricted military geographies, Orford Ness possesses an ambivalent relation to the national space in which it lies.[25] During the time of its military occupation, the Ness was off-limits to ordinary citizens, cut out of public space. Yet behind its fence the defense of the realm took place. There's a tension, then, between the Ness's ideological and infrastructural integrity to the state and its physical separation and enclosure from the surrounding countryside. The site's strategic usefulness depends on what—to return one last time to Agamben's useful (if limited) formulation—we must call its existing *outside within* the territory. It's not just the physical geography of the shingle spit, after all, that makes Sebald liken Orford Ness to foreign spaces such as an Asian penal colony. He also writes, in an obvious bit of hyperbole, that the Ness was once "no easier to reach than the Nevada desert or an atoll in the South Seas" (*ROS* 233/289). These aren't just any distant wildernesses. If the penal colony reference is partly explained by the architectural shape of pagodas, then these other geographical comparisons evoke the era of US nuclear weapons testing at the Nevada Testing Site and Pacific Proving Grounds. Sebald's similes don't just extend the figurative reach or reverberations of the extra-territorial; they situate Orford Ness historically, as one node within the archipelagic system of Cold War nuclear weapons development sites.

In the Orford Ness passage, natural and historical forms of extraterri-torial space overlap. The Ness's metaphorical qualities don't detract from its legal and political specificities, but they do help sharpen their signifi-cance. These days, the Ness is no longer a military base; it closed in 1983, long before Sebald took the walks strung together in *The Rings of Saturn*. When Sebald visited the Ness in the early 1990s, the AWRE structures had already begun to rot in the open as lightly managed modern ruins.[26] The National Trust now administers the site as a nature reserve, admitting visitors via motorboat in tightly controlled numbers. The vegetated shingle spit is a rare and fragile ecosystem; it is, as people like to say about such places, beautiful in an austere way. Look up and away and the shingle can seem for a moment like a desert floor. Yet the stones are strewn and filled with flowering vegetable growth, and the growth is littered with exploded ordnance and rusting industrial hardware. A scattering of laboratories and observation towers hugs the broad ridge of the peninsula; their mod-est heights offer views out to sea, to the bomb testing ranges, and back to the pretty village of Orford and the towers of its Norman castle and church. To the north of the AWRE structures looms a giant transmission facility, originally built as the Cobra Mist experimental early warning radar, later privatized and then leased by the BBC, who used it to broadcast the World Service radio. Once used to detect incoming Soviet missiles, later to proj-ect British "soft power" to the east, the huge semicircular antenna array is now abandoned and without purpose.

The connections I drew between Sebald, Kracauer, and Lukács raised the possibility that, if the novel is the genre of transcendental homeless-ness, then maybe it is also a genre inherently associated with the extrater-ritorial. Sebald's oeuvre suggests that, even when it addresses extraterrito-rial forms and themes, the novel is not homeless but, as we have seen throughout this book, is defined by the antithetical relation between oppo-sites that attract, whether home and away, extraordinary and ordinary, or then and now. To say that such structural irony is constitutive of the novel as such is, at one level, probably true. But to say that is also to lapse into New Critical generality of a pretty vapid kind, affirming a truth so familiar that it is, in the end, hardly sufficient for defining something as internally various and historically contingent as the novel.

Significant bodies of contemporary fiction, I wrote earlier, are trending extraterritorial. By that I meant that the analysis of political geographies can teach us much about how and the secondary worlds made in contemporary novels have taken on certain predictable spatial qualities, as well as how persons and affects of personhood at once float free of territorial determination without ever losing the stink of the destiny that is geography. Recognizing such qualities within the novel can teach us, in turn, how received ideas about globalization and the state often rest on the mistakenly normative status of the Westphalian myth or idea, with its idealized connection between sovereignty and territoriality.

Still, I resist, even in these concluding pages, the temptation to expand these historical and analytic claims to the contemporary novel as such. This book's literary-historical argument is pitched at a medium scale. I'm not tilting at windmills. And so, rather than aiming at whole genres or literatures, my political geography of contemporary fiction stakes its claim at the level of subgenres, such as the postapocalyptic and historical novels; oeuvres, as with the works of Ballard, Miéville, and Sebald; formal concepts, such as setting and chronotope; and, finally, through the deeply familiar method of literary-critical comparison. That middle range of evidence is deep and diverse enough to sustain my claim that the extraterritorial political plastic of twenty-first-century life has, consciously and unconsciously, affected the formal disposition of contemporary fiction. This isn't just a question of the ways writers such as Atwood or Miéville address overtly extraterritorial themes or ideas—the persistence of borders within the world after the flood, for instance, or the spatial logic of sovereign commands. For, as these writers address extraterritorial subjects and objects, they've also adapted existing literary techniques—point of view, diction, secondary world construction, and more—so as to better imitate and speculate about a world that, as we saw in *Wolf Hall*, is one because it faces both ways. Like extraterritoriality itself, my argument has had *personal* implications, rooted in the individual imaginations of talented artists, as well as *spatial* ones, grounded in the common geographic mediation of political forces and relations. And so it has emphasized both coercion or *closure* as well as *openness* or liberation—that is, the way our common history set limits at the same time it makes things possible.

At the beginning of this book, I outlined four types of extraterritoriality. It's been my business over the last many pages to describe and explain the crossings and contradictions between those four types of extraterritoriality. As I've done so, I've pursued an analysis of novelistic form and genre from the perspective of extraterritoriality, trying to remain sensitive to the politics of the built environment; to the natural world, especially as it is exploited by labor and the law; and to legal and political theory, especially the history of how sovereignty and territoriality meet the realities of governance. The extraterritorial, whether materialized in a social practice or spun into metaphor by artists and writers, gives the lie to zero-sum accounts of how humans, and the things they make, move across, under, through, or above borders. The territorial state was never the historical norm it has been supposed to be. The fragmented and parcelized nature of contemporary spatial experience is not the exception; it is a new development within a long history of doing sovereignty differently. The extraterritorial is more than a heuristic, giving discursive and aesthetic shape to the political geography of the past and present. It's a speculative resource, which in its oscillation between the one and the many, the coerced and the free, has enabled some of the most brilliant artists and writers of our young century to reimagine where we have come from, where we are, and where, in worlds weird and familiar, we might yet go.

NOTES

INTRODUCTION

1. For this context, see Benjamin Sutton, "To Avoid Contested Territory, Arabs and Israelis Show Art in International Waters," *L Magazine*, 9 September 2009, http://www.thelmagazine.com/TheMeasure/archives/2009/09/09/to-avoid-contested-territory-arabs-and-israelis-show-art-in-international-waters (accessed 28 April 2014).

2. All quotations in the remainder of this paragraph are drawn from the pages of the Exterritory Project website: http://exterritory-project.org/ (accessed 23 June 2015).

3. For Grotius, the sea is "one of those things . . . which cannot become private property. . . . no part of the sea can be considered as the territory of any people whatsoever." Grotius, *The Freedom of the Seas, or, The Right Which Belongs to the Dutch to Take Part in the East India Trade*, ed. James Brown Scott, trans. Ralph Van DeMan Magoffin (New York: Oxford University Press, 1916), 84.

4. Elizabeth DeLoughrey, "Satellite Planetarity and the Ends of the Earth," *Public Culture* 26, no. 2 (2014): 258.

5. For the sailing boat image, see Alice Pfeiffer, "Probing Boundaries in Extraterritorial Waters," *International Herald Tribune*, 23 June 2011, M4.

6. Exterritory Project.

7. Gerhard Richter, *Thought Images: Frankfurt School Writers' Reflections from Damaged Life* (Stanford, CA: Stanford University Press, 2007), 112.

8. Reem Fekri, "Ex-territory," *Art Dubai Journal* 6 (2009): http://web.archive.org/web/20091202064942/http://www.artdubai.ae/journal/2009/november/exterritory.html

(accessed 23 June 2015). Amir draws on Michel Foucault's concept of "heterotopia," which he exemplifies via the space of the free seas and the pirate ship and defines as "counter-sites, a kind of effectively enacted utopia in which the real sites, all the other real sites that can be found within the culture, are simultaneously represented, contested, and inverted." Foucault, "Of Other Spaces," trans. Jay Miskowiec, *Diacritics* 16, no. 1 (1986): 24.

Brett Neilson and Ned Rossiter point out the limitations of Foucault's embrace to the ship's heterotopic potential: "It is not that we are unsympathetic to dreams, adventure and pirates. Our inclinations are quite the contrary. Rather, we are unaware of civilizations without boats. In today's world, even a landlocked country such as Switzerland hosts MSC, one of the world's largest shipping lines. Similarly, a nation as remote from the ocean as Mongolia runs a thriving ship registry. . . . Today capitalist globalization at once creates a single global order and constantly divides it through multiple and shifting practices of bordering. Paradoxically, these practices of bordering, among them those that establish different legal jurisdictions across land and sea, are essential to maintain the singularity of this same global order." Nielson and Rossiter, "Still Waiting, Still Moving: On Labour, Logistics and Maritime Industries," in *Stillness in a Mobile World*, ed. David Bissell and Gillian Fuller (New York: Routledge, 2011), 53.

9. In the ensuing violence, nine civilians (eight Turks and one Turkish American) died, and a diplomatic rift opened up between Israel and Turkey. Israel's use of military force on the high seas was condemned by Richard Falk, UN Special Rapporteur on Human Rights, as an offense against the freedom of navigation enshrined in Article 87 of the UN Convention on the Laws of the Sea. "Secretary-General 'Shocked' by Deadly Raid on Gaza Aid Flotilla," UN News Centre, 21 May 2010, http://www.un.org/apps/news /story.asp?NewsID=34863&Cr=gaza&Cr1#.UxpjivSwKKk (accessed 7 March 2014). A UN report upheld the legality of Israel's Gaza blockade but condemned the IDF's "excessive and unreasonable" military response to a civilian flotilla many miles from Israeli territorial waters. Sir Geoffrey Palmer, Alvaro Uribe, Joseph Chiechanoer Itzhar, and Süleyman Özdem Sanberk, "Report of the Secretary-General's Panel of Inquiry on the 31 May 2010 Flotilla Incident," United Nations, http://www.un.org/News/dh/infocus /middle_east/Gaza_Flotilla_Panel_Report.pdf (accessed 7 March 2014).

10. Maritime space includes such juridical areas as "contiguous zones," "exclusive economic zones," and "ecological protection zones," the last two of which can extend two hundred miles or more from shore. Sometimes maritime jurisdiction stretches through three dimensions, encompassing surface waters, subsurface waters, seabed, underground resources, and the airspace above. And those three dimensions can be divisible. In an exclusive economic zone, for instance, states can claim sovereign rights over biological, energy, and mineral resources found under the seas but cannot restrict movement over or under the surface. This is why Eyal Weizman argues that we must consider political geography not as a cartographic *area* divisible only by two dimensions but as a three-dimensional *volume*. Weizman, "The Politics of Verticality," openDemocracy, 23 April 2002, https://www.opendemocracy.net/en/article_801jsp/ (accessed 8 August 2019).

11. European Parliament Directorate General for Internal Policies, Policy Department B, Structural and Cohesion Policies: Fisheries, "Jurisdictional Waters in the Mediterranean and the Black Sea: A Study," 2009, http://www.eurocean.org/np4/file/2063/download .do.pdf (accessed 10 March 2014), 26.

12. Hugo Grotius, *De Jure Belli ac Pacis* (1625); quoted in China Miéville, *Between Equal Rights: A Marxist Theory of International Law* (Leiden: Brill, 2005), 213.

13. European Parliament, "Jurisdictional Waters in the Mediterranean," 26.

14. See, e.g., Peter Osborne's dictum that "the fiction of the contemporary is a global or a planetary fiction" (*Anywhere or Not at All: Philosophy of Contemporary Art* [London: Verso, 2013], 26). For the idea of the contemporary novel as a "global form," see, e.g., Debjani Ganguly, *This Thing Called the World: The Contemporary Novel as Global Form* (Durham, NC: Duke University Press, 2016): "If the industrial age saw the rise of the novel as a genre representing a new space-time configuration enabled by print capitalism that then created the conditions under which the 'nation' could be imagined (as Benedict Anderson has taught us), the radical spatiotemporal shifts generated by the information age produce the global novel that helps imagine the new chronotope 'world'" (2). In her theory of "born translated" fiction, Rebecca L. Walkowitz describes novels that, because they are published simultaneously in multiple languages, are written in the expectation of translation and therefore "start as world literature" (*Born Translated: The Contemporary Novel in an Age of World Literature* [New York: Columbia University Press, 2015], 2). Other literary critics emphasize the historical longevity of writing beyond the nation— see, especially, Wai Chee Dimock, *Through Other Continents: American Literature across Deep Time* (Princeton, NJ: Princeton University Press, 2007). But the point is not that there exist global literary histories that are not contemporary; it's that contemporary literary histories regularly aspire to an expanded geographic scale.

15. Indeed, in terms of actual scholarly production, the particular and the contextual arguably retain numerical and methodological hegemony. For a full-throated assault on the reign of "actually existing nuance" in the social sciences, see Kieran Healey, "Fuck Nuance," *Sociological Theory* 35 (2017): 118–27. For a defense of generalization that's skeptical about the humanities' commitment to the singular, see Caroline Levine, "Model Thinking: Generalization, Political Form, and the Common Good," in *New Literary History* 48, no. 4 (Autumn 2017): 633–53.

16. See, e.g., Sarah Brouillette, *Postcolonial Writers in the Global Literary Marketplace* (New York: Palgrave Macmillan, 2007), 49–61.

17. Miwon Kwon, Response to "Questionnaire on 'The Contemporary,'" ed. Hal Foster, Julia Bryan-Wilson, Grant Kester, James Elkins, Miwon Kwon, Joshua Shannon, Richard Meyer et al., *October* 130 (2009): 13.

18. The criticism for and about world literature is voluminous. For a useful account of the field, which attends to the ways in which the object "world literature" is discursively and institutionally constructed, see Stefan Helgesson and Pieter Vermeulen, "Introduction: World Literature in the Making," in *Institutions of World Literature: Writing, Translation, Markets* (New York: Routledge, 2016), 1–23.

19. For "sovereignty-territory ideal," see Mark B. Salter, *Rights of Passage: The Passport in International Relations* (Boulder, CO: Lynn Rienner, 2003), 121.

20. Robert Tally, *Spatiality* (New York: Routledge, 2012), 45.

21. Tally, *Spatiality*, 80.

22. Felicity D. Scott, *Outlaw Territories: Environments of Insecurity/Architectures of Counter-insurgency* (New York: Zone, 2016), 15–16.

23. Eyal Weizman, *Hollow Land: Israel's Architecture of Occupation* (London: Verso, 2007), 5.

24. Anselm Franke, Ines Gleisner, and Eyal Weizman, introduction to "Islands: The Geography of Extraterritoriality," special section of *Archis* 6 (2003): n.p.

25. For "structural forces" and an account of the internet as a "co-constructed" medium in which the very idea of territoriality is put to the test, see Miyase Christensen, André Jansson, and Christian Christensen, "Introduction: Globalization, Mediated Practice and Social Space: Assessing the Means and Metaphysics of Online Territories," in *Online Territories: Globalization, Mediated Practice, and Social Space*, ed. Miyase Christensen, André Jansson, and Christian Christensen (New York: Peter Land, 2011), xi. For a narrower meditation on extraterritoriality, the law, and the internet, see Mireille Hildebrandt, "Extraterritorial Jurisdiction to Enforce in Cyberspace? Bodin, Schmitt, Grotius in Cyberspace," in *Extra-Territorialities in Occupied Worlds*, ed. Mayaan Amir and Ruti Sela (Brooklyn: Punctum, 2016), 173–201.

26. For the extraterritorial status of the black sites operated by the Central Intelligence Agency in the early 2000s, see Marko Milanovic, *Extraterritorial Application of Human Rights Treaties: Law, Principles, and Policy* (Oxford: Oxford University Press, 2011), 122–23.

27. DeLoughrey, "Satellite Planetarity," 257–80.

28. For partial exceptions, see Amir and Sela, eds., *Extra-Territorialities in Occupied Worlds*; and Franke, Gleisner, and Weizman, introduction to "Islands."

29. Oliver Clemens, Jesko Fezer, Kim Förster, and Sabine Horlitz (writing as *An Architektur*), "Extra-territorial Spaces and Camps: Judicial and Political Spaces in the 'War on Terrorism,'" in *Territories: Islands, Camps, and Other States of Utopia*, ed. Anselm Franke, Rafi Segal, and Eyal Weizman (Berlin: KW Institute for Contemporary Art, 2003), 26.

30. The idea of an international legal personhood can sound odd, given how accustomed we are to thinking of states as the subjects of international law. Sanford R. Silverburg reminds us, however, that "originally the only recognized subjects of international law were individuals" and it was only in the sixteenth and seventeenth centuries, especially following the Peace of Westphalia, that "the traditional subject of international law came to be the dominant nation-state" ("The Palestine Liberation Organization in the United Nations: Implications for International Law and Relations," *Israel Law Review* 12, no. 3 [1977]: 366). I am indebted to Joseph R. Slaughter for this insight and citation.

31. United Nations, "Convention on the Privileges and Immunities of the United Nations," *United Nations Treaty Series* 1, no. 4 (1946–47): 16–32, https://treaties.un.org/doc/Publication/UNTS/Volume%201/volume-1-I-4-English.pdf (accessed 10 January 2017).

32. United Nations, "Agreement Between the United Nations and the United States of America Regarding the Headquarters of the United Nations," *United Nations Treaty Series* 11, no. 147 (1947): 20, 18, https://treaties.un.org/doc/Publication/UNTS/Volume%2011 /volume-11-I-147-English.pdf (accessed 10 January 2017). For an analysis of the limits to the headquarters district's autonomy, see Hans Kelsen, *The Law of the United Nations: A Critical Analysis of its Fundamental Problems* (New York: London Institute of World Affairs/Prager, 1950; Clark, NJ: Lawbook Exchange, 2008), 348–56.

33. Kelsen, *Law of the United Nations*, 18.

34. Kelsen, 20, 27–29, 30–32.

35. For Carl Schmitt, to whose ideas we will return in the next chapter, the very idea of politics depends on the existence of more than one locus of power and authority. See *The Concept of the Political*, trans. George W. Schwab (Chicago: University of Chicago Press, 1996), 53.

36. Embassies and consulates enjoy the protection, codified under Article 22 of the Vienna Convention, that they are legally inviolate. Although this inviolability does not depend on the physical presence of the ambassador, Garrett Mattingly explains that the idea that embassies amounted to "little islands of alien sovereignty" emerged out of the practical need to extend extraterritorial protections from the ambassador to his staff and family, especially when it came to the free exercise of religion. Mattingly, *Renaissance Diplomacy* (Baltimore: Penguin, 1955), 242–44.

37. Martin Jay, "The Extraterritorial Life of Siegfried Kracauer," in *Permanent Exiles: Essays on the Intellectual Migration from Germany to America* (New York: Columbia University Press, 1986), 152–97.

38. For the relevant passage in Latin, see Hugonis Grotii, *De Iure Belli Ac Pacis Libre Tres, In Quibus Ius Naturae Et Gentium, Item Juris Publici Praecipua Explicantur,* ed. P. C. Molhuysen (Leiden: A. W. Sijthoff. 1919; Clark, NJ: Lawbook Exchange, 2005), 338. For a recent English translation, see Hugo Grotius, *On the Law of War and Peace,* ed. Stephen C. Neff, trans. Francis W. Kelsey (Cambridge: Cambridge University Press, 2012), 263.

39. I say "Englishness" (although "Anglo-Welshness" would be even better) because the United Kingdom contains three relatively autonomous legal systems (Northern Ireland, Scotland, and England and Wales), only the last of which applies to government employees overseas.

40. "Extraterritoriality," in *West's Encyclopedia of American Law,* 2nd. ed. (St. Paul, MN: West Group, 1998), 295; capitalization and formatting in the original.

41. Thus, e.g., the Military Extraterritorial Jurisdiction Act (2000) extended US jurisdiction over military personnel deployed abroad. After 2004, this act was expanded to cover civilian contractors and other government employees working to support the Department of Defense. United States Congress, Military Extraterritorial Jurisdiction Act of 2000, 18 USC Title 18—Crimes and Criminal Procedure, part 2, chapter 212, http://www .pubklaw.com/hi/pl106–523.pdf (accessed 2 April 2010).

42. United Kingdom of Great Britain and Northern Ireland, Terrorism Act 2000, part 4, section 59(1)-(2), http://www.legislation.gov.uk/ukpga/2000/11 (accessed 9 January 2015).

In such an eventuality, the standard applied is whether the action would have been illegal had it actually occurred in the United Kingdom.

43. For a survey of developments in the extraterritorial application of the law in the United States, including the Foreign Corrupt Practices Act and the Military Extraterritorial Jurisdiction Act, see Anon., "Developments in the Law: Extraterritoriality," *Harvard Law Review* 124 (2011): 1226–1304.

44. See, e.g., Georg Friedrich von Martens, *The Law of Nations: Being the Science of National Law, Covenants, Power &c. Founded on the Traditions and Customs of Modern Nations In Europe*, trans. William Cobbet (London: William Cobbet, 1829), 119–20.

45. Along with the common hyphenated form, there developed, over the nineteenth and twentieth centuries, new contractions of "extraterritorial" such as "exterritorial" and "extrality." Per the *OED*, the last of these is an obsolete syncopation for "extraterritorial" briefly popular in the 1920s. The term "exterritorial" was, however, not just a contraction. At one point it named a real (if often unobserved) legal distinction. Thus, in *Exterritorial: The Law Relating to Consular Jurisdiction and to Residence in Oriental Countries* (London: William Clowes, 1892), Sir Francis Taylor Piggott reserves "exterritorial" for the privileges afforded to ambassadors and diplomats or to overseas nationals who, by virtue of treaty laws, are subject to the jurisdiction of their own consuls. He uses "extra-territorial" to refer to the actions of governments who exert power overseas (28–29). Thus, e.g., a British banker in Shanghai ca. 1892 enjoys "exterritorial" freedoms; the British government who prosecutes that banker for fraud acts in an "extraterritorial" manner. Though "exterritorial" is still used today, Piggott's distinction between the actions of individuals and states has fallen out of use and the terms are today generally synonymous.

46. Alexander H. de Groot, "The Historical Development of the Capitulatory Regime in the Ottoman Middle East from the Fifteenth to the Nineteenth Centuries," in *Oriente Moderno* 83, no. 3 (2003): 575–604. There is debate over how to periodize the capitulatory system. Capitulations were agreed between the Ottoman Empire and a number of mercantile city-states (e.g., Genoa and Venice) during the fourteenth and fifteenth centuries. However, the capitulation agreed with France ca. 1535–36 is often misleadingly treated as if primordial (Umut Özsu, "Ottoman Empire," in *The Oxford Handbook of the History of International Law* [Oxford: Oxford University Press, 2012], 434–35). In a similar vein, Turan Kayaoğlu distinguishes between a later imperialist system of extraterritorial jurisdiction in the Ottoman Empire, comparable to the practices also imposed upon Japan and China, and an early modern system in which foreign mercantile communities practiced forms of self-rule (*Legal Imperialism: Sovereignty and Extraterritoriality in Japan, the Ottoman Empire, and China* [Cambridge: Cambridge University Press, 2010], 104–5). Özsu argues, on the contrary, that the history of the capitulations cannot be reduced to the question of their usefulness to imperial hegemony, whether Western or Ottoman ("Ottoman Empire," 445–47).

47. This summary follows Özsu, "Ottoman Empire," 433–45; and De Groot, "The Historical Development of the Capitulatory Regime," 575–604. It's important to note that

diplomatic immunity is also not a one-size-fits-all proposition. The UK government, e.g., recognizes different privileges according to diplomatic rank, with some foreign government workers afforded complete immunity from civil and criminal jurisdiction and some only protected in relation to acts committed as part of official duties (Crown Prosecution Service, "Diplomatic Immunity and Diplomatic Premises," http://www .cps.gov.uk/legal/d_to_g/diplomatic_immunity_and_diplomatic_premises/ [accessed 18 June 2015]). Degrees of diplomatic immunity also vary from place to place. Recognizing this, the UK Diplomatic Privileges Act (1964) enshrines a principle of parsimonious reciprocity, such that a representative of, say, Thailand in Britain would only be afforded the same protections as a British diplomat in Thailand (http://www.legislation.gov.uk /ukpga/1964/81/section/3 [accessed 8 January 2020).

48. Giorgio Agamben, "Beyond Human Rights," in *Means Without End: Notes on Politics*, trans. Vincenzo Binetti and Cesare Casarino (Minneapolis: University of Minnesota Press, 2000), 16, 24. I return to Agamben's use of "extraterritorial" in chapter 2.

49. Kal Raustiala, *Does the Constitution Follow the Flag? The Evolution of Territoriality in American Law* (New York: Oxford University Press, 2009), 8.

50. For this point, see Eyal Weizman, "On Extraterritoriality," opening address to the symposium Archipelago of Exception: Sovereignties of Extraterritoriality, Centra de Cultura Contemporània de Barcelona, 10–11 November 2005, http://www.publicspace.org /en/text-library/eng/b011-on-extraterritoriality (accessed 18 July 2015).

51. Quoted in William S. Dodge, "Understanding the Presumption Against Extraterritoriality," *Berkeley Journal of International Law* 16, no. 1 (1998): 85.

52. And territoriality is, in itself, not simple—thus, for instance, the distinction within international law between *subjective* and *objective* territorial jurisdiction. Charles Chatterjee applies this principle to the case of the Lockerbie aircraft bombing incident of 21 December 1988, in which Libyan nationals in Malta loaded a bomb onto a plane that later exploded over Scotland, killing the passengers on board as well as people on the ground. Chatterjee argues that the principle of subjective territoriality allows a state to claim jurisdiction over "crimes connected with the State but completed or consummated abroad. If one applies this principle, then Malta could have assumed jurisdiction [over the Lockerbie homicide cases] as the bomb is said to have been loaded aboard the aircraft in Malta. The objective territoriality principle is applied to assume jurisdiction when an essential constituent or component of a crime or act is consummated on the territory of a State even though it was initiated outside its territory" (Chatterjee, *International Law and Diplomacy* [London: Routledge, 2010], 51). Thus, because Pan American Flight 103 exploded over Scotland, the Scottish courts assumed *objective* territorial jurisdiction over foreign nationals who were never in Scotland and were accused of loading the bomb in a third country. Malta could have (but did not) assume *subjective* territorial jurisdiction, even though the bomb exploded over Scotland, on the basis that crimes executed elsewhere were planned and initiated within its own jurisdiction.

53. In saying this, we have immediately to concede that there are groups of people—e.g., nomads—who don't identify power over people with power over land. We must also

acknowledge that forms of legal and administrative pluralism are hardly modern inventions—e.g., the ancient Roman custom in which a *prateor peregrinus* (foreign praetor) would "utter law (ius dicit [exercise jurisdiction]) between foreigners." A. Arthur Schiller, *Roman Law: Mechanisms of Development* (Berlin: Walter de Gruyter, 1978), 403.

54. I draw here on Stephen Krasner's understanding of sovereignty as containing several aspects, one of which (international legal sovereignty or mutual recognition) is associated with traditions of diplomatic relations and consular immunity. Krasner, "Abiding Sovereignty," *International Political Science Review/Revue internationale de science politique* 22, no. 3 (2001): 229–51, 232.

55. Roland Barthes, "Criticism as Language," *Times Literary Supplement*, 27 September 1963, 739–40. For the French phrase, see Roland Barthes, *Essais Critiques* (Paris: Seuil, 1991), 253.

56. I use "topological" here, and below, to distinguish between logical or geometric spaces (e.g., the relations between the subordinate parts of an argument, or the abstract space of a line or a circle) and spaces that might be materialized in absolute and relative terms. The distinction between absolute and relative space is from David Harvey, "Space as a Key Word," in *Spaces of Global Capitalism: Towards a Theory of Uneven Geographical Development* (London: Verso, 2006), 120–23. This same sort of topological relation applies to T. W. Adorno's use of "extra-territorial" (*exterritorial* in the German) to describe how Berthold Brecht's *The Resistible Rise of Arturo Ui* (1941) wrongly comprehends the class composition of the Nazi elite: "The group which engineered the seizure of power in Germany was also certainly a gang. But the problem is that such elective affinities are not extra-territorial: they are rooted within society itself." Adorno, "Commitment," trans. Francis McDonagh, *New Left Review* 1, nos. 87–88 (1974): 81.

57. Fredric Jameson, *Postmodernism, or, The Cultural Logic of Late Capitalism* (Durham, NC: Duke University Press, 1991), 49.

58. Fredric Jameson, "Science Fiction as a Spatial Genre: Generic Discontinuities and the Problem of Figuration in Vonda McIntyre's 'The Exile Waiting,'" *Science Fiction Studies* 14, no. 1 (1987): 44–59.

59. Fredric Jameson, *Archaeologies of the Future: The Desire Called Utopia and Other Science Fictions* (London: Verso, 2005), 4–5.

60. Adrian Franklin, "The Tourist Syndrome: An Interview with Zygmunt Bauman," *Tourist Studies* 3, no. 2 (2003): 210, 212.

61. Zygmunt Bauman, "Reconnaissance Wars of the Planetary Frontierland," *Theory, Culture & Society* 19, no. 4 (2002): 81–82; emphasis in original.

62. Lukasz Galecki, "The Unwinnable War: an Interview with Zygmunt Bauman," openDemocracy, 1 December 2005, https://www.opendemocracy.net/globalization-vision_reflections/modernity_3082.jsp (accessed 29 May 2015).

63. In this light, see also Steiner's lectures on the idea of Europe. Celebrating what he sees as Europe's preeminence in the histories of philosophy and mathematics, he says: "Again, there are philosophic moments and systems extraterritorial to Europe. But the sovereign stream of supposition and argument . . . flows . . . from the pre-Socratics to

Wittgenstein" (Steiner, *The Idea of Europe* [New York: Overlook Duckworth, 2015], 47). Note the near-synonymy of "extraterritorial" and "foreign." Note also, in the light of the argument to follow, the idea of a sovereign stream of thought, moving across space and time from classical Greece to an Austrian's rooms in Cambridge, potent precisely because of its dynamic movements across languages, cultures, places, and times.

64. George Steiner, *Extraterritorial: Papers on the Literature and Language Revolution* (New York: Athaneum, 1976), 11.

65. Compare Steiner's conception of extraterritoriality to what Peter Stallybrass and Allon White say about the limits of Bakhtin's account of the Rabelesian marketplace as an "open, extraterritorial space. . . . a place-beyond-place, a pure outside." Stallybrass and White, *The Politics and Poetics of Transgression* (Ithaca, NY: Cornell University Press, 1986), 28.

66. I borrow the line about history and necessity from Fredric Jameson, *The Political Unconscious: Narrative as a Socially Symbolic Act* (London: Routledge, 1989), 102.

67. This doesn't require, however, that extraterritorial enclaves embody an *explicitly* colonial logic of importation from outside—e.g., the CIA black site in which the intelligence services of another NATO government were paid by US authorities to allow the creation of an extralegal detention facility outside either country's criminal jurisdiction. This sort of clandestine arrangement between allied states and intelligence agencies is perhaps better understood in the language of US hegemony than neocolonial invasion. Adam Goldman, "The Hidden History of the CIA's Prison in Poland," *Washington Post*, 23 January 2014, http://www.washingtonpost.com/world/national-security/the-hidden-history-of-the-cias-prison-in-poland/2014/01/23/b77f6ea2-7c6f-11e3-95c6-0a7aa80874 b.c._story.html (accessed 3 June 2015).

68. A case in point: Deleuze and Guatarri's language of de- and reterritorialization. In their *Anti-Oedipus*, the planetary space of the whole Earth serves as a metonym for absolute deterritorialization: the planet figures as a plane or body utterly decontextualized, unmarked by stratification. Judged by this standard, a space such as the high seas would be at best only *relatively* deterritorialized, since naming it as oceanic involves making distinctions between maritime and terrestrial geographical orders. Gilles Deleuze and Felix Guattari, *Anti-Oedipus: Capitalism and Schizophrenia*, trans. Robert Hurley, Mark Seem, and Helen R. Lane (Minneapolis: University of Minnesota Press, 1983), 34. But, despite this superficial resemblance between the logic of relative deterritorialization and my account of the extraterritorial, I dissent from Deleuze and Guattari's conceptual geography for three reasons:

(i) They stereotype the state as a coercive and immobilizing force opposed to dynamic nomadism: "It is a vital concern of every State not only to vanquish nomadism but to control migrations and more generally, to establish a zone of rights over an entire 'exterior,' over all flows" (*A Thousand Plateaus: Capitalism and Schizophrenia*, trans. Brian Massumi [Minneapolis: University of Minnesota Press, 1987], 385). By contrast, chapter 1 of this book explores how the how the state also produces, rather than only inhibits, such "flows."

(ii) The "relative" twofold movement between de- and reterritorialization is a rigged game: a "perpetual immanence of the absolute" persists within any relative deterritorialization, such that the latter always remains regrettably "oriented toward the absolute" (*Thousand Plateaus*, 56–57). My approach maintains the dialectical tension between these poles.

(iii) It's not clear what absolute deterritorialization would even look like. The whole Earth is only nonstratified if it is considered as a discrete singularity abstracted from any cosmological or astronomical context (e.g., the moon, solar system, galaxy). But, even if we put aside the problem of infinite regress that such hypostatization would involve, why would we even want to consider the Earth thus? For what citizen of the Earth is it ever in fact a whole singularity?

69. Andrew Thacker, "The Idea of a Critical Literary Geography," *New Formations* 57 (Winter 2005–6): 60.

70. M. M. Bakhtin, "Forms of Time and the Chronotope in the Novel: Notes toward an Historical Poetics," in *The Dialogic Imagination: Four Essays*, ed. Michael Holquist, trans. Caryl Emerson and Michael Holquist (Austin: University of Texas Press, 1981), 84.

1. ZONE

1. David Segal, "Swiss Freeports Are Home For a Growing Treasury of Art," *New York Times*, 21 July 2012, http://www.nytimes.com/2012/07/22/business/swiss-freeports-are -home-for-a-growing-treasury-of-art.html?_r=1 (accessed 5 October 2016).

2. From a 2017 report by the consulting firm Deloitte Luxembourg and the London-based art market analysis firm ArtTactic: "With an estimated US$1.62 trillion in art and collectible wealth held by [Ultra High Net Worth Individuals] in 2016 and an estimated US$2.7 trillion by 2026, wealth managers seem to realize both the financial and emotional value attached to art and collectibles. . . . Despite the auction market volatility seen in the last two years, the global auction market saw total sales growth of 319 percent between 2000 and 2016, and with more wealth allocated to art and collectibles, this positive trend is likely to continue." Art and Finance Report 2017, https://www2.deloitte.com/lu/en/pages/art-finance/articles/art-finance-report.html (accessed 21 March 2019).

3. Thierry Ehrmann, president of art market information service Artprice, quoted in Marie-Noëlle Blessig/Agence France-Presse, "Geneva Duty-free Art Warehouses Under Fire," Local.ch, 3 June 2015, https://www.thelocal.ch/20150603/geneva-duty-free-art -storage (accessed 6 October 2016). The value of goods stored in freeports "is thought to be in the hundreds of billions of dollars, and rising," though it's not clear what evidence lies behind this surmise. "Über-warehouses for the Ultra-rich," *Economist*, 23 November 2013, http://www.economist.com/news/briefing/21590353-ever-more-wealth-being -parked-fancy-storage-facilities-some-customers-they-are (accessed 5 October 2016).

4. Says one insurance agent: "We can't actually calculate how much we have insured at the Freeport. . . . There are insurers who could be so overexposed that in the event of disaster they will be unable to pay" (Quoted in Segal, "Swiss Freeports").

5. "Über-warehouses for the Ultra-rich." The Geneva Freeport "allows temporary postponement of VAT and customs duty payments until such time as the goods reach their final destination. Goods may be stored in transit for an unlimited period of time" ("Free Port Status," http://geneva-freeports.ch/en/#sous-douane [accessed 5 October 2016]). The Geneva Freeport is 86-percent owned by the Swiss canton of Geneva, which shares in the facility's operating profit in lieu of unpaid taxes and customs duties.

6. The Geneva Freeport has its origins in the bonded warehouses that, long popular the world over, offer importers of foreign goods exemption from duties and taxes until such time as those items are sold to a domestic buyer or removed to another fiscal zone. The logistics company Crozier Fine Arts contends that "bonded warehouses are synonymous with freeports because freeports are merely clusters of bonded warehouses in one location; however, freeports may have different tax implications." Diana Wierbecki and Amanda A. Rottermund, "Freeports for the Art World: A Guide to their Uses," Wealth Management, 19 February 2016, http://www.wealthmanagement.com/art-auctions-antiques-report/freeports-art-world (accessed 4 January 2017).

7. Keller Easterling, *Extrastatecraft: The Power of Infrastructure Space* (London: Verso, 2014), 15.

8. Easterling, *Extrastatecraft*, 15.

9. Easterling, 33.

10. Easterling, 16–17. The Dubai International Finance Center places a key role in Joseph O'Neill's novel *The Dog* (New York: Pantheon, 2014), in which an American lawyer exploits the legal freedoms associated with the financial free zone to enrich his Lebanese employers and yet, when those same employers frame him for their own crimes, is swiftly subject to the sovereign power of the Emirati state.

11. Easterling, 15.

12. Aihwa Ong, *Neoliberalism as Exception: Mutations in Citizenship and Sovereignty* (Durham, NC: Duke University Press, 2006), 78 and 75–96. Ong associates graduated sovereignty regimes with the kinds of space—technology zones, regional trade networks, ports, telecommunications networks—that are at the center of Easterling's study

13. For a profile of Bouvier, see Sam Knight, "The Bouvier Affair: How an Art-World Insider Made a Fortune by Being Discreet," *New Yorker*, 15 February 2015, http://www.newyorker.com/magazine/2016/02/08/the-bouvier-affair (accessed 5 October 2016). Knight focuses on the possible prosecution of Bouvier by the US government for allegedly defrauding his former art client Dmitry Rybolovlev. That case against Bouvier was dropped in late 2017. Christian Berthelsen, "Russian's Da Vinci Windfall Undercuts U.S. Probe of Art Dealer," Bloomberg, 29 May 2018, https://www.bloomberg.com/amp/news/articles/2018-05-29/russian-s-da-vinci-windfall-undercut-u-s-probe-of-art-dealer (accessed 21 March 2019).

14. Knight, "The Bouvier Affair."

15. Cris Prystay, "Singapore Bling," *Wall Street Journal*, 21 May 2010, http://www.wsj.com /articles/SB10001424052748703691804575255551995870746 (accessed 6 October 2016).
16. Quoted in "Über-warehouses for the Ultra-rich."
17. "Facilities," Le Freeport Corporate, http://www.lefreeport.lu/facilities/ (accessed 6 October 2016).
18. Stefan Heidenreich, "Freeportism as Style and Ideology: Post-Internet and Speculative Realism," *E-Flux Journal* 71 (March 2016): http://www.e-flux.com/journal/71/60521 /freeportism-as-style-and-ideology-post-internet-and-speculative-realism-part-i/ (accessed 6 October 2016).
19. Susanna Davies-Crook, "The Topic Is the Birth and Evolution of Worms," ExBerliner, 13 November 2012, http://www.exberliner.com/culture/art/for-each-new-project-i-go -back-to-basics/ (accessed 6 October 2016).
20. Jean Kay, interview with Katja Novitskova, AQNB, 19 June 2013, http://www.aqnb.com /2013/06/19/an-interview-with-katja-novitskova/ (accessed 6 October 2016).
21. Luca Francesconi, "Interview with Katja Novitskova," *Mousse Magazine*, 2013, http:// moussemagazine.it/blog/wp-content/uploads/Katja-Novitskova-ANG.pdf (accessed 6 October 2016).
22. Heidenreich, "Freeportism as Style and Ideology."
23. This argument begs a question: Why can't the two objects, and the kinds of cultural and economic value they create or decreate, be thought of outside the logic of derivation or belatedness? That is, even if we acknowledge that Novitskova's Instagram posts are remediations of a complex kind, why must we see them as the digital "second life" of a manufactured physical object, rather than part of an expanded "first life" that involves the production of multiple objects and images in multiple media, none of which have absolute temporal priority? Some further questions: Does the physical object only accrue value if images of it circulate online? Might the object's online remediation not possibly cause its depreciation as a commodity? Would the "post-internet" artwork become a bad investment if it didn't circulate as an image on the internet to which it is said to be posterior?
24. For the "dynamics of digital extraterritoriality," see Victoria Bernal, "Extraterritoriality, Diaspora, and the Space of Cyberspace," in *Extraterritorialities in Occupied Worlds*, ed. Maayan Amir and Ruti Sela (Brooklyn: Punctum, 2016), 157–70.
25. Hito Steyerl, "Duty-Free Art," *E-Flux* 71 (March 2015): http://www.e-flux.com/journal /63/60894/duty-free-art/ (accessed 6 October 2016).
26. Hito Steyerl, "Duty-Free Art," *E-Flux* 71 (March 2015), http://www.e-flux.com/journal /63/60894/duty-free-art/ (accessed 6 October 2016).
27. Peter Osborne, *Anywhere or Not at All: Philosophy of Contemporary Art* (London: Verso, 2013), 25.
28. Osborne, *Anywhere or Not at All*, 35.
29. Osborne, 22–23.
30. Hito Steyerl, "Duty-Free Art."
31. Steyerl borrows the terms of Easterling's *Extrastatecraft* here.

32. Hito Steyerl, "Duty-Free Art."

33. Osborne, *Anywhere or Not at All*, 22.

34. Mark B. Salter, *Rights of Passage: The Passport in International Relations* (Boulder, CO: Lynn Rienner, 2003), 121.

35. John Griffiths, "What Is Legal Pluralism?," *Journal of Legal Pluralism and Unofficial Law* 24 (1986): 4.

36. Griffiths, "What Is Legal Pluralism?," 3.

37. Griffiths, 39.

38. Harold Laski, *Authority in the Modern State* (New Haven, CT: Yale University Press, 1919), 24.

39. Michael Mann, *The Sources of Social Power, Vol. II: The Rise of Classes and Nation-States, 1760–1914* (Cambridge: Cambridge University Press, 1993), 88.

40. Mann, *Sources of Social Power*, 75.

41. Mann, 75.

42. Mann, 56.

43. Michael Mann, "The Autonomous Power of the State: Its Origins, Mechanisms and Results," in *States in History*, ed. John A. Hall (Oxford: Blackwell, 1986), 112.

44. Mann, *Sources of Social Power*, 56.

45. Krasner, "Abiding Sovereignty," 232.

46. Michael Keating, *Plurinational Democracy. Stateless Nations in a Post-Sovereignty Era* (Oxford: Oxford University Press, 2001), 11.

47. For this description, see Giovanni Arrighi, *The Long Twentieth Century: Money, Power, and the Origins of Our Times* (London: Verso, 1994), 43. In Michel Foucault's words, after 1648 it was "finally recognized that the Empire"—whether Roman, Roman Catholic, or Holy Roman—"is not the ultimate vocation of all states," and that Europe would henceforth conceive of itself as "a multiple state space" within a "temporally open history." Foucault, *Security, Territory, Population: Lectures at the Collège de France 1977–1978*, ed. Michel Senellart, trans. Graham Burchell (New York: Picador, 2004), 290–91.

48. Friedrich Kratochwil, "Of Systems, Boundaries, and Territoriality: An Inquiry into the Formation of the State System," *World Politics* 39, no. 1 (1986): 29.

49. Kratochwil, "Of Systems, Boundaries, and Territoriality," 29. For a similar comparison, see John Gerard Ruggie, "Territoriality and Beyond: Problematizing Modernity in International Relations," *International Organization* 47, no. 1 (1993): 139–74, especially 148–52. Somewhat unhelpfully, though, it turns out that neat distinctions between territorial and kinship-based forms of community are hard to make in practice. Even resolutely nomadic peoples sometimes make privileged or proprietary claims to such things as pasturage or migration routes. Both Kratochwil and Ruggie draw on Owen Lattimore's studies of nomadic property rights in Mongolia, which show how the nomadic "sovereign importance of movement" was not in fact absolute, thereby troubling firm distinctions between territorial and non-territorial forms of sovereignty and community-formation (Ruggie, "Territoriality," 149; quoting Lattimore, *Studies in Frontier History* [Oxford: Oxford University Press, 1962], 535).

50. Emile Durkheim, "Progressive Preponderance of Organic Solidarity" (1893), trans. George Simpson (1933), in *Emile Durkheim on Morality and Society*, ed. Robert N. Bellah (Chicago: University of Chicago Press, 1973), 63–85.

51. Dukrheim, "Progressive Preponderance of Organic Solidarity," 73.

52. Durkheim, 74.

53. On the historical inaccuracy of the equation between political modernity and the overcoming of intrasystemic territorial divisions, see Michael Keating, "Thirty Years of Territorial Politics," *West European Politics* 31, nos. 1–2 (2008): 60–62.

54. Jean-Jacques Rousseau, *The Discourses and Other Early Political Writings*, ed. and trans. Victor Gourevitch (Cambridge: Cambridge University Press, 1997), 164; italics in original. Quoted in Stuart Elden, *The Birth of Territory* (Chicago: University of Chicago Press, 2013), 1. Elden makes plain that, for Rousseau, "civil society" does not name an alternative to the state; it describes government in general, so that territorial division is positioned right at the heart of political life.

55. Saskia Sassen, *Territory, Authority, Rights: From Medieval to Global Assemblages* (Princeton, NJ: Princeton University Press, 2007), 32–73, especially 72–73.

56. Perry Anderson, *Lineages of the Absolutist State* (London: New Left, 1974), 37–38.

57. Leo Gross, "The Peace of Westphalia, 1648–1948," *American Journal of International Law* 42, no. 1 (1948): 20; emphases added. By "certain," Gross doesn't mean only "particular" or "acknowledged" but "defined"—that is, states with territorial integrity, not just spatial extension and limits.

58. See Article 2, Paragraph 1 ("The Organization is based on the principle of the sovereign equality of all its Members"); Article 2, Paragraph 4 ("All Members shall refrain in their international relations from the threat or use of force against the territorial integrity or political independence of any state"); and Article 2, Paragraph 7 ("Nothing contained in the present Charter shall authorize the United Nations to intervene in matters which are essentially within the domestic jurisdiction of any state." Charter of the United Nations: Chapter 1: Purposes and Principles, http://www.un.org/en/documents/charter/chapter1.shtml (accessed 24 July 2015). The principle of nonintervention is the one that Krasner concedes might reasonably be called "Westphalian" ("Abiding Sovereignty," 232). For a general dismissal of the Westphalian settlement as a touchstone of modern international relations, see Stephen Krasner, "Sovereignty," *Foreign Policy* 122 (January–February 2001): 21–22.

59. Gross, "Peace of Westphalia," 28.

60. John H. Herz, "Rise and Demise of the Territorial State," *World Politics* 9, no. 4 (1957): 474. Compare Martin Heidegger's description of the twentieth century as the first in which it became possible to imagine the world as a picture. Among Heidegger's examples of what makes the image of worldedness possible: "The destruction of great distances by the airplane." Heideigger, "The Age of the World Picture," in *Off the Beaten Path*, ed. and trans. Julian Young and Kenneth Haynes (London: Cambridge University Press, 2002), 69).

61. Arrighi, *Long Twentieth Century*, 65. Article 2 of the UN Charter in fact predicts exactly this dialectic of expansion and supersession, concluding Paragraph 7's defense of domestic jurisdiction with the caveat that "this principle shall not prejudice the application of enforcement measures under Chapter Vll ['Action With Respect To Threats To The Peace, Breaches Of The Peace, And Acts Of Aggression']," which establishes a basis in international law for the UN Security Council to contravene domestic jurisdiction so as to "maintain or restore international peace and security" (Article 39).

62. Arrighi, *Long Twentieth Century*, 66–67.

63. Jean-Marie Guéhenno, *The End of the Nation-State*, trans. Victoria Elliott (Minneapolis: University of Minnesota Press, 1995), 7–8.

64. Arjun Appadurai, "Disjuncture and Difference in the Global Cultural Economy," *Public Culture* 2, no. 2 (1990): 1–24. In this seminal essay of 1990s globalization theory, Appadurai mentions the territorial state only once, in the following context: "By *production fetishism* I mean an *illusion* created by contemporary transnational production loci, which *masks* translocal capital, transnational earning-flows, global management and often faraway workers . . . in the idiom and *spectacle* of local . . . control, national productivity and territorial sovereignty" (16; emphases added). From Gross's gateway to the future to Appadurai's spectacular fetishistic illusion in less than half a century!

65. Arjun Appadurai, "Sovereignty Without Territoriality: Notes for a Post-National Geography," in *The Anthropology of Space and Place: Locating Culture*, ed. Setha M. Low and Denise Lawrence-Zuñiga (Oxford: Blackwell, 2004), 347. For the "last legs" remark, see Arjun Appadurai, *Modernity at Large: Cultural Dimensions of Globalization* (Minneapolis: University of Minnesota Press, 1996), 19.

66. Arrighi, *Long Twentieth Century*, 55. For Arrighi, hegemony must be understood not as power alone but as power plausibly exercised in the language of the general interest (27–28).

67. Another way of putting this is that the Westphalian myth aggrandizes the political at the expense of the economic. On this topic, see Wendy Brown, "Sovereignty and the Return of the Repressed," in *The New Pluralism: William Connolly and the Contemporary Global Condition*, ed. David Campbell and Morton Schoolman (Durham, NC: Duke University Press, 2008), 250–72. Brown argues that the resurgence of sovereignty-speak in postmillennial political theory (especially in work that draws on Carl Schmitt) evinces an unaddressed anxiety that politics might in fact never again exercise sovereignty over the economy.

68. This is the central insight that leads to the powerful double vision of Arrighi's world-systems theory, which contains two linked narratives—one defined by what John Ruggie calls "spaces of places," the other by "spaces of flows" ("Territoriality and Beyond," 172; quoted by Arrighi, *Long Twentieth Century*, 84). In the broadly territorial account, we have a succession of world hegemons in which the most advanced form of capitalism is identified with particular states—e.g., the Netherlands in the seventeenth century, the United States after World War I. In the second story of market flows, we have a

nonterritorial genealogy of systemic cycles of accumulation that are precisely not identified with one particular state. The world system, for Arrighi, is determined by the dialectic between these contrary narratives, with the story (at least, up to the emergence of China as the potential hegemon of the twenty-first century) gradually tipping toward the nonterritorial side of things. Thus, while the British hegemonic cycle is described as part-capitalist and part-territorial, the United States is said to become hegemonic in the twentieth century partly because, next to its major rivals, it is comparatively less concerned with winning a territorial empire. It is here, however, that one can argue with Arrighi: for the United States can only be described as a nonterritorial global hegemon to the extent that one ignores its imperialist expansionism on the North American continent—not to mention its annexations and land grabs in the Caribbean and the Pacific, the latter of which may involve the occupation of small parcels of land but that enables the strategic domination, through a combination of naval and aerial power, of vast swathes of the Earth's surface. Arrighi acknowledges this in passing, but there's still something off-putting about his reference to US expansionism as taking place "at home" (59; quoting Gareth Steadman-Jones). One feels obliged to ask, with one's mind very much on the genocide of indigenous Americans, *whose home?*

69. Ruggie, "Territoriality," 172.

70. Anderson, *Lineages of the Absolutist State*, 38.

71. Ruggie, "Territoriality," 165.

72. Sassen, *Territory, Authority, Rights*, 10–11.

73. See also the academic literature on the state's central role in funding and supporting many of the iconic institutions, business practices, and technological innovations associated with globalized capitalism—e.g., Marianna Mazzucato, *The Entrepreneurial State: Debunking Private v. Public Sector Myths* (London: Anthem, 2014); and Fred Block and Matthew R. Keller, eds., *State of Innovation: The U.S. Government's Role in Technology Development* (St Paul, MN: Paradigm, 2011).

74. Sassen, *Territory, Authority, Rights*, 14.

75. Saskia Sassen, *Losing Control? Sovereignty in an Age of Globalization* (New York: Columbia University Press, 1996), 6.

76. Sassen, *Territory, Authority, Rights*, 381.

77. For a brief account of typical ways in which the territorial space of the national state has long been punctured, see Kal Raustiala, "The Geography of Justice," *Fordham Law Review* 73 (2005): 2510–11.

78. Wendy Brown, *Walled States, Waning Sovereignty* (New York: Zone, 2010), 21; emphasis in original. For a different account of the political and temporal implications of the "post-" prefix, see Ella Shohat, whose argument implies that a prefix such as "neo-" would be more appropriate to the "after but not over" temporality identified by Brown. I tend to agree. Shohat, "Notes on the 'Post-Colonial," *Social Text* 31, no. 32 (1992): 99–113, especially 106.

79. James C. Scott, *The Art of Being Governed: An Anarchist History of Upland Southeast Asia* (New Haven, CT: Yale University Press, 2009), 67–68.

80. For extraterritorial law and governance in Africa before the Berlin Conference of 1884–85, see Siba N'Zatioula Grovogui, *Sovereigns, Quasi-Sovereigns, and Africans: Race and Self-Determination in International Law* (Minneapolis: University of Minnesota Press, 1996), especially chapter 2, "Partial Recognition to the Barbarous," 43–76. My thanks to Joseph Slaughter for this insight and reference.

81. See, e.g., Shih Shun Liu, "Extraterritoriality: Its Rise and Its Decline," *Columbia University Studies in the Social Sciences* 118, no. 2 (1925): 1–235.

82. On this topic, see Par Kristoffer Cassel, *Grounds of Judgment: Extraterritoriality and Imperial Power in Nineteenth-Century China and Japan* (New York: Oxford University Press, 2012), especially 6–11. Cassel notes that extraterritorial jurisdiction has Asian as well as European ancient and early modern contexts; in both East and West, "imperial and royal sovereigns usually claimed sovereignty over people rather than over territories" (8). Accounts of extraterritoriality in China cannot begin by presuming the normative status of Westphalian territorial sovereignty.

83. Andreas Osiander, "Sovereignty, International Relations, and the Westphalian Myth," *International Organization* 55, no. 2 (2001): 251–87.

84. In the post-1648 world, Teschke writes, "territories remained an adjunct of royal marriage politics and inter-dynastic wars of succession." Benno Teschke, *The Myth of 1648: Class, Geopolitics, and the Making of Modern International Relations* (London: Verso, 2003), 11.

85. Anderson, *Lineages of the Absolutist State*, 28.

86. Anderson, 21, 408.

87. John Agnew, "The Territorial Trap: The Geographic Assumptions of International Relations Theory," *Review of International Political Economy* 1, no. 1 (1994): 54, 66–67.

88. For information about eruvim, see Zvi Kaplan, "Eruv," *Encyclopaedia Judaica*, 2nd ed., vol. 6, ed. Michael Berenbaum and Fred Skolnik (Detroit: Macmillan Reference USA, 2007), 484–85.

89. "The Jewish Religious Landscape: Eruvim," Pluralism Project, 2004, http://www.pluralism.org/reports/view/160 (accessed 29 April 2014).

90. For maps of the Manhattan eruv, see "The Extended Manhattan Eruv: The Online Guide to the Virtual Wall," https://sites.google.com/site/manhattaneruv/. For similar information about the London eruv, see "Northwest London Eruv," http://nwlondoneruv.org/. Both sites accessed 29 April 2014.

91. Yad Vashem International Institute for Holocaust Research, http://db.yadvashem.org/deportation/place.html?language=en&itemId=5436623 (accessed 29 April 2014).

92. On this topic, see, e.g., James Young, *Textures of Memory: Holocaust Memorials and Meaning* (New Haven, CT: Yale University Press, 1993); and "Memory and Counter-Memory: The End of the Monument in Germany," *Harvard Design Magazine* 9 (Fall 1999): 1–10.

93. Keating points out that Britain—which from its founding in 1707 contained established churches with distinct theological characters in England and Scotland—never met the *cuius regio* standard (*Plurinational Democracy* 105). The former Prince-Bishopric of Münster was, from the Reformation onwards, also a regular site of struggle between different

Christian denominations, be they Catholic, Lutheran, or Anabaptist. If the Westphalian settlement tried to align the secular and religious identity of territories such as Münster, then *Zone* reminds us that that relationship was persistently off-kilter.

94. This is an obviously incomplete list, biased toward major world religions with established written legal codes.

95. John Griffiths, "What Is Legal Pluralism?," 6. Obviously, the histories of extraterritoriality briefly offered in my introduction (e.g., the Ottoman Capitulations) suggest a longer temporality than is implied by Griffiths's reference to the East India Company. Lauren Benton and Richard J. Ross note that the Western academic study of legal pluralism emerged out of the study of European imperialism, a fact that I suspect explains Griffiths's oddly foreshortened historical genealogy ("Empires and Legal Pluralism: Jurisdiction, Sovereignty, and Political Imagination in the Early Modern World," in *Legal Pluralism and Empires, 1500–1850*, ed. Lauren Benton and Richard J. Ross [New York: New York University Press, 2013], 1–2). I borrow the phrase "company-state" from Philip J. Stern, whose revisionary history of the East India Company as "a state in disguise as a merchant" does much to advance our sense of the historical complexity of the state form. Stern, *The Company-State: Corporate Sovereignty and the Early Modern Foundations of the British Empire in India* (New York: Oxford University Press, 2011).

96. For a classic example of such borderless thinking, see, e.g., the pair of books by organizational theorist Ken'ichi Ōmae, *The Borderless World: Power and Strategy in the Interlinked Economy* (New York: Harper Business, 1990); and *The End of the Nation-State* (New York: Simon & Schuster, 1995).

97. On territorial sovereignty as a three-dimensional practice, see Eyal Weizman, "Introduction to the Politics of Verticality," openDemocracy, 23 April 2002, http://www .opendemocracy.net/ecology-politicsverticality/article_801.jsp (accessed 10 March 2014).

98. Étienne Balibar, *We, the People of Europe? Reflections on Transnational Citizenship*, trans. James Swenson (Princeton, NJ: Princeton University Press, 2003), 1.

99. Étienne Balibar, *Politics and the Other Scene*, trans. Christine Jones, James Swenson, and Chris Turner (London: Verso, 2002), 78.

100. For this latter argument, see Sandro Mezzadra and Brett Neilson, *Border as Method, or, the Multiplication of Labor* (Durham, NC: Duke University Press, 2013). If anything, Mezzadra and Neilson have too generous a sense of what counts as a border. For this critique, see Linn Axelsson, "Temporalizing the Border," *Dialogues in Human Geography* 3, no. 3 (2013): 325. Wendy Brown does acknowledge that the contemporary moment is not only defined by wall-building projects such as those at the US-Mexico border, briefly noting that "we confront not only barricades, but passageways through them segregating high-end business traffic, ordinary travelers, and aspiring entrants" (*Walled States* 20).

101. For these examples, and for a longer consideration of the "mobility" and "differentiation" of borders in the twenty-first century, see Chris Rumford, "Theorizing Borders," *European Journal of Social Theory* 9, no. 2 (2006): 155–69.

102. For these details of checkpoints operated on the US/Mexico border, see US General Accountability Office, Report to Congressional Requesters: Border Patrol, August 2009, http://www.gao.gov/new.items/d09824.pdf (accessed 27 July 2105). For accounts of US Border Patrol checks made far from the Canadian border, see the interviews with international scholars at the University of Maine's Orono campus in Colin Woodard, "Far From Border, US Detains Foreign Students," *Chronicle of Higher Education*, 9 January 2011, http://chronicle.com/article/Far-From-Canada-Aggressive/125880/ (accessed 27 July 2015).

103. Balibar, *Politics and the Other Scene*, 91; emphases in original.

104. Balibar, 92; emphases in original.

105. For the history of the French legislation and the eventually successful constitutional challenges to it, see the judgment of the European Court of Human Rights, *Amuur v. France*, Application No. 19776/92, 25 June 1996, http://hudoc.echr.coe.int/sites/eng/pages/search.aspx?i=001-57988 (accessed 8 January 2015).

106. Balibar, *Politics and the Other Scene*, 83.

107. Mark Wallinger, *The Russian Linesman: Frontiers, Borders, and Thresholds* (London: Hayward, 2009), 76. Nureyev's defection scene is memorably narrated in Rudolf Nureyev, *Nureyev: An Autobiography with Pictures* (New York: Dutton, 1963), 13–23.

108. This discourse has been especially vital in Latinx and Chican@ Studies, especially as those fields focus on the US/Mexico border. To give just a few classic examples: Gloria Andalzúa famously described the US/Mexico border as "una herida abierta [open wound] where the Third World grates against the first and bleeds. . . . the lifeblood of two worlds merging to form a third country—a border culture" (*Borderlands/La Frontera: The New Mestiza* [Berkeley: University of California Press, 1987], 3). José David Saldívar invokes the US/Mexico border as "a paradigm of crossing, resistance, and circulation" that, far from reifying nation-state identities, "has contributed to the 'worlding' of American studies" (*Border Matters: Remapping American Cultural Studies* [Berkeley: University of California Press, 1997], xiii). And Walter Mignolo uses similar language in developing a concept of "border thinking" as a "worldly culture" that multiplies "epistemic energies in diverse local histories . . . and its unavoidable obscure companion, the history of colonialism" (*Local Histories/Global Designs: Coloniality, Subaltern Knowledge, and Border Thinking* [Princeton, NJ: Princeton University Press, 2000], 39). An early bibliography of research on the US/Mexico borderlands lists over two hundred books and articles and concludes that they share, above all, a "focus on the paradoxical, on the contradictory, and on the conflicts of cultural practices and identity." Robert Alvarez Jr., "The Mexican-US Border: The Making of an Anthropology of Borderlands," *Annual Review of Anthropology* 24 (1995): 462.

109. See, e.g., Diane Abbott, MP, "Brian's Banners Were a Necessary Mess," *Evening Standard*, 24 May 2006, 12.

110. United Kingdom of Great Britain and Northern Ireland, Serious Organized Crime and Police Act 2005, Part 4: Public Order and Conduct in Public Places Etc.: Demonstrations in Vicinity of Parliament: 138 (1)-(3), http://www.legislation.gov.uk/ukpga/2005/15/pdfs/ukpga_20050015_en.pdf (accessed 13 November 2014).

111. David Blunkett, MP, quoted in Joe Murphy, "Parliament Protesters Face Fines and Prison," *Evening Standard*, 24 November 2004, D2.

112. Amity lines traditionally demarcated the border between the European law of nations and a zone of anomie and lawlessness. See Carl Schmitt, *The Nomos of the Earth in the International Law of the Jus Publicum Europaeum*, trans. G. L. Ulmen (New York: Telos, 2003), 92–99.

113. In a letter to the editor of the *Guardian*, Charles Thomson of "anti-anti-art" group the Stuckists complains that the exclusion zone actually ends north of Tate Britain ("Letters: As We Like It," *Guardian*, 18 January 2007, http://www.theguardian.com/news/2007 /jan/19/leadersandreply.mainsection1 (accessed 11 April 2014). Wallinger responded in the same venue: "As the wall labels in the gallery clearly state, I took the 1km exclusion zone of the act literally. The act states that the zone 'at no point . . . may be more than one kilometre in a straight line from the point nearest to it in Parliament Square'" ("Letters: Boundary Dispute," *Guardian*, 29 January 2007, http://arts.guardian.co.uk /art/news/story/0,,2000890,00.html [accessed 11 April 2014]). That is, his taped line is more than one kilometer from where Haw's protest actually was but never more than one kilometer from Parliament Square.

114. The common law tradition protects free speech and assembly via the principle of "no prior restraint," in which rights can be assumed and acted upon where not explicitly denied or regulated in law. Since the passage of the Human Rights Act 1998, and certainly during the events described in this chapter, when the United Kingdom was a member state of the European Union, common law also had to be consistent with the constitutional protections enshrined in Section I of the European Convention on Human Rights (ECHR), including Article 10 (Freedom of Expression) and Article 11 (Freedom of Assembly and Association). See Eric Barendt, *Freedom of Speech*, 2nd ed. (Oxford: Oxford University Press, 2005), 39–47.

115. For the official Russian justification for Snowden's extended stay in the airport, see "US Whistleblower Snowden 'Still in Moscow Airport,'" BBC News, 26 June 2013, http:// www.bbc.com/news/world-europe-23053915 (accessed 8 January 2015).

116. United Kingdom of Great Britain and Northern Ireland, Terrorism Act 2000, Section 40(1)(b), http://www.legislation.gov.uk/ukpga/2000/11/section/40 (accessed 9 January 2015).

117. A contemporary summary of the Miranda case and of significant early reporting is provided by Daniel Isenberg, "David Miranda Special Edition—Human Rights Roundup," UK Human Rights Blog, 26 August 2013, http://ukhumanrightsblog.com/2013/08/26 /david-miranda-special-edition-the-human-rights-roundup/ (accessed 9 January 2015).

118. United Kingdom of Great Britain and Northern Ireland, Immigration Act 1971, Part I, Section 11 (1), http://www.legislation.gov.uk/ukpga/1971/77/pdfs/ukpga_19710077_en.pdf (accessed 1 September 2015).

119. Lord Justice Laws, *David Miranda v. The Secretary of State for the Home Department and The Commissioner of the Police of the Metropolis* ([2014] EWHC 255). http://www.bailii .org/ew/cases/EWHC/Admin/2014/255.html (accessed 8 January 2015). Laws quotes here

the judgment of Lord Justice Gross in the case of *Sylvie Beghal v. Director of Public Prosecutions* ([2013] EWHC 2573), http://www.bailii.org/ew/cases/EWHC/Admin/2013/2573 .html (accessed 9 January 2015).

120. Justine Lloyd, "Departing Sovereignty," *Borderlands E-Journal* 1, no. 2 (2002): http://www .borderlands.net.au/vol1no2_2002/lloyd_departing.html (accessed 9 January 2015). It's worth pointing out that airports are generally not located "in the heart of" global (or provincial) cities. On the contrary, like most such infrastructural zones, they are located in what Marion Shoard calls "edgelands": "The apparently unplanned, certainly uncelebrated and largely incomprehensible territory where town and country meet." Shoard, "Edgelands," in *Remaking the Landscape*, ed. Jennifer Jenkins (London: Profile, 2002), 118.

121. Lloyd, "Departing Sovereignty," para. 38.

122. Martin Herbert, *Mark Wallinger* (London: Thames & Hudson, 2011), 105–12. I am indebted to Herbert's monograph for several details in the paragraph that follows.

123. Herbert, *Mark Wallinger*, 112.

124. Gaston Bachelard, *The Poetics of Space*, trans. M. Jolas (Boston: Beacon, 1994), 218; Jacques Derrida, *Of Hospitality*, trans. Rachel Bowlby (Stanford, CA: Stanford University Press, 2000), 123.

2. CITY-STATE

1. For "the weird," old and new, see Jeff VanderMeer, "The New Weird: 'It's Alive?,'" in *The New Weirds*, ed. Ann VanderMeer and Jeff VanderMeer (San Francisco: Tachyon, 2007), xi–xviii. For the paraliterary (there hyphenated as "para-literary"), see Darko Suvin, "On the Poetics of Science Fiction as a Genre," *College English* 34, no. 3 (1972): 372–82. Suvin's landmark essay argues that SF should be distinguished from the paraliterary as such, since "the criteria for the sufficiency of most SF is to be found in the genre itself. This makes SF in principle . . . equivalent to any other 'major' literary genre" (380). For Miéville's critique of how Suvin's embrace of SF depends on an hierarchical distinction between SF and fantasy, see "Afterword: Cognition as Ideology: A Dialectic of SF Theory," in *Red Planets: Marxism and Science Fiction*, ed. Mark Bould and China Miéville (London: Pluto, 2009), 231–48. "The weird" is, among much else, a means of dissolving this kind of hierarchical distinction among popular and speculative genres.

2. An obviously incomplete list: the length and number of Miéville's novels, combined with his brilliant idiosyncrasy, make for a long catalog of characteristic terms, tropes, and themes. On the prefix "ab-" (from the Latin for "away") see Kirsten Tranter, "An Interview with China Miéville," *Contemporary Literature* 53, no. 3 (2012): 417–36. On Miéville's neologisms, see Carl Freedman, *Art and Idea in the Novels of China Miéville* (London: Gylphi, 2015), 87–88.

3. Tranter, "Interview with China Miéville," 423, 421.

4. For the figure/ground analogy as a way of conceiving of setting as a matrix for defining not itself but character, see Seymour Chatman, *Story and Discourse: Narrative Structure*

in Fiction and Film (Ithaca, NY: Cornell University Press, 1978), 138–41. For the complaint that "setting . . . so readily symbolic, becomes, in some modern theories, 'atmosphere' or 'tone,'" see Rene Wellek and Arthur Warren, *Theory of Literature* (New York: Harcourt, Brace, 1948), 224.

5. Mieke Bal, *Narratology: Introduction to the Theory of Narrative*, 3rd ed. (Toronto: University of Toronto Press, 2009), 139.

6. Roger Luckhurst, "The Weird: A Dis/Orientation," *Textual Practice* 31, no. 6 (2017): 1057.

7. For the history and context of Harrison's first coinage of "New Weird," see VanderMeer, "New Weird," ix and 317–31.

8. Luckhurst, "Weird"; quoting Mezzarda and Nelson, *Border as Method*, 6.

9. Roger Luckhurst, "In the Zone: Topologies of Gothic Weirdness," in *Gothic Science Fiction, 1980–2010*, ed. Sarah Wasson and Emily Alder (Liverpool: Liverpool University Press, 2011), 23.

10. For "errant geography," see China Méville, *Iron Council* (New York: Del Rey, 2004), 479. Hereafter cited parenthetically as *IC*.

11. China Miéville, *The City & the City* (New York: Del Rey, 2010), 80. Hereafter cited parenthetically as *CC*.

12. W. G. Sebald, *Austerlitz*, trans. Anthea Bell (New York: Random House, 2001), 29; W. G. Sebald, *Austerlitz* (Munich: Carl Hanser Verlag, 2001), 43. Hereafter cited with the German pagination following the English, thus: *Austerlitz*, 29/41.

13. This is a quality that, in his meditation on *Austerlitz*, Eric Santner reads in terms of Agamben's political theory. Santner, *On Creaturely Life: Rilke, Benjamin, Sebald* (Chicago: University of Chicago Press, 2006), 132.

14. Giorgio Agamben, *State of Exception*, trans. Kevin Attell (Chicago: University of Chicago Press, 2004), 23.

15. Plato, *Symposium*, trans. Alexander Nehamas and Paul Woodruff (Indianapolis: Hackett, 1989), 26–27.

16. For an account of *The City & the City* as depicting sovereignty in three dimensions, see Robert Duggan, "The Geopolitics of Inner Space in Contemporary British Fiction," *Textual Practice* 27, no. 5 (2013): 899–920, especially 911–18.

17. Carl Schmitt, *Political Theology*, trans. George Schwab (Chicago: University of Chicago Press, 2005), 36.

18. On this topic, see Agamben's restatement of what he dubs the "perfect" correspondence between Schmitt's theory of the state of exception and Nicolas Malebranhce's account of the relation between miracles and the general will. Agamben, *The Kingdom and the Glory: For a Theological Genealogy of Economy and Government*, trans. Lorenzo Chiesa with Matteo Mandarini (Stanford, CA: Stanford University Press, 2011), 267–68.

19. Bodin, *On Sovereignty*, 23.

20. Schmitt, *Political Theology*, 7.

21. Schmitt, 5; emphases added. See also Jean Bodin, *On Sovereignty*, ed. and trans. Julian H. Franklin (Cambridge: Cambridge University Press, 1992), 56.

22. China Miéville in Annalee Newitz, "Ask China Miéville Anything You Want about *The City & the City*,'" io9, 29 July 2010, http://io9.gizmodo.com/5600009/ask-china-mieville -anything-you-want-about-the-city—the-city (accessed 5 August 2010).

23. China Miéville, "Theses on Monsters," *Conjunctions* 59 (2012): 143.

24. Joan Gordon, "Reveling in Genre: An Interview with China Miéville," *Science Fiction Studies* 30, no. 3 (2003): 365.

25. China Miéville, *Un Lun Dun* (New York: Del Rey, 2008), 99.

26. China Miéville, *Looking for Jake: Stories* (New York: Del Rey, 2005), 55–77. My thanks to Kirsten Tranter for making this connection.

27. VanderMeer hails *Perdido Street Station* as the novel that "crystallized" the New Weird tendency into self- and popular awareness ("New Weird," ix-xii).

28. China Miéville, *Perdido Street Station* (New York: Del Rey, 2000), 144. Hereafter cited parenthetically as *PSS*. *PSS* was nominated for the 2002 Nebula Award and Hugo Awards and won the Arthur C. Clark Award for 2001. *The Scar* (2002) was again nominated for the Hugo, nominated for the Arthur C. Clark Award and Philip K. Dick Award, and won the 2003 British Fantasy Award. *Iron Council* (2004) won the 2005 Locus Fantasy Award and repeated *Perdido Street Station*'s victory in the 2005 Arthur C. Clark Award competition.

29. Peter Lamborn Wilson, *Pirate Utopias: Moorish Corsairs and European Renegadoes*, 2nd rev. ed. (New York: Autonomedia, 2003).

30. China Miéville, "Floating Utopias: Freedom and Unfreedom of the Seas," in *Evil Paradises: Dreamworlds of Neoliberalism*, ed. Mike Davis and Daniel Bertrand Monk (New York: New Press, 2007), 256.

31. Freedman, *Art and Idea in the Novels of China Miéville*, 49–54. For Miéville's sympathy with radical pirate/maroon history, see his admiring reference to Peter Lunebaugh and Marcus Rediker's *The Many-Headed Hydra: Sailors, Slaves, Commoners, and the Hidden History of the Revolutionary Atlantic* (Boston: Beacon, 2000) in "Floating Utopias," 257, 315n18.

32. Freedman, *Art and Idea*, 47.

33. China Miéville, *The Scar* (New York: Del Rey, 2004), 106. Hereafter cited parenthetically as *S*.

34. For Miéville and the western, see Lou Anders, interview with China Miéville, *Believer*, April 2005, http://www.believermag.com/issues/200504/?read=interview_mie ville (accessed 19 July 2016).

35. On the relation between constituted and constituent power, see Martin Loughlin, "The Concept of Constituent Power," *European Journal of Political Theory* 13, no. 2 (2014): 218–37. I use both of these terms literally, to highlight how Iron Council rules in the name of its constituents without making sovereignty claims, and metaphorically, to suggest how the train's constant movement stops it from taking final geographical form.

36. Yet another example: before its revolutionary apotheosis, as the industrial magnate Weather Wrightby drives his railroad through the wilderness, the train is followed by a group of prostitutes whose mobile habitation is called "Fucktown." The train's transformation into Iron Council begins when the women of Fucktown go on strike, a series of

events that leads the revolutionaries to "make flags for [the] sudden new country" they
have made of the train (*IC* 250). Bellis Coldwine says in *The Scar* that people believe "any
city . . . is better than none" (339).

37. Aristotle, *The Politics*, trans. Carnes Lord (Chicago: University of Chicago Press, 1984),
35. In this vein, Christopher Palmer suggests that the plot of saving the city is a repeated
element of Miéville's fiction. Palmer, "Saving the City in China Miéville's Bas-Lag Novels," *Extrapolation* 50, no. 2 (2009): 224–38.

38. Those of Miéville's novels set in the "real" territorial state called the United Kingdom—
King Rat (1998), *Un Lun Dun* (2007), and *Kraken* (2010)—initially appear to follow territorial business as usual: London is the capital city of a state, the United Kingdom, that
it dominates but in which it is also subsumed. Any sense of normality is, of course, soon
disturbed by weird happenings that imply, as with *King Rat*'s occult animal kingdoms,
that the sorts of political decisions taken in Parliament are merely epiphenomenal to the
true workings of power. More basically still, Miéville's nominally British territories
remain peculiarly metropolitan, as if London were an adequate synecdoche for the kingdom as a whole. He takes his readers on journeys across the deserts and oceans of
Bas-Lag, but his "British" fictions seldom if ever leave the capital's urban terrain, which
suffices as an imaginative world in itself.

39. President Bush's comment ("I'm the decider, and I decide what is best") was made in a
press conference on 18 April 2006, long after *Iron Council* went to press. Bush made the
remark while defending his right to determine the future of defense secretary Donald
Rumsfeld, following public criticism of his handling of the wars in Iraq and Afghanistan. Critics were quick to associate this remark with the Bush Administration's centralization and personalization of executive power: see, e.g., Caroline Read, "Bush's
'Imperial' Presidency," *Financial Times*, 5 July 2006, https://www.ft.com/content/d97
b1b48-0c4f-11db-86c7-0000779e2340 (accessed 20 September 2016).

40. Gordon, "Reveling in Genre," 357. Two of Miéville's hand-drawn maps of Bas-Lag are
collected in China Miéville, "Miscellany Concerning the World of Bas Lag and the City
of New Crobuzon," in *Flotsam Fantastique: The Souvenir Book of the World Fantasy Convention 2013*, ed. Stephen Jones (Brighton: World Fantasy Convention, 2013), 158–59.

41. See, e.g., the several maps of Bas-Lag posted on the Tumblr page Fuck Yeah Fictional
Maps: http://fuckyeahfictionalmaps.tumblr.com/ (accessed 9 January 2020). See also
the massive selection of fan art Bas-Lag for Beginners: A Visual Guide: http://per
manentsatisfactions.tumblr.com/post/37155225973/bas-lag-for-beginners-a-visual-guide
(accessed 9 January 2020). According to Miéville, the *Perdido Street Station* map of Bas-
Lag contains an error (Jones, *Flotsam Fantastique*, 158).

42. Gordon, "Reveling in Genre," 366. A note, here, on Miéville's use of the word "genre":
he is irreverent about distinctions between subgenres such SF, fantasy, noir, and so on.
This attitude tends to lead him, as here, to adopt the encompassing label "genre," rather
than emphasizing the diversity of popular genres or subgenres. This doesn't mean that
he ignores generic tropes. For instance, knowing that *Iron Council* would be inspired by
the western, Miéville decided that he "had to go away and read a lot of westerns so I

didn't seem to be patronizing this genre that was relatively new to me. If I've done my job well, *Iron Council* is not a kind of postmodern, ironic wink at the western. It's a fucking *western*. It's got cowboys in it, for fuck's sake" (Anders). On the other hand, *Iron Council* is, by any measure, a very unfaithful western. Alongside the usual horsey loners, it features golems, robots, interdimensional spiders, sorcerers, elemental beings, and more.

43. Robert H. Sherard, "Jules Verne Re-visited," T.P.'s Weekly, 9 October 1903, http://jv .gilead.org.il/sherard2.html (accessed 9 January 2020). Verne misspoke here; Wells's antigravitational metal takes his explorers to the Moon, not Mars.

44. The ab-canny is to the uncanny as the weird is to the hauntological: "The Weird is not the return of any repressed," writes Miéville in an essay on M. R. James. That's to say, the weird is not characterized by the figure of the revenant, by the horror of the familiar thing out of place or time; it is the horror of sheer alterity. Miéville, "M. R. James and the Quantum Vampire," *Collapse* 4 (29 November 2011): http://weirdfictionreview.com /2011/11/m-r-james-and-the-quantum-vampire-by-china-mieville/ (accessed 4 August 2016).

45. Wells's "domesticate the impossible hypothesis" remark is quoted approvingly by China Miéville in his introduction to H. G. Wells, *The First Men in the Moon*, ed. Patrick Parrinder (London: Penguin, 2005), xvii. For the line in original context, see H. G. Wells, "Preface to The Scientific Romances" (1933), *H. G. Wells's Literary Criticism*, ed. Patrick Parrinder and Robert M. Philmus (Brighton: Harvester, 1980), 240–45.

46. Miéville, "Afterword," 238–39. For further discussion of cognition and genre, see Rhys Williams, "Recognizing Cognition: On Suvin, Miéville, and the Utopian Impulse in the Contemporary Fantastic," *Science Fiction Studies* 4, no. 3 (2014): 617–33.

47. Gordon, "Reveling in Genre," 357.

48. Seymour Chatman, *Story and Discourse*, 139. See Kurt Vonnegut, *Slaughterhouse-Five* (New York: Dial, 2009), 7. The idea that setting is in part constituted by the distribution of minor characters—which is to say, the combination of their location, attitude and relative density—is implied by notion of "character space" in Alex Woloch, *The One Versus the Many: Minor Characters and the Space of the Protagonist in the Novel* (Princeton, NJ: Princeton University Press, 2003), especially 12–24. Consider also, in this regard, the nonhuman actors that, in considering setting through the concept of the social sites, David J. Alworth reads as tantamount to fictional persons. Alworth, *Site Reading: Fiction, Art, Social Form* (Princeton, NJ: Princeton University Press, 2015), 20.

49. My reference to Edgeworth replicates the chronology proposed by Vera Kreilkamp's *The Anglo-Irish Novel and the Big House* (Syracuse, NY: Syracuse University Press, 1998). The fact that a novel such as *Castle Rackrent* (1800) is better known as an example of the gothic than the "big house" subgenre also reminds us that such categories are far from clean or exclusive—an obvious point, but one Miéville mobilizes to radical ends.

50. Steampunk thus represents a deliberate rebuff, immanent within novelistic form, to the idea that paraliterary genres ought to be distinguished from each other in hierarchical terms. Miéville believes strongly in the equality of speculative subgenres and on the

fungibility of distinctions among them. See, e.g., his remarks in conversation with John Newsinger, "Fantasy and Revolution: An interview with China Miéville," *International Socialism* 88 (Autumn 2000): http://www.marxists.de/culture/sci-fi/newsinger.htm (accessed 9 January 2020). Fredric Jameson suggests that SF depends for its identity on endless disputes about what can be admitted to its canon, such that it "is constituted by generic recognition (or its accompanying opposite number, generic undecidability)" (*Archaeologies of the Future: The Desire Called Utopia and Other Science Fictions* [London: Verso, 2005], 68). Miéville argues that Jameson's special focus on the utopian content of SF, and criticism of the nostalgic and ethical character of fantasy, reproduces Suvin's elevation of SF above fantasy ("Afterword," 231–32, 245–46, 246n9).

51. For the story of Jack Half-a-Prayer, see Miéville, *Iron Council*, 65–67; and "Jack," in China Miéville, *Looking for Jake: Stories* (New York: Ballantine, 2005), 199–212.

52. Miéville, "Floating Utopias," 260.

53. Miéville, 260–61.

54. Miéville completed a PhD in International Relations at the London School of Economics in 2001.

55. China Miéville, *Between Equal Rights: A Marxist Theory of International Law* (Leiden: Brill, 2004), 54, 63; emphases in original. Hereafter cited parenthetically as *BER*.

56. "Brilliant but sinister" is Alex Callinocos's phrase, quoted in *BER*, 27.

57. Carl Schmitt, *The Nomos of the Earth in the International Law of the* Jus Publicum Europaeum, trans. G. L. Ulmen (New York: Telos, 2003), 70, 79. This passage is quoted, in a slightly different form, by Miéville, *BER*, 29.

58. Not fully or singly extraterritorial, however. To say otherwise would be to ignore indigenous legal regimes, with their own attitudes toward the relation between land and law, not to mention differences among and within settler-colonial regimes.

59. "Agonal" is from Schmitt, *Nomos of the Earth*, 99. Miéville cites Jörg Fisch's objection that there is no evidence for amity lines in European treaties, as well as Fisch's thesis that they were "an invention of the French and the English in the 17th century . . . as an instrument against Spanish claims" (*BER* 180n119, quoting personal correspondence with Fisch; ellipsis in original). Miéville avers, however, that "even if Fisch is right that the Spanish never agreed these terms . . . the very fact of their being so posited early in the seventeenth century, disputed or not, is evidence that the model they embedded was functional to the new global thinking of (at least some) European powers" (*BER* 181n119).

60. Agamben, *Homo Sacer*, 159.

61. Agamben, 15; emphasis added.

62. Agamben, 18, 21, 175; emphases in original.

63. Keller Easterling, *Enduring Innocence: Global Architecture and Its Political Masquerades* (Cambridge, MA: MIT Press, 2005), 3.

64. Easterling, *Enduring Innocence*, 14.

65. Eyal Weizman, "On Extraterritoriality."

66. For the conference and subsequent edited volume, see the website for Archipelagos of Exception: Sovereignties of Extraterritoriality, Centre de Cultura Contemporània de

Barcelona, 10–11 November 2005, http://www.cccb.org/en/activities/file/archipelago-of
-exception/218418 (accessed 4 August 2016).

67. An Architektur, "Extra-Territorial Spaces and Camps," 23–28.

68. See, e.g., Sari Hanafi, "Palestinian Refugee Camps in the Palestinian Territory: Territory of Exception and Locus of Resistance, in *The Power of Inclusive Exclusion: Anatomy
of Israeli Rule in the Occupied Territories*, ed. Adi Ophir and Michal Givoni (Cambridge,
MA: MIT Press, 2009), 495–518; Simon Turner, "Suspended Spaces: Contesting Sovereignties in a Refugee Camp," in *Sovereign Bodies: Citizens, Migrants, and States in the Postcolonial World*, ed. Thomas Blom Hansen and Finn Stepputat (Princeton, NJ: Princeton
University Press, 2005), 312–32; and Trevor Paglen, *Blank Spots on the Map: The Dark Geography of the Pentagon's Secret World* (New York: New American Library, 2010), especially
16. Hanfi and Turner differ from Agamben in that they both emphasize the complexity
of political identity and experience in refugee camps, which are at once zones of subjec-
tion and resistance to sovereign power.

69. Giorgio Agamben, "What Is a Camp?," in *Means Without End: Notes on Politics*, trans.
Vincenzo Binetti and Cesare Casarino (Minneapolis: University Minnesota Press, 2000),
39; emphasis added.

70. Agamben, *State of Exception* 3.

71. Agamben, "Sovereign Police," in *Means Without End*, 104.

72. Agamben, "Beyond Human Rights," in *Means Without End*, 24.

73. Agamben, "Beyond Human Rights," 25.

74. Agamben, 24.

75. Agamben, 24. The language of region used here is inherently indeterminate (a region
can be small and subnational, like the West Midlands, or huge and transnational, like
West Africa). Worse, it's mealy-mouthed. Two or more groups might happily cohabit
within a region—history is full of such examples. The point seems to be that "region"
seems to sidestep the ideological toxicity associated with "nation" while still gesturing
toward some kind of relation, however eccentric, between locality, sociality, and representation. Still, what kind of "regional" political institutions, legitimated on what
basis, are up to the job of distributing scarce resources and adjudicating competing
claims for justice? Agamben's sentences beg the question of how one establishes
a framework for determining regional (and interregional) priorities, as well as for
generating extracommunal social solidarities, without recourse to institutions such as
citizenship.

76. Agamben, 24.

77. Agamben, 24.

78. Agamben, 26.

79. In the Italian text of "Al di là dei diritti dell'uomo," the word translated into English as
"extraterritoriality" is the Italian Latinate expression "extraterritorialità" (Giorgio Agamben, *Mezzi Senza Fine: Note sulla Politica* [Torino: Bollati Boringhieri, 1996], 19. In
Homo Sacer, the phrase translated into English as "delimits an extratemporal and extraterritorial threshold" reads "delimita una soglia extratemporale ed extraterritoriale."

Giorgio Agamben, *Homo Sacer: Il potere sovrano e la nuda vita* (Torino: Einaudi, 1995), 177.

80. Miéville's specific target in this section of *Between Equal Rights* is John Austin's "command theory of law," as articulated in his 1832 *The Province of Jurisprudence Determined*, ed. W. Rumble (Cambridge: Cambridge University Press, 1995).

81. Pavlos Eleftheriadis, "Law and Sovereignty," *Law and Philosophy* 29, no. 5 (2010): 561.

82. Agamben, *State of Exception*, 86.

83. An exception: David Peace's *Red Riding Quartet* (1999–2002), in which the price exacted on "good" policemen is at once tremendous (death, the end of one's career, madness) and in which being "good" means going against the interests of the state.

84. Agamben, *State of Exception*, 6, 48.

85. Sebald, *Austerlitz*, 30/44–5.

86. Michel de Certeau, *The Practice of Everyday Life*, trans. Stephen Rendall (Berkeley: University of California Press, 1984), 36–37.

87. Sebald, *Austerlitz*, 30/44.

88. Evgeny Pashukanis, *The General Theory of Law and Marxism*, in *Pashukanis: Selected Writings on Marxism and Law*, ed. Piers Beirne and Robert Sharlet (London: Academic Press), 69. Quoted in *BER*, 130; emphasis added by Miéville.

3. STRING THEORY

1. United States Department of Education, "Equity of Opportunity," http://www.ed.gov/equity (accessed 11 January 2015). The text of this webpage has changed over the writing of this chapter. See an archived version at https://web.archive.org/web/20150111055000/http://www.ed.gov/equity (accessed 24 August 2016).

2. For a critique of the power of education to alleviate social inequality, see John Marsh, *Class Dismissed: Why We Cannot Teach or Learn Our Way Out of Inequality* (New York: Monthly Review, 2011).

3. United States Department of Agriculture Economic Research Service, "Rural Poverty and Well-being: The Geography of Poverty," 17 December 2015, http://www.ers.usda.gov/topics/rural-economy-population/rural-poverty-well-being/geography-of-poverty.aspx#.U8VZvordUms (accessed 24 August 2016).

4. KaNin Reese and Jasen Taciak, "A Geographic Comparison of Child Poverty and Adult Poverty, 2006–2009," United States Census Bureau poster, presented at the Annual Meeting of the Population Association of America, 31 March 2011, http://www.census.gov/did/www/saipe/publications/files/Reese%20&%20Taciak%20PAA%20poster%204-13-11.pdf (accessed 24 August 2016).

5. John Lanchester, struggling to explain the June 2016 Brexit vote in the United Kingdom, is even more emphatic about the relationship between geography and social identity and status: "What strikes you if you travel to different parts of the country, though, is that the primary reality of modern Britain is not so much class as geography.

Geography is destiny. And for much of the country, not a happy destiny." Lanchester, "Brexit Blues," *London Review of Books*, 28 July 2016, http://www.lrb.co.uk/v38/n15 /john-lanchester/brexit-blues (accessed 24 August 2016).

6. Kenneth T. Jackson, "Race, Ethnicity, and Real Estate Appraisal: The Home Owners Loan Corporation and the Federal Housing Administration," *Journal of Urban History* 6, no. 4 (1980): 447. For a reassessment of Jackson's influential argument, suggesting that federal government policy and long-standing racial biases among private actors were more influential in the history of redlining than the New Deal–era Home Owners Loan Corporation, see Amy E. Hillier, "Redlining and the Home Owners Loan Corporation," *Journal of Urban History* 29, no. 4 (2003): 394–420. My thanks to Donovan Finn for these citations.

7. Rita Felski also advocates for what she calls "mid-level reading," which would be neither "close" (rooted in the singular close reading) nor "distant" (based on quantitative analysis or abstract literary-historical models). For Felski, mid-level reading is connected to Latour's actor-network theory, with its distributed model of social agency: "If we take the lessons of actor-network theory to heart, we are thus less inclined to pore over a single text to draw out its hidden plenitude of aesthetic, philosophical, or sociopolitical truth. . . . Yet actor-network theory also pulls out the rug from under the sociologist's dispassionate analysis of a literary system: from such a bird's-eye view, everything looks remarkably similar, things blur together, and essential details are lost" ("Latour and Literary Studies," *PMLA* 130, no. 3 [May 2015]: 741). To be clear, this is not what I'm suggesting. The model of social power operative in this book is, as we saw in chapter 1, drawn from Michael Mann's distributed polymorphic account of the interaction between ideological, economic, military, and political forces. But, while Mann offers a distributed account of social power, that theory does not minimize the subject/object distinction or aggrandize the agency of nonhuman objects. By "medium scale," then, I mean no more or less than: (1) the selection of a range of analytical objects sufficiently large, and sufficiently similar, to make reasonable conjectures at the level of a genre or type; and (2) the restriction of that range of analytical objects to a set small enough to allow for some attention to literary form—and, thus, to how generic patterns manifest themselves at the "lower" levels of diction and point of view. (And, while we're here in the definitional weeds, let me finally add that by "sufficiently similar" I mean here published within a few years of each other, written in the same language, by authors who straddle the literary/popular divide, and set in Britain or North America.)

8. Ernest Hemingway, *The Sun Also Rises* (New York: Scribner, 1996), 127.

9. Eric Hayot, *On Literary Worlds* (New York: Oxford University Press, 2012), 46.

10. Raymond Chandler, *Later Novels and Other Writings* (New York: Penguin/Library of America, 1995), 620. See also Hayot, *On Literary Worlds*, 43–47.

11. Hayot, 46–47.

12. Hayot, 47.

13. Erich Auerbach, *Mimesis: The Representation of Reality in Western Literature*, trans. Willard R. Trask (Princeton, NJ: Princeton University Press, 2003), 473.

14. Hippolyte Taine, *Histoire de la littérature anglaise*, 4 vols. (Paris: Hachette, 1863–64).

15. Samuel R. Delany, *The Jewel-Hinged Jaw* (Elizabethtown, NJ: Dragon, 1977), 149; cited in R. B. Gill, "The Uses of Genre and the Classification of Speculative Fiction," *Mosaic: A Journal for the Interdisciplinary Interpretation of Literature* 46, no. 2 (2013): 72.

16. Margaret Atwood, "*The Handmaid's Tale* and *Oryx and Crake* in Context," *PMLA* 119, no. 3 (2004): 513. It makes little sense to make scientific plausibility a standard by which we say something is *not* SF. For instance, the loose subgenre of "hard SF" is so strongly associated with values of scientific and technological accuracy and plausibility that Kathryn Cramer begins her survey with the provisional definitions that "a work of sf [*sic*] is hard sf if a relationship to and knowledge of science and technology is central to the work" and that "[the] primary characteristic for defining a work as hard sf is its relationship with science" ("Hard Science Fiction," in *The Cambridge Companion to Science Fiction*, ed. Edward James and Farah Mendlesohn [Cambridge: Cambridge University Press, 2003], 187, 188). It's also far from clear whether all the elements in Atwood's own speculative fictions satisfy her condition of scientific plausibility. What science, for instance, underlies the "spray guns" that pop up throughout the *MaddAddam* trilogy? These future weapons are never described in detail and lack any obvious connection to current military technology. They're powered by something called "cellpacks," which can run out and might be batteries, or might be some sort of magazine. We don't know what kind of munitions they fire. Overall, they seem like a near-future version of a submachine gun: deadly, easy to use, but not especially efficient. Atwood's "spray guns" are therefore not different in kind from many kinds of SF hardware: a piece of technology, more potent than ours (and therefore deserving of the sinister adjective "spray") but familiar enough (the verb "spray" is commonly used to describe automatic gunfire) that it needs neither expository elaboration nor scientific justification.

17. See, most influentially, Ursula Le Guin's rejoinder to Atwood's rejection of the label "science fiction," which she explains thus: "She doesn't want the literary bigots to shove her into the literary ghetto." Review of Margaret Atwood, *The Year of the Flood*, *Guardian*, 29 August 2009, https://www.theguardian.com/books/2009/aug/29/margaret-atwood -year-of-flood (accessed 10 August 2016).

18. John Rieder, "What Is SF? Some Thoughts on Genre," in *A Virtual Introduction to Science Fiction*, ed. Lars Schmeink (2012): http://virtual-sf.com/?page_id=137 (accessed 5 July 2016). Although the term "speculative fiction" was coined by science fiction pioneer Robert Heinlein in 1947, it was popularized by the US author and editor Judith Merril as she worked to boost British "New Wave" SF authors such as J. G. Ballard, whose work tended to eschew extraterrestrial settings and an emphasis on scientific progress. See Helen Merrick, "Fiction, 1964–1979," in *The Routledge Companion to Science Fiction*, ed. Mark Bould, Andrew M. Butler, Adam Roberts, and Sherryl Vint (New York: Routledge, 2009), 105.

19. Mark Bould and Sherryl Vint, *The Routledge Concise History of Science Fiction* (New York: Routledge, 2011), 19.

20. Mark Bould and Sherryl Vint, "There Is No Such Thing as Science Fiction," in *Reading Science Fiction*, ed. James Gunn, Marleen Barr, and Matthew Candelaria (New York: Palgrave Macmillan, 2009), 43.

21. Quantitative analysis suggests weaknesses in the nominalist position. For instance, Ted Underwood argues that—in the case of SF, the detective novel, and the gothic—"a genre's past does an excellent job of predicting its future." See Underwood, "The Life Cycles of Genres," *Journal of Cultural Analytics* (23 May 2016): http://culturalanalytics.org/2016/05/the-life-cycles-of-genres/ (accessed 5 July 2016). For a recent account of genre in contemporary fiction, which balances "a set of relatively stable norms and a heterogeneous, historically variant set of practical instantiations," see Jeremy Rosen, *Minor Characters Have Their Day: Genre and the Contemporary Literary Marketplace* (New York: Columbia University Press, 2016), 12.

22. This list is illustrative, not comprehensive. Gill points out that the Internet Speculative Fiction Database contains entries relevant to a much wider array of genres: "Science fiction, fantasy, utopian and dystopian fiction, magic realism, fantastic voyages, ghost stories, and the Gothic with supernatural elements" ("The Uses of Genre," 72). Most definitions of speculative fiction assume, at least, the triad SF-fantasy-horror. See, e.g., N. E. Lilly, "What Is Speculative Fiction?," Green Tentacles, March 2002, http://www.greententacles.com/articles/5/26 (accessed 5 July 2016).

23. Theodore Martin, *Contemporary Drift: Genre, Historicism, and the Problem of the Present* (New York: Columbia University Press, 2016), 6.

24. Martin, *Contemporary Drift*, 7.

25. For the *Parable* series as "Mundane SF," as well as an account of the trilogy informed by the manuscripts of the unfinished *Parable of the Trickster*, see Gerry Canavan, "'There's Nothing New / Under The Sun, / But There Are New Suns': Recovering Octavia E. Butler's Lost Parables," *Los Angeles Review of Books*, 9 June 2014, https://lareviewofbooks.org/article/theres-nothing-new-sun-new-suns-recovering-octavia-e-butlers-lost-parables/ (accessed 13 February 2017).

26. See, e.g., Abby Aguire, "Octavia Butler's Prescient Vision of a Zealot Elected to 'Make American Great Again,'" *New Yorker*, 26 July 2017, https://www.newyorker.com/books/second-read/octavia-butlers-prescient-vision-of-a-zealot-elected-to-make-america-great-again (accessed 20 August 2019).

27. Thus, Samuel R. Delany argues that, rather than being defined by its "content," speculative fiction is characterized by a stylistic or subjunctive element: "No matter how disciplined [a speculative novel's] creation, to move into 'unreal worlds' demands a brush with mysticism" (*The Jewel-Hinged Jaw* [Elizabethtown, NJ: Dragon, 1977], 13). The mystical element in Butler's *Parable* series is framed both by biblical narrative—the *Exodus* story and the wanderings of the early Christians—as well as the voyages and sojournings of diasporic African history: the middle passage, the underground railroad, the great migration, and much more.

28. Chang-rae Lee, *On Such a Full Sea* (New York: Penguin/Riverhead Books, 2014), 10. Hereafter cited parenthetically as *OFS*.

29. There's a double allusion at work in the word "Charters." It connotes the royal charters through which towns in medieval Europe were granted self-governing authority, thereby helping to shape the parcelized territorial sovereignty of the feudal world. But it also has a contemporary resonance: the present-day charter school movement, with its new potential to divide the social space of the nation along socioeconomic and racially demographic lines and that therefore serves as a kind of implicit metonymy for the privatization of urban space.

30. Keller Easterling, *Extrastatecraft: The Power of Infrastructure Space* (London: Verso, 2014).

31. A recent study suggests that "almost half of the Chinese companies [operating in Uganda] have [fewer] than three quarters of their workers from Uganda. In 17 percent of the cases less than half the number of workers [are] from the host country." Ward Warmerdam and Meine Pieter van Dijk, "New Light on Chinese Enterprises in Africa: Findings from a Recent Survey of Chinese Firms in Kampala, the Capital of Uganda. ISS Staff Group 3: Human Resources and Local Development," Maastricht School of Management, 2012, http://hdl.handle.net/1765/39413 (accessed 30 September 2016).

32. In the final chapter, the narrators revert to "where you are" in attempting to describe Fan's boldness, which was "not [a quality] that simply pushed her forward but rather fixed her, solid, on the very spot she found herself. *Where you are*" (*OFS*, 348; emphasis in original). It's not a bad metaphor for Fan's resolve and self-sufficiency, and it's one Lee returns to again in the novel's final lines, which address Fan directly, enjoining her to "Stay put for now" and "not come back for us" (352). The idea that this finally settles the meaning of "where you are" is, however, undercut by the obvious irony that the phrase reappears just as Fan is preparing to hit the road again, leaving her brother's home in the Charters, her final destination unknown. Likewise, "stay put for now" is preceded by the acknowledgment that, in order to escape her brother's betrayal, she must travel "swift and wide and far" (351).

33. Ursula K. Le Guin, review of *On Such a Full Sea*, *Guardian*, 30 January 2014, https://www.theguardian.com/books/2014/jan/30/on-such-full-sea-chang-rae-lee-review (accessed 16 June 2016).

34. Le Guin, review of *On Such a Full Sea*.

35. See Min Hyoung Song, "Between Genres: On Chang-rae Lee's Realism," *Los Angeles Review of Books*, 10 January 2014, https://lareviewofbooks.org/article/chang-rae-lees-realism/ (accessed 16 June 2016).

36. It also bears noting that while Le Guin criticizes Lee for insufficiently developing his secondary world, Diane Johnson complains that he describes it in tedious detail. Johnson, "Let's Go to Dystopia," *New York Review of Books*, 5 June 2014, http://www.nybooks.com/articles/2014/06/05/chang-rae-lee-dystopia/ (accessed 21 June 2016).

37. Thus, for Geoff Mak, "*On Such a Full Sea* tells the story of a futuristic, dystopian America after China has colonized the United States," but for Joanna Biggs it depicts the transformation of the US into a new federated entity called "the Association" (Mak, "Chang-rae Lee's Dystopian America," *Los Angeles Review of Books*, 5 February 2014, https://lareviewofbooks.org/article/chang-rae-lees-full-sea/ [accessed 21 June 2016];

Biggs, "We: Chang-rae Lee's *On Such a Full Sea*," *New Yorker*, 27 January 2014, http://www.newyorker.com/magazine/2014/01/27/we-4 [accessed 21 June 2016]). Both interpretations strike me as overreadings. There's no positive evidence that the "directorate" that controls B-Mor is under Chinese state control or that its powers stretch throughout the former United States. The "Association," meanwhile, appears to govern only the Charters—at least, the novel never says that "directorate" and "Association" are part of the same nexus of power. The point is that the nature of political control in Lee's secondary world remains opaque to his narrators.

38. Le Guin herself implies this in her backhanded remark about Lee's "complex subtlety of point of view" (review of *On Such a Full Sea*). The difference is that, in her judgment, literary "subtlety" is often an alibi for not taking SF seriously enough.

39. Lee resists even the abrupt and arbitrary kind of closure found in Homer's original oral *Odyssey*, in which only the gods' angry commands bring an end to the hero's adventure—and only then with barely a handful of lines to go.

40. Le Guin, review of *On Such a Full Sea*. For more on systematicity and world creation, see chapter 2.

41. Sarah Hall, *Daughters of the North* (New York: Harper Perennial, 2007), 7, 1. Hereafter cited parenthetically as *DN*.

42. On the figure of the inimicus or "unjust enemy," see Ian Baucom, "Cicero's Ghost: The Atlantic, the Enemy, and the Laws of War," in *States of Emergency: The Object of American Studies*, ed. Russ Castronovo and Susan Gillman (Chapel Hill: University of North Carolina Press, 2009), 124–42.

43. Paolo Bacigalupi, *The Water Knife* (New York: Knopf, 2015).

44. Jeanette Winterson, *The Stone Gods* (New York: Houghton Mifflin, 2008); Hugh Howey, *Wool: Omnibus Edition (Wool 1–5)* (New York: Simon & Schuster, 2012); David Mitchell, *Cloud Atlas* (London: Sceptre, 2004).

45. Henry James, "Preface to the New York Edition," in *Roderick Hudson*, ed. Geoffery Moore (London: Penguin, 1986), 37.

46. Emily St. John Mandel, *Station Eleven* (New York: Knopf, 2015), 267. Hereafter cited parenthetically as *SE*. This novel was a finalist for the National Book Award and the PEN/Faulkner Award as well as winner of the Arthur C. Clarke Award for science fiction. If *Station Eleven* is a decidedly literary dystopia, then St. John Mandel's previous work—e.g., *The Lola Quartet* (Denver: Unbridled, 2012)—is most often associated with genre conventions derived from the thriller and noir.

47. The regularity with which St. John Mandel's characters say "collapse" is too persistently jarring to be accidental; she clearly wants her reader to reflect on the language of catastrophic change. Consider the scene in which the shipping executive Miranda, surveying mothballed ships off the coast of Malaysia "just before the old world ended," finds herself "a little amused by the memory of how casually everyone had thrown the word collapse around, before anyone truly understood what the word meant, but in any event, there had been an economic collapse and now the largest shipping fleet ever assembled lay fifty miles east of Singapore Harbor " (217). The irony here is triple: (1) Miranda

understands "collapse" better than the people who threw the word around before the 2008 crash; but (2) because we already know she doesn't survive the end of the world, we know she can't understand "collapse" in all its implications; and yet (3), by the end of the novel, even the end of the world emerges as a kind of new beginning—thus, "collapse" never in fact means the total and permanent breakdown it threatens to mean. Andrew Hoberek comments upon this same aspect of *Station Eleven* in "The Post-Apocalyptic Present," *Public Books*, 15 June 2015, http://www.publicbooks.org/fiction/the-post-apocalyptic-present (accessed 24 August 2016).

48. Like the Symphony itself, most of those exceptions are familiar from folklore and fantasy: religious wanderers, traveling merchants, brigands, and so on. These are all figures who possess a kind of glamour and mystery by being avatars of movement in a world defined by isolated settlements.

49. See *SE*, 144, 176, 177, 188, and 234. The motif is well enough known that a popular version (perhaps the image that concludes the well-known title sequence to season 1 of the AMC zombie drama *The Walking Dead*) becomes the object of wry comment in Whitehead's *Zone One*: "In the cinema of end-times, the roads feeding the evacuated city are often clear, and the routes of town clotted with paralyzed vehicles. . . . It makes for a stark visual image, the crazy hero returning to the doomed metropolis to save his kid or gal or to hunt down the encrypted computer file that might—just might!—reverse disaster, driving a hundred miles an hour into the hexed zip codes when all the other citizens are vamoosing. . . . In Mark Spitz's particular apocalypse, the human beings were messy and did not obey rules, and every lane in and out, every artery and vein, was filled with outbound traffic" (*Zone One* [New York: Doubleday, 2011], 136). In *Station Eleven*, as in Whitehead's novel, "gridlock [is] absolute" (*SE* 176).

50. By "temporal referent" I mean the kind of phrase that might establish a relationship of proximity or simultaneity ("That night, in the summer of Year Fifteen" [*SE* 269]); or of precedence ("Seven years before the end of the world" [167]; or succession ("Later they have a house in the Hollywood Hills" [91]); or of a mixed time, such as when succession gives way to precedence in a qualifying clause ("Two weeks later, just before the old world ended" [217]). These kinds of temporalizing phrase might indicate an amount of time passed or yet to come; or they might simply indicate the general time at which something happened—for instance, a season ("The first winter in the Severn City Airport" [242]) or a time of day ("The Symphony arrived . . . in the midafternoon" [43]). The key qualities are the specificity of temporal relation, whatever the chronological scale invoked, the phrase's presence in the first three sentences, and—above all—the fact that this happens over and over.

51. This formulation comes from Alexander Beecroft, "On the Tropes of Literary Ecology: The Plot of Globalization," in *Globalizing Literary Genres: Literature, History, Modernity*, ed. Jernej Habja and Fabienne Imlinger (New York: Routledge, 2016), 195–213. I return to this argument about the formal aspect of "global" fictions in chapter 4, with reference to Amitav Ghosh's *Ibis* trilogy of historical novels.

52. Beecroft, "On the Tropes," 199.

53. George Orwell, *Nineteen Eighty-Four* (New York: Penguin/Signet Classics, 1961), 187.

54. Orwell, *Nineteen Eighty-Four*, 187.

55. J. G. Ballard, *The Complete Stories of J. G. Ballard* (New York: W. W. Norton, 2009), 23. Hereafter cited parenthetically as *CSB*.

56. In Morressy's novel, such formal extraterritoriality of person is symbolically amplified by the way that Selkirk's memory is wiped in-between his foreign assignments, so that he is not only legally exempt from punishment by those he harmed but—or so he at first believes—invulnerable from the moral problem of guilt.

57. John Morressy, *The Extraterritorial* (New York: Laser, 1977), 7. Hereafter cited parenthetically as *E*.

58. Margaret Atwood, *In Other Worlds: SF and the Human Imagination* (New York: Doubleday/Nan A. Talese, 2011), 66.

59. George Steiner, *Extraterritorial: Papers on the Literature and Language Revolution* (New York: Athaneum, 1976), 11.

60. Atwood, *In Other Worlds*, 69.

61. Atwood, 69.

62. Atwood, 69.

63. Atwood, 70.

64. To say this is to take the common route of describing genre as a kind of Wittgensteinian family resemblance. The key point here is that no common feature is dispositive of family membership: lacking an archipelagic setting no more precludes a text from membership in the group of dystopian novels than having such a feature guarantees membership in the absence of other qualities. See Ludwig Wittgenstein, *Philosophical Investigations*, trans. G. E. M. Anscombe (Oxford: Blackwell, 1986), §§ 66–77. For histories and evaluations of literary critics' use of Wittgenstein's notion, see Alastair Fowler, *Kinds of Literature: An Introduction to the Theory of Genres and Modes* (Oxford: Oxford University Press, [1982] 2002), 41–42; and David Fishelov, *Metaphors of Genre: The Role of Analogies in Genre Theory* (University Park: Penn State University Press, 1993), 54–68.

65. This list of transnational social and environmental phenomena, all of them with some presence in *Station Eleven*, is compiled from the subject headings in Lance Saker, Kelly Lee, Barbara Cannito, Anna Gilmore, and Diarmid Campbell-Lendrum, "Globalization and Infectious Disease: A Review of the Linkages," *Special Topics in Social, Economic and Behavioural Research* 3 (2004). Steering Committee for Social, Economic and Behavioural Research, UNICEF/UNDP/World Bank/WHO: Special Program for Research and Training in Tropical Diseases, World Health Organization, Geneva, http://www.who.int/tdr/publications/documents/seb_topic3.pdf (accessed 6 August 2016).

66. David Harvey, *The Condition of Postmodernity: An Enquiry in the Nature of Cultural Change* (Oxford: Blackwell, 1990), 284–307, especially 294.

67. For the importance of allegories of connectedness to environmental thought, see Ursula K. Heise, *Sense of Place and Sense of Planet: The Environmental Imagination of the Global* (New York: Oxford University Press, 2008). Heise contrasts representations of

planetary connection that "[rely] on summarizing the abstract complexity of global systems in relatively simple and concrete images that [foreground] synthesis, holism and connectedness" (63) to those that demonstrate how different "places are inexorably connected to the planet as a whole and to the perception that this wholeness encompasses vast heterogeneities" (64). In suggesting that the catastrophic plague in *Oryx and Crake* might be conceived as a parody of one Earth-style thinking, I do not mean to say that Atwood endorses that ecological vision. On the contrary, by yoking it to Crake's sociopathic activity, she might be thought to reject it.

68. It's therefore possible to object that, in addition to the time needed for any virus to spread and incubate, the BlyssPluss virus is still initially transmitted via a physical object (a pill) that needs to be packaged and distributed throughout space. But that objection is pedantic. *Oryx and Crake* goes to great lengths to root the erstwhile natural event of pandemic disease in the very kinds of infrastructural and economic development that Harvey sees as characteristic of globalization and which underpin his thesis about the new spatiotemporal disposition of the present.

69. Le Guin, review of Margaret Atwood, *Year of the Flood*.

70. Le Guin, review of *Year of the Flood*.

71. The word "theodicy" names that primordial theological question: If God is entirely good and powerful, why is there evil in the world? By "generic theodicy," I imply something like the question: If the apocalypse is supposed to be transformative, why does the world that comes after the fall in dystopian fiction look so much like the one before?

4. A BORDER THAT IS NOT A BORDER

1. The "rise and rise" line about Cromwell's career up to 1535 comes from the jacket copy to the British first edition of Hilary Mantel, *Wolf Hall* (London: 4th Estate, 2009). Hereafter cited parenthetically as *WH*.

2. Franco Moretti, *Atlas of the European Novel, 1800–1900* (New York: Verso, 1999), 33, 35.

3. Moretti, *Atlas of the European Novel*, 39.

4. See, respectively, Françoise Lionnet, "World Literature, Postcolonial Studies, and Coolie Odysseys: J. M. G. Le Clézio's and Amitav Ghosh's Indian Ocean Novels," *Comparative Literature* 67, no. 3 (2015): 287–311; Alexander Beecroft, "On the Tropes of Literary Ecology: The Plot of Globalization," in *Globalizing Literary Genres: Literature, History, Modernity*, ed. Jernej Habjan and Fabienne Imlinger (New York: Routledge, 2016), 195–212; and Jonathan Arac, "Amitav Ghosh's *Ibis* Trilogy in American World Literature," in *American Literature as World Literature*, ed. Jeffrey R. Di Leo (New York: Bloomsbury, 2018), 149–64.

5. György Lukács, *The Historical Novel*, trans. Hannah Mitchell and Stanley Mitchell (Lincoln: University of Nebraska Press, 1962), 53.

6. Lukács, *Historical Novel*, 53.

7. Caren Irr, *Toward the Geopolitical Novel: US Fiction in the Twenty-First Century* (New York: Columbia University Press, 2014), 4. Although Irr primarily focuses on fiction written by US nationals or residents, her book also features chapter sections on fiction by writers from South Asia (including Amitav Ghosh), South America, West Africa, and the former Soviet Union.

8. Irr, *Toward the Geopolitical Model.*

9. England, we might object, is not actually an island, but, my, how the fiction persists.

10. To be clear, the so-called great statute of praemunire of 1393 did not abolish papal authority in England and Wales; it merely invalidated papal bulls and instruments that constrained the monarch's authority over secular affairs, and only then incompletely. The historical record suggests that neither Richard II nor his successors considered the 1393 act to apply "to all encroachments of the papacy on the temporal sphere" (W. T. Waugh, "The Great Statute of Praemunire," *English Historical Review* 37, no. 146 [1922]: 174–75). Moreover, the pope's authority in spiritual matters remained relatively unconstrained in law until the passing, under Cromwell's leadership, of the 1532 Ecclesiastical Appeals Act and the 1534 Act of Supremacy. In *Wolf Hall*, the clearest evidence of this reality lies in the scene in which Henry VIII and Katherine of Aragorn both appear at the 1529 Legatine Court called by Wolsey and Cardinal Campeggio; the court fails to affirm Henry's petition, and so he refuses to concede to its judgments, but both its very existence and the fact that Henry does not immediately marry Anne confirms that the king was for a long while willing to recognize papal authority over church law (*WH* 144–46). Moreover, Mantel's narrator makes it clear that even the lawyers who drew up the charges against Wolsey weren't sure about the implications of the 1393 act: "The law of praemunire dates from another century. No one who is alive now quite knows what it means. From day to day, it seems to mean what the king says it means" (165).

    There's reason to believe, however, that the period around Wolsey's downfall did indeed see an expansion of the statute of praemunire's meaning and purpose. J. A. Guy explains how, between 1529 and 1532, the reach and implications of the 1393 act were broadly extended, though without that extension amounting to a wholesale assault on the rights of the English clergy ("Henry VIII and the *Praemunire* Manoeuvres of 1530–31," *English Historical Review* 97, no. 384 [1982]: 481–503). In *Wolf Hall*, by contrast, Cromwell worries that the assault on Wolsey will end in "the downfall of the priests of England. . . . For if the cardinal is guilty of a crime in asserting his jurisdiction as legate, are not all those clerics . . . who assented to his legacy, also guilty?" (186). Interestingly, Guy argues, somewhat *contra* Mantel, that Cromwell ought not to be identified as the author of the period's enhanced legal conception of praemunire (487–88).

11. Given the pope's status as a prince in Italy, the church's great wealth as a landowner, and the very real social and political power wielded by bishops and clergy in England, the distinction between temporal and spiritual power should not be overstressed.

12. Mary Robertson, "Thomas Cromwell's Servants: The Ministerial Household in Early Tudor Government and Society," PhD diss., University of California, Los Angeles, 1975,

13. Robertson, "Thomas Cromwell's Servants," 13. Elton also features in Robertson's acknowledgements, where she thanks him for allowing her to attend a 1971 Cambridge University seminar on Tudor history. She also corresponded with Elton "for years" about their common historical interests (Stevens, "Booker Club," 7).

14. G. R. Elton, *The Tudor Revolution in Government: Administrative Changes in the Reign of Henry VIII* (London: Cambridge University Press, [1953] 1962, 3.

15. Elton, *Tudor Revolution in Government*, 3–4.

16. G. R. Elton, *England under the Tudors* (New York: Routledge, [1955] 1991), 160.

17. Elton, *England under the Tudors*, 161.

18. Indeed, Elton's strong hypothesis attracted controversy quite quickly—see, e.g., the debate inaugurated by Penry Williams and G. L. Harriss in "A Revolution in Tudor History?," a special section of *Past & Present* 25 (1963): 3–8, 8–39, 39–58, with responses by Elton and others in subsequent issues. For a survey of the historiographical origins of Elton's thesis, including its indebtedness to earlier work by Victorian historians such as J. A. Froude and twentieth-century predecessors T. F. Tout and A. P. Newton, see Ian Harris, "Some Origins of a Tudor Revolution," *English Historical Review* 126, no. 523 (2011): 1355–85. Of particular interest is Harris's argument that the idea of "revolution" provides more of an "artistic" than "structural" unity in *The Tudor Revolution in Government*, with the language of "reform" tending to predominate in the book's main chapters (1383–84).

19. See, e.g., the essays gathered in Christopher Coleman and David Starkey, eds., *Revolution Reassessed: Revisions in the History of Tudor Government and Administration* (Oxford: Clarendon, 1986), especially Starkey, "Which Age of Reform?," 13–27. C. S. L. Davies's slightly later objection is characteristic, holding that Elton's work is "remarkable" on the particulars of Tudor administration but "falls down in its attempt to chart a spurious and procrustean 'medieval-modern' divide, differentiating 'informal' or 'household' from 'bureaucratic' types of administration" ("The Cromwellian Decade: Authority and Consent," *Transactions of the Royal Historical Society* 7 [1997]: 177–78). Diarmaid MacCulloch's recent biography of Cromwell is repeatedly in dialogue with Elton's thesis, even to the point that Elton (his former tutor) is MacCulloch's dedicatee. MacCulloch's argument doesn't so much reject Elton's thesis as modify and disperse it across and between persons, institutions, and periods. For instance, he concludes that Cromwell's evangelism certainly paved the way for the "religious "Revolution in Government'" that occurred during the reign of Edward VI and under the leadership of Cromwell's ally Thomas Cranmer (*Thomas Cromwell: A Revolutionary Life* [New York: Viking, 2018], 542). And he argues that "there was revolution enough, in Cromwell's steady, careful plans to make all the Tudor realms work in the same way, on the model of England, which was a polity with a unique degree of centralization in Europe and, by the standards of the time, exceptionally well run even before Cromwell took over its supervision" (543–44).

20. I use the word "country" advisedly: when Cromwell is elevated to the king's council, the narrator explains the absence of the Dukes of Norfolk and Suffolk by saying they are "in their own countries, holding their Christmas courts" (280). "Country," of course, does not necessarily connote "state" or "nation" in the sixteenth century; it was often synonymous with "county." Still, Mantel takes pains to remind us of the powers exercised by feudal lords in the early sixteenth century. Norfolk, we learn later, "still has serfs on his lands, and even if the law courts move to free them the duke expects a fee from it" (586).

21. An example: when Cromwell makes no headway in pleading for the release of John Petyt, a protestant merchant and member of Parliament, he "knows he has gone to the brink and must feel his way back" (303).

22. I refer to Ernst H. Kantorowicz, *The King's Two Bodies: A Study in Medieval Political Theology* (Princeton, NJ: Princeton University Press, [1957] 2016). Mantel is clearly familiar with Kantorowicz: "The king has two bodies. The first exists within the limits of his physical being. . . . The second is his princely double, free-floating, untethered, weightless, which may be in more than one place at one time" (*WH*, 480).

23. For a full sense of Mantel's attitude to More, see "A Letter to Thomas More, Knight," in Hilary Mantel and Xavier F. Solomon, *Holbein's Sir Thomas More* (New York: Frick Collection/D Giles, 2018), 11–17. The reference is to Ali Smith, *How to Be Both* (New York: Anchor, 2014).

24. In *Thomas Cromwell*, Diarmid MacCulloch casts doubt on Mantel's version, of Cromwell's departure, suggesting that accounts of his father Walter Cromwell's bad reputation have been exaggerated (15–16). He argues, instead, that the impulse behind Cromwell's ca. 1500 departure for Flanders and Italy was "the restlessness and original intelligence which characterized his public career, and which had made him a 'ruffian' [Cromwell's own phrase] in his youth" (22).

25. "Remodeled society" is Mantel's description of England after Cromwell, found in her character notes to Mike Poulton, Wolf Hall *and* Bring Up the Bodies: *The Stage Adaptation* (New York: Picador, 2014), 10.

26. Mike Poulton, Wolf Hall *and* Bring Up the Bodies, 11. For similar descriptions of Cromwell's household in Robertson, see "Thomas Cromwell's Servants," chapter 2, section 2, "The Domestic Household: Development and Education": "Where rising young men had once sought to attach themselves to Wolsey, they now [ca. 1531] turned to Cromwell" (67). See also chapter 5, part 4, "Education" (368–70), emphasizing not just the number of Cromwell's young men who had attended Oxbridge or the Inns of Court, but also their informal knowledge of classical and modern languages and experience in French and German universities.

27. Hilary Mantel, "Hilary Mantel: How I Came to Write Wolf Hall," *Guardian*, 7 December 2012, https://www.theguardian.com/books/2012/dec/07/bookclub-hilary-mantel-wolf-hall (accessed 31 May 2018). Regarding Cromwell's reputation as an historical villain, see Stephen Greenblatt's review of *Wolf Hall*, which begins by comparing him to "Stalin's sinister henchman Lavrenti Beria ("How It Must Have Been," *New York Review*

of Books, 5 November 2009, http://www.nybooks.com/articles/2009/11/05/how-it-must -have-been/ [accessed 30 May 2018]). Marianne Brace likewise contrasts Mantel's depiction of Cromwell as learned, wry, tolerant, calculating with his "dark" reputation ("Wolf Hall, by Hilary Mantel," *Independent*, 8 May 2009, https://www.independent.co .uk/arts-entertainment/books/reviews/wolf-hall-by-hilary-mantel-1680694.html [accessed 30 May 2018]). But the easiest way to exemplify critics' reluctance to take Mantel at her word when she says she's not come to flatter Cromwell, is to sample the critiques written by defenders of More. Thus does Charles Krauthammer write that "*Wolf Hall*'s depiction of Cromwell as a man of great sensitivity and deep feeling is even harder to credit" than its representation of More as "little more than a cruel heretic-burning hypocrite" ("Men Wielding Power in Hellish Times," *National Review*, 1 May 2015, https://www.nationalreview.com/2015/05/men-wielding-power-hellish-times-charles -krauthammer/ [accessed 30 May 2018]).

28. Angiola Codacci, interview with Amitav Ghosh. *L'Espresso Magazine*, 24 November 2011, https://www.amitavghosh.com/interviews.html#gpm1_8 (accessed 30 May 2018).

29. According to the US Census Bureau, the trade deficit with China in June 2018 is $185,721,300,000. In November 2011, when Ghosh's remarks about the deficit were published, it stood at $295,249,700,000 (US Census Bureau, "Foreign Trade: Trade in Goods with Chinam," 2018, https://www.census.gov/foreign-trade/balance/c5700.html [accessed 31 August 2018]). For a summary of the trading relations between China and the East India Company, including discussion of the relative flow in silver specie, see Paul A. Van Dyke, "The Canton Trade, 1700–1842," *Oxford Research Encyclopedia of Asian History*, ed. David Ludden (Oxford: Oxford University Press, 2017), https://oxfordre.com/asianhistory /view/10.1093/acrefore/9780190277727.001.0001/acrefore-9780190277727-e-127 (accessed 7 March 2019).

30. See, e.g., Elleke Boehmer and Anshuman A. Mondal, "Networks and Traces: An Interview with Amitav Ghosh," *Wasifiri* 27, no. 2 (2012): 34.

31. Quoted in Tim Teeman, "'Opium Was the Single Largest Sector of the Empire's Economy': Amitav Ghosh Talks to Tim Teeman About Colonial Wars, Imperial Power—and a Controversial Literary Prize," *Times*, 11 June 2011, 42.

32. Codacci, interview with Amitav Ghosh.

33. Amitav Ghosh, *The Great Derangement: Climate Change and the Unthinkable* (Chicago: University of Chicago Press, 2016), 93–115, especially 103–11. Hereafter cited parenthetically as *GD*.

34. Moretti's terms are "filler" and "turning point," but he says they're basically compatible with other theories about the relation between exceptional and everyday events in the novel, such as Seymour Chatman's distinction between narrative "kernels" and "satellites," and Roland Barthes's between "cardinal functions" and "catalyzers." Moretti, "Serious Century," in *The Novel, Vol. 1: History, Geography, and Culture*, ed. Franco Moretti (Princeton, NJ: Princeton University Press, 2006), 366–67.

35. The tendentiousness of Ghosh's argument is clearest when he finally considers genres such as SF, which habitually escape the gravity of the everyday. Drawing on Margaret

Atwood's problematic distinction between SF and speculative fiction (on which see chapter 3 above), Ghosh concludes that "the Anthropocene resists science fiction: it is precisely not an imagined 'other' world apart from ours; nor is it located in another 'time' or another 'dimension.'" As Ursula K. Heise notes, this is an "oddly literalist" account of SF, which "of course always addresses its audience's here and now through the detour of imagined futures." Heise, "Climate Stories: Review of Amitav Ghosh's *The Great Derangement*," b2o: the Online Community of the boundary2 Editorial Collective, 19 February 2018, https://www.boundary2.org/2018/02/ursula-k-heise-climate-stories -review-of-amitav-ghoshs-the-great-derangement/ (accessed 21 March 2019).

36. Compare Ghosh's historical novels to David Mitchell's *The Thousand Autumns of Jacob de Zoet* (2010), in which historical realism is interrupted by a gothic romance in which sorcery and mysticism have real-world effects. I have previously written about Mitchell's mixture of the historical and fantastic. See Matthew Hart, "Globalism and Historical Romance," in *The Cambridge Companion to Post-1945 British Fiction*, ed. David James (New York: Cambridge University Press, 2015), 207–23.

37. Ghosh, *Great Derangement*, 61–62.

38. Moretti, at least, is clear that the era of the "serious" bourgeois novel was a limited one, which in the twentieth century gave way to modernist antirealism and "magical" realist reenchantment ("Serious Century" 400). I find it hard to believe that Ghosh would want to exclude the forms of magical realism that have proved so important to the postcolonial novel—and that, as in the work of Marquez and Rushdie, so often traverse expanses of time and space—from the "mansion of serious fiction," never mind the vast number of speculative fictions, from Thomas More through Ursula LeGuin, that can claim canonical status. But we should be content, for now, that he does not exclude this possibility.

39. Ghosh draws on the common opposition between *place*, as a bounded and experiential geographic realm, and *space*, as an abstract location'; see, e.g., Yi-Fu Tuan, *Space and Place: The Persepective of Experience* (Minneapolis: University of Minnesota Press, 2001), 6. But there are modes of spatial thinking in which a sense of local "place" remains inextricable from its national or transnational relation and extension. See, e.g., David Harvey's account of "militant particularism" in the novels of Raymond Williams, in which the experiential particularity of the South Wales borderlands can only be articulated in and through an understanding of their enmeshment in a global system of capitalist modernity; see "Militant Particularism and Global Ambition: The Conceptual Politics of Place, Space, and Environment in the Work of Raymond Williams," in *Spaces of Capital: Toward a Critical Geography* (New York: Routledge, 2012), 158–87. There's no necessary reason to associate "place" with finitude or scalar smallness.

40. Emphasis on *primary* commitment, since, as noted via the Henry James quotation in the previous chapter, while "really, universally, relations stop nowhere," all novels face the challenge of drawing some kind of apparently non-arbitrary limit somewhere. James, "Preface to the New York Edition," in *Roderick Hudson*, ed. Geoffrey Moore (London: Penguin, 1986), 37.

41. Isabel Hofmeyer, "The Complicating Sea: The Indian Ocean as Method," *Comparative Studies of South Asia, Africa and the Middle East* 32, no. 3 (2012): 585.

42. Alexander Beecroft, "On the Tropes of Literary Ecology: The Plot of Globalization," in *Globalizing Literary Genres: Literature, History, Modernity*, ed. Jernej Habjan and Fabienne Imlinger (New York: Routledge, 2016), 195.

43. Beecroft, "On the Tropes," 201.

44. Paul Stasi, "Amitav Ghosh's *Sea of Poppies* and Postcolonial Modernism," *NOVEL: A Forum on Fiction* 48, no. 3 (2015): 341.

45. Rudrani Gangopadhyay, "Finding Oneself On Board the *Ibis* in Amitav Ghosh's *Sea of Poppies*," *WSQ: Women's Studies Quarterly* 45, nos. 1–2 (2017): 59–60.

46. Amitav Ghosh, *Sea of Poppies* (New York: Picador, 2008), 11. For a comparative reading of Atlantic chattel slavery and indentured labor in the Indian Ocean region, see Nandini Dhar, "Shadows of Slavery, Discourses of Choice, and Indian Indentureship in Amitav Ghosh's *Sea of Poppies*," *Ariel: A Review of International English Literature* 48, no. 1 (2017): 1–35. See also Françoise Lionnet, "Shipwrecks, Slavery, and the Challenge of Global Comparison: From Fiction to Archive in the Colonial Indian Ocean: 2012 ACLA Presidential Address," *Comparative Literature Studies* 64, no. 4 (2012): 446–61.

47. For "The *Ibis* Chrestomathy," see *Sea of Poppies* 473–515; and http://amitavghosh.com/chrestomathy.html (accessed 6 March 2019).

48. Amitav Ghosh, *Flood of Fire* (New York: Farrar, Strauss & Giroux, 2015), 608.

49. Sanjay Krishnan, *Reading the Global: Troubling Perspectives on Britain's Empire in Asia* (New York: Columbia University Press, 2007), 6–11.

50. Citing Kenneth Pomeranz, *The Great Divergence: China, Europe, and the Making of the Modern World Economy* (Princeton, NJ: Princeton University Press, 2000), 46. Pomeranz is cited a further four times in *The Great Derangement*, the title of which also owes something to Pomeranz's example (90, 97, 120). Pomeranz is also thanked, along with Dipesh Chakrabarty and Julia Adeney Thomas (two more renowned historian critics of Eurocentric theories of modernity), in Ghosh's acknowledgments (163).

51. Ghosh quotes here from Sanjay Subrahmanyam, "Hearing Voices: Vignettes of Early Modernity in South Asia, 1400–1750," *Daedalus* 127, no. 3 (1998): 99–100.

52. Beecroft, "On the Tropes," 205–6.

53. Lukács, *Historical Novel*, 58.

54. Ritu Birla, *Stages of Capital: Law, Culture, and Market Governance in Late Colonial India* (Durham, NC: Duke University Press, 2009), 236.

55. Birla, *Stages of Capital*, 236–37.

56. James Hevia, *Cherishing Men from Afar: Qing Guest Ritual and the Macartney Embassy of 1793* (Durham, NC: Duke University Press, 1995), 25.

57. Viscount Palmerston to Lord Napier, 25 January 1834, *Correspondence Relating to China: Presented to Both Houses of Parliament, by Command of Her Majesty, 1840.* (London: T. R. Harrison), 4.

58. Palmerston to Napier, 25 January 1834.

59. Plamerston to Napier.

60. Palmerston to Napier.

61. Lord Napier to Viscount Palmerston, 14 August 1834, *Correspondence Relating to China*, 12.

62. Napier to Palmerston, 14 August 1834, 14.

63. Napier to Palmerston, 14 August 1834, 13.

64. Lord Napier to Earl Grey, 21 August 1834, *Correspondence Relating to China*, 26.

65. Mao Haijin, *The Qing Empire and the Opium War: The Collapse of the Heavenly Dynasty*, ed. Joseph Lawson, trans. Joseph Lawson, Craig Smith, and Peter Lavelle (Cambridge: Cambridge University Press, 2016), 5.

66. Haijin, *Qing Empire*, 5–7.

67. Lord Napier to the Governor of Canton, 26 July 1834, *Correspondence Relating to China*, 10–11.

68. Governor of Canton to the Hong Merchants, 21 July 1834, *Correspondence Relating to China*, 17.

69. Governor of Canton to the Hong Merchants, 27 July 1834, *Correspondence Relating to China*, 18. The term "Hong" refers to the business houses allowed to conduct foreign trade at Canton; they were gathered together as a guild called the "Cohong." In English documents from the period, these words are sometimes used interchangeably. For simplicity's sake, I refer in what follows to the "Hong merchants."

70. Lord Napier to Viscount Palmerston, 14 August 1834, *Correspondence Relating to China*, 9.

71. Napier to Palmerston, 14 August 1834, 9.

72. Napier to Palmerston, 14 August, 1834, 8.

73. Lydia H. Liu, *The Clash of Empires: The Invention of China in Modern World Making* (Cambridge, MA: Harvard University Press, 2004), 2–3 and 46–51.

74. Lawson, "Translator's Preface," *Qing Empire*, x.

75. Joanna Waley-Cohen, "China and Western Technology in the Late Eighteenth Century," *American Historical Review* 98, no. 5 (1993): 1528.

76. Hevia, *Cherishing Men from Afar*, 10.

77. Hevia, 27.

78. For more on the legal basis of extraterritorial jurisdiction in China, as well as its effects on social life and urban geography, see chapter 5.

79. The Innes subplot in *River of Smoke* draws on a real event, the outline of which is narrated in Captain Elliot to Viscount Palmerston, 8 December 1838, *Correspondence Relating to China*, 323–24. The jurisdictional problem that Ghosh dramatizes via the Innes incident has an earlier precedent in the 1835 dispute between the firm Messrs. Turner & Co. and a Mr. Keating, in which the latter claimed to be immune from English and Chinese jurisdiction and in which it became clear that British officials had no legal authority to regulate commercial disagreements among foreign merchants. Elliot's predecessor, Sir G. B. Robinson summed up Keating's position as follows: "Entertaining opinions that there is an absence of all power and authority over him, [he] takes advantage of that supposed state of circumstances, to retain in his hands a sum of money claimed by another person, in spite of the concurrent opinions of several of the most respectable merchants in the place, to whom the case was submitted by his own consent" (99).

80. Immanuel C. Y. Hsu, *The Rise of Modern China*, 6th ed. (New York: Oxford University Press, 2000), 151.

81. Hisu, *Rise of Modern China*, 150–51.

82. Cassel, *Grounds of Judgment*, 40. Here Cassel cites William C. Jones, trans., *The Great Qing Code* (New York: Oxford University Press, 1994), 67–68.

83. The British flag is the biggest, and stands before "a chapel with a clock-tower" that "keeps time for all of Fanqui-town," so that the merchants' activities are symbolically associated with nation, church, and the rational order of clock-time (*RS*, 172).

84. The strange thing about the painting is that Chinnery has dated it July 1839, but the thirteen factories of Fanqui-town were in fact not destroyed by fire until 1856, during the Second Opium War: says Neel, "it seems that Robin saw it in a dream" (*RS* 516).

85. Anon., "Interview with Amitav Ghosh," *History of the Present: A Journal of Critical History* 2, no. 1 (Spring 2012): http://historyofthepresent.org/2.1/interview.html (accessed 6 March 2019).

86. "Amitav Ghosh—The Shadow Lines," BBC World Book Club Podcast, 26 May 2012, https://www.bbc.co.uk/programmes/p00s473j (accessed 12 March 2019).

5. SETTLEMENT

Epigraph: J. G. Ballard, *High-Rise* (London: Harper Perennial, 2006), 76.

1. "Consortium Invests $50M in China Housing," *Private Equity Week* 4, no. 20 (19 May 1997): https://advance-lexis-com.ezproxy.cul.columbia.edu/api/permalink/609772a2 -3cd2-45c5-b2ee-6d3b6cb41c7b/?context=1516831 (accessed 12 February 2019).

2. Geoff Hiscock, "Shanghai the Missing Link for Suppliers," *Australian*, 9 December 1997, https://advance-lexis-com.ezproxy.cul.columbia.edu/api/permalink/465306c5-50bd -49b1-b1f3-7ea9651bcd31/?context=1516831 (accessed 12 February 2019).

3. See Leu Siew Ying, "Growing Expatriate Community Fosters Club Revival in Shanghai," Agence France Presse, 10 December 1997, https://advance-lexis-com.ezproxy.cul .columbia.edu/api/permalink/2120fa86-d99e-47fa-8277-e43322b37708/?context=1516831 (accessed 12 February 2019).

4. "Beacon Keeps on Buying . . . Zell/Zuckerman Duke It Out," *National Real Estate Investor*, July 1997, https://advance-lexis-com.ezproxy.cul.columbia.edu/api/perma link/7edfaaa4-fe85-4518-9e8c-f720f0278de5/?context=1516831 (accessed 12 February 2019).

5. Richard McGregor, "Trouble in a Tranquil Zone of Shanghai: A US-style Retreat Has Turned into an Embarrassing Headache for the Chinese City," *Financial Times*, 15 March 2002; Tony Wong, "Shanghai Takes Flight," *Toronto Globe and Mail*, 4 August 2002.

6. For the Hansens' counterclaims against a wide range of entities, see the website they set up to defend themselves: http://www.shanghailinks.com/shanghai_links_litigation.html (accessed 14 February 2019).

7. "Damages Cannot Reduce in Time," *Times* (London), 17 December 2002, https://advance
-lexis-com.ezproxy.cul.columbia.edu/api/permalink/3f3452dd-fe0e-4cf5-a982-cb3ed
5455321/?context=1516831 (accessed 12 February 2019).

8. See, e.g., Jerry Borrell, "A Story to Give One Pause," *Venture Capital Journal*, 1 May 2005,
https://advance-lexis-com.ezproxy.cul.columbia.edu/api/permalink/b313a986-4592-438b
-944d-e09ffa209f39/?context=1516831 (accessed 12 February 2019); Richard McGregor,
"Shanghai Pressed to End Land Dispute," *Financial Times*, 9 December 2002, https://
advance-lexis-com.ezproxy.cul.columbia.edu/api/permalink/3d5f5101-5601-402c-957c
-1fbc9fde498f/?context=1516831 (accessed 12 February 2019); and Richard McGregor,
"Investors Regain Golf Course," *Financial Times*, 2 March 2005, https://advance-lexis
-com.ezproxy.cul.columbia.edu/api/permalink/a73bf0e7-666d-4965-a5cc-b71caacdaea2
/?context=1516831 (accessed 12 February 2019).

9. Sean Snyder, "Shanghai Links, Hua Xia Trip, 2002," in *Territories: Islands, Camps, and
Other States of Utopia*, ed. Anselm Franke, Rafi Segal, and Eyal Weizman (Berlin: KW—
Institute for Contemporary Art, 2003), 38.

10. Snyder, "Shanghai Links," 38.

11. Snyder, 38; bold and italic text in the original.

12. The Empire of Japan occupied the Chinese-governed precincts of the city in November 1937, following the three-month-long Battle of Shanghai. The International Settlement remained inviolate until December 1941, when it was occupied by the Japanese one day after the attack on Pearl Harbor. The United Kingdom and the United States finally renounced extraterritorial jurisdiction in China in 1943, as a condition of Chinese support for the Allied war with Japan. During the 1941–45 Japanese occupation of the International Settlement, the French Concession persisted under the administration of the Vichy government. See K. C. Chan, "The Abrogation of British Extraterritoriality in China 1942–43: A Study of Anglo-American-Chinese Relations," *Modern Asian Studies* 11, no. 2 (1977): 257–91; and Christine Cornet, "The Bumpy End of the French Concession and French Influence in Shanghai," in *In the Shadow of the Rising Sun: Shanghai Under Japanese Occupation*, ed. Christian Henriot and Wen-Hsin Yeh (Cambridge: Cambridge University Press, 2004), 257–76.

13. Pál Nyíri, "Extraterritoriality. Foreign Concessions: The Past and Future of a Form of Shared Sovereignty," inaugural oration delivered at Amsterdam Free University, 19 November 2009, http://www.espacestemps.net/articles/extraterritoriality-pal-nyiri/ (accessed 18 February 2019).

14. Sean Snyder, "Temporary Occupation," in *Territories*, 30–37.

15. Mark Prince, "Southfork Ranch Romania," *Art Monthly* 264 (March 2003): http://www
.artmonthly.co.uk/prince.htm (accessed 31 March 2010).

16. For a description of areas of extraterritorial jurisdiction in China as "anomalous zones," see Eileen P. Scully, *Bargaining with the State from Afar: American Citizenship in Treaty Port China, 1844–1942* (New York: Columbia University Press, 2001), 107.

17. Simon Sellars, "J. G. Ballard Live in London," Ballardian, 7 October 2005, http://www
.ballardian.com/jg-ballard-live-in-london (accessed 14 January 2019).

18. J. G. Ballard, *Miracles of Life: Shanghai to Shepperton: An Autobiography* (London: Fourth Estate, 2008), 11.

19. For the claim that the period between 1911 and 1931 represented the peak of foreign influence in China, see Jürgen Osterhammel, "Semi-Colonialism and Informal Empire in Twentieth-Century China: Towards a Framework of Analysis," in *Imperialism and After: Continuities and Discontinuities*, ed. Wolfgang J. Mommsen and Jürgen Osterhammel (London: Allen & Unwin, 1986), 300. For a sense of this as, simultaneously, an era of crisis, see Bickers's argument that "the beginnings of the road to Hong Kong in 1997" (when that colony returned to Chinese sovereignty) "lay in Hankou 1927," when a crowd of nationalist demonstrators took over the British extraterritorial concession in that city, starting the "dismantling of the British presence in China" (*Britain in China*, 15–16).

20. Lewis Burke Frumkes, "Kazuo Ishiguro," in *Conversations with Kazuo Ishiguro*, ed. Brian W. Shaffer and Cynthia F. Wong (Jackson: University Press of Mississippi, 2008), 190. For the details about Toyota, see "An Interview with Kazuo Ishiguro" Bookbrowse, https://www.bookbrowse.com/author_interviews/full/index.cfm/author_number/477/kazuo-ishiguro (accessed 7 February 2020).

21. M. M. Bakhtin, *The Dialogic Imagination: Four Essays*, ed. Michael Holquist, trans. Caryl Emerson and Michael Holquist (Austin: University of Texas Press, 1981), 84.

22. Shih Shun Liu, "Extraterritoriality: Its Rise and Its Decline" (PhD diss., Columbia University, 1925). I quote from the republication, under this same title, in *Columbia University Studies in the Social Sciences* 118, no. 2 (1925), 28. The dissertation was also published in book form as *Extraterritoriality: Its Rise and Its Decline* (New York: Columbia University Press, 1925).

23. Shih Shun Liu, *Extraterritoriality*, 234.

24. H. L., "The End of Extraterritoriality in China," *Bulletin of International News* 20, no 2 (23 January 1943): 53.

25. H. L., "End of Extraterritoriality," 234–35.

26. The short biography of Shih Shun Liu provided in *Columbia University Studies in the Social Sciences* says that he "was sent by the Chinese Government in 1920 to pursue higher studies in the United States" (237). The internationally recognized government in 1920 was the so-called Beiyang or warlord government at Beijing; that was still the case when he completed his doctorate in 1925. Its legitimacy was contested, however, by Sun Yat-sen's rival Kuomintang administration in Guangzhou, the leadership of which passed to Chiang Kai-shek in 1925. I have not been able to discover which of these administrations sent Liu to the United States.

27. Robert Bickers, *Britain in China: Community, Culture, and Colonialism, 1900–1949* (Manchester: Manchester University Press, 1999), 128. The census of 1925 counted the combined foreign population of the International Settlement and French Concession as 37,638. Recent research into the native Chinese population lists it as over two million in 1915, rising to two and a half million by 1927. For these figures, see Nicholas R. Clifford, *Spoilt Children of Empire: Westerners in Shanghai and the Chinese Revolution of the 1920s* (Hanover, NH: Middlebury College Press/University Press of New England, 1991), 7, 9.

28. Aldous Huxley, *Jesting Pilate: An Intellectual Holiday* (New York: George H. Doran Co., 1926), 271.

29. "The system which the claim and grant of foreign jurisdiction has called into being is artificial in the extreme. It recognises the existence of two separate communities in the same country. Where one is savage and the other is civilised, the points of disturbance are few. But where the foreign community is a large one carrying on a prosperous trade; and where the native community is also prosperous and busy, has its own laws, police, courts, and the whole system of executive government, the points of disturbance are many." Sir Francis Taylor Piggott, *Extraterritoriality: The Law Relating to Consular Jurisdiction and to Residence in Oriental Countries* (London: William Clowes & Sons, 1892), 3.

30. Piggott, *Extraterritoriality*, 272. For a classic example of the European description of Asia as defined by unchangeable antiquity, see G. W. Hegel: "The History of the World travels from East to West, for Europe is absolutely the end of History, Asia the beginning (*The Philosophy of History*, trans. J. Sibree [New York: Dover, 1956], 103). See also Edward W. Said's critique of the Marxian notion of the "Asiatic Mode of Production" as premised on a timeless and undifferentiated orient in *Orientalism* (New York: Vintage, 1979), 153–56.

Huxley's interwar Orientalism is repeated in Vicki Baum's German-language bestseller *Shanghai '37* (1937), in which an illiterate rickshaw coolie Yen receives a letter from his son that expresses an "astonishing mixture of modern schooling and Confucian politeness," a quality of semifeudal untimeliness that suffuses almost all Baum's otherwise sympathetic engagements with her Chinese characters (*Shanghai '37*, trans. Basil Creighton [New York: Doubleday, Doran, 1939], 303). Even contemporary historians fall victim to this canard, as with Harriet Sergeant's offensive assertions that, with the Communist takeover of Shanghai in 1949, "the interior, so long despised for its backwardness, nevertheless proved to be the true China" and that "without foreign protection [Shanghai] was powerless to withstand the Chinese peasant" (*Shanghai* [London: John Murray, 1991], 27–28).

For more nuanced treatments of the modernity of interwar Shanghai, see Marie-Claire Bergère, *Shanghai: China's Gateway to Modernity*, trans. Janet Lloyd (Stanford, CA: Stanford University Press, 2009); Leo Ou-fan Lee, *Shanghai Modern: The Flowering of Urban Culture in China, 1930–1945* (Cambridge, MA: Harvard University Press, 1999); and Wen-Hsin Yeh, *Shanghai Splendor: Economic Sentiments and the Making of Modern China, 1843–1949* (Berkeley: University of California Press, 2007). Yeh valorizes the "lure of modernity" as also "the lure of a good life of moral as well as material respectability" (8), while Lee and Bergère defend Shanghai modernity against accusations that it was insufficiently Chinese or wholly shaped by foreign capitalism (Bergère 367–406; Lee 307–23). Such suggestions were common after 1949, when Shanghai's urban history conflicted in certain ways with the agrarian and anti-imperial ideology of the People's Republic of China. Shu-mei Shih adopts the most nuanced position on the politics of Shanghai's interwar culture, which she sees as sufficiently committed to Western commodity capitalism that it "expressed an ambivalent, and at best oscillating, allegiance to nationalism and critique of the colonial presence" (*The Lure of the Modern: Writing Modernism in Semicolonial China, 1917–1937* [Berkeley: University of California Press, 2001], 232). Nevertheless, she describes Shanghai as a space of "strife-ridden . . . cultural fluidity [that] created the possibility of a cosmopolitanism. . . . fully explained in neither the language of compadorism [*sic*] nor that of nationalism" (238).

31. Shih Shun Liu, "Extraterritoriality," 28.

32. Shih Shun Liu, 425–26.

33. J. G. Ballard, *Empire of the Sun: A Novel* (New York: Simon & Schuster, 2005), 23. Hereafter cited parenthetically as *E*.

34. Ballard, *The Kindness of Women* (New York: Harcourt, Brace, , 1991), 3. Hereafter cited parenthetically as *K*.

35. Ernst Bloch, "Nonsynchronism and the Obligation to Its Dialectics," trans. Mark Ritter, *New German Critique* 11 (Spring 1977): 22–38.

36. Writes Bloch: "Obviously, the entirety of earlier development is not yet 'sublated' in capitalism and its dialectics. World history, as the bourgeois revolutionary Ludwig Borne has said, is a house that has more stairways than rooms. And, if Marx himself emphasizes the relatively more bearable aspect of the precapitalist condition, if even he characterizes Greek art and epic as 'in a certain respect the norm and unattainable ideal' (introduction to the Critique of Political Economy), then this 'social childhood of humanity' is a barely dissolved attraction for him or, in any case, capitalism is not the only house in history that could be dialectically inherited" ("Nonsynchronism," 36–37).

37. Bloch, "Nonsynchronism," 26. Of course, there are many differences between Bloch's general philosophy of history and the peculiar fictional space-times studied in this chapter. And perhaps the most important of those differences is that Ballard and Ishiguro, despite being "creative" writers, treat extraterritoriality with more historical literalism than does the political philosopher. Bloch uses "extraterritorial" as a metaphor to describe the cultural effect of a general temporal disjunction within fascist ideologies, which articulates its assault on "relativism" and "nihilism" through the symbolism of "a time long past" (27). By contrast, the Shanghai narratives discussed in this chapter foreground the mutual constitution of untimeliness and *actual* juridico-political extraterritoriality—that is, in these novels, extraterritoriality is never just a metaphor but a concrete technology of and for the operation of imperial power.

38. "Treaty of Nanjing (Nanking), 1842," East Asian Studies Documents, University of Southern California-University of California Los Angeles Joint Asia Institute, http://www.international.ucla.edu/eas/documents/nanjing.htm (accessed 14 June 2011).

39. "Treaty of the Bogue," http://en.wikisource.org/wiki/Treaty_of_the_Bogue (accessed 14 June 2011). Because these two treaties granted diplomatic consuls jurisdiction over their respective citizens, they enshrined what came to be known as a system of "consular jurisdiction," a phrase that's often used in the historical literature as a synonym for "extraterritoriality."

40. Ching-Chun Wang, *Extraterritoriality in China* (London: John Murray, 1937), 1.

41. Ching-Chun Wang in fact argues that the principle of extraterritorial jurisdiction in China was only fully systematized with the Sino-American Treaty of Wanghia in 1844 (*Extraterritoriality in China*, 1). It is indeed clear the Sino-American treaty exceeds the 1843 Supplementary Treaty in its clarity, even as it claims the same privileges for American citizens as the British had already negotiated for their own: "Subjects of China who may be guilty of any criminal act towards citizens of the United States, shall be arrested and punished by the Chinese authorities according to the laws of China: and citizens of the United States, who may commit any crime in China, shall be subject to be tried and punished only by the Consul, or other public functionary of the United States, thereto authorized according to the laws of the United States" (http://en.wikisource.org/wiki /Treaty_of_Wanghia, accessed 14 June 2011).

42. For the history of the Mixed Court system, and its relationship with Manchu jurisdictional practices, see Par Cassel, "Excavating Extraterritoriality: The 'Judicial Sub-Prefect' as a Prototype for the Mixed Court in Shanghai," *Late Imperial China* 24, no. 2 (2003): 156–82.

43. W. Somerset Maugham, *On a Chinese Screen* (New York: George H. Doran, 1922), 225. Hereafter cited parenthetically as *OCS*.

44. Dong Wang, *China's Unequal Treaties: Narrating National History* (Lanham, MD: Lexington, 2005), 10–11. In the Mixed Court system, moreover, the foreign administrative and legal staff "constantly encroached upon [this Chinese magistrates'] prerogatives" and by 1911 the court operated under de facto foreign control (Bergère, *Shanghai*, 112). For an introduction to legal practice in Shanghai, see Clifford, *Spoilt Children*, 28–32.

45. Immanuel Chung-yueh Hsü, *The Rise of Modern China* (New York: Oxford University Press, 1970), 239. The phrase "unequal treaty" was seldom if ever used in the nineteenth century and in fact dates from the early 1920s—that is, the period of Republican nationalism. Wang, *China's Unequal Treaties*, 1–2, 9–10.

46. A note on nomenclature: writers differ as to whether *semicolonial* takes a hyphen or not. With the exception of quotations, I follow Shu-mei Shih's unhyphenated use in *Lure of the Modern*.

47. Derek Attridge and Marjorie Howes, introduction to *Semicolonial Joyce*, ed. Attridge and Howes (Cambridge: Cambridge University Press, 2000), 8.

48. Vladimir Ilyich Lenin, *Imperialism: The Highest Stage of Capitalism* (Chippendale, AU: Resistance Books, 1999), 86.

49. Here, I echo Shih (*Lure of the Modern*, 371) in tacitly reversing the title terms of Ranjit Guha's study, *Dominance Without Hegemony: History and Power in Colonial India* (Cambridge, MA: Harvard University Press, 1997).

50. See Ernest Mandel, "Semicolonial Countries and Semi-Industrialized Dependent Countries," *New International* 2, no. 5 (1983), 156; and Osterhammel, "Semi-Colonialism and Informal Empire," 296.

51. Mao Zedong, "Why Is It That Red Political Power Can Exist in China?," Marxists Internet Archive, http://marxists.org/reference/archive/mao/selected-works/volume-1/mswv1_3 .htm (accessed 12 July 2011).

52. Shih, *Lure of the Modern*, 32–33. Bickers similarly describes China as a zone of "informal empire" that was "subject to multiple imperialism, which competed and cooperated. It was never subject to power relations and domination on the mainstream colonial pattern" (*Britain in China*, 8).

53. Shih, *Lure of the Modern*, 371.

54. See Bergère, *Shanghai*, 109–21.

55. Bergère, 28.

56. As Bergère summarizes it, in managing their relations with the British, local officials in Shanghai "adopted the classic Chinese strategies" for controlling outside groups, drawing on their long history of relations with foreign trading populations: "Segregation, collective responsibility, and partial integration into the Chinese administrative structures" (*Shanghai*, 30). For the broader history of the Chinese state's practice of governing foreign and minority populations via principles of graduated sovereignty, see Pär Kristoffer Cassel, *Grounds of Judgment: Extraterritoriality and Imperial Power in Nineteenth-Century China and Japan* (New York: Oxford University Press, 2012).

57. Clifford, *Spoilt Children*, 19. For the semisovereignty of the Shanghai Municipal Council, see Bickers, *Britain in China*, 126–28.

58. Paul French, *Old Shanghai A-Z* (Hong Kong: Hong Kong University Press, 2010), 53. See also Clifford, *Spoilt Children*, 28.

59. For these effects, see Ching-chun Wang, *Extraterritoriality in China*, 4–7; and Harriet Sergeant, *Shanghai* (London: John Murray, 1991), 10–30.

60. André Malraux, *La condition humaine* (Paris: Gallimard, 1982), 16.

61. Christian Henriot and Wen-Hsin Yeh, introduction to *In the Shadow of the Rising Sun*, 6. See also Frederic Wakeman, *The Shanghai Badlands: Wartime Terrorism and Urban Crime, 1937–1941* (Cambridge: Cambridge University Press, 1996), 2, 6–15. I am indebted, for these references and this term, to Alexander M. Bain, "International Settlements: Ishiguro, Shanghai, Humanitarianism," in "Ishiguro's Unknown Communities," ed. Lisa Fluet, special issue, *NOVEL: A Forum on Fiction* 40, no. 3 (Summer 2007): 240–64, especially 243–44.

62. Wen-Hsin Yeh argues that the great political irony of the 1937–41 period was that the extraterritorial zones become the only guarantee of the Chongqing government's influence in the region. Although they continued to interrupt the territorial fabric of the Republic, they now enhanced its claims to sovereignty rather than, as previously, undermining it. Yeh, prologue to *Wartime Shanghai*, ed. Wen-Hsin Yeh (London: Routledge, 2005), 8–10.

63. Wakeman, *Shanghai Badlands*, 2.

64. Aihwa Ong, "Graduated Sovereignty in South-East Asia," *Theory, Culture & Society* 17, no. 55 (2000): 58. See also *Flexible Citizenship: The Cultural Logics of Transnationality* (Durham, NC: Duke University Press, 1999), especially 1–28; and *Neoliberalism as Exception: Mutations in Citizenship and Sovereignty* (Durham, NC: Duke University Press, 2006), especially 75–97.

65. Shih, *Lure of the Modern*, 34.

66. This is why Shih spends so much time, for instance, finding precedents for forms of extra-territoriality not predicated upon "the special situation of a defective legal system in non-Christian Powers" (*Extraterritoriality*, 40).

67. To be clear: the anachronistic qualities of extraterritorial law do not make it the antith-esis of the modern; rather, we know extraterritoriality to be modern precisely because its anachrony speaks to the developmental unevenness of our world. "Time," writes Roberto Schwarz, "can become so uneven, when it is stretched far across space, that . . . forms which are already dead in the first [world] may still be alive in the second" ("A Brazilian Breakthrough," *New Left Review* 36 [2005]: 92). The situation Shih protested is a func-tion of China's modernity, not the symptom of its backwardness: although qualitatively different, "center" and "margin" remain coeval.

68. Arthur Ransome, *The Chinese Puzzle* (London: George Allen & Unwin, 1927), 28. For a similar, and more recent, view of foreign privilege in Shanghai, see Clifford, *Spoilt Chil-dren of Empire*, 14–15.

69. Clifford, 28–29.

70. W. H. Auden and Christopher Isherwood, *Journey to a War*, in W. H. Auden, *Prose and Travel Books in Prose and Verse, Vol. 1: 1926–1938*, ed. Edward Mendelson (Princeton, NJ: Princeton University Press, 1996), 512.

71. Benedict Anderson, *Imagined Communities: Reflections on the Origin and Spread of Nation-alism* (London: Verso, 1991), 26.

72. Anderson, *Imagined Communities*.

73. Jacques Derrida, *Specters of Marx*, trans. Peggy Kamuf (New York: Routledge, 1994), 6. Natalie Melas desribes how Derrida opens up "a space for anachrony as a disjunctive rela-tion between times." Melas, "Untimeliness, or Négritude and the Poetics of Contramo-dernity," *South Atlantic Quarterly* 108, no. 3 (2009): 565.

74. Kazuo Ishiguro, *When We Were Orphans* (New York: Knopf, 2000), 30, 7. Hereafter cited parenthetically as *O*.

75. Kazuo Ishiguro, *An Artist of the Floating World* (London: Faber & Faber, 1986).

76. *The White Countess*, directed by James Ivory (2005; Sony Pictures Classics), DVD.

77. M. Akbar Abbas, "Cosmopolitan De-scriptions: Shanghai and Hong Kong," *Public Cul-ture* 12, no. 3 (2000): 775.

78. Peter Bradshaw, review of *The White Countess*, *Guardian*, 31 March 2006, https://www.theguardian.com/culture/2006/mar/31/4 (accessed 8 February 2019).

79. Frumkes, "Kazuo Ishiguro," 192.

80. Cynthia F. Wong, "Like Idealism Is to the Intellect: An Interview with Kazuo Ishig-uro," in *Conversations with Kazuo Ishiguro*, 184.

81. Wong, "Like Idealism Is to the Intellect," 184–85.

82. Frumkes, "Kazuo Ishiguro," 192.

83. Christopher Bigsby, "In Conversation with Kazuo Ishiguro," in *Conversations with Kazuo Ishiguro*, 20. The mistaken assumption that Ishiguro ought to be read primarily in rela-tion to the history of Japan stems, first, from his Japanese ancestry and, second, from

the way his first two novels, *A Pale View of Hills* (1982) and *An Artist of the Floating World* (1986), deal with themes of war and militarism in 1930s and 1940s Japan.

84. Kazuo Ishiguro, *The Unconsoled* (New York: Vintage, 2005), 16.

85. Edward Said, *Reflections on Exile and Other Essays* (Cambridge, MA: Harvard University Press, 2000), 182. Quoted in Shao-Pin Luo, "Living the Wrong Life: Kazuo Ishiguro's Unconsoled Orphans," *Dalhousie Review* 83, no. 1 (2003): 44.

86. Like the servants and officials that direct Ryder around the unnamed city of *The Unconsoled*, Morgan assumes Banks's complicity in his plans and Banks, again like Ryder, is inexplicably unwilling to contradict him.

87. Brian Finney, *English Fiction Since 1984: Narrating a Nation* (New York: Palgrave Macmillan, 2006), 141.

88. Bain, "International Settlements," 243–44.

89. Nina Auerbach, *Romantic Imprisonment: Women and Other Glorified Outcasts* (New York: Columbia University Press, 1985), 64. If *When We Were Orphans* engages any orphan tale in particular, it is Charles Dickens's *Great Expectations*. For a comprehensive account of Ishiguro's allusions to *Great Expectations*, see Henry Carrington Cunningham III, "The Dickens Connection in Kazuo Ishiguro's *When We Were Orphans*," *Notes on Contemporary Literature*, 34, no. 5 (2004): 4–6. This intertextual relation has also been explored by Wai-chew Sim, *Kazuo Ishiguro: A Routledge Guide* (New York: Routledge, 2010), 70.

90. Brian W. Shaffer, "An Interview with Kazuo Ishiguro," in *Conversations with Kazuo Ishiguro*, 166.

91. Finney, *English Fiction Since 1984*, 153.

92. P. D. James, *Talking About Detective Fiction* (New York: Knopf, 2009), 174. See also David A. Grossvogel's description of the genre as predicated on "the *expectation* of a solution. The detective story offers confirmation and continuity at the price of a minor and spurious disruption." Grossvogel, "Agatha Christie: Containment of the Unknown," in *The Poetics of Murder: Detective Fiction and Literary Theory*, ed. Glenn W. Most and William W. Stowe (New York: Harcourt Brace Jovanovich, 1983), 254; emphasis in original.

93. Ron Hogan, "Kazuo Ishiguro," in *Conversations with Kazuo Ishiguro*, 159.

94. Tzvetan Todorov, *The Poetics of Prose*, trans. Richard Howard (Ithaca, NY: Cornell University Press, 1995), 46. This is true of all the crimes in *When We Were Orphans*, the only exception being the war crimes being committed in Chapei. Such crimes exceed—at the epistemological, as well as political, level—his ability to render a judgment.

95. Todorov, *Poetics of Prose*, 46.

96. Todorov, 45.

97. Hogan, "Kazuo Ishiguro," 159.

98. Michael Dirda, review of *The Complete Stories of J. G. Ballard*, *Washington Post*, 17 September 2009, C4; Dwight Garner, "His Twists and Turns, on Paper and in Life: J. G. Ballard's Memoir *Miracles of Life*," *New York Times*, 6 February 2013, C7; China Miéville, "J. G. Ballard: Five Years On—A Celebration," *Guardian*, 4 April 2014, https://www.theguardian.com/books/2014/apr/04/jg-ballard-celebration-five-years-writers-books-reissued (accessed 18 May 2016).

99. "Ballardian," Collins English Dictionary, https://www.collinsdictionary.com/us /dictionary/english/ballardian (accessed 18 May 2016).

100. J. G. Ballard, *Running Wild* (New York: Farrar, Strauss & Giroux, 1998), 82.

101. J. G. Ballard, *Cocaine Nights* (Berkeley: Counterpoint, 1998), 224.

102. Ballard, *Miracles*, 7.

103. J. G. Ballard, *Extreme Metaphors: Collected Interviews*, ed. Simon Sellars and Dan O'Hara (London: Fourth Estate, 2014), 384.

104. Martin Amis, "Ballard's Worlds," *Observer Magazine*, 2 September 1984, https://www .jgballard.ca/media/1984_sept2_observer_magazine.html (accessed 20 March 2013).

105. Joan Gordon, "Reveling in Genre: An Interview with China Miéville," *Science Fiction Studies* 30, no. 3 (2003): 366.

106. Gordon, "Reveling in Genre," 366.

107. J. G. Ballard, *Super-Cannes* (New York: Picador, 2000), 258.

108. J. G. Ballard, *Cocaine Nights* (Berkeley: Counterpoint, 1998), 60–61.

109. Sianne Ngai, *Ugly Feelings* (Cambridge, MA: Harvard University Press, 2005), 271.

110. Giorgio Agamben, *Homo Sacer: Sovereign Power and Bare Life*, trans. Daniel Heller-Roazan (Stanford, CA: Stanford University Press, 1998), 20.

111. J. G. Ballard, *Millennium People* (London: Harper Perennial, 2004), 109, 265, 294.

112. J. G. Ballard, *Kingdom Come* (London: Fourth Estate, 2006), 213, 218.

113. J. G. Ballard, *A User's Guide to the Millennium: Essays and Reviews* (New York: Picador, 1996), 199.

114. Ballard, *User's Guide to the Millenium*.

115. "Shanghai to Shepperton" is the title of a memoir first published in the Northeast London Polytechnic review of science fiction, *Foundation* 24 (1982). In a miniature allegory of Ballardian circulation and canonization (his work moving from the parastate funded institutions of the London underground scene, to the global traffic in cult fiction, to the academic sphere) it was then republished in a 1984 Ballard edition of the Bay Area journal *RE/Search* before being reprinted again in an academic trade anthology, *The Profession of Science Fiction* (1992). "Shanghai to Shepperton" later provided the title to the "Autobiographies" section of *A User's Guide to the Millennium* (1996) and the subtitle to the full-dress memoir *Miracles of Life* (2008). The academic conference, organized by Jeanette Baxter (Anglia Ruskin University), was held at the University of East Anglia on 5–6 May 2006.

116. Roger Luckhurst, *"The Angle Between Two Walls": The Fiction of J. G. Ballard* (Liverpool: Liverpool University Press, 1997), 45.

117. Self, *Junk Mail*, 360.

118. Ballard, *Extreme Metaphors*, 229.

119. Chris Beckett, "The Progress of the Text: The Papers of J. G. Ballard at the British Library," *Electronic British Library Journal* 12 (2011): 15.

120. J. G. Ballard, *The Drowned World and The Wind from Nowhere* (New York: Doubleday, 1965), 62, 162.

121. Self, *Junk Mail*, 360.

122. F. T. Ranson, letter to J. G. Ballard, 20 October 1984, ADD. Ms. 88938/2/1/6: Letters Received from Lunghua Camp Internees Following Publication of *Empire of the Sun* (1944–1991), Papers of James Graham Ballard, Western Manuscripts Collection, British Library, London. Hereafter cited as Ballard Papers.

Was this F. T. Ranson, who identifies himself as a Fellow of the Royal College of Surgeons, the inspiration for the character Dr. Ransome in *Empire*? If so, it's a connection denied or repressed, for Ranson writes to Ballard: "I cant [*sic*] recognise Dr Ransome unless it is meant to be Cater" (Ranson). In her history of Allied internment by the Japanese military, Bernice Archer refers to a "Dr Cater" (like Ranson, she gives no first name) who taught a medical class in Lunghua (100–101).

123. G. S. Dunkley, Letter to J. G. Ballard, 31 October 1984, ADD. Ms. 88938/2/1/6: Letters Received from Lunghua Camp Internees Following Publication of *Empire of the Sun* (1944–1991), Ballard Papers.

124. Indeed, the Ballard Papers also contain letters from former internees who found the experience of reading *Empire* "oddly vindicating" and congratulate Ballard on having "caught the flavour of the place." Julia Reilly, Letter to J. G. Ballard, 20 October 1984, ADD. Ms. 88938/2/1/6: Letters Received from Lunghua Camp Internees Following Publication of *Empire of the Sun* [1944–1991], Ballard Papers.

125. In the end, the Japanese did not enforce this regulation—though the worst conflicts between the Japanese, the Allied civilians, and the officers of the BRA tended to occur in the wake of detainee escapes, when the Japanese camp commandant would routinely hold the BRA responsible for discouraging and preventing escapes. William Braidwood, "Escapes," ADD Ms. 88938/2/1/7/4: British Residents' Association—Minutes, Memoranda, and Reports, Ballard Papers.

126. William Braidwood, "The Lunghua Civilian Assembly Centre," ADD Ms. 88938/2/1/7/2: Plans of Lunghua ["Lunghwa"] Camp, and Documents Concerning the Construction and Condition of its Buildings, Ballard Papers.

127. Braidwood, "Lunghua Civilian Assembly Centre."

128. Mark Mazower, "Foucault, Agamben: Theory and the Nazis," *boundary 2* 35, no. 1 (2008): 30–32.

129. Elaine Scarry, *Thinking in an Emergency* (New York: W. W. Norton, 2011), 15.

130. Giorgio Agamben, *State of Exception*. Trans. Kevin Attell (Chicago: University of Chicago Press, 2005), 6, 48.

131. Scarry, *Thinking in an Emergency*, 14.

132. Braidwood, "Lunghua Civilian Assembly Centre."

133. William Braidwood, Speech to the Shanghai British Residents Association, 30 November 1945, ADD Ms. 88938/2/1/7/4: British Residents' Association—Minutes, Memoranda, and Reports, Ballard Papers.

134. Ballard, *Miracles*, 21.

135. Ballard, 4–5.

136. Ballard, 99.

137. Ballard, *User's Guide*, 185.
138. Ballard, 185.
139. Ballard, 185.

CONCLUSION

1. The theme of extraterritoriality has been noticed by several Sebald scholars, but none have explored it at length, nor has anyone considered that word in relation to its legal and political history. See, e.g., Stephen Clingman, *The Grammar of Identity: Transnational Fiction and the Nature of the Boundary* (Oxford: Oxford University Press, 2009), 189; Jan Cueppens, "'Das belgische Grabmal' Sebalds 19. Jahrhundert," in *W. G. Sebald: Intertextualität und Topographie*, ed. Irene Heidelberger-Leonard (Berlin: LIT Verlag, 2008), 94; Cynthia Ozick, "The Posthumous Sublime," *New Republic*, 16 December 1996, 34; Gunther Pakendorf, "Als Deutscher in der Fremde: Heimat, Geschichte und Natur bei W. G. Sebald," in *W. G. Sebald: Schreiben ex patria/Expatriate Writing*, ed. Gerhard Fischer (Amsterdam: Rodopi, 2009), 91; Judith Ryan, "'Lines of Flight': History and Territory in *The Rings of Saturn*," in *W. G. Sebald: Schreiben ex patria*, 48–50; and Eric Santner, *On Creaturely Life: Rilke, Benjamin, Sebald* (Chicago: University of Chicago Press, 2006), 132n47.

2. W. G. Sebald, *Campo Santo* (München: Carl Hanser Verlag, 2003), 186; W. G. Sebald, *Campo Santo*, trans. Anthea Bell (New York: Random House, 2005), 143. From this point I quote from the authorized English translations of Sebald's work, referring to the German for emphasis or clarification. Subsequent citations refer first to the English edition, then to the equivalent page of the German text. A scholar of literary translation, Sebald oversaw the English translations of his works, even significantly revising *Schwindel, Gefühle* (1990) upon its translation as *Vertigo* (1999). Mark McCulloh therefore concludes that, "as befits Sebald [the translations] are works of literature in their own right" ("Introduction: Two Languages, Two Audiences: The Tandem Literary Oeuvres of W. G. Sebald," in *W. G. Sebald: History, Memory, Trauma*, ed. Scott Denham and Mark McCulloh [Berlin: de Gruyter, 2006], 18). I follow McCulloh in treating Sebald's English editions as neither autonomous from the German, nor subordinate to them. One might even say that the English texts possess an extraterritorial relation to the German.

3. Mark M. Anderson, "The Edge of Darkness: On W. G. Sebald," *October* 106 (2003): 105–6.

4. W. G. Sebald, *The Emigrants*, trans. Michael Hulse (New York: New Directions, 1996), 181; W. G. Sebald, *Die Ausgewanderten: vier lange Erzählungen* (Frankfurt am Main: Eichborn Verlag, 1992), 270

5. Sebald, *Austerlitz*, 236/335.

6. W. G. Sebald, *The Rings of Saturn*, trans. Michael Hulse (New York: New Directions, 1998), 237; W. G. Sebald, *Die Ringe des Saturn: Eine englische Wallfahrt*. Frankfurt am

Main: Eichborn Verlag, 1995), 290. Hereafter cited parenthetically as *ROS*, followed by references to the English, then German, editions.

7. Gertrud Koch, *Siegfried Kracauer: An Introduction*, trans. Jeremy Gaines (Princeton, NJ: Princeton University Press, 2000), 10.

8. Jay, "Extraterritorial Life of Siegfried Kracauer," 155.

9. György Lukács, *Theory of the Novel: A Historico-Philosophical Treatise on the Forms of Great Epic Literature*, trans. Anna Bostock (Cambridge, MA: MIT Press, 1971), 41 and 29–39.

10. Lukács, *Theory of the Novel*, 40–41.

11. Lukács, 34.

12. Lukács, 33.

13. Quoted in Jay, "Extraterritorial Life," 153.

14. Jay, 153.

15. Siegfried Kracauer, *History: The Last Things Before the Last* (New York: Oxford University Press, 1968), 66.

16. Kracauer, *History*, 67.

17. Kracauer, 68.

18. Tara Forrest, *The Politics of Imagination: Benjamin, Kracauer, Kluge* (Bielefeld: Verlag, 2007), 119.

19. Kracauer, *History*, 82–83.

20. See Ian Baucom's *Out of Place: Englishness, Empire, and the Locations of Identity* (Princeton, NJ: Princeton University Press, 1999) for an account of Pierre Nora's theory of *lieux de mémoire* (places of memory) as "cultic phenomena, objects of pilgrimage and veneration . . . cultural ensembles possessed by a need to stop time or . . . launch a voyage of return to the past" (19).

21. W. G. Sebald, *Vertigo*, trans. Michael Hulse (New York: New Directions, 1999), 186.

22. William Shakespeare, *Hamlet*, ed. Harold Jenkins (London: Routledge, 1982), 3.1.79–80. This metaphor provides Sebald with the title of an essay on the death motif in Kafka's *The Castle*, which he interprets as embodying "the fear of a perpetual habitation in the no-man's land between man and thing" (Sebald, "The Undiscover'd Country: The Death Motif in Kafka's Castle," *Journal of European Studies* 2, no. 22 [1972]: 34). Sebald's self-allusion suggests that *Rings* develops an implicit comparison between its narrator and Kafka, with the difference that the "no-man's land" of Orfordness is both the (extra) territory of death and a place from which he can return.

23. John Zilcosky, "Lost and Found: Disorientation, Nostalgia, and Holocaust Melodrama in Sebald's *Austerlitz*," *Modern Language Notes* 121, no. 3 (2006): 680–81; emphasis in original. Zilkoscy finds the germ of this paradox in the title of Sebald's volume of academic essays on Austrian literature, *Unheimliche Heimat: Essays zur österreichischen Literatur* (St. Polten, Austria: Residenz Verlag, 1995). The phrase translates as "uncanny home," with the clear connotation of "unhomely." Sebald clearly alludes to Sigmund Freud's "The Uncanny" (1919) in which the etymology of *unheimlich* is excavated to show how the logic of repression binds together the language of the frightening and the familiar or home-like (*heimisch*).

24. For this history, see Paddy Heazell, *Most Secret: The Hidden History of Orford Ness* (London: History Press/National Trust, 2010).

25. For an analysis of military installations in these terms, see Rachel Woodward, *Military Geographies* (Oxford: Blackwell, 2004).

26. In *The Rings of Saturn*, Sebald makes it clear that he first saw the Ness in 1972, when it was impossible to gain access to it (231/290). The opening pages of the book date his first walk on the Ness as taking place "in the dog days of 1992" (3/9), but in fact the National Trust didn't take ownership of the property from the Ministry of Defence until 1993. These temporal complications are perhaps explained by the fact that, when I visited Orford in 2011 and 2013, I met several locals who claimed to know "Max" Sebald and said he regularly walked on or near Orford Ness. The apocalyptic visions narrated in *Rings of Saturn* appear to synthesize elements of several walks.

INDEX

location: language of, in *On Such a Full Sea*, 116; Thacker on, 24. *See also* place; space(s)

Lockerbie aircraft bombing incident, 243n52

The Lola Quartet (St. John Mandel), 269n46

London, England: Ballard on, 223; eruvim in, 54

Long, Jeff, 127

The Long Goodbye (Chandler), 108

The Long Twentieth Century (Arrighi), 47–48

Lovecraft, H. P., 87

Low, Judah (*Iron Council* character), 82–83

Luckhurst, Roger, 70–71, 215

Lukács, György, 145–46, 167, 227, 229

Lu Kun, 171

Lunghua Civilian Assembly Center, 215–16, 218–24, 290n125

Lunghwa Academy, 219

Luo, Shao-Pin, 204–5

Luxembourg, Le Freeport, 35

Macao, China, population of (1836), 176

MacCulloch, Diarmaid, 274n19, 275n24

MaddAddam (Atwood), 137

MaddAddam trilogy (Atwood), 27, 107, 111, 135–40, 266n16

magic realism, 277n38

Mak, Geoff, 268–69n37

Malraux, André, 198

Malta, Lockerbie aircraft bombing incident and, 243n52

Manhattan, New York City, eruvim in, 54

Mann, Michael, 41, 101, 265n7

Mantel, Hilary: on administrative changes of 1530s, 152; on Austin Friars, 158; critiques of, 276n27; Cromwell, depiction of, 157, 276n27; on feudal lords, power of, 275n20; historical past, depiction of, 146; influences on, 151; Kantorowicz, familiarity with, 275n22; *The Mirror and the Light*, 153; on More, 154; present tense, use of, 154; theoretical approach

to, 27; on *Wolf Hall*, 158–59. *See also Wolf Hall*

Mao Zedong, 195–96

Mare Liberum (Grotius), 3, 5

maritime law, European Parliament report on, 5

maritime space, zones in, 238n10

market, influence of, 48

Martens, Georg Friedrich von, 16

Martin, Theodore, 111

Marx, Karl, 284n36

Matsuda, Mr. (*The White Countess* character), 203

Mattingly, Garrett, 241n36

Maugham, W. Somerset, 193–94

Mayer, Hans, 227

Mazower, Mark, 220, 221

McCulloh, Mark, 291n2

meaning, anthological localization of, 58–59

Mediterranean, international waters of, 5

medium scale, description of, 265n7

Melas, Natalie, 287n73

Melville, Herman, 87

Memory-Temples, 179

Merrill, Judith, 266n18

Messrs. Turner & Co., 279n79

metropolitan modernity, 199

Mexico, descriptions of US/Mexico border, 255n108

Mezzadra, Sandro, 70, 254n100

mid-level reading, 265n7

Miéville, China: about, 69; on amity lines in European treaties, 262n59; conclusions on, 234; critiques of critics of, 77–78; education, 262n54; on figurative interpretations, 78; genre, use of term, 260–61n42; on international law, 92–93, 103; narrative settings of writings of, 70; political geography of, 77–85, 87; secondary world creation, methodology for, 85–91; signature elements of fiction of, 69–70; sources for, 87; on speculative

INDEX

Piggott, Francis Taylor, 190, 242n45, 283n29
pirates, nature of, 80
place: creation of extraterritoriality of, 14;
space versus, Ghosh on, 277n39.
See also space(s); zone(s)
planetary connections, Heise on, 272n67
Plato *Symposium*, 75
pluralism, legal and administrative, 244n53
pluriverses, 123
poetics: borders, Wallinger's interest in
visual poetics of, 57–58; of exile, 21–22;
extraterritorial narrative poetics,
121–24; of interstitiality, 59; of liminality,
59, 62
points of disturbance, 189–92
Poitras, Laura, 63
police, Agamben on, 96
political demonstrations exclusion zone,
256n113
political geography: of *The Carhullan Army*,
121–22; criminal law, relationship with,
60–62; in *The Extraterritorial*, 132;
extraterritorial cartographies, double-
sidedness of, 140–41; in Heavenly
Dynasty conception of foreign relations,
170–71; literary form and, 23–25; in
MaddAddam trilogy, 136–40; Miéville's,
77–85, 87; in *Nineteen Eighty-Four*,
129–30; of Shanghai, 198; of Shanghai
Links, 186–87; in *Station Eleven*,
125–26; in *On Such a Full Sea*, 117–18,
119, 120; as three dimensional, 238n10;
of twenty-first century, extraterritoriality
of, 9–10; in *When We Were Orphans*,
209; in *Wolf Hall*, 159. *See also*
disaggregated political geography and
globalization
politics: political plastic (politics in matter),
9; political power, Miéville's approach
to, 26, 92; political space, divisibility of,
15; Schmitt on, 241n35
Pomeranz, Kenneth, 28, 166–67, 278n50

Pomerleau International (construction firm),
184
pope, authority in England and Wales,
273n10
ports of entry, 57, 63
postapocalyptic genre, 8, 133–41
postapocalyptic novels, settings for, 105–41;
The Extraterritorial, 131–33;
extraterritorial cartographies, 133–41;
extraterritorial narrative poetics, spatial
characteristics of, 121–24; overview of,
26–27; reality, weight of, 117–21; setting
as destiny, 105–13; spatial simplification
in, 123; *Station Eleven*, 124–29; *On Such a
Full Sea*, 113–17; total space, dystopian
fiction and, 129–30
postinternet artworks, 25
"Postmodernism, or, The Cultural Logic of
Late Capitalism" (Jameson), 19–20
post-Westphalianism, 50–53
poverty, geographic persistence of, 106
power: absolute power, domination versus,
41; coercive power, 103; geography of, 23;
over people versus land, 243n53; political
power, Miéville's approach to, 26, 92; of
states, 40–42; uneven spatial distribution
of, 62
praemunire, 148–49, 273n10
present, anthropology of, 47
preservation by absence, 113
presumption against extraterritoriality, 18
Prince, Mark, 186
Proust, Marcel, 228
psychopathology, Ballard on, 216
publishing, impact of globalization on, 6

Qing dynasty, attitude toward trade, 170–73
quasi-extraterritorial zones, 17

Raad, Walid, 38
Rabelesian marketplaces, 245n65
Railsea (Miéville), 87

309